Federalism

A Political Theory for Our Time

P.I.E. Peter Lang

Bruxelles · Bern · Berlin · Frankfurt am Main · New York · Oxford · Wien

Lucio Levi, Giampiero Bordino,
Antonio Mosconi (eds.)

Federalism

A Political Theory for Our Time

Federalism
Vol.7

Spinelli's Commitment for the European Constitution 97
John Pinder, 3/2007

In What Respects Will European Federalism Be Different? 105
Robert Toulemon, 1/2008

Steps towards European and World Federalism 113
John Pinder, 1/2006

Multi-level Governance and Federalism 119
Lucio Levi, 3/2010

Democratic Decisions vs. Diplomatic Decisions 123
Ludo Dierickx, 2/2000

States Vote, People Do Not 127
Tommaso Padoa-Schioppa, 1/2000

Proposals for Europe: a Political and Moral Essay 131
Robert Lafont, 1/2001

Towards a Federal United Kingdom 139
Ernest Wistrich, 1/2001

Meade's Social Dividend 143
Alfonso Iozzo, 3/2011

Re-inventing the Welfare State 151
Barbara Spinelli, 2/2012

What Future for Federalism? 155
Fernando A. Iglesias, 3/2014

Part Two

European Unification: an Unaccomplished Project 163
Giampiero Bordino

Back to the Dream 167
Barbara Spinelli, 1/2013

From War to Peace 171
Tommaso Padoa-Schioppa, 1/2002

European Democracy is Valuable Too, not Just the Monetary Union ... 175
Amartya Sen, 3/2011

Europe Needs a Government ... 179
Fernand Herman, 2/2002

A Democratic Constitution for the European Union ... 183
Romano Prodi, 3/2003

Europe Needs to Renew its Vows for Federal Union ... 187
Guy Verhofstadt, 3/2013

The Unaccomplished Way Toward the European Unity ... 189
Lucio Levi, 1/2007

A European Government to Get out of the Crisis ... 193
Andrew Duff, 1/2014

The Crisis and the Weakness of the European Demos ... 199
Josep Borrrell, 3/2015

Europe and the World ... 203
John Pinder, 3/2004

The Union of the Peoples of Europe and the Example of Mandela ... 209
Tzvetan Todorov, 2/2014

Europe's Place in the World in the 21st Century ... 211
Peter D. Sutherland, 2/2007

The Search for a European Identity: Who Are We? ... 217
Giampiero Bordino, 3/2006

Where Do the Boundaries of European Integration Lie? ... 221
Heinz Timmermann, 2/2009

The Eurozone, the Dynamic Core of a European Federation ... 229
Dusan Sidjanski, 1/2014

The Eurozone in the IMF ... 233
Daniel Gros, 1/2011

A Federal Europe for Promoting a New Model of Growth ... 237
Alberto Majocchi, 1/2011

Europe by the People ... 245
Carsten Berg, 1/2003

European Citizenship to Residents ... 249
Paul Oriol, 2/2004

Strong European Political Parties for a Democratic EU ... 255
Jo Leinen, 1/2007

The European Citizens' Initiative ... 261
Sylvia-Yvonne Kaufmann, 2/2011

Part Three

The Integration Processes at the Regional Level ... 269
Giampiero Bordino

Rethinking the "European Common Home" ... 273
Antonio Mosconi, 1/1999

New Myths about Russia and NATO ... 277
Ira Straus, 1/2002

For a Euro-Mediterranean Community ... 281
Pier Virgilio Dastoli, 3/2011

The Arab Spring, Federalism and Euro-Arab Relations ... 289
Hazem Hanafi, 3/2011

Federal/Confederal Solutions to the Israeli-Palestinian-Jordanian Conflict ... 295
Daniel J. Elazar, 1/2002

What Is Israel's End-Game? ... 303
Seyla Benhabib, 2/2009

Reflections on Middle Eastern Regional Integration ... 311
Yossi Amitay, 3/2000

Reconciling the Irreconcilable ... 317
John Parry, 3/2006

Recent Developments of Regionalism in East Asia and Their Implications for Europe ... 323
Ken Endo, 1/2010

The Regional Unification Processes in Asia 327
James W. Arputharaj, 3/2009

The Regional Integration Process of Central America 333
Giannis F. Papageorgiou, 3/2001

A Regional Criminal Court Against Transnational Organized Crime 337
Fernando A. Iglesias, 1/2014

Federalism and Decolonization in Black Africa 341
Jean-Francis Billon, 1/2011

PART FOUR

The Contradictions of Globalization without Government 345
Antonio Mosconi

Who is Controlling Globalisation? 353
Peter Ustinov, 1/2000

September 12: The World is not at Zero-Point 355
Tommaso Padoa-Schioppa, 2/2002

How Is the State Changing in the Globalization Process? 363
Giampiero Bordino, 3/2007

For a UN Emergency Force 369
Sir Brian Urquhart, 1/2007

Terrorism and World Government 373
Lucio Levi, 3/2001

World Security through World Law 377
Garry Davis, 3/2001

The Global Promise of the Responsibility to Protect in Libya 379
Fergus Watt, 2/2011

From Hiroshima to Fukushima 383
Kenji Urata, 3/2011

A Global Climate Community 387
David Grace, 1/2011

From a League of Failing Nations to a Global Community for the Environment 391
Joan Marc Simon, 1/2012

Global Warming: with a View to the 2015 UN World Conference in Paris 395
Roberto Palea, 2/2015

The Foundation of a Cooperative Global Financial System 403
Alfonso Iozzo and Antonio Mosconi, 2/2006

The World Supremacy of the Dollar at the Rendering (1917-2008) 413
Antonio Mosconi, 1/2009

Adding the RMB into the SDR Basket: an Evaluation 421
Yide Qiao and Jiafei Ge, 1/2015

A Constitution for the Internet 427
Stefano Rodotà, 1/2006

A People's Assembly for the UN 431
Jo Leinen, 3/2004

Problems of Democratization 435
George Modelski, 1/2008

Opinion on World Government in the USA 439
Joseph Baratta, 3/2010

The Security Council Reform 445
Lucio Levi, 3/2004

The ICC is a Reality International Law Applied over Individuals 449
William R. Pace, 2/2002

Reforming the United Nations by the Convention Method 451
Antonio Papisca, 1/2006

Editors/Authors 459

Introduction

Lucio LEVI

The present book is a collection of articles published between 2000 and 2015 in the review *The Federalist Debate*[1]. The authors belong to different disciplines, political affiliations and nationalities. The distinguished names of many of them show that federalist ideas have found dissemination channels among the protagonists of European and world politics, the broad universe of civil society movements and intellectuals. It is sufficient to mention the Nobel Prize Amartya Sen, the former President of the European Commission Romano Prodi, several members of the European Parliament such as its former President, Josep Borrell and Andrew Duff, Barbara Spinelli, Jo Leinen, Guy Verhofstadt, UN officers, like the former Undersecretary-General Brian Urquhart, or the actor, writer and world federalist leader Peter Ustinov, the leaders of civil society movements like Carsten Berg, Garry Davis, Ludo Dierickx, Fernando Iglesias, Paul Oriol and Bill Pace, distinguished writers and analysts like Daniel Elazar, Daniel Gros, George Modelski, John Pinder, Stefano Rodotà, Dusan Sidjanski, Tzvetan Todorov, Nadia Urbinati.

It is up to the readers to assess the merits and faults of this book, but what seems unquestionable is that, although the vision and viewpoints of the texts collected here are rooted in different and, at times, distant cultural and political experiences, they share largely convergent interpretations of the main trends of contemporary history. As regards the task of detecting the sense of contemporary history, political debate assumes a crucial importance, since the confrontation between different ideas and cultural experiences, the free exchange of opinions is the most effective method for gradually approaching truth through the constant questioning of every aspect of a problem and the continuous testing of hypotheses against facts. This is the method adopted in the choice of the texts reproduced here. They offer hypotheses, formulated in the spirit of dialogue, which can contribute to improve the understanding of some of the most important problems of the contemporary world and to the debate on their solution.

1 On *The Federalist Debate* see the notes at page 6. The review's issue in which the articles included were published is specified both in the Index and in the footnotes of each article.

In our time, the dynamics of history is driven by the search of ever wider human aggregations including many states and many nations. We are in an age of transition from the time of nation-states to the era of multinational states and global politics. The fact is that European unification – and other regional integration processes, which are in progress according to an uneven development all over the world – and the strengthening and democratization of the United Nations are issues on the political agenda since the end of the Second World War. This means that, in spite of the shortcomings of the regional organizations and the UN, due to the fact that the construction of those institutions is still unaccomplished, they have become necessary elements of the international political and economic landscape.

Federalism is a new paradigm of politics, a new political thinking which allows to understand and govern this transition process. The title of this book – *Federalism. A Political Theory for Our Time* – has been chosen in order to suggest the topical interest of federalism as political thought which aims to abolish war and build peace through law, and more precisely through the extension of the rule of law to international relations. The significance of the federalizing processes, in progress in the world according to a principle of uneven development, lies in the overcoming of the separation between domestic and international politics through the constitutionalization of international relations.

Federalism did not assert itself overnight. The world is changing and federalism has changed with it. Today, federalism still exists in an unfinished state. It is not a closed and static political project nor a timeless theoretical system. It is an unaccomplished theory, which is constantly evolving in response to the new problems which history is raising relentlessly. It has been ripening slowly along three stages of development.

The Federalist Debate has strived to offer a modest contribution to the interpretation of the main trends in contemporary history. Moreover, federalism has challenged nationalism and the division of the world into sovereign states, which have been put progressively on the defensive. The need for peace and unity is asserting itself slowly but constantly first in Europe, then globally. Therefore, I devote this introduction to sketch the framework within which the historical and political evolution of federalist thinking took place.

*

* *

The birth of federalism dates back to 1787, when the members of the Philadelphia Convention drafted and signed the Constitution of the United States of America, a new form of state, that it has become customary to call "Federation". At the beginning, the political project to which we are used to give the name of "Federalism" had a regional size and an institutional aspect only. For a long time it remained a marginal political model, if we consider that until World War Two only three other states adopted a federal constitution: Switzerland (1848), Canada (1867) and Australia (1901). It is to be noted that they were established in peripheral regions of the world, where the centralizing pressure exerted by power politics and class struggle was weaker than in the leading centres of world politics. The establishment of federalism in one part of the world started to show its contradictions when in the 1900s the historical conditions for isolationism became obsolete and the United States started to gradually transform itself into a great power. Such a weak form of political organization as the federal is, in which sovereignty is not concentrated in one centre, but is articulated on two – and potentially several – government levels, could only establish itself in a marginal region. The North American federal institutions have survived since then because they were a sort of political island shielded by the sea from the power clashes that always have divided the States in international politics. When the United States was compelled to intervene in the two World Wars and after 1945 it became one of the two pillars of the world order, it was driven to modify its institutional structure in the direction of authoritarianism, nationalism and militarism. Today, it is the living example of how federalism is destined to degenerate in one country while its full realization can occur only at world level.

The prevailing form of political organization was the unitary state, based on the national ideology, whose structure was adapted to ensure cohesion between classes and regions and the states' survival in a world of sovereign nations clashing with one another. In the Westphalian world, where states do not recognize any supranational authority, mankind's division in sovereign states was an insurmountable obstacle. All Federations in existence so far are sovereign states in a world divided into sovereign states. Therefore, the first forms of federal government belong to the same phase in history in which the national states were formed and share their logic of division and antagonism. They have not questioned the principle of the division of mankind into antagonistic states, but have accepted international anarchy, power politics and war as necessary and permanent features of political life. Thus, the form of political unity they have pursued does not substantially differ from that of the decentralized unitary states.

*

* *

The First World War marks a turning point in contemporary history, the moment which saw the birth of the new concept of "crisis the of nation-state", the foundation stone of the autonomous vision of history of federalism in our time. It has the same relevance that the concepts of "crisis of absolute monarchy" and "crisis of capitalism" have respectively in the liberal and in the socialist and communist theories. The importance and function of these concepts is to identify a basic contradiction and to formulate a comprehensive assessment of a phase of history. What distinguishes contemporary federalism is that it challenges and questions the pretense of nationalism to be the theory of the highest form of political community. The stream of history, spurred by the second phase of the industrial mode of production, aimed irresistibly to enlarge the dimension of economic, social and political processes from the nation-state to the multinational state. This is the second phase in the history of federalism.

As the nation-state was the product of the industrial revolution and the driving force of coal and steam-engine, likewise the second phase of industrial revolution, fostered by the driving force of electricity and the internal combustion engine, promoted the formation and the predominance of multinational states and the decline of nation-states. The bedrock of the international system, the sovereignty of the nation-state, was subject to substantial erosion. Therefore, a world state system, led by the United States and the Soviet Union, replaced the declining European state system.

It is worth recollecting that two leading figures of the liberal (Einaudi) and the communist movement (Trotsky), in spite of the distance of their viewpoints, have come to largely convergent interpretations of World War One. At the start of World War One, Trotsky wrote:

> At the root of the present war there is the revolt of the productive forces brought up by capitalism against the way the national state employs them [...]. The old national states [...] are obsolete and have turned into chains for the further development of the productive forces. The war of 1914 constitutes first of all the crisis of the national state as a self-sufficient economic area [...]. In such historical conditions, the solution for the European proletariat cannot but imply the defence of the obsolete fatherland, which has become the main obstacle to economic progress: the mandatory task is to create a new fatherland, much more powerful and stable, the United States of Europe as a transitional phase towards the United States of the world.[2]

Einaudi, in two articles published in *Corriere della Sera* in 1918, finds the root of the crisis of the national state, along the same line of Trotsky's interpretation, in the strong increase of economic interdependence:

> "When matters subject to discussion and deliberation have an international nature, they cannot be discussed and decided by municipal Parliaments. Above the states, become small, almost as big counties, and their deliberating

2 Trotsky, Lev D., *Der Krieg und die Internationale* (München: Futurus Verlag, 1914, pp. 3-6).

bodies, there must form, there have been ideally constituted already, larger states, government bodies different from the normal ones".[3]

Exactly like Trotsky, Einaudi defines war as a sign of the need of Europe's unity:

"The present war is the condemnation of European unity imposed by force by a bold Empire; but it is also the bloody effort to frame a political form of a higher order".[4] He too considers European unity as a stage on the road to world unity: "To the United States of America there should be opposed or associated the United States of Europe, awaiting the birth in a later moment of human civilization of the United States of the world".[5]

Unlike Trotsky, Einaudi is aware of the institutional innovation brought by the Philadelphia Convention, which drafted the federal Constitution of the United States of America, "transforming a shadow, an unreal society of nations ready to split and fight each other, into a single State of a higher order than the 13 confederated states".[6] Moreover, according to the federalist tradition, Einaudi believes that state sovereignty is the ultimate cause of war. Therefore, peace cannot be but the result of unity of the states under a Constitution giving birth to a democratic government, granted the necessary powers to forbid and avert the use of force in the relations among states. What is peculiar to the federalist theory is that the cause of war is not ascribed to certain internal structures of the state (for example, the capitalist system, as maintained by the Marxist theory), but to the mere division of the world into sovereign states, as a consequence of which, whatever the political regime and production system it must yield to the law of force to defend its independence. If international anarchy is a typical feature of the international relations, it can only be overcome by federal institutions. The novelty of this phase of development of federalist thinking lies in the fact that federal institutions present themselves not only as a new form of state, but also as a new form of international organization, i.e. a step toward constitutionalizing international relations first at the European level, then worldwide. This means that the overcoming of the separation between domestic and international politics becomes conceivable. At the same time, federalism appears as an alternative to traditional ideologies, which have accepted the nation-states as the natural framework for their action and have been dragged along the downward phase of their trajectory. From this time on, federal institutions do not appear only as the vehicle for the merger

3 Einaudi, Luigi, *La guerra e l'unità europea* (Bologna: Il Mulino, 1986, p. 34).

4 *Ibid.*

5 *Ibid.*, p. 27.

6 *Ibid.*, p. 26.

of a group of states and the creation of a new state on the area covered by many states. They become to be viewed as the vehicle to pursue a universal end: uniting Europe to unite the world. In other words, European Federation can pave the way to uniting the peoples of all countries in a World Federation and to building perpetual peace.

The European system of sovereign states, codified with the Peace of Westphalia (1648), was supplanted in 1945 after the end of the Second World War by the world system composed of two superpowers of macro-regional dimensions, the United States and the Soviet Union. This date marks the beginning of a new era: the era of international organizations, which is characterized by the need to submit international relations to the rule of law. Governments' answer to global interdependence and globalization has been international cooperation, not by choice, but due to the absence of alternatives. In fact, there is no national answer to global problems. The ever more frequent creation of international organizations at the regional and global levels represents the way taken by governments for finding a solution to problems that they cannot solve alone. A quantitative datum is sufficient to appreciate the importance of the phenomenon: the incredible speed at which their number grew during the 20th century. According to a comprehensive criterion (utilized by the *Yearbook of International Organizations*) for classifying international organizations, that includes not only the ones instituted by states at regional and world level, but also those promoted by international organizations, they were 37 in 1909, and have grown to 7,608 in 2011.[7]

World War One was concluded with the founding of the League of Nations and World War II with the creation of the United Nations. Those institutions represent the first attempt to ensure world peace through specific institutions, but they were not endowed with an independent power to pursue that goal. Owing to their confederal – not federal – structure, they were subordinate to the member states. Therefore, the scourge of war has continued to lash the world.

In this new historical context, federalism presents itself as the most radical and innovative political proposal in comparison with the weaker formulas of international cooperation or international organization. In fact it puts forward the establishment of an independent supranational level of government, coordinated with the lower levels of government, and the extension of democracy from the national to the international plane.

Until the end of the Second World War, both European and world federalism appeared as distant final goals, which had no possibility to influence history. In fact, only during the second post-war period have

---

[7] *Yearbook of International Organizations* (Leiden-Boston: Brill-Martinus Nijhoff, 2011, vol. I, pp. 32-35).

the first political movements been constituted with the aim to pursue the goals of European (1946) and World Federation (1947).

There is no doubt that the most important achievement in the construction of peace in the post-2nd world war period was the establishment of the European Communities and the European Union. After centuries of warfare, Europe has never before lived so long in peace. The *Ventotene Manifesto* is the most significant document of the European Resistance movement. It was written by Altiero Spinelli and Ernesto Rossi with a preface by Eugenio Colorni in 1941, when Hitler, after the conquest of France, launched the attack on Russia and swastika flags were waving all over the European continent. The *Manifesto* marks the overcoming of the old vision of the world according to which the nation-state is the centre of the political universe and the world rotates around it. The significance of Spinelli's work lies in his commitment to free himself from the state-centric point of view. The most important message launched by the *Manifesto* is that, in the age of the crisis of the nation-state and the internationalization of the production process, a new dividing line cuts across the forces of progress and those of conservatism: the line that separates federalism and nationalism. Those who choose the nations as the ground of their political commitment, even if their goal is to realize more democracy or more socialism, place themselves on the side of conservatism, because their political action consolidates the national states. Consequently, the objective to be pursued, first of all by those who want to promote progress, is the commitment to overcome Europe's and the world's division into sovereign states. European unification has proceeded more slowly than the authors of the *Manifesto* expected. But what proves their far-sightedness is that the first European Community (the European Coal and Steel Community) was created only ten years after the *Manifesto* was written.

The end of the Second World War marked the starting point of European unification under the protecting shield of the United States and the Atlantic Alliance. It is the expression of the need of the European nation-states to federate in order to acquire a macro-regional dimension and to enable them to compete with giant states which have risen to the leadership in world economy and politics, like the United States, the Soviet Union, China and India.

World War II marked the defeat of the last attempt at unifying Europe under the hegemony of the mightiest state of the system (Germany), but also the decline of the sovereignty of the European winners of the war (France and Great Britain), and the start of European unification. What distinguishes the institutions of the European Union is a general tendency towards constitutionalizing international relations. Institutions like the

European Parliament – directly elected and endowed with a legislative co-decision power with the Council and a control power towards the European Commission – or the euro, the single European currency, show that the Union has gone beyond the traditional forms of cooperation which characterize international organizations. The constitutional construction site of the European Union is the laboratory of a new form of statehood.

On the other hand, the constitutional gradualism which characterises the construction stages of European unification – which is far from being concluded – shows that the overcoming of nations consolidated by centuries of independent state life cannot occur through a big qualitative leap, but requires an incremental approach. It is to be underlined the profound difference between American and European federalism. While the thirteen states of North America were small states which had just acquired their independence and had trifling power in world politics, the novelty of European federalism lies in its attempt to unify the historical nations of the Old Continent some of which have been established after centuries of conflicts and wars. This observation is sufficient to conclude that European federation cannot be achieved through a qualitative leap (examplified by the precedent of the Philadelphia Convention, which in four months drew up a federal constitution), but rather through an incremental process.

The EU is an example of how nation-states can change their way of settling disputes by moving from power politics to the rule of law. Violence as an instrument for interstate conflict resolution has been abandoned and replaced by a mutually agreed legal order. European unification is the process of constructing peace through a progressive constitutionalization of inter-state relations. The Commission, the Parliament, the Court of Justice, the Central Bank now regulate what were once considered the domestic affairs of the nation-states. Therefore, the EU can be defined as a post-Westphalian community.

In spite of this success, the EU is an unaccomplished project, it still has limited capacities for action. Its budget is below 1% of the European GDP, its foreign and security policy has not been unified yet. Two visions of the future coexist in the EU: the one of the Eurozone countries, which tends to a political union, and the British one, which conceives the EU as a market. It is an alternative that can be solved only through a two-speed Europe with a federal core and a less integrated outer ring. The perspective of a two-speed Europe is not to be feared. It is already a reality, as the euro and Schengen free movement space show. What is important is that the core of states which want to proceed toward the federal target stays open in order to avoid exclusions and discriminations.

*
* *

Globalization marks the beginning of the third phase of development in the history of federalism.

Globalization is the product of a turning point in the evolution of the modes of production, which dates back to second half of the last century: the scientific revolution in material production. There is a specific relation between the globalization process, which is nothing but a process of economic and social integration at the world level, and the scientific mode of production. In our time, scientific knowledge has become the main force of production, the driving power of economic and social progress. The scientific revolution changes the form and size of the economic and social life. Automation frees man from the fatigue of manual labor and increases the quantity of material goods necessary to satisfy basic needs. The revolution in communications and transport technologies has intensified the world-wide flow of capital and commodities and large-scale migrations, and has facilitated the circulation of information and cultural models. The social integration process extends itself beyond state boundaries, and creates the bases for unification of mankind. Scientific revolution imposes, in sum, on all the sectors of social life a much wider dimension than that of sovereign states, even the biggest ones. This process creates the economic and social conditions not only for a global civil society and global market, but also for worldwide political institutions. In other words, the great technological and social changes of our time require parallel changes in the sphere of political institutions.

The most significant aspect of globalization affects the sphere of politics. Its peculiar character lies in the contradiction between a market and a society that have been taking global dimensions and a system of states that has remained national. Therefore, globalization triggers a tension between the development of those forces of production that are unifying the world and the structures of the states, which should, but cannot, govern the process because of their dimension.

European unification and globalization belong to two different phases of history: they represent, respectively, the second stage of the industrial mode of production, requiring a state organization over spaces with the dimensions of a great region of the world, and the scientific mode of production, posing the problem of political unification of the world. European unification weakens national governments, drives them to cooperate in order to be in a position to solve together the problems they are not able to cope with separately, creates a European civil society side by side with the national civil societies, creates European institutions that represent a mechanism for shaping political decisions which progressively dispossesses the national institutions. The process has reached such an advanced stage that a war between member states of the European Union has become impossible, and the European Constitution currently represents a key aspect of the political debate in Europe.

While European unification is still under way and all the great regions of the world are involved, with an uneven degree of development, in a similar integration process, another integration process is taking place simultaneously at the global level, which includes all the regions of the world. The federalizing process, conceived as the answer to the crisis of the sovereign state, does not generate only the need for a power transfer toward international organizations, but also toward regional and local governments. It represents the reversal of three hundred years of centralization policies within the framework of the territorial states and the tendency to create new forms of statehood which overcome the national state model from above and from below, and create new levels of government above nations and inside them.

What happened in 1989 was not merely a change in the world system of states (the end of bipolarism and of Cold War). There began to shape up a process in which globalization started to produce its first visible effects on the international system through the erosion of states' sovereignty and the decline of power politics. The fundamental concepts we were used to attach to the state – sovereignty, independence, non-intervention – are now questioned. They do not reflect the reality of today's world any longer. The dominant political phenomenon is the end of the international order based on territorial states, whose sovereignty is questioned by the rise of non-state actors, who are undermining the primacy of the state over civil society. States are downgraded to the rank of actors of a global civil society, which compete with non-state actors for the decision-making power at world level. They are no longer exclusive protagonists of international relations.

There is an analogy between the evolution of the European system of states after World War II and that of the bipolar world system after the fall of the blocks and the end of the Cold War. For a long time, the history of both systems has been dominated by the struggle for hegemony. After the failure of the attempt by the most powerful states at prevailing over each other through force, it became possible to take the road of cooperation, which in Europe opened the way to economic integration and political unification. This happened because the reasons driving to cooperation were stronger than those of antagonism, and the existence of higher common interests has been acknowledged.

On the other hand, the undoing of the institutions of the epoch of Cold War shows that the world is getting out of control and the direction to be taken by international politics is the strengthening and democratization of the UN and the other international institutions. The disastrous cycle of the American monopolarism, inspired by the George Bush's megalomaniac dream to transform the United States into a world empire, and the refusal to abide by the discipline of international organizations and the constraints of multilateral agreements, is concluded. The United States is becoming aware of the decline of its power. The end of the Cold War did not mark only the collapse of the Soviet system, but also the retreat of the American power in the world, as shown by the failure of military interventions carried out in the last four decades, from Viet Nam to Iraq. And these facts have been accompanied by the rise of the EU, China, India, Brazil and by the recognition of the need for a cooperative management of world politics.

The Federalist Debate has been monitoring and analyzing the evolution of world politics from the end of the bipolar world order to the ephemeral affirmation of the American monopolarism to the current disorder, characterized by the temptation of a return to the troubles of power politics and Cold War. I summarize here the most significant results of our research.

The end of the Cold War's bipolar balance of power was not the starting point of the formation of a new world order, nor of the affirmation of new binding rules in international relations. What we can assert with certainty is that the world is evolving towards a multipolar order, as shown by the emergence of the so-called BRICS, the new protagonists of world economy and politics. Facing globalization and the erosion of state sovereignty, the world has to respond to four challenges.

The first challenge is the increasing number of problems of such a magnitude that cannot find a solution within the borders of individual states, also of the states that include wide regions of the world. This means that the crisis of the sovereign state affects also those giant states which formerly we were used to call superpowers. The great issues of peace, security, protection of human rights, the regulation of the global market, poverty, international justice and environment protection have taken on global dimensions. The states, which are progressively losing control of their essential functions – economic development and security – are not able to face problems of global dimension. But also international organizations and international regimes are increasingly inadequate to this task. The difficulties that the negotiations on the main items on the global agenda are facing confirm that. The IMF and G-20 have been so far unable to open the way to a reform of the international monetary system, i.e. the replacement of the dollar as a reserve currency with a basket of currencies, conceived as a step toward a world reserve currency. The Kyoto Protocol has been unsuccessful in fighting against climate change and hopes that it could be supplanted by a World Environmental

Organization endowed with binding powers have been so far deceived. The nuclear non-proliferation negotiations have failed in the attempt to address the issue of a universal and controlled nuclear disarmament.

The second challenge generated by globalization is the rise of global non-state actors, whose action escapes states' control. Banks, stock exchanges, rating agencies, multinational companies are taking the world market away from states' control. Religious organizations, research centers, Foundations, Universities are working out and spreading around cultural models on the world plane. Global TV networks (CNN, Al Jazeera, etc.) shape global public opinion. Nuclear disarmament or environmental movements are activating the first forms of citizens' mobilization at the world level. Criminal and terrorist organizations are threatening the monopoly of violence held by the states. In sum, globalization is digging an ever deeper ditch between the states, which remain national, and the market and civil society, which are taking on a global dimension. Thus, the states, having lost the power to decide on the issues that will determine the future of mankind, show their inadequacy to govern globalization.

A third challenge is represented by the fact that the citizens feel that they have lost control of their destiny, because the most important decisions are taken at world level while democracy stops at states borders. Beyond those borders, relations of force dominate between states and non-state actors competing with one another for determining the lines of world policies. There ensues a crisis of consent towards political institutions and of legitimization of public powers. Consequently, the decline of the state brings about the triumph of private interests connected with the market and the decline of collective values which politics is supposed to promote. A new ideology is taking shape: market fundamentalism. Hans Tietmeyer, former governor of the German Federal Bank, in 1998 endorsed the idea that global markets are more democratic than parliamentary elections, praising national governments for preferring: "The permanent plebiscite of global markets to the plebiscite of the ballot box".[8] In fact, citizens vote and choose their government, but those elected too often obey the dictates of private interest groups not accountable to the people. The new ruling class – consisting of 1% of the population, as "Occupy Wall Street" repeats –, has deprived the people of the power to decide its own destiny. The powerlessness of democratic institutions is rooted in the weakness of national governments and parliaments with regard to the global decision-making power of financial oligarchies. Faced with this dilemma, it is no exaggeration to say that the survival of democracy is at risk.

A final challenge lies in the fact that, with nuclear weapons and climate change, for the first time in history, humankind has acquired such

8 Žižek, Slavoj, "How Capital Captured Politics", *The Guardian*, 13 July 2014.

a destructive power as to threaten the continuation of life on the planet, but has not yet developed the power to govern it. This is a clear signal that we have entered in a new epoch of history. Albert Einstein wrote: "The unleashed power of the atom has changed everything save our modes of thinking, and thus we drift toward an unparalleled catastrophe".[9] The alternative facing humanity is then extinction or a world government. In the face of the global character of the destructive forces threatening the survival of mankind, the Kantian project of perpetual peace through world Federation does not appear any longer a distant ultimate goal of universal history, but takes on the features of a concrete political proposal offering a practical solution to the immediate problems troubling humanity.

For centuries the states have been regulating the market and civil society through a system of laws and institutions tasked with keeping order and the repression of behaviors contrary to the norms of civil coexistence. The answer to the loss of state's control over the enforcement of norms and public order cannot but come from politics. This is indeed the field where the efforts to govern the historical process may be successful.

Terrorism, climate change and the financial and economic crisis are three issues to which *The Federalist Debate* has devoted special attention. They are consequences of globalization without government. Only political institutions can stop the dissemination of violence that is an outcome of the retreat of politics. Moreover, the current financial and economic crisis has unquestionably revealed the flaws in the present system: the lack of coercive rules to combat the abuses committed by the speculators and the inability of governments to take effective action. Yet, economic order implies both rules and a government to enforce them, i.e. a political order.

The mainstream political reaction to the globalization process, championed by the majority of policy makers, is "global governance". It is the most popular formula widely used in reference to a minimum amount of norms necessary to assure the global order without the support of an organized government. It represents one of the possible ways of extending the sphere of action of politics to the global level. It manifests the need to assure guidance to international politics and economy, without resort to new powers at international level or to a world government. Whereas it recognizes a role to state governments, it considers non-essential the institution of higher levels of government on the regional and world planes.

This idea has been welcomed by governments, because it considers cooperation between states the only way for addressing international

9 Nathan, Otto and Norden, Heinz (eds.). *Einstein on Peace* (New York: Simon & Schuster, 1960, p. 376).

issues and does not question national sovereignty. But the financial and economic crisis has unquestionably shown the flaws of a lack of government and coercive rules to combat the abuses committed by the speculators and, more generally, to govern globalization. The fact is that the economic order implies rules and a government, i.e. a political order. Without adequate institutions and rules, globalization cannot be regulated. Today the only effective response to the need of a new world order can only come from politics and more precisely from the return of the primacy of politics over markets. In this perspective, global governance can be conceived as a step on the way leading to world government.

The idea of a world government continues to raise distrust and hostility not only on the part of the supporters of national sovereignty, i.e. the nationalist circles, but also on the part of many figures of the democratic thought, for instance Ulrich Beck.[10] The fear is that an authoritarian and uncontrolled power, a kind of planetary Leviathan, can come about.

The achievement of world peace is a process tending to constitutionalize that sphere of political life that still belongs to the state of nature and that is the field of the diplomatic and military confrontation between states. Peace is not just the absence of war or, more precisely, the "truce" in the interval between two wars, as the term is understood to this day in common language (negative peace), but rather the situation, described by Kant in *Perpetual Peace*, that does not seek "merely to stop one war," but "seeks to end all wars forever" (positive peace)[11]. The transfer of the monopoly of coercive force to a world authority is the main instrument to eliminate war and solve all conflicts through law. As a matter of fact, with a world government it will be possible to eliminate a traditional function of government, i.e. defense, which is necessary only in a world divided into sovereign states. Universal and controlled disarmament is necessary for building a lasting peace. As Clark and Sohn asserted, disarmament "should be accomplished by carefully verified stages and subject to a well-organized system of inspection".[12] This does not mean that the world government will be in a position to fulfill its functions without armed forces. Although it will not wage war, nor have foreign relations, it will have the obligation to keep public order. Thus, the armed forces will play only a police role.

In addition, the elimination of war will weaken one of the strongest factors of tyranny and despotism, the search of security in the face of external threats, which often has driven the states to limit the freedom

---

10 Beck, Ulrich. *What is Globalization?* (Cambridge: Polity Press, 1999, p. 164).

11 Kant, Immanuel. "Perpetual Peace", in Ted Humphrey (ed.), *Perpetual Peace and Other Essays* (Indianapolis: Hackett, 1988, p. 117).

12 Clark, Grenville and Sohn, Louis B. *World Peace through World Law: Two Alternative Plans* (Cambridge, MA: Harvard University Press, 1966, p. XVI).

of individuals and to erode the institutions created for protecting human rights against the abuses of public powers. There is "no example of modern autocratic government [...] which does not draw its internal strength from an external threat," noted Eric Weil. Therefore, since "in a World State, threat and possibility of aggression would disappear," power concentration to face security threats would become unnecessary.[13] But there is another unobserved consequence. Owing to the fact that it will not have to wage war, world government would likely be the weakest form of government experienced in human history.

The way leading to world government is long and tortuous. But, as Tommaso Padoa-Schioppa used to say, "we are not at zero-point". To realize that the first step has been taken, it is sufficient to mention the institution of the International Criminal Court in 1998, which is empowered to incriminate and sentence individuals guilty of genocide, war crimes, crimes against humanity and aggression. It is the sign that the world is approaching an order in which the subjects of international law are the individuals, and no longer the States only. This means that the premises are being created for overcoming the distinction between domestic and international law, and for the recognition of a cosmopolitan law. This important achievement is simply a starting point on the way of the world government.

I would like to conclude with a quotation taken from an article that Tommaso Padoa-Schioppa wrote for *The Federalist Debate* a few weeks after the destruction of the Twin Towers: "In the construction of a world political order within which to pursue that part of peace, liberty, prosperity, justice (I say "part" because not all peace, liberty, etc. are dependent on the state of the world: there is one peace in the family and one in the city, a local and a universal justice) which is realisable only on a global scale, the path is steep. But we must know that we are not at zero-point. We sensed and turned onto that path almost a century ago. The same failures endured up to now have something to teach us. What Altiero Spinelli said on the subject of European unity is valid for the creation of a world political order: the strength of an idea is revealed not by the fact that it imposes itself without friction at its first appearance, but from its capacity to be reborn out of defeat. If an idea contains in itself what I call the beginning of the solution to a question that torments humanity, to that idea people will come back, trying again and again. The failings of repeated attempts will not succeed in erasing it from people's mind and will."[14]

Let us follow his invitation to concentrate our efforts and mental capacities on this great constructive task.

---

13 Weil, Eric. *Philosophie politique*. (Paris: Vrin, 1984, p. 240).

14 Padoa-Schioppa, Tommaso. "September 12: The World is not at Zero-Point", *The Federalist Debate*, XV, 2002, 2, p. 39.

Part One

Old and New Shapes of Federalism

Lucio Levi

The concept of "crisis of the nation-state", illustrated in the introduction, enables to formulate a comprehensive historical judgment on our time and, more specifically, to point out the relationship between the crisis of the European states system and German imperialism, world wars, international economic disorder and the authoritarian degeneration of the structure of nation-states. Furthermore, that concept shows that the nation-states are powerless to cope with the basic trends of contemporary history (internationalization of the production process, formation of a world system of states, primacy of states with macro-regional dimension).

Federalism presents itself as the political project which enables to control and give impulse to a double process of reorganization of the nation-states through a transfer of powers toward higher and lower levels of government, i.e. the international organizations, established at the macro-regional and global levels, and the territorial communities smaller than the nation-states. Federal institutions promote the overcoming of the closed and centralized structures of the nation-state with the formation, downstream, of genuine regional and local autonomies, and the realization, upstream, of effective forms of political and social solidarity between nation-states and regional groupings of states.

Federalism is a form of political organization which aims to tame and domesticate the violent and authoritarian nature of the nation-state, by raising internal and external limits to it. Federal institutions are the most developed shape of limited government, as citizens are subject to at least two – but potentially several – independent governments and to a multilevel legal and fiscal order. They add to the traditional division between legislative, executive and judicial powers, the one between federal government and federated governments. Moreover, since citizens belong at the same time to several territorial communities – city, county, region, nation, great region of the world and the world –, they hold multiple loyalties that operate on different levels and therefore do not conflict with each other. Thus, with federal institutions a new form of citizenship takes shape, which could be called "multidimensional citizenship". At the same time, federalism is the only political system which ensures that democracy can express itself at all levels, from local to the world, and thus combines local with international democracy. Diericks and Padoa-Schioppa carefully distinguish the difference between the international (or confederal) and the constitutional (or federal) approach and assert that only the second one enables to expand the sphere of democracy and the rule of law to the international level.

It is generally maintained by scholars – in this book by Nadia Urbinati – that the subsidiarity principle defines the specific character of federal institutions. It is true that this principle suggests how powers are to be distributed between various levels of government. However, it is to be noticed that this principle is compatible with the most different forms of government, particularly with the confederation and the unitary decentralized state. In a confederation, the confederal authority is subordinate to the governments of the confederated communities. In a unitary decentralized state, regional and local authorities are subordinate to the central government. Instead, in a federal Constitution, powers are shared between the government of the whole constituent political community (federal government) and the governments of the entities of which it is composed (federated governments). Each government is independent in its own sphere, separate from the other ones. Therefore, in federalist theory, the word "independence" must not be understood in absolute terms. In fact, regional governments have limited powers. In the same way, the federal government has limited powers too. Everyone exercises a legislative power within its own sphere. None of these governments is subordinate to the others. Each governmental level is at the same time "independent and co-ordinate", according to the formula coined by Kenneth C. Wheare.[1] The federal system allows the conciliation of independence of all power centers, even the smallest ones, with the unity of a large territory, which in the future may potentially include the whole world through the United Nations reform.

A process of power devolution from the national governments to the regions is in progress all over Europe. For instance, Ernest Wistrich maintains that this process underway in the UK is evolving towards a federal destination. At the same time, the most vital part of regionalist movements has decided to support European unification and to abandon the obsolete idea of micro-nationalism, that would lead to an entrenchment within the regional borders. But in these circles is very popular a questionable idea, upheld in this book by Robert Lafont: the so-called "Europe of Regions", which would imply the purpose of erasing the nation-states and transforming the regions into direct members of the European federation. Considering that national governments should be eased from the burden of addressing the problems of regional or local

[1] Wheare, Kenneth C, *The Federal Government* (London: Oxford University Press, 1966, p. 11).

dimensions and, at the same time, supranational issues, the fact is that the national governments still have a reason to survive: the existence of several problems of national dimension, which need national solutions. F.i., as Robert Toulemon argues, "there is a consensus about maintaining at the national level the mechanisms of social welfare". Likewise, the protection of national languages and cultures is a function that should remain under control of national governments. Whereas the federalizing process "has gone far in important aspects of the Union's internal affairs", in the field of foreign and security policy it "remains at an early stage", has observed John Pinder. The consequence is that the EU is unable to speak with one voice in international affairs. As Barbara Spinelli argued, "without a government, Europe may well be more democratic, but is absolutely without any weight." On the other hand, it is to be noted that regions have insufficient dimensions and powers to exercise an effective countervailing power toward the European institutions. Therefore, nation-states still keep a role: that of intermediate articulations between the regions and Europe. A European federation composed of a mosaic of regional-dimension states, in which the national level is eliminated, would be destined to oscillate between anarchy and centralism. After all, the difficult problem the construction of the European unity has to solve is "Making Europe without unmaking France"[2] and we should add "and any other nation". Of course, Monnet considered acceptable this formula borrowed from George Bidault provided that making Europe would mean to proceed on the way of delegation of sovereignty.

*

* *

Einaudi's forerunning federalist interpretation of contemporary history has been quoted in the introduction to this book. His writings together with the British federalist literature represent the main sources of post-war federalism. For these thinkers, federalism is not a political priority, but remains an idea ancillary to liberalism and socialism. They conceive federalism simply as a method for the organization of power, a constitutional technique which abolishes armed conflicts among states which have subscribed to a federal pact. In other words, federation appears as an alternative to war and not the response to the main problems of the current phase of history characterized by the transition from the time of nation-states to the era of multinational states and global politics. Conceived in these terms, federalism is simply the completion of liberalism and socialism, a means to protect the values promoted by these ideologies from the negative consequences of international anarchy.

---

2 Monnet, Jean. *Mémoires* (Paris: Fayard, 1976, p. 463).

Unlike Lord Lothian[3], one the most eminent exponents of British federalism, who died in 1940 during World War Two, Lionel Robbins lived until 1984. Thus, he witnessed the development of European unification until the direct election of the European Parliament. He never repudiated either the idea of the decline of the nation-states or his attachment for the concept of federalism. The need for a larger political unit than nation-states is imposed by the technology of industrial era. Therefore, the alternative that Europe was facing before WWII according to Robbins was a union "by mutual agreement or by caesarian conquest."[4] The defeat of nazism paved the way to the construction of the European unity by consent. What is paradoxical is the fact that Robbins, who had been one of the most brilliant advocates of European federalism before and during the war, gave up this specific cause by just at the moment, after the war, when the political conditions for European unification were ripening. He opposed the project for the European Coal and Steel Community and supported the idea of an Atlantic Community, as he believed that Europe was unable to ensure its independence without the aid of the United States. Likewise, Ernesto Rossi, a co-author of the *Ventotene Manifesto*, gave up his commitment for European unification after the fall of the European Defence Community in 1954, when, owing to the thawing of the Cold War, the danger of a Third World War began to lessen. Lastly, the limit of Einaudi's federalist commitment – to which he remained faithful also when he became President of the Italian Republic – lies in the fact that no political proposal on how to carry out the federalist design can be found in his writings. Once he had illustrated the nature of the objective to be pursued, he considered his task accomplished.

What is important to recall here is that the first attempt to create a European federation with the support of a government and a public opinion movement occurred during WWII. Charles Kimber, one of the three founders of Federal Union, described the story of the birth of this organization, occurred in 1938. It is a milestone in the history of federalism, the first example of a federalist movement made up of a group of active members capable of exerting an influence on political, intellectual and social circles and public opinion, organized over the territory with local branches (over 200, according to Kimber's assessment) and a newsletter. This organizational model is not substantially different from that applied by post-war federalist movements. The action of Federal Union was so penetrating that it can "claim, with some justification to have brought the

3 It is worth quoting here his masterpiece *Pacifism is not Enough (nor Patriotism Either)*, (London: Oxford University Press, 1941).

4 Robbins, Lionel, *The Economic Causes of War* (New York: Howard Fertig, 1968, p. 107).

offer of union with France within the 'art of the possible' (at least in that desperate moment). But it also can claim to have put federation at the top of the agenda of such public discussion of 'war aims'" (Kimber C., 2005, 49). John Parry offers in his contribution a detailed account of this attempt to create the core of a European federation, starting from an Anglo-French Union. Winston Churchill on 16 June 1940 for strengthening the resistance to Nazism, proposed to France, which was about to fall under German rule, to join Great Britain, instituting a Parliament, a government, and an army in common. When Churchill wrote in his memoirs of the War Cabinet's discussion about the proposal that "France and Britain shall no longer be two nations, but one Franco-British Union", he expressed his surprise when he saw "the staid, solid, experienced politicians engage themselves so passionately in an immense design".[5]

The author of Churchill's plan was Jean Monnet, who devoted the first chapter of his *Memoirs*[6] to the narration of this event. When France was occupied by the Nazi army, he was at London, where he was President of the Franco-British co-ordination committee, created to organize a joint military action. Monnet's special talent lay in his capacity to influence crucial decisions, working far from the limelight, in the background where the future is prepared patiently. After the war he became a protagonist of European unification.

In the moment of the collapse of the European system, for the first time a national government, reversing the system's historical tendency to work on the principle of the balance of power among independent states, was formulating a proposal of federal unification. The significance of that proposal is clear: the federal principle had become an operational political objective. Unfortunately, that proposal did not find in the defeated French government an interlocutor ready to accept such a revolutionary project, and it was dropped. Thus, Europe did not enter a road that could have led it to its federal unification around a Franco-British core.

Aside from that episode, Churchill always pursued the UK independence in relation to Europe and the United States. In a 1930 article he stated: "We have our own dream ... We are with Europe, but not of it"[7]. In other words, Churchill envisaged European unification only for the countries of the continent, not for Britain. This is the fundamental meaning of the message he launched from the University of Zürich in 1946, when he supported

---

5 Churchill, Winston S., *The Second World War. Vol. 2: Their Finest Hour* (London: Cassell, 1949, pp. 180-184).

6 Monnet, Jean, *op. cit.*

7 Churchill, Winston S., "The United States for Europe", *Saturday Evening Post*, 15 February 1930, quoted in Coudenhove-Kalergi, Richard, *An Idea Conquers the World* (London: Hutchinson, 1953, p. 163).

again the idea of "a kind of United States of Europe", but keeping for Britain the role of a sponsor from the outside. For him, a united Europe was first of all the necessary bulwark against Soviet expansionism. We can assert that, at the distance of seventy years, the British attitude towards European unification has not substantially changed.

*

* *

The need to look in depth into the evils of the World Wars epoch led the founding fathers of the federalist movement to conceive a grandiose plan for Europe freed from fascism and nazism not limited to the construction of peace, but including social protection, freedom from need and active democracy. On this subject, it is important to mention William Beveridge, one of the towering personalities of British federalism, to point out that, among post-war aims conceived by federalists, peace – for sure the most important and the most difficult objective to attain – is only one chapter of a more comprehensive plan, which included the invention of the Welfare State. In the preface to the *The Price of Peace*, published in 1945, he stressed that three main objectives had to be pursued: "peace, a job when one can work, an income when one cannot work".[8] This concern did not worry only the British federalists. Ernesto Rossi, co-author of the *Ventotene Manifesto* wrote in 1942 during confinement before the Beveridge Plan a book titled *Abolishing Misery*.[9] In agreement with the Beveridge Plan, he supports the idea of a health care system. But the most original and forerunning proposal is a sort of compulsory civilian service for young people after school.

The goods and services produced by the youth work would provide people in need with sustenance as an alternative to monetary aid, a source of waste and inefficiency. Barbara Spinelli argues that the pursuit of the objectives of full employment and basic income for those who for any reason are unable to work has a great relevance to face the current financial and economic crisis the world is confronted with.

Another author who advocated an extensive reform of economic institutions is James Meade. One of his major contributions to think the contemporary world is *Agathotopia*[10]. This word means "a good place". In fact, Meade used economics to help make the world not a perfect but a better place to live in. Agathotopia is an imaginary island-nation,

---

8 Beveridge, William H., *The Price of Peace* (London: Pilot Press, 1945, p. VII).

9 Rossi, Ernesto, *Abolire la miseria* (Milano: La Fiaccola, 1946).

10 Meade, James E., *Agathotopia: The Economics of Partnership* (Aberdeen: Aberdeen University Press, 1989).

where firms are organized in a way that capitalists and employees hold shares which receive equal dividends. Therefore, the employees receive a dividend instead of wages and are transformed into entrepreneurs. Alfonso Iozzo underlines the significance of Meade's approach for leading the transition from the industrial to scientific mode of production and to a sustainable economy not based on debt, but on public patrimony. In the measurement of GDP, Meade suggests to take into account of the value of non-renewable resources and recommends to return to the use of the concept of patrimony to assess the wealth of a nation. This is the way to evaluate whether future generations will have a greater or lesser amount of natural resources available.

The Maastricht Treaty marks a turning point on the way of the affirmation of the principle of solidarity between generations. As it prescribes not to burden future generations with debts contracted by the current one, it takes a step on the way of the extinction of public debt. But this is not enough. A European investment plan for sustainable development and employment supported by European own resources, foreshadowed by the Juncker Plan promoted by the President of the European Commission after the European elections of 2014, should complement the efforts to reduce the public debt. In the long term, owing to the constant depletion of natural goods, it is necessary to replace public debt with a sovereign wealth fund in order to build a significant stock of public capital to be used to fund the Welfare State and especially citizens' basic income. This fund is necessary to protect citizens against unemployment in times of crisis or against the consequences of quick technological progress, like the reduction of the demand for labor and the increase of income inequalities. A significant example is the Norwegian pension fund fostered by oil and gas revenues. Meade advocated a social dividend as a central ingredient of a just and efficient economy.

The power of new ideas has been the most influential factor in history. It has received less attention from scholars than action. But action can succeed provided that it is inspired by a project capable of promoting progress. The attraction power of the federalist message and its capacity to mobilize support lies, as pointed out by Francesco Rossolillo, in its cultural autonomy and more precisely in its alternative vision of history and politics to what is still considered the natural order of things, i.e. the state-centric paradigm. Like all political projects which want to change the world, federalism has an active attitude towards politics. The great contribution of the federalist movements, according to Fernando Iglesias, lies in the creation of new institutions, like the European Parliament – the laboratory of international democracy – or the International Criminal Court – the laboratory of international justice –. He warns federalists not to fall in the temptation of confining their commitment to the management of the existing institutions instead of engaging themselves in the full accomplishment of their project through the creation of new institutions.

The analysis of the institutions of the federal States established so far makes us appreciate the importance of the institutional innovations necessary for bringing to conclusion the construction of the European unity. What makes European unification an undertaking without precedents in history is the attempt to build a Federation of national States. The pluri-national nature of the EU fosters a new form of citizens' loyalty, that Toulemon defines on the wake of Jürgen Habermas "constitutional patriotism", the political attachment to the values embodied in the Constitution.

Firstly, it is to be remarked that all the Federations established so far have been unions of cantons, provinces or regions. Never has a federal order been created that includes a group of national States proud of their independence, which have determined for centuries the trends of world politics and are the most thorough expression of the idea itself of sovereign State. For these reasons they demand to keep within the European federal institutions in the making a degree of independence greater than any other in the past. The substance of the new shape of federalism embodied by the EU lies in the formula "Union of States and Citizens".

Among the most significant innovations of the European federalizing process there is to point out: a) the awarding to the European Council, i.e. the Heads of State and Government, of the power to appoint the President of the Commission, thus assigning the role of Presidency of the Union to a collegiate body; b) the awarding to the Council, in which each state is represented by its government, of the power to participate in the Union's legislation; c) the arranging of the Union with three levels of government (European, national and regional); d) the European Central Bank's independence from governments whose primary objective is to maintain price stability, protect citizens against inflation and prevent governments from financing public expenditure through money emission.

Secondly, all Federations have felt the negative burden of power politics, which, especially in the era of the world wars and during the cold war, has brought about everywhere the strengthening of the federal governments to the detriment of the regional governments and hence a general tendency to the centralization of power. In turn, the class struggle has caused a deep social fracture, which has hindered the formation of the solidarity required for developing the typical dialectic of federal societies between the smaller territorial communities and the whole society. In sum, the class struggle has strengthened the tendency to centralization.

This is the most serious degenerative aspect that has characterized the institutional evolution of Federations in the contemporary world.

Hence the necessity to test a new federal model that could ensure in a more efficient fashion the independence of the member States. Actually, it is something more than a mere necessity. It is a real possibility, if one considers that the European Federation will be born in a world where the globalization process and the decline of power politics have fostered powerful tendencies to cooperation and international organization, which it will contribute to consolidate. At the same time, the overcoming of the class struggle has eliminated another factor of centralization of power.

*

* *

The most engaging challenge federalism has to face in our days is constitutionalizing globalization. This means, in other terms, to govern the globalization process by building a world order that has the federalist constitutionalism as its cornerstone. It is a long-run objective that requires years and even decades of effort.

The power to govern human communities has shifted from the national to international level and from politics to economics. The old maps provided by the traditional political thinking, embodied by liberal, democratic and socialist political parties have lost their capacity to plan the future, since they are imprisoned in the steel cage of nation-states. The division of the world into sovereign states survives within the framework of the globalization of markets and civil society. This is the main obstacle on the way of the economic and social progress. The scene, for the time being, is occupied by the globalist liberalism and xenophobic nationalism, which clash against each other, and try to keep federalism out of the scene.

The old and obsolete state-centric paradigm rests on two axioms: the supremacy of the state over market and civil society and the predominance of the states in the sphere of international politics. These axioms no longer correspond to the reality of our times. Globalization has questioned these two postulates of the state-centric paradigm, which put the state at the center of political thought and action. In fact the most significant consequence at the political level of globalization is the erosion of state sovereignty. On the one hand, with the formation of the global civil society, globalization puts in a critical position the principle of state supremacy over market and civil society, whose dynamic escapes state control. On the other hand, international relations are conditioned in an increasingly glaring way by non-state actors (multinational corporations and banks, non-governmental organizations, criminal and terrorist groups etc.), which threaten the control that the states used to exert exclusively over international relations and compete with the states for the decision-making power on the great issues of international politics.

If we ask ourselves how the crisis of the sovereign state will be resolved and how politics will be able to govern the globalization process, an important indication may come from an analysis of European unification. The institutions of the European Union are an expression of a general tendency towards constitutionalizing international relations. Institutions like the European Parliament, endowed with legislative co-decision and control powers towards the European Commission, or the euro, the single European currency, show that the Union has gone beyond the traditional forms of cooperation which characterize international organizations. The constitutional construction site of the European Union is the laboratory of a new form of statehood. It should be pointed out that this process creates a new level of government in Europe, which does not substitute but rather joins those existing nationally, regionally and locally. However, it has the power to interfere in the domestic affairs of the states as regards its areas of competence, such as monetary, trade and competition policies. It is to be underscored that the latter is based on the bestowal of an antitrust authority to the European Commission. If we want to govern globalization, it is obvious that like powers must be instituted at the international level.

The end of the Cold War and the apparent inability of the United States to continue to play the role of the world's policeman and banker, have contributed to put in the world agenda the United Nations reform, whose institutions were devised at the end of World War Two, in a world very different from the present one. The emergence of the European Union as a global player – so far only in the monetary and trade sectors – together with the rise of China, India and Brazil as economically and politically influential developing countries will allow international equilibria to evolve towards multilateralism. This is the condition for awarding to the UN the role of custodian of the international order, based on law instead of on force.

The institution of the International Criminal Court (ICC) represents the first success of the political commitment of world federalists. The application of international law to individuals guilty of genocide, war crimes and crimes against humanity is a principle that indisputably reproduces on the international plane a state-peculiar prerogative and is the expression of the ongoing process of constitutionalization of international relations. It is worth underlining a non-fortuitous fact: the then fifteen members of the European Union have all voted in 1998 for instituting the ICC, whereas the US has voted against. It is the confirmation that the primary objective of the EU's foreign policy is the creation of an international order founded on the rule of law.

*

* *

This leads to address the problem of political action. In this field Spinelli's work made a really innovatory impact. He defined the strategy to achieve the European federation. This objective has a dual nature. On the one hand, it is a treaty in which states agree to give up part of their power to a supranational government, and on the other it is a Constitution defining the structure of this union of states. Since the nature of the objective determines the character of the means to be used, Spinelli concluded that progress towards the construction of a European federation would not be practicable without the agreement of the states, even though the latter represent the main obstacle to the transfer of powers to the European level. This obstacle can be overcome only through a movement from below.

The model of the Philadelphia Constitutional Convention was constantly in his mind. Following this example, Spinelli specified the characteristics of the constituent method which he saw as the only procedure possible for the successful construction of a European democratic power. It required on the one hand a European constituent assembly representing all the peoples and political forces of Europe. This would be the only body entitled to act since its legitimacy would derive from the citizens' election and therefore had the authority necessary to draft and propose a Constitution. On the other hand, as a democratic assembly it would take its decisions publicly and by majority vote together with procedures permitting a clear identification of responsibilities and therefore enabling democratic and productive decision-making. This is, namely, the opposite of the diplomatic method which is based on decisions taken behind closed doors and by unanimity, without the participation of the political parties, media and public opinion: a process which protects national sovereignty and leads to compromises that have to take the individual interests of every participating state into account.

The Spinelli's design would have remained longtime at the stage of a project had Monnet not been able to start the European integration process with the European Coal and Steel Community. The European federation was the ultimate goal of his political commitment. It is explicitly mentioned in the Schuman Plan. But the underlying idea of the Plan was that "Europe will not be created at a stroke", but "upon concrete achievements which first create a *de facto* solidarity"[11]. Monnet and Spinelli were endowed with a special ability to exploit the contradictions of the European politics in order to introduce a new element in it and to

[11] Monnet, Jean, *op. cit.*, p. 355.

change the course of history. Monnet exercised it in starting unification process, Spinelli in seeking to conclude it. In other words, their role was determinant in different stages of European unification.

When the first European institutions were established, Spinelli's strategic goal became the bestowal of the constitutional mandate on the parliamentary bodies which were a significant aspect of those institutions. On the basis of this constitutional strategy, Spinelli twice succeeded in bringing Europe to the threshold of a federal union. First, he tried to put the European army – in course of construction between 1951 and 1954 – under a European political power. Second, in 1984, as a member of the European Parliament he tried again with the draft Treaty of European Union. In both cases it was a parliamentary body – the enlarged Assembly of the European Coal and Steel Community and the European Parliament – that drafted the constitutional document. And in both cases the constitutional project was defeated by a single government: France in the first instance, and then Britain. The Convention summoned in 2001 to frame a European Constitution was the most recent incarnation of Spinelli's constitutional strategy, though at the same time it contained an innovatory element, namely a constitutional procedure based on co-decision between associated national and European institutions and their governmental and parliamentary organs.

Questioning himself about the Spinelli's legacy, John Pinder observed, "the final destination of his odyssey is not yet in sight. But his life remains an inspiration for those who are continuing the journey, and in particular for those who wish to complete it."

The Birth of Federal Union*

Charles KIMBER

Federal Union was born in September 1938 at the time of 'Munich'; by anger out of desperation.

'Munich' finally forced everyone to declare themselves. One side saw Chamberlain's journeys and signature as a brave action, vindicating his policy of appeasement. We and our children should be eternally grateful; war had been averted. The other side saw it as a shameful surrender in a long line of surrenders. Antagonisms became passionate: long-time friends stopped speaking to each other, families became divided. And Hitler ranted on regardless.

Chamberlain's policy of 'appeasement' was the product of a government dominated by a generation of men who had been too old to fight in 1914. They had thought to restore their own pre-war Victorian values; the right to separate nationhood, and of each nation to decide its own foreign policy backed by its own armed forces to defend that independence. The individual sovereignty of each nation was held to be sacrosanct; it was the duty of its young male citizens to die for it if necessary. Any difference of interest between nations would be solved reasonably by diplomats from the parties involved.

The sons of that older generation had fought in the trenches. But those who had survived did not take over. They retired into themselves and the nightmares of what their forbears had called on them to do; and what they had seen and done. It was a generation which took little part in government, leaving it to the old men, now joined by the 'profiteers who had done well out of the war', to carry on. Those of them who did take part in government such as Eden and Macmillan, dismissed by Neville Chamberlain as the 'Boys Brigade', had been brought up in their fathers' values. They could differ with their elders but could not find it in themselves to break with them. They could approve the idea of a League of Nations bound by a communal alliance, but not at the expense of diplomacy between individual states and the creation of alliances and counter alliances; these remained the order of the day. The umbilical cord proved too strong and proved lethal. The idea that the League of Nations should be a body, which could override one to one diplomacy between

* Published in Issue 1/2005.

nations, and take action in its own name on behalf of them all, in the way that the Covenant of the newly created League seemed to make possible, was no part of their thinking. The League, in fact, had neither authority nor power to do so. Its constitution laid down that each member remained free to conduct its own diplomacy, backed if necessary by its own forces. It was an escape hatch for those who wanted to renege on collective action.

That generation was followed by one which had been too young to fight in 1914; but was just the right age to be called on now in 1939.

It was a generation which had been brought up with the writings of Norman Angell, H.G. Wells and Bertrand Russell and many others, together with a host of journals, as well as talk in the many branches of the League of Nations Union up and down the country. All identified 'national sovereignty' as the menace and the root from which wars developed. It had been brought up to regard 'collective security' under the Covenant of the League of Nations as a pledge that their fathers had not sacrificed their lives in vain; 'Covenant', with its biblical connotation, was an appropriate word. Though of age to fight it was a generation which was not experienced enough to take part in government – even Eden and Macmillan from the previous generation, were treated as no more than promising apprentices to be ignored or sidelined by their elders. The old men in control, however, found 'collective security' a useful vote winner; but privately held the idea in contempt. The young were naive enough to believe that they meant what they said.

The moment of truth came in 1935 when Mussolini began threatening to invade Abyssinia. In June eleven million people in Britain voted for sanctions against Italy if Mussolini carried out his threats – nine million of them for military sanctions. "Terribly mischievous" according to 66 year old Neville Chamberlain, already prime minister in waiting.

A paraphrase of Harold Macmillan's account (Wind of Change) of what followed may be cited. On 11 September the British foreign secretary, Samuel Hoare made what he described as 'a revivalist appeal to the Assembly of The League. At best, he said, it might start a new chapter of League recovery. The speech, however, had been minutely vetted by the Foreign Office and Neville Chamberlain. Nevertheless Hoare boldly proclaimed:

> "The League stands, and my country stands with it, for the collective maintenance of the Covenant in its entirety [...] If the burden is to be borne, it must be borne collectively. On behalf of His Majesty's government, I can say that in spite of these difficulties, that Government will be second to none in its intention to fulfil, within the measure of its capacity, the obligations which the Covenant lays upon it".

The following day two battle cruisers and a cruiser squadron arrived in Gibraltar, supporting his words.

The effect throughout the world, Macmillan recorded, was sensational. Belgium's representative at the League, for example, reported: "the British have decided to stop Mussolini, even if it means using force". In Britain, Macmillan wrote, the 'response was immediate and impressive; the sense of national unity and pride was aroused'; 'Once more we were going to take our right place in the world. America was neutral, Germany hostile; the democratic nations now looked to us, and we would not fail them. Britain was back in the lead'.

Mussolini called the old men's bluff; went ahead and invaded Abyssinia. There was then a pause while Baldwin called a general election; it had the effect of giving the old men a breathing space to recover from their shock. Baldwin fought the election on a policy which included support for the League and of rearmament as support for collective security. In the meantime the diplomats and Neville Chamberlain among others, quietly got to work to undo the damage which, in their eyes, Hoare's speech had done.

Having won the election on a policy of support for the League, however, the government, as Macmillan wrote, were in 'honour bound, in spite of a sentence here or there of reservation, to stop Mussolini. When the House of Commons met in November, no one – inside or outside Parliament – doubted that this was their firm purpose'. The Foreign Secretary and the Foreign Office thought otherwise. Within a fortnight the British Foreign Secretary, Samuel Hoare, stopped off in Paris on way to a holiday in Switzerland; the head of the Foreign Office just happened to be in Paris too; and the deal with Pierre Laval leaving Mussolini free to occupy almost all of Abyssinia, was agreed and signed without any consultation with London. Abyssinia was left with what the Times famously described as "a corridor for camels", to reach the sea.

In his biography of Neville Chamberlain, written some quarter of a century later, Iain Macleod judged correctly. "Historically", he wrote, "the Abyssinia crisis has often been presented as a side-show compared with the main drama of Germany's advance to world conquest. In fact it was the turning point of the thirties. Hitler was not slow to act upon this evidence of our weakness". Within a couple of months his troops occupied the Rhineland in violation of Versailles. Like Mussolini in Abyssinia, he was unopposed.

Hoare's squalid betrayal of Abyssinia finally killed off the League of Nations; it had been shown to be terminally impotent without leadership. Britain had had its chance to take the lead and had funked it. Hoare and his elderly associates had successfully put an end to any future action in the name of the League. The deception that 'collective security' could be relied on to work, and the treachery which had ensured that it didn't, had been uncovered. The memorial to the millions who had died in the 1914 war had been demolished without shame. The old men were seriously taken aback by the public reaction and discussed desperately where to lay the blame; finally they had to sacrifice Hoare and let Eden take his place.

But as 1936 went on all attention became concentrated on the gathering pace of events – the Rhineland occupation, Hitler's and Mussolini's participation in the Spanish Civil War on the side of a fellow dictator, and Britain's non-intervention, then the murder of Dollfuss and the occupation of Austria. Many of the young had already taken sides and had been so outraged that they had gone to Spain to fight against the dictators. But in general public opinion only began to feel the stirrings of fear; while remaining incredulous. Few were ready to think the unthinkable: that the dictators might have ideas beyond putting right what many felt had been wrong with the Peace Treaty of 1919. However useful they might be as a 'bulwark against Communism', the dictators might after all, be mad enough to be heading for a repeat of past horrors: a revenge war which would reassert their national pride. A divide in public opinion was beginning to open which would become a chasm at Munich. In the following year Neville Chamberlain, now Prime Minister, effectively took charge of relations with the Dictators, acting behind Eden's back; and the divide inevitably widened.

It was against this background, not surprisingly since it was all their futures which were at stake, that very many of the young were debating among themselves the reasons for the failure of the League of Nations in which they had been encouraged by their elders to invest so much confidence. In 1935 two young men who had attended the same school and left Oxford only two years previously found themselves working for the same boss, One, Derek Rawnsley, soon left in order to start two businesses of his own; both to do with pictures. The other, Charles Kimber, stayed on in the press and political division of oil companies, aiming for a career in politics. They took to lunching together more or less weekly and were often joined by others. Inevitably the same question arose and a general agreement emerged that heads of states, each acting in the name of his state (echoes of *l'état c'est moi*) could not be trusted to act collectively. The League itself should have had power to act; that to do so it needed forces under its own command; and should have consisted of elected members to authorise their use, rather than party political heads of state, each claiming to represent even those in opposition to him.

Munich was more than Rawnsley could stomach. He rang Kimber and said "Charles, we must do something. If you leave old Mudlitup, (our nickname for our boss) you can have a room in my office in Gordon Square and we'll start an organisation". Kimber feeling no less strongly, at once resigned his job and transferred to Rawnsley's offices at 44 Gordon Square. There, he set about writing a pamphlet which was to set out what the organisation should stand for. As he did so, the two were introduced to Patrick Ransome, a freelance journalist with a first class degree in international law. He told them that what they were proposing was a federation; and offered to come in with them.

The pamphlet was agreed between the three and duplicated. All three then sent copies to any of their friends who might be interested and an enthusiastic meeting of some sixty or seventy people endorsed what had been written. What is more they put up money to have it printed and distributed, Kimber then selected some 400 names from Who's Who who had shown interest in international affairs, and posted the pamphlet under the title 'Federal Union' with a covering handwritten letter to each.

The response was astonishing; and he and Ransome (Rawnsley being preoccupied with his businesses) were kept busy interviewing those who had replied. Among them were some who offered personal help; and a meeting with those of them who had, was arranged. A 'Panel of Advisers' was recruited consisting of Lord Lothian, member of Milner's "Kindergarten" in South Africa's reconstruction after the Boer war and Lloyd George's personal secretary at the Versailles Peace Conference; Lionel Curtis, also one of Lord Milner's young men and founder of Chatham House (the Royal institute of International Affairs); Professor Barbara Wootton, Head of Social Studies at London University; Wickham Steed, ex-editor of the Times, and Kingsley Martin, current editor of the New Statesman, then a required weekly read for those politically involved.

They suggested a short 'Statement of Beliefs' which each of them undertook to circulate among the great and the good of their acquaintance for their signature. Any who signed it were expressing support for a supra national rather than an international body; but not as members of Federal Union, though their signatures could be used in propaganda for the organisation. The wording of the statement followed closely the wording of the official objects of the organisation. The list of well-known public figures who had signed, when it appeared, was impressive. It was published as a leaflet, copies of which, it is believed, are to be found in the Federal Union archives at the LSE, together with much else.

In the meantime Gordon Square had been planting letters in the press, both national and local, and what started as a trickle soon developed into a flood of letters in response. A large proportion said that 'this was just what they had been thinking'. A very substantial number enclosed money. In reply they were advised to do what the founders had done: arrange a meeting of likeminded friends and form a branch. Federal Union was on its way. First just one secretary, then a small staff supported by many young people who volunteered their help for free. A constitution was then agreed at a meeting of representatives of branches, providing for an elected General council and an Executive Committee.

It seems uncertain how many joined as paid up members. 14,000 is one figure, 60,000 another. There seems to be general agreement, however, that there were over 200 branches up and down the country. What is certain is that within eighteen months of posting that original pamphlet, Federal Union had become so well-known and had aroused so much interest, that a meeting in the old Queens Hall, home of Sir Henry Wood's Promenade concerts (soon to be bombed out of existence) filled all its two to three thousand seats.

In the year before Hitler finally went to war, and during most of the following year while he was concentrating elsewhere, Britain 'enjoyed' the 'phoney war'. Lord Lothian wrote a pamphlet 'The Ending of Armageddon' and gave it to Federal Union for distribution to its members. More and more branches were formed as membership and money from them increased. Federal Union never had one substantial backer. Other organisations were created, notably Sir Richard Acland's New Commonwealth, backed by Edward Hulton's Picture Post, and supportive of Federal Union. But as the months passed the call up began to bite; more and more members got called up for military service, membership – and contributions – began to fall.

On the outbreak of war, Sir William Beveridge fulfilled an undertaking that he had given Rawnsley who had been a student at University College while Beveridge was Master. Beveridge created a Federal Union Research Institute, with Ransome as secretary by recruiting a number of leading figures in their fields. He formed them into groups to discuss the effects of a European federation on their various fields and to get one from each group to write up its conclusions. Federal Union published the results in a series of 'Federal Tracts'. Professors Lionel Robbins, Ivor Jennings, Barbara Wootton, Dr C.E.M. Joad and Lord Lugard were among the authors.

The Institute survived the war and became the Federal Trust. The branches and the organisation as it had originated did not. When the bombs began to fall, Federal Union in that form, like all other voluntary organisations made up of local branches, was among the casualties. Rawnsley had been called up and was killed (accidentally); and Kimber resigned. R.W.G. Mackay, later an MP, took over, but died prematurely. The post war Federal Union which John Pinder joined 51 years ago, inevitably, was a very different animal from the pre-war Federal Union, founded over sixty years ago, though it shares the name.

What, if anything, had Federal Union achieved? The great and the good may have been ready to sign that pre-war Statement of Beliefs without committing themselves to joining the organisation. It was an important contribution. But it would not have been noticed if Federal Union had not been there to initiate and publicise it. Federal Union had made enough noise to be able to claim, with some justification, to have brought the offer of union with France within the 'art of the possible' (at least at that desperate moment). But it also can claim to have put federation at the top of the agenda of such public discussion of 'war aims' as Churchill's insistence on 'unconditional surrender' allowed.

"Europe must federate or perish", said Clem Attlee in 1938. With opinion in Britain now divided across party lines, party loyalties seem too strong to allow those who want a genuine union to get together. Unless they do, Attlee will be proved right and Europe will remain a gaggle of little self-centred states, each exercising its precious 'national sovereignty' by deciding to surrender to the bribery, bullying, or flattery of an overwhelmingly powerful American Empire.

A Complete and Indissoluble Union*

John PARRY

Seventy years ago, on June 16th, 1940, the British government under Winston Churchill took the remarkable step of offering complete and indissoluble political union with France. The proposal was one of the most innovative in the history of the two countries. It read as follows:

"DECLARATION OF UNION[1]

At this most fateful moment in the history of the modern world The Governments of the United Kingdom and the French Republic make this declaration of indissoluble union and unyielding resolution in their common defence of justice and freedom against subjection to a system which reduces mankind to a life of robots and slaves.
The two governments declare that France and Great Britain shall no longer be two nations, but one Franco-British Union.
The constitution of the Union will provide for joint organs of defence, foreign, financial, and economic policies.
Every citizen of France will enjoy immediately citizenship of Great Britain; every British subject will become a citizen of France.
Both countries will share responsibility for the repair of the devastation of war, wherever it occurs in their territories, and the resources of both shall be equally, and as one, applied to the purpose.
During the war there shall be a single War Cabinet, and all the forces of Britain and France, whether on land, see, or in the air, will be placed under its direction. It will govern from wherever it best can. The two Parliaments will be formally associated. The nations of the British Empire are already forming new armies. France will keep her available forces in the field, on the sea, and in the air. The Union appeals to the United States to fortify the economic resources of the Allies, and to bring her powerful material aid to the common cause.
The Union will concentrate its whole energy against the power of the enemy, no matter where the battle may be.
And thus we shall conquer."

---

* Published in Issue 2/2010.

1 Quoted in Winston Churchill, *Their Finest Hour*, p. 183.

It was an act of desperation. Europe was in crisis. During the seven years since Hitler took power he had incorporated first Austria and then the Sudetenland into the German Reich, occupied what remained of Czechoslovakia, and overrun Poland. To help Poland but also thwart any further expansion Britain and France had then declared war.

After some months of comparative calm – the period of the so-called 'phoney war' – Hitler's troops had launched their spring offensive through neutral Belgium and the Netherlands. Thus by-passing France's main line of defence (the Maginot line), hemming in the British at Dunkirk and pressing on towards Paris.

In the final days of May the British in Dunkirk had succeeded under heavy fire in evacuating 338,226 men (including 139,097 French) by ship, but at the high cost of six Royal Navy destroyers sunk and nineteen others damaged. The RAF lost 474 planes, while all the army's heavy guns, tanks, and military transport had to be abandoned.

Meanwhile the enemy had reached the heartland of France. To save Paris from destruction the capital was declared an open city while the French government withdrew first to Tours, then to Bordeaux. Fearing that Hitler and his fascist allies might become the unchallenged masters of continental Europe, Churchill – who had replaced Neville Chamberlain as prime minister – crossed the Channel several times for emergency meetings to encourage his French counterpart Paul Reynaud to continue the fight and in particular to ensure that the French fleet did not fall into German hands.

Already in March Britain and France had signed an agreement that neither country would make a separate peace with Hitler[2]. It also contained a clause that in due course the agreement "might be expanded so as to give some contractual form to the continuance of Anglo-French economic and military collaboration after the end of the war." Now, only two months later, the situation had changed radically.

Clearly something more was needed, some initiative which would raise the spirits of the defeated French – but what? The answer came not from the government but from the initiative of two civil servants, one British and one French, working in London as members of the Anglo-French Coordination Committee concerned with military supplies and at that moment dealing with the urgent need for more fighter aircraft. Arthur Salter and Jean Monnet had known each other since the 1914-1918 war when they had been engaged on a similar task. Conscious that only a grand gesture could keep the alliance intact they set about drawing up a draft declaration proposing a way of binding France and Britain more closely together: namely, that the two countries should become

2 Foreign Office file FO371/242962, p. 44.

a single, indissoluble political union[3]. But how would such a political union function? Salter's peacetime experience in the League of Nations administration had taught him that the "intrinsic weakness" of an interstate institution which leaves national sovereignty unimpaired is that it can lead to "a deterioration in the relation between its principal members (which) can quickly reduce it to impotence." His conclusion[4] therefore was that "a federation [...] is far preferable to an intergovernmental authority".

Jean Monnet shared Salter's views on the weakness of intergovernmental decision-making, though not his federalist aims. He deplored the allies' current lack of a common command structure which meant that until then – despite the existence of the Anglo-French Supreme War Council – Britain and France each seemed at times to be fighting its own war rather than confronting the enemy as a united force. In the prevailing situation such weakness could no longer be afforded.

Despite their differences the two men succeeded in producing a five-page draft plan which they could both support. It proposed neither a federation nor simply a strengthening of the Anglo-French alliance but something in between: namely that "France and Great Britain shall no longer be two nations, but one Franco-British Union." The two Parliaments would be united. There would be a single war cabinet and "all the forces of Britain and France whether on land, sea, or in the air, will be placed under its direction." In other words, the two countries would become a single unified state.

Getting Churchill even to read this proposal proved to be impossible, essentially because – according to Churchill's secretary Major Desmond Morton – Monnet lacked the necessary political standing to be able to speak for the French government. Persisting nevertheless, Monnet gathered together a small group to work on an improved draft. In addition to Salter and Major Morton it included the permanent secretary at the Foreign Office Sir Robert Vansittart and René Pleven of the French economic mission in London.

The deadlock was broken by the arrival in London of General Charles de Gaulle, newly appointed Secretary of State for War in the French Government[5]. "I am here to save the honour of France!" he is reported to have told Monnet's wife Sylvia, and it was no boast. He read the draft text at a meeting with Monnet and the French ambassador Charles Corbin and was impressed. This, he said, could give Prime Minister Reynaud the

[3] Jean Monnet, *Mémoires*, Chap. I.

[4] Lord Salter: *Memoirs of a Public Servant*, p. 201.

[5] Charles de Gaulle: *Mémoires de Guerre*, L'Appel, p. 62.

courage to continue the fight, if necessary from France's North African territories.

Winston Churchill states in his war memoirs[6] that he was "at a luncheon at the Carlton Club on the 15th of June when he first heard of the plan for an indissoluble Anglo-French union "with the object of giving M. Reynaud some new fact of a vivid and stimulating nature with which to carry a majority of his cabinet into the move to Africa and the continuance of the war." He does not mention that De Gaulle was also present and had handed him the draft text. His first reaction was "unfavourable". He was "by no means convinced" he wrote in his account of the meeting.

But Reynaud had already asked for France to be released from her obligations under the "no separate peace" agreement. It meant that Britain could be left isolated. At the June 16th cabinet meeting Churchill reported on his conversation with De Gaulle who had stressed that "some very dramatic move was essential [...] to keep M. Reynaud's Government in the war and that a proclamation of the indissoluble union of the French and British peoples would serve the purpose."

Vansittart was instructed to draft "some dramatic announcement which might strengthen M. Reynaud's hand." The Foreign Secretary Lord Halifax called together a small group consisting of Vansittart, Jean Monnet, René Pleven, and Major Morton to begin work immediately on drafting a brief, final revision of the Declaration of Union[7]. This was then discussed in Cabinet on the same day. Some minor changes were made and some major points dropped. Those excised included references to the establishment of a common Anglo-French customs area and a single currency. The provision that the two parliaments should 'unite' was altered to 'be formally associated'. Its final two paragraphs emphasized the need for France to continue the fight. This, for Churchill, was the essential point.

Once the text was agreed General de Gaulle dictated it by telephone to Paul Reynaud's office in France. He then made immediate arrangements to fly there in person, taking the written document with him. The following day Churchill was on his way for a meeting with Reynaud on board a British cruiser off the coast of Brittany when he received a telegram from the British ambassador in Bordeaux informing him that Marshal Philippe Pétain had replaced Reynaud as prime minister and was opening negotiations for an armistice. The plan had failed.

Whether an Anglo-French Union could have worked effectively at that point in time with most of France under enemy occupation is doubtful. Nor would it necessarily have survived in peacetime. For some British

6 Churchill, *op. cit.* Chap X.

7 Cabinet minutes CAB65/7, pp. 316-8.

government members it was intended only to be a temporary expedient which would no longer be necessary once the war had been won.

On the other hand in some circles the idea of a future Anglo-French political union had been unofficially discussed for some time. British Foreign Office files, for example, contain a report written by the historian Arnold Toynbee[8] together with Professor Sir Albert Zimmern describing their visit to Paris in March 1940 when they had been approached by France's previous Minister of Education, Senator André Honnorat with a suggestion that "the French and British governments should, without delay, conclude a treaty of perpetual association between France and Great Britain, and should submit this treaty for immediate adoption by the British and French parliaments."

Honnorat envisaged this treaty as

> "a brief and simple document providing for the pooling of defence, of the conduct of foreign policy, of the economic resources of the metropolitan territories and the non-self-governing dependencies of the two Powers. French citizens should have the passive rights of British subjects in the UK and the British Empire and British subjects should have the passive rights of French citizens in France, in the sense that neither French citizens on British soil nor British subjects on French soil should find themselves treated legally as aliens."

Emphasizing the need for bilingual education in both countries, he added that "the proposed organs of government in certain spheres should be placed under some kind of joint parliamentary control." And he concluded: "Even if Hitler's Greater Germany were to survive intact, it would henceforth be confronted by another European power of still greater calibre and staying power."

Attached to this report is a comment, possibly by Toynbee, stating that he was "struck by the fact that a number of Frenchmen whose reaction to the idea of 'federal union' in the abstract was hostile were prepared to think of this with approval as a nucleus to which other European countries might attach themselves at a later stage." And a further handwritten evaluation signed by J.G. Ward of the Foreign Office describes the plan as "an admirable first step towards an Anglo-French union or confederation" which "would be partly met by the latest draft of the proposed 'separate peace' declaration."

So the idea of independent nation states sharing some aspects of their sovereignty for their joint benefit was not unknown even during the darkest days of the second world war and although the proposed Anglo-French union was never realised it did arouse interest and even enthusiasm when it was first announced in the British press.

---

8 FO371/242962, p. 87.

It planted questions in the public mind about the relationship between states and, in doing so, it challenged nationalism. Perhaps, too, it influenced Winston Churchill's thoughts on the future shape of Europe. Speaking on the twin subjects of political unity and economic collaboration at the first Congress of Europe in The Hague in 1948 he pointed out[9] that "It is said with truth that this involves some sacrifice or merger of national sovereignty and characteristics, but it is also possible to regard it as the gradual assumption by all nations concerned of that larger sovereignty which can also protect their diverse and distinctive customs, and their national traditions."

---

9 Quoted in Hugo Young, *This Blessed Plot*, Chap. 1.

The Birth of the UEF*

Jean-Pierre GOUZY

15 December 1946, 9 rue Auber, Opera quarter in Paris: the Union of European Federalists (UEF) is established, at the headquarters of "La Fédération", the principal French federalist movement of the time.

This momentous occasion was not the result of coincidence... it would probably never have taken place without the repercussions of the 1941 Ventotene manifesto, without the European resistance of men like Henri Brugmans, Henri Frenay and Altiero Spinelli, future leaders, of, amongst other things, the UEF; without similar meetings, like that of the "Socialistes européens" in Montrouge in June 1946; that of intellectuals in Geneva like Jaspers, Spendler, de Rougemont, Lukács in September 1946, and of course the meeting in Hertenstein on the edge of the Quatre Cantons Lake from September 15 to September 22, 1946, the same year during which Churchill made his famous speech on September 19, in Zurich, in which he proudly said: "Stand up Europe! We have to create a United States of Europe".

The UEF was already starting to take shape in Hertenstein, but it would take another meeting, called for by the British leaders of Federal Union a month later in Luxembourg, to decide on the establishment of a European federalist secretariat in Paris and another one in New York for global federalists. In Paris, December 1946, after a last preparatory conference in November in Basel, the decision was taken to set up a Union of European Federalists, but many members remained captured by the idea of global federalism. Hence the first motto of the UEF: "One Europe in a united world".

Additionally, certain groups were only interested in the establishment of a European federation, others thought mostly about founding a new organization, others about organizing peace, and others still about global federalism. Some referred voluntarily to an Anglo-Saxon model of federalism; others, specifically French speakers, related to Proudhon and the libertarians of the preceding century or to the individualist thinking that emerged from debates and ideas during the course of the 1930s. For others, Hamilton still represented the essential reference.

---

* Published in Issue 1/2007.

Such a mixture of ideas was quite surprising. They needed to be channeled. This mixture made up the richness of the UEF, but in many ways it made life complicated for the movement over the course of the 1950s and even into the 1960s.

Could it have gone differently at the start of our grand adventure in that European wasteland in which everything had to be rethought and rebuilt?

In Great Britain, for example, Miss Josephy, ex Vice-President of the Liberal Democrats, and one of the most active federalists of the time, was the incarnation of this mix of globalist, Atlanticist and European perspectives, representing one of the most symptomatic expressions of the Outre-Manche federalist tradition.

The constitutive meeting of the UEF took place on December 15, 1946, under the presidency of a man who incarnated the debates of the third French republic. Ex deputy of Ardèche, Gaston Riou was the President of a group named "Union économique et douanière européenne". Being the oldest member of the Assembly, he published in 1929 a premonitory work called "*Europe, ma patrie*" (*Europe, my Homeland*) which included a declaration by Aristide Briand. I must remind you that Aristide Briand, in the name of the French government of the time and with the support of Gustav Stresemann, called for the peoples of Europe – from the stage of the League of Nations – to tie a "federal knot" to each other.

The cospirators of rue Auber, despite their differences, decided unanimously to convene a first Congress, which was held in Montreux from 27 to 31 August, 1947. They also decided that the young UEF, which did not yet have a legal statute, would get one, conforming to Swiss legislation. The process was finalized with the establishment of its headquarters at Palais Wilson in Geneva. They then asked Alexandre Marc, journalist and 1930's avant-garde, to become the first Secretary General of the new organization, and Henri Brugmans, future dean of the College of Europe, to be its first President. The first task would be to control the post-war federalist explosion: about fifty clubs, circles, and unequal movements in about ten countries. There were, for example, no less than around fifteen in France alone and about twelve in Belgium.

I conclude by mentioning that as a young man, I myself had been involved in the federalist movement for several months. Six years later, I became Secretary General for France. I therefore personally knew the witnesses and actors who were involved in the events that I just related. This authorizes my testimony of the day.

When the delegates of that memorable gathering separated, into the bitter cold Paris night, immensely dark and sad, deprived of everything (because of the rations which disappeared definitively in 1949), the first post-war sign of European hope finally materialized: the UEF was born.

Albert Einstein, Pacifist*

Pietro GRECO

The greatest physicist of all times? Two hundred physicists interviewed in early 2000 by the specialized review Physics World had no doubts in answering with an overwhelming majority: Albert Einstein. The German scientist finished well ahead of colleagues of the caliber of Newton, Galileo, Archimedes, Maxwell.

The most representative personality of the 20th century? Experts in various disciplines, interviewed in the same weeks by Time magazine, once again had no doubt: Albert Einstein. He finished ahead of figures like Roosevelt, Stalin, Hitler, Mao, Picasso. Well, few know it, but the father of relativity, one of the three founding fathers of quantum theory (with Planck and Bohr), the most representative personality of the 20th century and perhaps of the entire millennium, the never-ending myth that became the very icon of science, was a pacifist. But not a detached and naïve pacifist, as somebody has described him. Rather, a militant pacifist, personally engaged and endowed with a great and secular capacity of interpreting his time and of fighting – yes, fighting — for building a desirable future.

It is worth reflecting further about this scientist who dedicated at least half of his public life to pacifist militancy. For two reasons: his extraordinary, topical relevance, and its extraordinary influence on the political history of the 20th century.

The story of the pacifist scientist with his head in the clouds, embraced even by some historians of science, is unjustified. Because Einstein, on the contrary, has often been a radical politician, but always with a very clear vision (the two things are not in contradiction). And he has been a militant pacifist always capable of modulating the intensity of his pacifism or, in different words, the quality of his requests on the basis of a detailed analysis of the context, or, to say it in the jargon of the physicists, of the boundary conditions. In short, Einstein's pacifism has never been absolute, but always modeled on the concrete historical reality.

One has just to have a look at his personal history to see that. Many of Einstein's biographers, starting with his friend Abraham Pais, ascribe his

* Published in Issue 1/2016.

pacifism to the fact that he could not countenance, since his boyhood and then adolescence, any form of authoritarianism and militarism. For this reason his pacifism has been defined "instinctive".

But it was not at all instinctive, at least not in its content, the first public display of the pacifist Einstein, which took place in 1914. A few months after his arrival in Berlin and few days after the outbreak of the First World War, the young man, just thirty five year old, unknown to the masses and admitted to the elite of Prussian physics on the recommendation of Max Planck, welcomed to Berlin with great honors by Kaiser Wilhelm in person, did not hesitate to sign a manifesto – his first manifesto – against Prussian militarism, in defiance of police prohibition. But there was not only courage in that act; there was also farsightedness. In the document, drafted together with the biologist Georg Nicolai, Einstein singles out a new character of modern war: the destruction of the cultural fabric and a regression of civilization: "While technology and commerce clearly compel us to recognize the bond between all nations, and thus a common world culture, no war has ever so intensively interrupted the cultural communalism of cooperative work as this present war does".

Einstein and Nicolai suggested a way out from the barbarism of the modern war then raging over the Old Continent:

> "We […] are firmly convinced that the time has come when Europe must act as one in order to protect her soil, her inhabitants, and her culture. We believe that the will to do this is latently present in many. In expressing this will collectively, we hope that it gathers force. To this end, it seems for the time being necessary that all those who hold European civilization dear, in other words, those who in Goethe's prescient words can be called "good Europeans" join together. […] We wish only to urge and appeal; and if you feel as we do, if you are similarly determined to lend the most far-reaching resonance to the European will, then we ask that you sign."

So, in the midst of war, thirty years before Altiero Spinelli, Ernesto Rossi and Eugenio Colorni, two scientists unknown to most people and with no significant political experience, Albert Einstein and Georg Nicolai, addressed themselves to all the citizens of the Old Continent, asking them to overcome the stockades of nationalism and engage themselves for the unity of Europe – a federation of the United States of Europe – as an antidote to war, and to embark on a virtuous path towards a universal, common civilization.

Their words sound extremely topical today, when the idea of a united Europe is in crisis not only in the economic plane, but also and perhaps foremost in the cultural one. Their "Manifesto to Europeans" did not have a great success. Nevertheless, Einstein will not reduce his political engagement. On the contrary, in some ways it was strengthened.

During the First World War he will be a militant in a pacifist party by then already underground. Then, after 1919, the year when his General Relativity Theory was tested, he became famous all over the world and able to touch the minds and also the hearts of the masses, from Paris to Tokyo; he then spent all his fame for the pacifist cause. "Do not forget to say that I am a convinced pacifist, who believes that the world has had enough of wars" he wanted to be assured by a journalist that had just interviewed him in 1921.

Einstein's peace militancy in those years was unshakeable. It was bolstered by good readings (Kant, Russell) and good contacts (Romain Rolland, the American President Woodrow Wilson, the philosopher Henri Bergson, Sigmund Freud). It was perfectly in tune with the pacifist wing of European rationalism, and proceeded along two main routes: internationalism, with the request, reiterated many times, of a democratic government of the world, and anti-militarism, with the request, this too reiterated many times, of a unilateral disarmament of the nations. So, we see Einstein taking part in the project of the Society of Nations and, at the same time, asking young people to refuse in each country to carry out military service.

This phase has been defined as that of Einstein's radical pacifism. Started in 1914, this phase ends between the summer of 1932 and the winter of 1933, when Einstein realizes that in Germany a force, the Nazis, is coming to power against which the instruments of pacifism have no effect. Even before Adolf Hitler took over power in December 1932, he left Germany. And to his wife Elsa who was leaving their house in Caputh, in the surroundings of Berlin, he said: "Take a look back, because you will not see it ever again".

Albert Einstein understands before and better than others the nature of Nazism. Its unprecedented violence, which threatens not only Jews and opposers in Germany, but the entire Europe. Or rather, the European civilization itself. To that organized force, Einstein believes, nothing can be opposed but organized force. And he states that publicly; he writes at the end of July 1933 to the Belgian pacifist Alfred Nahon:

> "What I am going to say will surprise you… Imagine that Belgium is occupied by today's Germany. Things would be much worse than in 1914, although they were indeed quite bad back then. Therefore, I must tell you candidly: were I a Belgian, I would not refuse, in the present circumstances, the military service, but rather I would carry it out diligently, certain that I would be doing it to save the European civilization. This does not mean that I am abandoning the principle I have been fighting for until now. I sincerely hope that the time will come when refusing the military service will become once again the best method for serving the progress of mankind."

The European pacifist movement was almost shocked by Einstein's analysis. But the political project he was promoting to counter Hitler was a close alliance between the USA, Great Britain, France and the Soviet Union; an alliance which will be made, but ten years later. Realizing before others that a power was being established so violent as to be impossible to counter it with the usual instruments of our civilization, and foreshadowing a political alliance that will be actually made a decade later are not for sure facts typical of a naïve politician. Nor of an unworldly pacifist. Einstein's thinking is always rational, based on a thoughtful analysis of the context.

And it is precisely such an analysis that drives him in the month of August 1939 to accept the invitation of three Hungarians – Leo Szilard, Eugene Wigner and Edward Teller–, and write to the American President Franklin Delano Roosevelt warning him that: a) physicists have realized the fission of the atom, discovering a new energy source; b) such a source can be utilized for the construction of mass destruction weapons of a devastating power; c) in Germany there are physicists able to develop such weapons; d) Hitler, after his invasion of Czechoslovakia, has come into possession of the needed raw material: uranium. It is necessary then that the United States commits itself to the construction of an atomic weapon: not for actually using it, but as a deterrent against the possible use of a German atomic bomb.

The effects of Einstein's letter to Roosevelt have been perhaps overestimated. For sure it did not have immediate results. In the USA, the Manhattan Project will only start two years later. Einstein is not involved at all. Also and in the first place because of the veto of the FBI, who consider him a dangerous extremist, maybe a friend of the communists. Therefore, it seems completely unfounded to associate him with the actual construction of the atomic bomb. Much less to associate the name of Einstein with the explosions of Hiroshima and Nagasaki.

On the contrary, before those two immense tragedies took place, in the Spring of 1945, Albert Einstein had already resumed his radical pacifism. In Europe the war is nearing its end. Nazism is defeated. Hence, Einstein believes, the reason for the construction of the atomic bomb has died away. The international context has changed, and he returns a militant and active pacifist. Here he is, then, writing a new letter to Roosevelt, soliciting him to listen to his friend Leo Szilard, who was pleading to suspend the Manhattan Project and block the construction of the mass destruction weapon. But Roosevelt dies and Szilard could not manage to get a fair hearing.

On August 6, 1945, a uranium bomb is dropped over Hiroshima. On August 8, the USSR declares war on Japan. On August 9, a plutonium bomb destroys Nagasaki. On August 15, Emperor Hirohito announces the surrender of Japan.

Now everything has changed. In the following months, the pacifist Einstein is once again in the field, alongside the Federation of Atomic Scientists that wants to oppose the "logic of the bomb". Once again his political clear-sightedness is all but naïve or simplistic.

Albert Einstein understands that the new mass-destruction weapon changes the relation between the military sphere and politics. The logic of the bomb has a dimension of its own, even superior to the logic of the political and ideological contest. And that it is that logic, this time, to jeopardize the survival of civilization. Maybe of mankind itself. Therefore it is necessary to act. On the one hand by resuming the idea of a world government, managed initially by the winning powers of the war – the USA, Great Britain, France and the USSR – to which the monopoly of the atomic weapon is to be entrusted. And on the other, by mobilizing the masses, in a close and unprecedented alliance with the scientists, in order to avoid becoming familiar with the bomb, and to build a global movement for nuclear disarmament.

On this project Einstein will work until his last days. And the work will reach a high point with the Russell-Einstein Manifesto signed by the German physicist one week before dying. Einstein's life ended on April 18, 1955. The manifesto was made public by Bertrand Russell the following July, and it became both the foundation for the Pugwash Conferences, the movement of scientists struggling actively and analytically for disarmament, and one of the basic texts of the mass movement for peace that, with changing fortunes and deep adjustments, is alive and active to this day.

Has the activity of the pacifist Einstein been that of a visionary, with no effect on the concrete reality of the world? Granted, the race to atomic rearmament was not stopped by the alliance between scientists and the masses envisaged by Einstein when he took in 1946 the Presidency of the Emergency Committee of the Federation of Atomic Scientists. Granted, mankind is still sitting on a powder-keg that could destroy it. But, as the historian Lawrence S. Wittner, of the New York State University, says, if after Hiroshima and Nagasaki the atomic bomb has never been used again, if it became a taboo for everybody, politicians and military people included, that is not due so much to the wisdom of governments and Chiefs of Staff, as to the movement for disarmament, able to mobilize the masses as Albert Einstein wanted.

Between October 11 and 12, 1986, in a summit held in Reykjavik, Iceland, Michail Gorbachev, the last Secretary of the Soviet Communist Party and last President of the USSR, proposed to Ronald Reagan,

President of the USA, to dismantle nuclear arsenals. Reagan was a stone's throw from accepting. The project vanished, but a process started for at least reducing the number of nuclear weapons. When, sometime afterwards, Gorbachev was asked where that idea was coming from, the USSR President replied: from Albert Einstein's books and from the proposals of the world pacifist movement. This confirms that the thought of the greatest physicist of all times did have a real influence on world history. An idea – the elimination of all nuclear weapons – as topical as ever.

Spinelli and the *Ventotene Manifesto**

John PINDER

It is now sixty years since Altiero Spinelli and Ernesto Rossi completed the *Ventotene Manifesto*. This article recounts how they came to do this, the impact on Spinelli himself and, through him, on events in Europe since then. It is an exciting, moving and inspiring story.

Spinelli was arrested for anti-fascist activities in 1927, when still less than twenty years old. He was confined for ten years in a prison cell then six in prison camp. He was, when arrested, a leading member of the Italian communist youth movement, which he had joined for three main reasons. He saw it as the only effective opponent of fascism in Italy; he found in it an all-embracing idea that would enable him to play his part in making the world better for mankind; and he wanted to dedicate his life to such a cause.

In prison he read and read and read: books on politics, philosophy, economics and history; literature in Italian, German, French, English, Russian, Spanish, Latin and ancient Greek. He had time to reflect – one of his favourite words – on what he read; and that led him to an uncomfortable conclusion. He realised that he had committed himself to the wrong idea. Stalinism was a monstrosity that stemmed from the denial of individual freedom, with which he was temperamentally and morally unable to live.

Spinelli, Rossi and the *Manifesto*

In 1939 two things happened that are crucial for this story. World War Two began; and Spinelli came to the prison camp on the island of Ventotene, seeking the right idea to which to devote his life. There he met Ernesto Rossi, a professor of economics who had been imprisoned for his anti-fascist activities in the social-liberal organisation 'Justice and Liberty', which was an early pioneer of the idea of combining liberal principles with social justice.

* Published in Issue 3/2001.

He was the ideal *maestro* for Spinelli's induction into the world of democratic politics.

Rossi had been a brilliant student of Luigi Einaudi, a more classical liberal of outstanding integrity who was to become the first President of the post-war Italian republic. There was wide latitude in what the prisoners confined on Ventotene could read, so Rossi and Spinelli were able to obtain a collection of essays by Einaudi, including two in which, in 1918, he had forecast that peace would not be preserved by a League of Nations based on the principle of national sovereignty, so a European federation was required. Rossi wrote to Einaudi asking him to send books on that theme.

It happened that the leading source of literature on the subject at that time was England, where a strong federalist movement had grown up in the late 1930s and leading intellectuals such as William Beveridge, Lord Lothian, Lionel Robbins and Barbara Wootton had been writing books and pamphlets on the subject. Einaudi sent Rossi some of these and the impact on Spinelli was decisive. He had found the cause to which he was to devote the rest of his life. In his own words, these books were for him 'a revelation', with 'the clean, precise thinking of these English federalists, in whose writings I found a very good method for analysing the chaotic state of affairs into which Europe was plunging and for drawing up alternatives[1]. Typically, what Spinelli got from these books was not only analysis as food for thought, but also alternative solutions as a basis for action.

Having found the right idea to replace the wrong one and spent a few months digesting it, Spinelli suggested to Rossi that they write a manifesto to advocate it. Rossi agreed. Spinelli did most of the drafting but they discussed it intensively, paragraph by paragraph. The result was the Ventotene Manifesto, completed in the late summer of 1941. They launched this democratic and federal challenge in remarkable circumstances. Hitler controlled almost the whole of continental Europe, including much of European Russia where his armies had been winning victory after victory. Many, perhaps most people on the Continent expected him to win the war. Churchill and de Gaulle were among those who did not. So also was Spinelli; and he intended the *Manifesto* to initiate a campaign to create a European federation when the forces of democracy had won.

The *Manifesto* contained an analysis of the contemporary crisis of European civilisation and a call for action to establish the federal solution. The crisis was the international anarchy caused by absolute national sovereignty. The federal solution was liberal democratic government

1 Altiero Spinelli, *Come ho tentato di diventare saggio*: *Io Ulisse* (Bologna: Il Mulino, 1984, pp. 307-8).

at two levels. The European federal institutions would comprise a two-chamber legislature with a house of the citizens and a house of the states, a federal executive responsible to the legislature and a court of justice as the supreme judicial authority for federal affairs. The federal powers would include foreign policy and defence, currency and trade, finance and the federal budget, and the guarantee of human rights. Other powers would remain with the member states.

Spinelli recalled later that these ideas were not new: others had already expressed them, 'certainly better than we did.' But the new ideas concerned the action to be taken. Federation was seen as an objective for action now; and the line of division between progressives and reactionaries would henceforth be, not the traditional one between left and right, but between those who focus on winning national power and 'those who see as their central task the creation of a solid international state.' Spinelli also pointed out a few 'political errors' in what was his first piece of federalist writing. One was the assumption that federation could be established rapidly after the war was over, before the old structures of the national states had been re-established. But he learnt to sustain his action through a much longer process. Another was that his idea of a dedicated leading group of federalists was expressed in a way that was 'too crudely Leninist'[2]. We must remember that he was still in the very early stages of learning how liberal democracy works. But he learnt remarkably quickly. One evidence of this is the first sentence of the *Manifesto*, with the fundamental affirmation of liberal political philosophy that 'man is not a mere instrument to be used by others but an autonomous centre of life'.

Already in 1941 the *Manifesto* began to exert its influence in Italy where it was circulated clandestinely; and it was published in 1944 after the fascist regime was overthrown. Spinelli was liberated in August 1943 and went immediately to Milan where he founded the *Movimento Federalista Europeo*, then took steps towards the foundation of the UEF. He was a great leader and played a decisive part in the development of both the Italian and the European organisation. But he was not an organisation man. His life was, rather, a saga of personal struggle to convert the vision of the *Manifesto* into the reality of a European federation. So the rest of this story will focus on six episodes in that struggle.

Spinelli, Monnet and the European Community

The first episode began in the summer of 1952 at a meeting with Jean Monnet who, having initiated the foundation of the European Coal and Steel Community and led the negotiations to establish it, was about

[2] *Ibid.*, pp. 311-12.

to become the first President of its High Authority. Monnet said how impressed he had been with the clarity of a paper drafted by Spinelli, in which he had proposed that the ECSC's parliamentary assembly be given the task of drafting a federal constitution. A few days later Monnet asked Spinelli to draft his inaugural speech to the High Authority[3]. Spinelli used the opportunity to identify the federal elements in the Community which would enable it to grow beyond the form of a traditional international organisation, depending for every action on the agreement of all the member states, into a launching pad for development into a federal union: a European executive, independent of the member states' governments; a parliamentary assembly, precursor of the European Parliament, to which the executive was to be responsible; a Court of Justice, supreme within the fields of competence of the Community; and a limited power to tax. In these respects the institutions, the speech affirmed, were federal – though it was certainly not Spinelli but Monnet who added *'disons le mot'* before the word federal, doubtless because, in France as later in Britain, the 'f' word was a cause of contention[4]. Spinelli became convinced that, although Monnet did not have 'the least idea' of what it meant to make a constitution, he was a federalist; and Monnet asked Spinelli to join the staff of the High Authority and write a series of speeches that could become the equivalent of *The Federalist* of Hamilton, Jay and Madison, which expounded the ideas behind the constitution of the United States. But Spinelli was determined to retain his independence until he could return to the European institutions in a political capacity: which, of course, he eventually did[5].

The second episode concerned the European army and the European Defence Community (EDC), which the six member states of the ECSC were planning to establish during the years 1950 to 1954. The governments' original idea was to give what would be the principal responsibility for the defence of the member states to a Council of Ministers, more intergovernmental than federal. Spinelli, who was fully versed in the principles of federal democracy, quickly realised that such responsibility could be given only to solidly democratic federal institutions. He persuaded the Italian government of this, which in turn persuaded the other five governments that an appropriate treaty should be drafted; and the task was given to the ECSC's parliamentary assembly, slightly adjusted for

3 Altiero Spinelli, *Diario europeo 1948/1969*, edited by Edmondo Paolini (Bologna: Il Mulino, 1989, pp. 142-3).

4 Jean Monnet, 'Speech to the Inaugural Session of the High Authority', in his *Les Etats-Unis d'Europe ont commencé: discours et allocutions 1952-1954* (Paris: Robert Laffont, 1955, pp. 55-8).

5 *Diario europeo*, pp. 142-3, 163.

the purpose[6]. Spinelli was active in advising the assembly's constitutional committee that drafted the treaty for a European Political Community, which would have provided a quasi-federal constitution for the EDC. But in August 1954 the project for the Defence Community, hence also the Political Community, was killed by the French Assemblée Nationale, where it was vehemently opposed by both communists and nationalists.

Federalists had to start again; and Monnet and Spinelli went in characteristically different directions. Monnet set up the Action Committee for the United States of Europe, whose members were the leaders of the main democratic parties and trade unions of the member states, and sought their support for further development of the Community. The result was the Messina Conference in 1955, which was to lead to the foundation of the European Economic Community in 1958. Spinelli thought that the Community project had reached the end of the road and Monnet was finished[7]. He continued to pursue the constitutional route towards European federation. Since the governments were evidently not prepared to set up an assembly to draft a constitution, he launched a campaign to do it without them, founding the Congress of the European People to organise elections of citizens' representatives to a constituent assembly. The campaign had some successes, but not nearly enough to create the nucleus of an assembly. It was a formative experience for the militants of the MFE which was to be important for their future work. But it came nowhere near to attaining its objective. Meanwhile, the great nationalist Charles de Gaulle had become President of France and Spinelli realised that so long as he remained President, the federal project would remain blocked. So the 1960s were, for Spinelli, what may be called his academic decade, when he shelved political action and concentrated on thought and analysis instead. He founded the *Istituto Affari Internazionali*, which did some pioneering work on federal projects and became the leading Italian institute of international affairs; and he became a visiting professor at the Bologna Center of the Johns Hopkins University. But in 1969 de Gaulle resigned and Spinelli seized the opportunity to return to political action.

The Commission and the Tindemans Report

One of the springs of Spinelli's dynamism was the tension between his federal idealism and his political realism. Spinelli the realist understood that his judgement of Monnet and the Community in the later 1950s

6 See Sergio Pistone, 'Il ruolo di Altiero Spinelli nella genesi dell'Art. 38 della Comunità Europea di Difesa e del progetto di Comunità Politica Europea', in G. Trausch (ed.), *La construction de l'Europe, du Plan Schuman aux Traités de Rome* (Brussels: Bruylant, 1992).

7 *Diario europeo*, p. 269.

had been wrong: that the Community could be seen as central to the development of a federal Europe and a vantage point from which to resume his federalist struggle. So, as he had told Monnet in 1952 that he would, Spinelli the idealist entered the European institutions in a political capacity, when the Italian government nominated him as a member of the Commission in June 1970.

He was an active Commissioner for industrial affairs, introducing new ideas that were in due course put into effect. But he was awaiting a chance to get the Commission to lead a campaign to convert the Community into a federation. In the spirit of one of his favourite metaphors, he was always seeking the Joan of Arc to put the crown on the head of the Dauphin thus causing him to exercise his sovereign rights: but the Dauphin was now the people of Europe and Joan of Arc was whoever would cause them to assume their federal sovereignty. Late in 1974 an opportunity to get the Commission to play this part presented itself, when the Heads of State and Government asked Leo Tindemans, the Belgian prime minister and a federalist, to produce a report on how to convert the Community into a European Union. For the next year Spinelli strove to persuade the Commission to press Tindemans to propose a federal reform of the Community. But the Commission went only part of the way; and Tindemans produced a report whose conclusions could, he hoped, be accepted by his fellow political leaders of the other member states, and were hence yet farther removed from what Spinelli wanted. Finding that route also a *cul-de-sac*, Spinelli resigned from the Commission in May 1974. His four years as a Commissioner had, however, given him experience in practical politics at the top level and the standing of a major political figure in the Community, which were to be important assets in the final, parliamentary phase of his federalist saga.

The European Parliament and the treaty constitution

The fourth episode, and the first in his parliamentary phase, started almost at once. In June Spinelli became a member of the *Camera dei Deputati*, as an independent on the Italian Communist Party's list. When I asked him why he had moved back towards the communists with whom he had broken some four decades before, his answer was threefold. First, as far as ideas were concerned, he had not moved towards them, but they had moved towards him, on the issue that they knew to be his overriding interest, the creation of a federal Europe; and their subsequent behaviour in the European Parliament was to confirm his judgement. Secondly, the political reality was that there was no other way for him to be elected to parliament; and the events of the next ten years were to show why he rightly believed that to be necessary. Thirdly, he had told the Communists that he would say what he chose, not what they might want him to say; and they had accepted this – doubtless because his name would help them in moving towards respectability in democratic politics.

Four months later Spinelli entered the European Parliament, whose members were not yet elected directly by the citizens, but indirectly by the parliaments of member states. His first action there was based on his understanding of a key event in the history of parliamentary democracy, when citizens' representatives in the English parliament gained control over public expenditure, hitherto the prerogative of the King. So Spinelli joined the Parliament's Budgets Committee and fought for parliamentary control over the Community's budget, hitherto largely the prerogative of the governments' representatives in the Council. Instigated by Spinelli, the Parliament fought battles on the issue and lost most of them. But Spinelli judged that the experience had radicalised the MEPs, preparing them for the critical struggle ahead: for the treaty constitution to convert the Community from a system still dominated by the member states' governments into a European federation.

The direct elections of June 1979 gave Spinelli, now seventy one years old, the opportunity for which his life had prepared him since he drafted the *Ventotene Manifesto* nearly four decades ago. The governments of the Community's member states had given him the citizens' elected representatives that he had tried in vain to secure through the Congress of the European People. He underlined the status of MEPs by saying that they were a normal cross-section of Europeans who shared one unique characteristic: all of them could say 'I have been chosen to represent the European citizens.' So they had the legitimacy to design Europe's future constitution.

This was his *rendez-vous* with destiny and he was determined not to fail. He wanted the Parliament to draft and approve a treaty that would provide the Community with a federal constitution. He formed the Crocodile group, named after the restaurant in Strasbourg where it first met, to help him promote the project. He then persuaded the Parliament to form an institutions committee, which would prepare the draft of the treaty, and to appoint him its general rapporteur. Although he had been renowned as too impatient and intolerant to work well with others, he co-operated in an exemplary way with all the main political groups and their MEPs to produce the text; and although he had generally been regarded as an all-or-nothing maximalist, he guided the committee to produce a draft treaty that he judged the Parliament would be able to accept. It was designed, not to by-pass the Community, but to reform it into a European Union, with institutions that were in substance federal but without the power over defence that a federation would have, though with an opening through which to move towards that too. His effort was rewarded on 14 February 1984 when a preponderant majority of MEPs voted for what was indeed a treaty-constitution.

The sixth and final episode in Spinelli's saga was his attempt to secure member states' ratification of the draft Treaty which, in order not to be subject to veto, was to enter into force when ratified by a majority of them with a population at least two thirds of the Community's total. After a meeting with Spinelli, President Mitterrand, in a speech to the European Parliament, offered warm support to its Treaty. But he was characteristically equivocal and went on to accept the Single European Act which fell far short of the Parliament's Treaty. The Single Act was the product of a confluence of the Parliament's initiative and that of Commission President Jacques Delors to create the single European market, with the use of qualified majority voting in the Council. The draft Treaty left its imprint on the Single Act in, among other things, the beginnings of legislative powers for the Parliament, which were to lead on to its substantial powers of codecision. More fundamentally, the Treaty demonstrated how the Community could be reformed into a federation: a source of inspiration and regeneration for the federalist cause after many years of stagnation.

Spinelli's life and legacy

Spinelli died in May 1985, three months after the Single Act was signed. Tragically, he thought it was useless: a *'topolino morto'* – a dead mouse – he called it. If he had lived longer he would have seen that it had in fact relaunched the Community, as the Rome Treaties had done in 1958. Thus the Single Act and the single market project, with the practice of majority voting and the start of legislative power for the Parliament, led on to the single currency, to the application of qualified majority voting and co-decision to the bulk of the Council's legislative decisions, and to various other federal elements in the Union's powers and institutions: in short, to a European Union that may be seen as over half way to becoming a federation. That represents great progress towards the federal Europe to which Spinelli devoted so much of his life; and the European Council at Laeken under Belgian Presidency in December 2001, to be followed by the Convention, offers federalists the opportunity to secure further federal reforms for the Union and a constituent process that should lead to a federal constitution.

Such was Spinelli's life and such is his legacy. His life, from Ventotene and the *Manifesto* to the European Parliament and his treaty-constitution, was a heroic struggle to convert his federalist vision into federal reality. His legacy is our chance to bring the struggle to a successful conclusion.

He combined in a remarkable way the capacities of thought and action. Observing the difficulties of British federalists, he wrote in his diary of their need for someone with 'the organisational sense of Mr x and the subtle intellect of Mr y'; and he added 'But I don't see him.' These qualities should, he thought, be found in one person. But we all have to contribute according to our abilities and in our own ways. The Ventotene seminar gives participants the opportunity to reflect on Spinelli's legacy and on what one's own contribution to this historic enterprise can be. It is a great merit of the MFE to have created this opportunity for us to do so.

Churchill and Hertenstein*

Raymond M. JUNG D'ARSAC

While still a student in July 1946, I was authorised by Europa-Union (Switzerland) to contact similar pressure groups in other countries inviting them to a conference to set up a federalist umbrella organisation to which we could all belong. The event took place at Hertenstein on the banks of Lake Lucerne and I was appointed rapporteur. Our conclusions – the Hertenstein Programme – set out the basic principles for a European Community on federal lines as 'a necessary and essential contribution to world union'.

These principles were publicly announced in Lucerne's large Congress Hall on the 19th of September 1946 while – by a happy coincidence – Britain's famous wartime prime minister Winston Churchill, speaking at Zurich University that very same day, called on our continent's war-torn countries to work together to create what he called a sort of United States of Europe. 'Let Europe Arise!' was the key message.

Over our long history many thinkers and political or military leaders from Charlemagne onwards have spoken of our continent's geographical and cultural unity. Some have tried to achieve political unity by force. But no such attempts succeeded. A Europe built by undemocratic inter-state agreements – that is, on a non-federalist basis – has no chance of survival.

With the collapse of the Austro-Hungarian empire after World War I the Viennese found themselves living in a world capital ten times larger than was necessary for the administration of a small country such as Austria. It was then that Count Coudenhove-Kalergi thought of restoring the empire in a new form: namely, a confederation extending over the whole of Europe with Vienna as its capital and the Hofburg occupied by a president, replacing the emperor. Coudenhove thus joined the long list of prominent persons aiming to unite Europe from the top down.

His campaign, under the name 'Pan-European Union', was the beginning of the modern movement advocating a European Union. By holding meetings, publishing books, but above all by organising congresses and influencing political leaders, Coudenhove won the support of the majority

* Published in Issue 2/2007. Edited extracts from the speech delivered at the 60th anniversary celebrations, September 2006.

of the contemporary heads of state and government such as Masaryk, Stresemann, Benesch, Mussolini, Briand, Dollfus and others – an élite circle with no democratic base who believed they could reach their goal without taking public opinion into account and without support from the citizens of those states they wished to unite.

Not only did this constitute what was later to be called 'unionism' – that is, *confederalism* as opposed to the creation of an American-style federal state nor following Switzerland which, with 22 sovereign states and four different languages, would seem the ideal embryonic model for Europe. It also anticipated the 'institutionalist' principle which postulates the primacy of the economy over politics.

Supporters of the pan-European idea undertook certain initiatives, among others in the League of Nations. The Briand Plan was one example. In the interwar period the French foreign minister Herriot and other statesmen also tried to put Coudenhove's ideas into practice, but without success. They were joined after World War II, and after Churchill's speech, by Robert Schuman (the Monnet Plan), Konrad Ardenauer, Paul-Henri-Spaak, etc. What they all had in common was that they were addressing the heads of state and government, and at best the national parliaments.

Coudenhove's initiative did not succeed in the interwar period, nor did it prevent the outbreak of a second World War. Nevertheless, it was in line with this tradition that, in 1946, Churchill re-launched the call for a European Union in his memorable speech at Zurich University. It found support in the European Movement led by his son-in-law Duncan Sandys and was later developed by the Belgian Paul-Henri Spaak and taken up by the two Frenchmen Jean Monnet and Robert Schuman, leading in the end to the European structure with which we are today familiar.

In parenthesis it must be said that under pressure from the changed situation after World War II, Coudenhove-Kalergi's organisation lowered its sights from the dizzy heights of prime ministers and heads of state and turned its attention to the level of parliamentarians.

But the history of the European Union can be viewed from another angle. The participants at the Hertenstein conference of September 1946 were not politicians nor government representatives. They were members of voluntary organisations representing no-one but themselves and their views were rooted in the general thrust of public opinion. For them, the European unification process should begin with the election of a constituent assembly to draw up a European constitution. These 'constitutionalists' or 'federalists' expressed doubts about the effectiveness of the alternative, inter-governmental approach.

At that time the Swiss branch of Coudenhove's Pan-Europe Union was led by Hans Bauer, then a young student, and the dramatic split in

1934 between these pioneers of the two different approaches will not be forgotten. Bauer dropped the word 'Pan', merged with the Young Europe organisation, and under the name 'Europa-Union' launched the Swiss Movement for the foundation of a United States of Europe by democratic means through the ballot box and on the basis of the majority expression of the will of the people. The historical impact of this change of direction, rooted in Switzerland's long democratic and federalist traditions, should not be under-estimated.

As the centre for all such activity was in French-speaking Switzerland, the task of organising the 1947 Europa-Congress in Montreux also became our responsibility. For this event so many people registered that it became necessary to hold two separate congresses: one aiming for a world federation, and the other for European unification. This last led to the foundation of the European Federalist Union under the leadership of Hendrick Brugmans.

There followed the May 1948 Congress at The Hague. All organisations promoting European unity were present, including Pan-Europa, the federalist UEF, and the unionist European Movement which dominated the proceedings. In the debates the dramatic and fundamental differences between the two approaches became very clear.

Under pressure from the institutionalist-orientated organisations and from the European Movement led by Churchill's son-in-law Duncan Sandys the 'constitutionalists' began to give way. The fatal idea, by then established in the European Movement, that economic ties would slowly and automatically lead Europe towards political union predominated, while the 'federalists' – including even committee members of their umbrella organisation, the Union of European Federalists – reacted passively, with disbelief, even naively to this development. The Congress, dominated by Winston Churchill, agreed to establish the Council of Europe and opened the door to 'institutionalism'.

Both approaches shared the strategic aim of unifying Europe though they were divided on tactics. The politicians' purpose was to foster a European awareness by establishing institutions such as the Coal and Steel Community, for example, which would lead more or less automatically to political union. Whether this 'institutional' or 'functionalist' tactic will lead to a clear *strategic* goal – namely, establishing what form of political structure Europe will adopt – is so far unclear. The evidence indicates that 'institutionalists' were and are mostly proponents of a looser European association – a position which led to the Rome treaties of 1951 and ultimately to the present status quo.

The question remains, is it possible – with their two different and often antagonistic visions of Europe – to celebrate the 60th anniversary of both the Churchill speech in Zurich and the Hertenstein conference? After a short hesitation the answer must be Yes! It was hard wrangling over disparate goals which led to the agreement to meet at Hertenstein in order to work out common positions which could form a programme for action.

For what is federalism? It is indisputable that the principle of equality first enunciated by the USA , then in the French Revolution, and accepted by western society is now the sine qua non of every community, whether long established or still in the process of formation. Federalism between nations is the equivalent of equality between human beings. If our aim is to unite peoples and nations through an inter-state system, we cannot ignore this principle of equality. Any lack of autonomous freedom, or of equality of opportunity and power could have the consequence of leading to conflict and possibly civil war.

The wheel of history has no reverse gear. But we can learn from history. Our contribution to Europe should be to restate the values set out in the Hertenstein Declaration and to bring into the ongoing process of unification the insights then achieved – namely, that Europe must be federal in structure and be built from the bottom up. "Let Europe Arise!" Yes, but as a federal state with a constitution which is close to the people and drawn up by the European Parliament.

The Relation between Politics and Culture in the Experience of the European Federalist Movement in Italy*

Francesco ROSSOLILLO

I.

The movements which compose the UEF have more or less different ideas as regards the relations between politics and culture in the federalist struggle, from which they have drawn different consequences as regards their organization and their character. So it cannot be denied that, within the UEF, we are confronted with pronounced diversities, with deep roots in the history of its component parts. It would therefore be unrealistic to think that the same model could be imposed everywhere. Such a purpose would produce only the consequence – catastrophic indeed – of breaking up our international organization. What matters in reality is that each of us respect the experience of the others, especially as we can see, within each of our movements, many admirable examples of self-denial and devotion to the cause of European unification. It must moreover be remembered that each of our movements, for all their differences, always represents in its country the vanguard in the struggle for European unification. This does not mean, of course, that we should refrain from comparing our points of view and seeking to identify as clearly as possible our divergences. As a matter of fact, each of our organizations, with its own identity stemming from sixty years of history, is a living and open reality and can thus find, in the experience of the others, important stimuli to evolve and enhance its capacity to act and to mobilize people's energy. That is why we must talk with each other and know one another better. I want therefore to express my appreciation to our friends Krause, Wessels and Schwartzer for having taken the initiative of organizing this meeting. As for myself, my aim is to explain briefly the concept of the relation between politics and culture on which the historical identity of the Italian MFE is founded.

* Published in Issue 2/2005.

II.

The idea which is at the basis of the historical identity of the MFE in Italy is that the problem of uniting Europe in a federation is not merely one of an institutional order and a regional scope, *but is the main political and cultural problem of world history in the second half of the twentieth century.* In this view, the federalist enterprise takes on the same global character as those which gave their sense to the great historical transformations of Europe in the last century. The liberal, democratic and socialist movements promoted both great institutional changes and great cultural revolutions. They affirmed new values, changed the terms of the political debate, brought in new canons of historical interpretation and above all fashioned the cultural instruments for thinking the future in a new way.

The great revolutions of modern history took place at points of time in which the culture produced by the existing order of things was no longer able to give men a vision of the future in terms of progress towards the emancipation of mankind, freedom from oppression, affirmation of reason. The effervescence of revolutionary historical phases is accounted for by the fact that a new culture, promoted by the agents of change gives back to men, and to young people in particular, the capacity to imagine a future, i.e. the perspective without which politics necessarily degenerate into a mere power-play, driving away from it the very best forces of society.

III.

We believe that the federalist turning-point of world history will have the same cultural significance. Federalism became a political movement in the course of World War Two. Some men, drawing their inspiration from the political reflections of Kant, the British federalists and Einaudi, understood that the destructive potential of war had by then reached such a monstrous degree as to give Kant's philosophical scheme the reality of a concrete political project. Federalism therefore started in Italy as a reflection on peace and a struggle for the realization of peace, and has since remained true to its original inspiration. Its relation to peace is the same as that of liberalism, democracy and socialism to liberty, equality and social justice. In this perspective, the struggle for European unification must be viewed as an episode of a much more long-term historical endeavor, aiming to realize peace through a world federation. Founding a European federation thus appears as the first step in the progress of federalism in world history. This significance can be already delineated, if only in embryo, in the segment of European integration which is already behind us. For, even though the federal unity of Europe is far from having been achieved, thanks to the presence of this goal an unprecedented work of peace-making has been realized in the ending of the historical enmity between France and Germany, which had been soaking Europe in blood during the whole course of modern history since German unification.

IV.

This is the kind of awareness which has formed the historical identity of the MFE in Italy. What had to be done in the years of its foundation, and still has to be done today, is to fight a battle which is both for an institutional change and for affirming a new culture: the culture of peace, which has to appropriate what is permanent in the cultures of freedom, equality and social justice and go beyond them in a larger perspective. In this way the character of federalism as a comprehensive cultural concept comes to the fore. In fact, it implies, on the one hand, the awareness that peace cannot be realized except by overcoming state sovereignty, and it presents us, on the other hand, with a difficult and fascinating intellectual challenge: to revise the Marxist conception of history as a history of class-struggle, and to go beyond it through laying the foundations of a new conception of history as a history of the coming of peace (a clear argument for the need for such a revision is to be found, among many examples, in the *impasse* of traditional historiography in face of the problem of interpreting European fascism). We have moreover to elaborate new models of society, whose realization would be made possible by overcoming state sovereignty. This means giving back to men and women, and to young people in particular the capacity to look to the future, to think of the history to come as a history of the accomplishment of what is specifically human in man. This is what the liberal, democratic and socialist ideologies are no more able to do. Hence, after having been the great driving force of the history of Europe in the nineteenth century, they are today but empty shells, deprived of any power to attract and to mobilize support.

V.

That the problem of peace is the crucial problem of our age is shown with the utmost clarity by the tremendous echo evoked by the initiatives of the peace movement in Europe. We have not, in this context, to take sides for or against the peace movement: as long as no institutional solution to the problem of peace is advanced, everybody is both right and wrong in the debate which is under way in Europe. It suffices to remark that, since the end of the war, no other problem has acquired the capacity to provoke such a vast and profound popular mobilization. Such a stirring does not happen by chance, for it is with respect to this problem that the destiny of Europe is at stake. But, if this is the case, the decisive challenge is to succeed in making the peace movement (and all those who, while not taking part in the public manifestations, are aware of the danger threatening Europe) become aware that there is no solution to the problem of peace except in federalism. It is – be it said once more a political task indeed, but also a cultural one: to bring the peace movement, and all those who want peace, to adopt the culture of peace.

VI.

Creating the culture of peace, however, is one of our responsibilities. It cannot be found ready-made in books. The official culture does not call state sovereignty in question. To be sure, the culture of peace has forerunners: from Kant up to the British federalists and Luigi Einaudi. But the federalist aspect of these great thinkers' works has been forgotten, almost removed by the culture of war. It is our task to reassess their thought, bringing its real value to the fore, to continue it and to deepen it.

VII.

The great institutional and cultural transformations of history occur when they are made possible by objective modifications of people's everyday behavior. When such modifications are so radical as to make the existing power structure obsolete, they are not understood by those in power, who always try to control the new reality – which eludes them – with the material and cultural instruments of the past, thus causing contradictions to accumulate and problems to become more and more intractable. *In reality the great historical transformations are never effected by the existing power structure.* In order for them to break through, a force must emerge able to take on in its own right the responsibility for effecting the change and to make this the reason for its political existence. This is our situation, and herein lies the great difficulty of our task. There is a passage in Machiavelli's *Prince* which has an important place in the cultural stock of the Italian MFE. It is said in it that "there is nothing more difficult to arrange, more doubtful, of success, and more dangerous to carry through than undertaking the introduction of new orders. The innovator makes enemies of all those who prospered under the old order, and only lukewarm support is forthcoming from those who would prosper under the new. Their support is lukewarm partly from fear of their adversaries, who have the existing laws on their side, and partly because men are generally incredulous, never really trusting new things unless they have tested them by experience".

VIII.

This is our situation. We must know that we cannot expect anything from the existing order, i.e. from the national one: neither from political nor from economic power nor from the media nor from official culture. This means that the essential condition of our survival as federalists (since we can always survive as an advertising agency of the European policy of national governments) resides in our capacity to build up, on our own account, the basis of our influence, to create our own information channels, to finance our organization ourselves and, first and foremost, to work out our own culture. That is, in a word, the primary requirement of *autonomy,* in the fields of politics, organization, finance and culture. Here is to be found the fundamental criterion which determined the basic choices that account for the specific nature and structure of the Italian MFE.

Let me point briefly to the way in which the choice of autonomy has been put into effect as regards i) our relations with political parties, ii) our criteria for selecting and training active members and iii) the raising of our financial resources.

i) Autonomy in our political relations has as its main manifestation *the refusal by the group of members who provide the leadership and management of the MFE to identify themselves with any national party.* We are but ourselves, neither right-wing nor left-wing, neither Christian Democrat nor socialist, since such distinctions belong to the order we want to overcome. It must be noticed, however, that it is just because of this position of independence (which is anyway compatible with tactical alliances) that we have been allowed to establish and maintain very good collaborative relationships with all democratic parties in Italy.

ii) The selection and training of active members are guided by the purpose to avoid restrictions which would be imposed on the movement by a too burdensome and costly administrative apparatus, which would inevitably depend, for its survival, on external funds. That is why *ours are all part-time active members,* each having a job which assures him economic independence, while leaving enough time to devote to federalist activity. In this way our organization is not expensive, and we are sheltered from any possible pressure or blackmailing by any center of political or economic power.

iii) The specific institution of financial autonomy, however, is self-financing. Every young man recruited in the Movement knows that being active in the organization will never procure him financial advantages, but rather will cost him money. Here lies the financial basis of our independence. To be sure, all this does not prevent us from receiving external contributions sometimes: but these are mainly used to finance particular actions, whereas the organization's permanent structure functions thanks to our own resources. This shelters us, once more, from any outside influence.

IX.

But the real foundation of all such choices is cultural autonomy. The sole motivation, in the absence of power and money, which can push active members to persevere, sometimes for decades, in a toilsome and difficult commitment, is the awareness of our irreplaceable historical role, i.e. of being those who are tracing a new way, who have a point of view allowing them to grasp, before others do, in their true sense the inarticulate ferments and aspirations of society in our epoch, that the others see with a biased eye, or do not see at all. Such awareness is a thoroughly cultural one. That is why we think that politics and culture are two inseparable aspects of our activity. This means, let me repeat once more, that it is the federalists themselves who have to produce their culture. This is the reason why each MFE section in Italy strives to be at the same time a center of political activity and of cultural creativity, in which lectures, training courses, etc. are given by the active members themselves. And it could not be otherwise, since federalist culture is in the making, and who could make it but the federalists? lt is a task that certainly could not be entrusted to academics, nor to other exponents of official culture, who represent the old order and who, as such, can have but the function of supporting the existing power.

X.

This figure of the activist, being at the same time a man of action and a man of culture, is the ideal to which the MFE has oriented itself throughout its history. To be sure, as always happens, reality has fallen short of the ideal from many points of view. Models, however, are important in the life of a movement which wants to be revolutionary (though this word, in the case of the MFE, has to be carefully stripped of any violent connotation). I am convinced that the influence exerted in Italy by the MFE lies in its always having attributed a primary importance to the selection and formation of men. Let me conclude with another quotation from Machiavelli. In the *Discourses* he asks whether it is true that money is "the sinew of war". And he answers that, "contrary to the general opinion, […] the sinews of war are not gold, but good soldiers; for gold alone will not procure good soldiers, but good soldiers will always procure gold". And good soldiers, in the current struggle for peace, can be found only if we are capable of working out a culture opening up a new outlook on the future of mankind.

The True Illusions*

Barbara SPINELLI

When the newly-elected President of the Italian Republic made reference on the island of Ventotene to the birth of the European unification project, many were probably asking themselves: how did that idea come about, how did it become the dominant idea of a continent, and how did it enter the lives of all of us in the form not only of a promise or a remorse for unaccomplished things, but also in the form of so many laws that nowadays have prevalence over national laws. There is to wonder why we insist in giving to that idea the name, noble but shaky, of a dream. Giorgio Napolitano vividly recalled what then, in the midst of a war between Europeans, seemed a fancy born in the minds of three anti-fascist confined – Altiero Spinelli, Ernesto Rossi, Eugenio Colorni. Indeed, so was considered what they envisaged: the birth of a Europe where there will never again be wars, and where a fundamental conviction regarding the nation-States will take roots. The nation-States had digged their own grave, by transforming their absolute State sovereignties into a mutual annihilation weapon, and finally into a self-annihilation one. As in a Greek tragedy, from sorrow and guilt a lesson was to come out, which will lead Europe to a new life. This was the catharsis proposed as a remedy in the *Ventotene Manifesto*.

To a close look, it was a quite special dream. It was more similar to a prophetic vision of a man looking for the unconfessed roots of his present time, and sketching on what he found the possible reality of tomorrow. It was supported by a very strong awareness of reality – which always imposes on one's political aspirations the respect of the conditions of the real world – and hence by a deeply-rooted practical sense, based on the experience and the memory of countless European wars. If it continued to be defined as a dream or utopia, it is because the States wanted that that be the general consideration of it, necessary for safeguarding their absolute national sovereignties. But it was not so for the founders of the Community: Adenauer, Monnet, Schuman, De Gasperi had clear in their minds the tragic sequel of Europe's history, and considered the Union to be essential in practice, not only desirable as an Utopia. But the guardians

* Published in Issue 3/2006.

of nationalism did not cease for decades to fight it with convenient expedients. Since the beginning, their main weapon has been to define the European adventure as an illusion, talked of to the past like other Utopias.

It would be worth reading again the papers that Alexander Hamilton, James Madison and John Jay wrote between the autumn of 1787 and the spring of 1788 in *The Federalist* under the pen-name of Publius, when there was to ratify the American Constitution approved by the Philadelphia Convention on September 17, 1787. In the sixth paper, Hamilton explains where the true illusions, the true "Utopian speculations", lie. Who was cherishing them were not the federalists, but their opponents, who supported the inviolable sovereignty of the thirteen American states or, at the most, partial confederations. Hamilton is stern: they believe possible "a continuation of harmony between a number of independent, unconnected sovereignties in the same neighborhood". They share the unwise optimism of those who believe that a republican spirit is substantially peaceful ("There have been, if I may so express it, almost as many popular as royal wars"). Reading Publius helps us reveal the deception of an Utopia that usually wraps itself in the mantle of a pragmatic respectability: "Is it not time to awake from the deceitful dream of a golden age, and to adopt as a practical maxim for the direction of our political conduct that we, as well as the other inhabitants of the globe, are yet remote from the happy empire of perfect wisdom and perfect virtue?", Hamilton writes.

Also for today's Europe that is true. Certainly those who see in the post-war founding principles something noble but no longer attracting are right: just because the Union partly exists already, it is not easy to contemplate new wars among Europeans. But that is not a reason for the European project to be seen as an Utopian desire, an old rhetoric for a world that does not exist. The threats from which the idea of Europe was born are still present, only the threats and the challenges have changed: they are called globalized economy, terrorism, scarcity and political use of energy. Today like yesterday the individual States cannot face them alone, and their rulers know it even when they are reluctant to delegate sovereignty. If they could look into their own history, they would know that theirs is not even real sovereignty: it is a shadow what they are clinging to. It is an illusion, as described in Abbagnano's *Dictionary of Philosophy*: "an erroneous appearance that does not cease when it is recognized as such [...] it is like seeing kinked a stick immersed in the water". By delegating decision-making powers to Europe, the States can regain a sovereignty that they have lost today.

Therefore it is for a sense of reality that we have to make Europe and give it a capacity to govern, just like in the Forties and Fifties. It is for a practical spirit that it is urgent to have a Union ready to act even when there is not unanimous agreement, instead of a Union blocked by the right of veto. Once again it is the historical experience that demands this, as called for by a prophetic dream, founded however on rationality. Today it is the nation-State to be under an illusion, when it pretends to be non-vulnerable and even wraps itself in the mantle of *real-politik* and pragmatism. The democratic rhetoric itself is a conjuring exercise, that risks to hide reality. Of course it is essential that Europe be accepted by the peoples. But without an efficient government it makes no sense to put that necessity as a priority: without a government, Europe may well be more democratic, but absolutely without any weight.

This too is a valuable lesson that comes from the American federalists of 1700. The generous democratic bursts may turn into a "torrent of angry and malignant passions"; "an over-scrupulous jealousy of danger to the rights of the people" may turn into "mere pretense and artifice, the stale bait for popularity at the expense of the public good", Publius says in *The Federalist.* The dangerous ambition is the one of those who "lurk behind the specious mask of zeal for the rights of the people", not of those who, taking the harder route, are concerned "for the firmness and efficiency of government" (Hamilton, Paper No. 1). Democracy, under certain conditions, may even become a deceit. The referendums on the adhesion of Turkey, promised in France and Austria, are in effect a way for expressing the right of veto by individual States over Europe's future foreign policy. More than respected, the peoples are thus made instruments.

A realistic dream of the Union is today the Constitution, and it is not by chance that it too is declared dead, as happens for Utopias condemned by reality. The two referenda in France and the Netherlands in May-June 2005 would have ditched the idea of a suitable European government, able to complement the national governments. Of course it is advisable to do something, waiting for France to elect a new Head of State in 2007; something pragmatic with the existing treaties, said the President of the Commission Barroso, proposing – in view of the European Summit on June 15 – a common security policy, domestic and against terrorism. But it will not be enough, as long as the decision-making powers in Europe will not be made clearer, besides being shared, and only a Constitution can do that. If possible, a Constitution approved this time by all the peoples simultaneously.

This project too is not illusive, and who has already ratified the constitutional Treaty knows it. Chancellor Angela Merkel said that she does not intend to give up: the German people and many other countries have voted for the Constitution, therefore the project cannot be dumped by some nations with easy presumption. Fifteen States out of 25 have ratified it (soon they will be 16, with Finland) and this means that a majority wants the Constitution. Also a majority of citizens – about 250 million out of 450 – want it. Reviving the realistic dream means to start from here, from this Europe that has already expressed herself by a majority for a working European government and for a continent that shall have a greater weight in the globalized economy and in an effective international policy. It is necessary to take into account those who are unsatisfied and denounce the faults of the Union, but also those who strongly want to complete the Union and give it a Constitution. To go back would be not only illusory, it would be a betrayal and a breach of the agreements, because all the governments have committed themselves to bring the Treaty to ratification in two years, when they signed it on October 29, 2004. It is important that Italy has got again a government team that has supported this project and is willing to even improve on it (for example, by abolishing the paragraph of the Treaty that requires a unanimous vote for constitutional revisions): President Napolitano will continue on this matter the struggle of former President Ciampi, and others will join in, starting with Prime Minister Prodi, who proposed an even more advanced constitutional Treaty – the Penelope Project – when he was President of the Commission. At that point it will indeed be a very good thing to revive the realistic dreams and put an end to the utopian national illusions: illusions that do not cease even when they are acknowledged as such.

Ex Uno Plures: the European Road to a Cooperative Federalism*

Nadia URBINATI

Multinational countries live in a state of permanent trouble, all the more so if economic anxiety makes solidarity an issue and ideologues and politicians dream of cultural homogeneity. Federalism has proved to be the most viable way to satisfy both the need for union and the desire for autonomy; it decentralizes sovereign power and civil society alike. My concern here, however, is not with discord within multinational states, but with the sentiments of disunion arising within countries marked by cultural and political unity. Perhaps an army forced them together, or ambitious or idealist intellectuals fostered their national feelings. Whatever their history, now these people display common characteristics even if they are also locally distinct. Political institutions contribute to constituting a nation no less than language, religion, and literary and folkloric traditions. A people that has been living under a unitary political system for several generations is, after all, a people without memories of federation. Today this elementary fact is acknowledged even by those intellectuals who dream of a federal Italy. "It is not easy," Gianfranco Miglio (a former leader of the Northern League) wrote, "to construct a federation in a country that does not have a 'federal culture.'" Nothing is more illogical than a Jacobin federalism. To *impose* a federation is like trying to bottle wine in the wrong season or shield it at the wrong temperature. Sooner or later the bottle will burst. As one cannot force the art of making wine, so one cannot force mutual trust. A federation needs both a strong sense of peripheral autonomy and an equally strong sense of national sympathy: these are the two souls of a "federal culture". The rationale of federalism is "subsidiarity," which denotes a system within which the units maintain the autonomy they need to deal with the spheres of action that pertain to them, but cede authority to a higher level in pursuit of common goals (security, peace, freedom, well-being). The retention of local autonomy may foster sympathy for the larger society. Neither autonomy nor sympathy, however, can be imposed by decree. My main concern here is with European single-state federalism. But in Europe today domestic and international dimensions are so intertwined

* Published in Issue 1/2011.

that notions of "inside" and "outside" are increasingly blurred. The road to single-state federalism crosses the highway of supernational federalism.

Both the unitary modern state and the idea of federation thrived in the age between the dynastic and religious wars of the sixteenth century and the two world wars of the twentieth. Two years after the St. Bartholomew Day massacre, Jean Bodin published *De la république,* a classic text celebrating the indivisible, unlimited, and centralized power of the state as the mighty guardian of domestic order. In the midst of the wars that followed the revocation of the Edict of Nantes, William Penn wrote *An Essay Towards the Present and Future Peace of Europe,* in which he argued that only a European confederation could guarantee a durable peace. Many of the men and women who fought against Nazism and fascism belonged to the tradition of Penn. Despite their different political allegiances and mutual isolation they reached similar federalist conclusions. The leviathan-state had put an end to social anarchy, but opened the door to a no less frightening international anarchy. The federalists of the 1940s interpreted World War II as a European *civil war,* and blamed the conflict on absolute state sovereignty. Attempts to unify Europe were not new, and they did not necessarily guarantee peace. After all, both Napoleon and Hitler were universalists. They sought to create a great Europe unified under the respective banners of Rationality (and Christianity) and Aryan civilization. The Napoleonic wars destroyed the myth of the territorial state as the guarantor of domestic and international order; World War II ended the nightmare of a continental leviathan. The two myths were complementary expressions of the hegemonic project of the nation-state. Napoleon's Europe was an expanded France; Hitler's, a vast Germany. Most World War II partisans saw continental federation as the only feasible alternative to the state's power vocation, domestic and supernational. They spoke of a new European order composed of a "network of local voluntary associations, vehicles of direct democracy, united within a European federation." Local autonomy and transnational co-operation would, in James Wilkinson's words, get rid of the "old nation-states [which were] bellicose and unresponsive to the needs of their citizens." All federalists prized political and cultural pluralism. Their models were the medieval city republics and the guilds. Harold Laski thought the modern theory of sovereignty was intrinsically statist, and portrayed himself as a "frank medievalist." Fragmenting sovereignty was a way of lightening its burden. Carlo Rosselli complained that the state gained power by expropriating from civil society all of its "numberless forms of association, as rich in their content as they were free and limited in extension." The many versions of federalism are all set against rationalist political ambition: to create a "mortal God" with an indivisible and irrevocable power over all its subjects. Modern right-

and left-wing federalism were born in reaction to Jacobin democracy. Both shared David Hume's admiration for the United Provinces and their ability to keep a people "from uniting into large assemblies" by dividing them "into many separate bodies" so that they could "debate with safety" and prevent "every inconvenience." Hume's preoccupation was shared by the authors of the *Federalist Papers* – a text that, notwithstanding its nationalist orientation, became a manifesto of latter-day European federalists.

Federalism fights on two fronts: the supernational and the domestic. On the one hand, it seeks to limit the power of each state in order to reach not a "mere suspension of hostility" but a condition of mutual trust. On the other hand, it advocates a division of sovereignty and rejects the principle of one-nation one-state. The architects of the European Union saw the new order not as a way of dissolving and weakening national identities, but as the only legitimate way "to preserve them and allow them to flourish vigorously in all their diversity." Their aim, Altiero Spinelli wrote, was not "one single European state, designed to become a European Nation, but a Federation of Nations in which citizens will jealously guard their own traditional home country while becoming at the same time citizens of the Community." The European Union is not likely to become another United States, where one defines oneself first as an American and then as someone who comes from Illinois. In the United States, identity goes from general to local. In Europe, things are different: one is first of all Italian, then European. Generally speaking, Europeans share multiple loyalties, which need not be a source of conflicts. Hence the role of the European Supreme Court, to which European citizens – both as individuals and as members of cultural groups – can appeal against their own states. Institutions of this kind are meant to generate the habit of multiple belonging while fostering a democratic culture of rights. Although the domestic and supernational strategies of federalism go together logically, historically they have been pursued separately. Until the last century, the federation remained a project of national unification. Carlo Cattaneo advocated a United States of Europe along with the United States of Italy, but his political commitment was to the latter. He thought one could construct a large federation by beginning with small ones. In the nineteenth century, the primary goal was political liberty rather than peace. The enemy was mass democracy and unlimited majority rule. The first generation of federalists were the Girondins, the second the Proudhonians, who opposed Mazzini's democratic nationalism as vehemently as their ancestors had opposed Rousseau's (and Robespierre's) republicanism. The horrors of world wars led federalists to switch their focus from the domestic to the supernational. Their main goal became peace and democracy. In his inaugural speech as the first president of the High Authority of the European Assembly (1950), Robert Schuman declared that the "essential political objective [of the federative process is]: to make a breach in the ramparts of national sovereignty which will be narrow enough to secure consent, but deep enough to open the way towards the unity that is essential to peace."

Altiero Spinelli, one of the spiritual fathers of the European Union, provided a very simple and convincing rationale for a supernational federalism. He thought that a European federation would open the door to domestic federations. He inverted the political strategy pursued by the federalists of the previous century: after almost a century of unitary statism, regions and local communities had lost the vigor to fight for a federation, but the federal enterprise could acquire new strength through Europe. Once the states begin to release portions of their traditional sovereign functions to the European Community, decentralization might "give birth again to a free local political life. "The European motto would then be *ex uno plures,* because the proliferation of peripheral autonomies proceeds from the very process of continental unification. Jurists and political scientists rightly insist on the "democratic deficits" of the European Union, which they trace to Jean Monnet's "functionalist" approach. Monnet's policy of dealing with prime ministers, while leaving the people temporarily outside, rested on the conviction that the union had to be prepared by transforming the habits of ordinary men and women in dealing with each other. Europeans had to be "persuaded" by practice that they could approach problems in "the same way," as nations that were different and divided but co-operating. As Spinelli had foreseen, the more the peoples of Europe perceived themselves *also* as Europeans, the more the centralized state would relax its ties. A supernational federation promoted one of the most interesting contemporary phenomena: a process toward autonomy and regionalism within the European nation-states. Until the early 1970s, only Germany was a federation among the states that became part of the European Community. Today other states have reached a stage of quasi-federation. The movement toward decentralization is particularly strong in those countries that have both a nondemocratic legacy and a strong centralist tradition. Italy implemented a system of regional government in 1970, Spain in 1978, and France in 1982. This process, however, began in the name of national unity, not federalism. The Italian, Spanish, and French constitutions proclaim the respective states to be "one and indivisible." They promote a certain degree of regional autonomy while assigning to the central state the task of redressing socio-economic disparities among the regions. Regional autonomy can be seen as a de facto federation, a physiological evolution of the unitary state once it becomes democratic and is no longer surrounded by potential enemies. Freedom and the loosening of fear encourage the expression of difference. A supernational federation unites what the territorial state had separated (internationally) and dissociates what the territorial state had unified (domestically). The novelty introduced by the European Union consists in the fact that, whereas federalism has traditionally been a process of unification (within a single state or among several states), today it can be both a *unifying* and a *divisive* force. Since its emphasis on autonomy and pluralism tends to re-open the arguments about national aggregations, in the short term decentralization may create instability. In the long term, however, it could bring former partners closer and even promote new kinds of associations. Historically, federalism designated a process of union. The United States became a country when its people united into a federal pact. Germany and Switzerland went from loose confederation to federal union. Until now the reverse process, a unitary state becoming a federation, has never happened without the state's falling apart. When federalism is used as a divisive tool, its natural conclusion is the dissolution of the state. Thus, Czechoslovakia became a federation shortly before it disappeared. This is the reason why regional autonomy may be seen as a safer form of decentralization than a full-blown federalism. But perhaps this is not necessarily so.

Spinelli's Commitment for the European Constitution*

John PINDER

The directly elected EP and the making of the Draft Treaty on European Union

Spinelli was, three decades after his initiative for creating a European Political Community (EPC) in the early 1950s, once again at the centre of a major endeavour to federate Europe. But this time the Monnet method of building federal Europe by a series of steps had provided him with a directly elected Parliament to act as a constituent, and, aged seventy five, he now had not only an idea for achieving it in the form of a treaty to establish a federal European Union but also a capacity for leadership through persuasion as well as example; and, in order to get the Parliament's structures and party groups on board for the voyage, he realised that he should begin by securing the commitment of a sufficient core of individual MEPs to the idea.

He opened his campaign in May 1980 in a debate on the budget, when he judged that their treatment by the Council had irritated MEPs sufficiently, by declaring that the Council's behaviour regarding the budget was such that the Parliament must initiate reform of the institutions: if this was to be done by the governments ignoring the Parliament, the result would be an intergovernmental reform that would change nothing; if by Parliament, it would deliver stronger, supranational institutions capable of dealing with the problems. He followed this with a letter to all MEPs and an invitation to a dinner at the Restaurant Crocodile, which was attended only by three other Italians, three British and two Germans, who did however found the Crocodile Club to promote the idea. Membership grew, regular weekly meetings were held and by the end of the year some eighty had expressed interest. A resolution was drafted for MEPs to sign, proposing an ad hoc working party representing all political groups and currents of opinion, to devote itself to the task of drawing up a constitution to present to the member states; and by June there were a hundred and seventy nine signatures, from all the significant party groups. But the largest group, the

* Published in Issue 3/2007.

Christian Democrats, was under-represented, evidently because, having been prominent in the Parliament's federalist initiatives, they saw Spinelli as an interloper: In discussion with them, however, Spinelli discovered that they would be satisfied if the resolution proposed a full parliamentary committee rather than a less formal working group, which he was ready to concede – and which was surely an important improvement.

The Parliament approved the resolution and the Committee on Institutional Affairs started work in January 1982, with a strong membership, balanced among the party groups and including three chairs from other committees. Spinelli wished to emphasise broad support rather than over-identification with himself. So chapters on the several aspects were drafted by six co-rapporteurs from the different party groups, within the framework of a basic general draft provided by himself as general rapporteur, underlining the principles of democratic and effective institutions and of competences attributed according to the principle of subsidiarity. The Committee repeatedly discussed and revised all the reports, until a full draft report was collated and edited by Spinelli, and it was debated, amended and approved by a large majority in the Committee. This vast task was completed and presented to plenary session, which, after discussing 185 amendments and adopting a few of them, approved the resolution in September 1983 by 202 votes to 37.

Four lawyers then worked with Spinelli on drafting a legal text, which included Article 82 stipulating that the Treaty could enter into effect when ratified by over half the member-states containing two-thirds of the Community's population. That was of course designed to prevent the whole enterprise from being torpedoed, like the EPC in 1954, by the veto of one or two member states. Knowing that this would be controversial, Spinelli had kept it until this stage so that MEPs could both appreciate the importance of the project and be confident that its implementation was legally well enough founded. That strategy was vindicated on 14 February 1984 when the plenary approved the legal text by the yet larger majority of 237 to 32.

The Parliament's Draft Treaty

Apart from Article 82, by-passing the veto on treaty amendment, the various provisions of the Draft Treaty establishing the European Union did not break with the method of building on the foundations of the European Community. Indeed many of the provisions have been put into effect in subsequent amending treaties. The distinction was, rather, in the scale of what was proposed, designed as a radically new departure to create a more powerful, democratic and effective Union.

Thus the European Union would inherit all the laws, practices and institutions of the European Community that were compatible with the new Treaty. The European Council would decide its own working methods and a new function would be to nominate the President of the Commission, who would select the list of other Commissioners to be presented for approval by the Parliament. The Council would decide mainly under the procedure of qualified majority and in legislative co-decision with the Parliament. The Commission would be strengthened and the Court of Justice aided by a Court of First Instance. The division of powers between Union and member states would follow the principle of subsidiarity. There would be a monetary union and timetable for completion of the internal market; and the provision for environmental and social policies would be more explicit. The distinction between agricultural and other expenditure would be abolished and the Union would have power to raise its 'own resources'. These provisions were all in the line of the Community's federal development. But cooperation in defence and political aspects of foreign policy was to be the responsibility of the European Council, which was to determine its own procedures, i.e. to work on a basis of consensus until it should decide otherwise.

Spinelli had carefully planned the next steps, towards winning enough support to ensure ratification of the Draft Treaty. The Parliament secured backing from the European associations of employers and trade unions as well from other elements of civil society. The Treaty was presented to member states' parliaments, was generally well received and was approved as it stood by the Belgian and Italian parliaments. But the breakthrough came when, two months after the European Parliament had approved the Treaty, Spinelli together with the President of the Parliament, Piet Dankert, and of the Institutional Committee, Mauro Ferri, visited President Mitterrand. Spinelli believed that French leadership would be the key to success. So he outlined the unique role that France, and hence Mitterrand himself, could play in launching the process of ratification and he proposed that Mitterrand should make a statement to that effect in his speech to Parliament in May 1984 as the current President of the European Council. Mitterrand was evidently impressed by what Spinelli said because he ended that speech by expressing his support for the Draft Treaty, adding that 'France is available for such an enterprise'; that he, as President, was willing, on behalf of France, 'to examine and defend your project, the inspiration behind which it approves; and, implicitly accepting the by-passing of the veto through Article 82, that consultations should begin leading up to a conference 'of the member states concerned'.

Meanwhile Parliament's delegation had visited Bonn, where Spinelli found parties and members of the Bundestag largely supportive. But the reaction of the Chancellor's office was that the time was not yet ripe to consider alternatives to all the member states going forward together, with particular mention of the occupying powers, i.e. the UK as well as France. The preference for steps taken by all member states was a settled element in Germany's European policy; and it may well be that the political situation in the Soviet Union, where Gorbachev was to succeed to the leadership in a year's time, weighed heavily with Chancellor Kohl, who had long combined what seemed to many to be, for his generation, the contradictory ambitions of achieving both European and German unification – the latter requiring the consent of all four occupying powers.

Mitterrand then secured the agreement of the European Council in June to set up an *ad hoc* Committee of the heads of governments' personal representatives, which became known as the Dooge Committee after the Irish Senator who chaired it, to prepare the ground for the proposed conference; and Mitterrand appointed as his own representative Maurice Faure, who had been one of the signatories of the Rome Treaties and could be relied on to draft a report for the Committee incorporating the main features of the Draft Treaty. This he indeed did in the Committee's Interim Report, presented to the European Council in December 1984, with the reservations of the British, Danish and Greek members expressed in numerous dissenting footnotes.

Spinelli had by now identified Germany as the 'weak point' among the states whose support for the Draft Treaty was necessary; and Kohl proposed postponement of the decision on the Committee's final report, with presentation only to the foreign ministers in March and to the European Council not until June. Spinelli perceived that this delay was a danger for the Draft Treaty.

From Draft Treaty to Single European Act

The destiny of the Draft Treaty had indeed been profoundly affected by another decision of the European Council under Mitterrand's Presidency: to appoint Jacques Delors as President of the Commission starting in January 1985. Delors was determined to get the Community moving again after two decades of relative stagnation but, like Monnet, he sought what he thought politically possible while being at the same time necessary, whereas Spinelli put all his effort into making his vision of the necessary possible. So Delors spent the latter part of 1984 visiting the heads of member states' governments to ascertain which they would accept among what he identified as four major necessary projects: monetary union, common defence policy, reform to make the institutions more effective and democratic, or completion of the internal market. Needless to say, the one that gained unanimous assent, including that of Mrs Thatcher, was the single market. So Delors began his Commission Presidency preparing, with great speed and energy, a very detailed White Paper on a programme for completing the internal market by 1992, for presentation to the European Council in 1985.

Spinelli was encouraged when Delors told him, in September 1984, that he was now convinced that institutions were decisive. But Delors was doubtless thinking of institutional reforms that would be required to make a project such as the single market effective, rather than those of the Draft Treaty as a whole; and this offered a way through Kohl's dilemma by providing for a significant reform which all the member states were likely to accept.

Delors had the advantage of a close relationship with Mitterrand, including recent service as finance minister in his government; and this, combined with the Presidency of the Commission, helped to give him privileged access to Kohl. So it was perhaps not surprising that before the meeting of the European Council in June, both Kohl and Mitterrand made it known that they favoured reforms such as a move towards qualified majority voting in the Council, increases in power for the Commission and the Parliament, and an extension of Community competences, corresponding to what was to be required for what became the Single European Act rather than the full Draft Treaty.

This evidence that Mitterrand had abandoned the Draft Treaty was extremely disturbing for Spinelli, who underwent a major cancer operation on 22 May which seriously weakened him throughout the summer and prevented him from travelling until October. Mrs Thatcher, who preferred trying to create the single market through a 'gentlemen's agreement' rather than treaty amendment, was against the proposal for an intergovernmental conference. But the Italian presidency called a vote, in which the six founder states plus Ireland prevailed over the negative votes of Britain, Denmark and Greece. While this was encouraging, the IGC was based on the Commission's White Paper and the Dooge Committee's report, not the Parliament's Draft Treaty. So the main institutional reforms incorporated in the Single European Act agreed by the European Council in December 1985 were confined to provision for qualified majority voting on single market legislation, a "cooperation" procedure that gave the Parliament a foot in the door to legislative power and an assent procedure for accession treaties and association agreements; and there were some new competences in fields such as the environment, social policy and a fund to support the Community's less-developed regions, together with a commitment to the aim of monetary union.

Spinelli's first journey after his operation was to Bonn, in early October, where he was well received at the Bundestag, which had however delayed delivering its report, recommending that the Draft Treaty be the basis for the government's position, until after the IGC had been completed – perhaps because the Christian Democrats wished to express their support for the more federalist project while not embarrassing Kohl before the day of decision on the Single Act in the European Council. Spinelli followed this with a visit to Brussels for lunch with Delors, who said that not only Britain but also France and Germany were now opposed to the Draft Treaty and that the Commission, more realistically than the Parliament, was seeking a compromise; and after the European Council's meeting, Delors told the Parliament that what had been agreed was not enough, but nevertheless a significant step.

The Single European Act was signed in February 1986. Spinelli tried, despite his failing health, to rally MEPs into promoting a campaign to secure support from a group of member states for giving the Parliament a constituent role after the next European elections. But MEPs no longer had the stomach for it. So he died on the twenty third of May, believing that the result of all his efforts had been 'only a miserable little mouse, which many suspect is a dead mouse'.

Spinelli's legacy

The legacy of the second great episode of Spinelli's European federal odyssey, from 1970 to 1986, was twofold. He put the idea of a European constitution back on the political map from which it had been deleted since the mid-1950s, and he made a major contribution to the relaunching of the process of the Community's federal development, after the stasis initiated by de Gaulle.

Delors, in his *Mémoires*, was to express himself as 'surprised and hurt' that Spinelli had criticised the Single European Act so severely, pointing out that, without the impact of the Draft Treaty, he would not have been able to insert so many 'factors of progress' in it. The SEA did indeed initiate a period of dynamism in the Community during which important federal elements of the Draft Treaty came into effect. The Act's apparently modest institutional reforms led on, through subsequent treaties, to the application of the principles of qualified majority voting and codecision for most legislative decisions; to nomination by the European Council of the Commission's President subject to approval by the Parliament; and to the establishment of the Court of First Instance. Subsidiarity became a basic principle for the division of responsibilities between the member states and what is now called, as in the Draft Treaty, the Union. The Single Act's commitment to 'the progressive realisation of economic and monetary union' was honoured by the creation of the euro and the European Central Bank, for which British and Danish vetoes were circumvented by what amounted to a specific application of the principle of Article 82; and there is now an Amsterdam Treaty provision for this precedent to be followed by member states wishing to go farther and faster towards a federal polity.

All this confirmed the constructive synergy of Monnet's and Spinelli's approaches to the building of a federal Europe. It had been Monnet's creation of the ECSC and initiation of the proposal for an EDC that gave Spinelli the opportunity to promote his project for a federal EPC; and from this in turn emerged the project of the common market for the relaunching of Monnet's Community process, with the successful extension of its scope in the EEC. It was thanks to the provision in the ECSC and subsequent Treaties for direct elections that Spinelli was able to go so far towards realising, in the form of the Parliament's Draft Treaty, his vision of the citizens' representatives drafting a federal constitution, which led on to the federal elements in subsequent treaties, as well as keeping the aim of a federal European constitution on the agenda.

Spinelli recognised this synergy when he said, on the day after the Parliament's first massive vote in favour of the Draft Treaty in September 1983, that "Monnet has the great merit of having built Europe and the great responsibility to have built it badly", and while it was surely not feasible in 1950 to "build Europe well" in the full sense that Spinelli doubtless had in mind, his radical initiatives in 1951-53 and 1981-84 not only kept the aim of a European federal constitution on the agenda but were also major impulses towards building the Union better. Twenty years later the Convention put the idea of a constitution on the agenda again, though as the name for a less federal and more complicated project than the Parliament's Draft Treaty, and the outcome is almost certain to be some further federal steps. So the final destination of his odyssey is not yet in sight. But his life remains an inspiration for those who are continuing the journey, and in particular for those who wish to complete it.

In What Respects Will European Federalism Be Different?*

Robert TOULEMON

According to many superficial observers for European reality, the widening of the European Union (EU) would mean the end of all perspective of federal evolution. On the contrary, the increase of the number of its members leaves no choice but between either paralysis or federalism. Some people, for example in France, believe they can find an alternative solution in a directorate of the bigger States. They forget that such an orientation is rejected by the others and that its efficiency is far from being guaranteed. Its first result would be to foster inner tensions and push smaller states towards an extreme pro-American attitude. This return to interstate tensions would be a definite step backward. It would not allow Europe to achieve a real political presence.

Federalism is the organizational form the best adapted to the community of peoples and States of Europe, which corresponds the most exactly to the motto proposed for the Union, "Unity in Diversity", combining the greatest autonomy of the federated entities, in other words subsidiarity, a federalist term par excellence, and a supra-state authority in the fields of common competence. However, to federate nations several of which in turn have occupied first rank positions in the world and which still believe themselves to be first rate powers, is a difficult undertaking. The federal systems of the American States, of the German *Länder*, of the Swiss Cantons, of the Canadian provinces, of the States of Australia or India, while they provide useful examples, cannot simply be transposed to Europe. In the present period of constitutional crisis we are going through, it is not without interest to consider the lessons offered by historical experiences in federalism, but also to define the peculiar features of a future European federal model.

The lessons we can draw from historical experiences

The historical examples are first to be considered from the point of view of the institutions. But how much freedom of choice is kept by the federated entities in their inner policies is also a matter to be carefully considered.

* Published in Issue 1/2008.

Institutions

The first experience to be considered is ours. The distribution of competences between different levels, some being exclusive and others shared, the decision-taking by majority vote, the primacy of community law over States' law, the existence of a common currency managed by a Central Bank are the federal elements to which the EU owes its main achievements. In the same way, the semi-proportionality of citizens' votes in the Council and representations in the Parliament is not far different from the current systems of representation of federated entities in existing federations. Some combine equal representation in one assembly (the Senate in the US, the Council of States in Switzerland) with the representation of populations in another assembly (the House of Representatives in the US, the National Council in Switzerland). Others add to the assembly representing the populations another chamber where the federated States have a semi-proportional representation; such is the case in Federal Germany. The provision in the European Constitutional treaty of a double majority of States and population in the Council of Ministers is inspired by the same philosophy. Indeed, the ambition of federal systems is to find a balance between the equality of States and the equality of citizens. History tells us that this equilibrium is not easy to reach nor to preserve. The crises of federalism may lead to conflicts; the most bloody was the one which tore the US during the Civil war. The adversaries of federalism put forward these crises to support the thesis that all federations are threatened by a sudden breakdown. They quote the example of the Soviet Union or Yugoslavia. So doing they forget that those federations were purely formal constructions which hardly masked the dictatorship of a single party and a crushing hegemony in the former USSR as in the present Federation of Russia. There remains that keeping the balance between the influence of the most populated and less populated States is as essential as the balance between the federated States and the federation.

The tensions peculiar to federal systems result most of the time from the sharing of competences and their exercise. The feeling that "Brussels" meddles too much in minor matters which could remain in the field of responsibility of the States, or even local entities, feeds the demand for a better respect of the subsidiarity principle. The constitutional treaty gave national Parliaments a power of caution in this field, the last word pertaining to the Court of Justice. The existence of a strong judiciary is necessary to the good functioning of federalism. The greatest merit of federalism is to substitute judicial arbitration to armed conflicts. This substitution means that the arbiter must be recognized as independent of the federated entities and of the federal institutions as well. The independence of judges depends as much on the duration of their mandate and the conditions of its renewal as on the authority who designates them. The extreme solution is the appointment for life, as in the Supreme Court of the USA.

Until now the member-States of the EU have refused to extend the competence of the Court of Justice to matters of defense and foreign policy; in the same way they refuse to extend the competence and the power of initiative of the Commission to these same fields. As it had been remarked by the founder of the College of Bruges, Henri Brugmans, until now Europe has just practiced federalism the wrong way round. Without competence for the questions which normally pertain to federalism, it often deals with matters which, somewhere else, concern the States themselves. The formula contemplated by the Constitutional Treaty that creates a Minister of Foreign Affairs linked to the Council and the Commission, with a diplomatic service of its own, would be a real step toward a federalism going in the right direction.

Another lesson drawn from federal examples: the necessity to have a strong executive at the head of the federation, strong meaning legitimate and visible. In this respect the Constitutional Treaty marked only a limited progress. The creation of a President of the European Council with a larger mandate and no longer fulfilling national functions is useful, but the appointment procedure is far from democratic and creates a duality with the president of the Commission. However, the supporters of a Federal Europe must see to it that these dispositions are adopted, whatever the fate of the Constitutional Treaty.

What Autonomy for the States?

The promoters of federalism have to answer the fundamental question posed by their adversaries: what autonomy will be left to the federated States in a European Union? From this point of view the experience of the other federal systems deserves to be considered. Everywhere education remains the concern of the federated entities, as well as, for an important part, the tax system, welfare policies and protection of the environment. We may, for instance, notice the choice by California to endorse the Kyoto Protocol that the USA government has not ratified. Be that as it may, political and social choices are basically made or arbitrated by the federal elections in the Federal State. In a European Federal Union these choices will be decided, for a large part, as they are now, by national elections, but the importance of European elections should increase together with the competences of the Union. However that may be, European states will keep more latitude in the choice of their economic, social or environmental model. For example, differently from other federal states, there is a consensus about maintaining at the national level the mechanisms of social welfare and to exclude the taxes on individuals from a fiscal harmonization, however advisable the latter may be. The system of ownership of firms will equally remain a national competence, even if the necessity of a fair competition, essential condition for the single market, remains under the competence of the Union. Nevertheless, there is the field of ethical values and fundamental rights where, even today, the EU has greater powers than the US. Such is the case, for example, of the abolition of the death penalty. However, the jurisprudence of the Supreme Court in Washington tends to place the fight against discrimination above the traditional States' rights.

The Specifics of a European Federalism

The particular character of a European federation will be to be pluri-national. The US, Germany, India, Switzerland, in spite of the latter being plurilingual, conceive themselves as forming one nation. Only the Belgian federation is bi-national, but its recent and very complex structure combining regions and linguistic communities makes it a model difficult to transpose. Rather than a federal State, Europe will define itself as a federal "Union of States and Citizens", a formula which seems to me more accurate than Jacques Delors' "federation of Nation States" – which was coined to appease the "souverainistes". Indeed, to quote Jean Monnet: "we do not form a coalition of States, we unite men". Moreover, several members of the EU, for example the United Kingdom, are pluri-national.

The first consequence of the pluri-national character of the EU is that it must foster a patriotism of values, of citizenship, a constitutional patriotism, and, in no case, an ethnic or geographical patriotism. This form of patriotism seems to me of a superior ethical level and certainly better adapted to the aspirations of younger generations, consequently it will be easier to make them share it. It is also a response to the perpetual adversaries of the EU who like to caricature it as an empire designed to be dominated by Germany, while one of its essential values is the refusal of any hegemony. A second consequence concerning the institutional organization of the federation: national organs, governments and parliaments will have to work together with the federal government, especially in the fields of foreign policy, defense and domestic security. In existing federations, federated entities only partake more or less in the Union government through their representative assembly: the US Senate, the German *Bundesrat*, the Council of States in Switzerland. But neither the Governors of the American States nor the Minister-Presidents of the *Länder* take part in the definition of the federal foreign policy. It should not be the same in the European federation.

The institution of a President of the European Council relieved of national functions was one of the most important innovations of the constitutional treaty. It raised reservations among federalists and supporters of the communitarian method, who could see it as a strengthening of the "Europe of States". We hope that a president who has only European responsibilities will act as the champion of the common interest. His role will be to associate the chiefs of national Governments to the management of EU's affairs.

From this innovation two evolutions seem possible. The more likely, at least for some time, will be the division of the government of the EU into a community domain where the Commission will have the main influence and an inter-governmental domain mostly concerning the States. In the medium term another evolution would be advisable: the two domains progressively coming together. This merging could take place by a progressive community of decisional procedures (an extension of the majority vote to foreign policy and defense, being understood that, as long as no integrated army is in existence, the minority would not be obliged to take part in an armed intervention that they would not approve of), by the fusion of presidencies and the creation of a European Cabinet composed of several ministers with a double function, on the model of the Minister of Foreign Affairs, another innovation of the Constitutional Treaty. It would be a clever means of conciliating the desire of each State to have a Commissioner and the necessity to ensure the coherence of the Community's Executive. Each of these ministers would have a vast range of responsibilities and would receive a power of coordination over the corresponding commissioners. In this way it would not just be Foreign Affairs, but also defense, domestic security, the economy, sector policies, the quality of life, including the environment and welfare, education, communication, culture and youth, which would represent seven or eight portfolios. Chosen without consideration of nationality by the President of the Commission, with the approval of the Parliament and the European Council, these ministers would constitute a select cabinet within the Commission. They would be closer to the government but they would benefit from the independence of the Commission; they would, so to speak, realize "smoothly" the passage from the inter-governmental to the community method before the completion of the federal system. The existence of a restricted cabinet sitting under a unified presidency would reduce the risk of incoherence deriving from the multiplication of the number of commissioners. The mode of designation of the federal President and his cabinet is another subject which requires specific solutions. Several formulas can be envisaged according to the system to be preferred: more parliamentary or more presidential. A strictly parliamentary or definitely presidential one would not be well adapted to European complexity. The keeping of double presidencies, a solution retained in the Constitutional Treaty, leads to parliamentarism, the president of the Commission acting as a Prime Minister. Nevertheless, it remains only half parliamentary, the essential role in defense and foreign policy being devolved upon the President of the European Council. The merging of the presidencies would leave the option open.

An evolution toward a parliamentary system could take place through the creation of a real post of Prime Minister, when the conditions of transfer of governmental power in all fields to a Cabinet responsible to Parliament are obtained. On the contrary, the election of the President of the European Council by universal suffrage would lead to a presidential system. A more original formula might perhaps better answer European specificities. It would be to propose to popular suffrage a reduced and collegial team on the model of the Swiss Federal Council. In this hypothesis the federal President designated by an agreement between the governments and the Parliament would keep his (or her) role of representation and arbitration, and the main powers would be endowed to the executive college.

These speculations about the various possible forms of a European government may seem irrelevant in the present day when the EU goes through an existential crisis. But we can also argue that we may seize the opportunity of the crisis to ponder over the medium and longer term institutions. Indeed, one of the causes of today's difficulties lies precisely in the lack of vision and the absence of debates on the future.

The emergence of a strong executive cannot be conceived without the strengthening of the role of the Parliament, which should be endowed with the initiative to introduce laws and the power to control the Executive, which would be conceived according to the more parliamentary or more presidential model which will finally prevail.

Recognizing the part played by national parliaments in the affairs of the EU is already, and will be even more tomorrow, an original feature of the European federal system. Beyond the control of subsidiarity, for which the national parliaments will be called to play an ever increasing role, it would be useful to give them the possibility to deliberate with the European Parliament on the general policy of the Union. In the same way, they could be associated to the process of amendment of the federal Constitution, thanks to a Convention composed of national and European MPs and representatives of the various Executive authorities. These revisions would not be submitted to the unanimity rule, but to a reinforced qualified majority, for example two thirds of the States and populations; minority states would be allowed to exert their right to opt out.

This right to abstain recognized in the constitutional treaty would be another specificity of a European Federal Union, different from a federal State. One of the European values is the settlement of conflicts by law and conciliation. The recourse to force against a member state is not conceivable within a European federation. On the other hand, economic sanctions must be allowed in case of breach of contract and, if necessary, political sanctions in case of severe or persisting default. Indeed, this possibility does exist today. The withdrawal from the EU is not a sanction but a safety valve; it should render it possible a relaxation of the amendment procedure: minority States would have a choice to opt out, and ask for a special dispensation or to transform their membership into an association.

Less radical than withdrawal, the granting of the possibility to opt out could conciliate the desire of a majority to move forward and the timidity of some members. In this way, a vanguard could be constituted, not by selection but by voluntary self-exclusion. The result would be the same, but the political impact would be quite different. Selection is unacceptable for those who are not chosen, but those who exclude themselves must consider it is their own decision and should be able to go back to the majority at any time. The failure of "enhanced cooperations" can be explained by the fact that this formula is felt as selective rather than dispensational. We must add that the term cooperation was poorly chosen to name ambitious actions. Rather than "hard core" it should have been "soft core". It would be much better to say consolidated integration. The opting out formula can lead to an improved integration, as can be seen with the monetary union. It can be observed that a temporary exclusion of a country which has the will, but not the capacity, to take part raises no difficulty, since it will be resolved at the proper time. Finally there is the question of the voting right at the Council and Parliament for countries which are temporarily excluded or opting out on the issues in question; it would seem logical, at least, to ask countries who opt out not to exercise their voting right.

To reflect upon federal forms adapted to European specificities is all the more useful as in several countries, among others France and the United Kingdom, federalism meets with a hostility which comes from a lack of understanding. For many Frenchmen and Englishmen federalism means centralization, for others, the Germans for example, it offers a guarantee against the encroachments of centralization. Therefore the battle for federalism is difficult. We must rely on a clear vision of what is possible in a Europe which remains more attached to national sovereignties than it was in the post-war years. The worst criticism from which federalists must defend themselves is that they advocate the death of sovereign States. By devising formulas which will allow the states not to alienate their sovereignty forever, thanks to the right to opt out, to preserve some freedom of choice in domestic policies, especially in social and fiscal matters, and to take part in the definition and running of the affairs of the Union, it may be possible to convince those of our adversaries who are sincere and in good faith.

Steps towards European and World Federalism*

John PINDER

We need 'an active and capable EU' to 'make an impact on a global scale' and thus 'contribute to an effective multilateral system leading to a fairer, safer and more united world.'[1]. Such was the conclusion of the strategy paper agreed by the EU Council in December 2003; and it corresponds to what surveys and other evidence show to be a prevalent aspiration among citizens of member states. Thus the question is not what the citizens and their governments want in this respect, but rather what the Union could do to bring it about; and the purpose of this article is to show how the federal idea, as manifested in the European experience since 1950, can make the only genuinely effective contribution to the process.

The first lesson from that experience is that the basic driving force for introducing substantial federal elements into the relationships among European states has been a deeply felt need to deal with the danger, in an unreformed interstate system, of the possible recurrence of intra-European war. That motive, along with the need to deal with common economic problems, has carried the Union far towards federal arrangements for the economy as well as to the establishment of permanent peace among the member states. But this application of the federal idea to its internal polity has not been accompanied by an equivalent process in its relationship with the rest of what is becoming an increasingly dangerous world. While the Union's strategy paper points in the right direction, it fails to convey a sense of how urgently action is required to confront the dangers facing Europeans today, including in particular from atomic, biological and chemical weapons in the hands of an increasing number of states and, potentially, of non-state terrorists; from various forms of pressure arising out of global poverty; and from catastrophic climate change. Nor does it indicate that the proper response is to introduce substantial federal elements into the Union's arrangements for external policy, as a major step towards a European federation.

But whereas the federal process has gone far in important aspects of the Union's internal affairs that are appropriate for it according to the criterion of subsidiarity, in the field of foreign policy, jealously guarded

* Published in Issue 1/2006.

1 *A secure Europe in a better world* (Brussels: Council of the European Union, December 2003), concluding paragraph.

by most of the member states, the process remains at an early stage. The Union's structure, however, and many of its internal policies provide a basis on which a federal foreign and security policy can be built; and there is one field of external policy that already, for the last four decades, offers an astonishingly successful example.

Trade, money, aid, environment, defence

The Community's common external tariff had been put in place by the mid-1960s and the US responded to a suggestion from Jean Monnet by proposing the Kennedy round of Gatt negotiations, in which the participating states agreed to cut tariffs by an average of one third. As the Brookings Institution's expert on the subject put it:

> 'The dominant position of the United States in Gatt evaporated with the implementation of the Rome Treaty [...] the Common Market is now the most important member of Gatt, and can determine in large measure the success or failure of any attempt to liberalise trade. When Europeans instruct Americans in the realities of the new international economic situation they are demonstrating the change in relative power that has taken place.'[2]

The consequence of this shift from hegemonic to bipolar leadership was not the trade wars and the mutual hostility that many opponents of a more powerful Union claim would follow from such a relationship with the US, but on the contrary a process of continued trade liberalisation with the EC/EU and the US as the principal actors, leading to the creation of the World Trade Organisation as the prime example of an effective rule of law in world affairs; and this stemmed from the Rome Treaty's provision not only of a federal instrument (the common tariff), but also a federal executive as negotiator (the Commission), with a federal procedure for accountability (qualified majority voting in the Council which, even if not often used, provides a deterrent to disruptive use of the veto).[3]

In almost all other fields, the American relationship with Europeans, as with others, remains hegemonic, with an inevitable drift towards policies with imperial characteristics, which make the world neither safer, nor fairer, nor more united. But Europeans have not yet, four decades later, shown much sign of having learnt from this remarkable example of how they could, in most fields of policy, replace the American hegemony by a genuine partnership that is equally beneficial to both.

---

2 Laurence B. Krause, *European Economic Integration and the United States* (Washington, DC: The Brookings Institution, 1968, pp. 224-5).

3 For the role of the Community institutions in the Kennedy round, see David Coombes, *Politics and Bureaucracy in the European Community* (London: George Alien & Unwin, 1970, pp. 166-216).

Thus although the euro has since 1999 become a counterweight to the dollar in international money markets, it remains far from that in the field of international monetary policy. Neither the eurozone nor the Union has the necessary federal elements in its institutions. The eurozone ministers and the Ecofin Council take their decisions without a procedure for majority voting; the European Central Bank is represented but there is no significant role for the Commission; and the eurozone does not dispose of a common vote in the IMF. But the eurozone could, with an effective common external monetary policy, preferably supported by Britain and other EU states, do much to promote a just and effective world monetary system, less vulnerable to the export of US domestic financial problems.

The EU provides over half the world's development assistance, four times that of the US. Most goes towards the attack on poverty. But a robust economy and good governance are more important for general welfare; and the Union has shown itself capable of providing, for example in the West Balkans, valuable assistance in a range of areas relating to public institutions, civil society and the economy. The EU aims to raise its contribution to 0.7 per cent of GDP; and the interests of both the recipients and the Union would be well served if a growing proportion is used to help enhance the contribution that the recipients can make to security and good governance as well as to their participation in an effective multilateral system.

The significant federal elements in the Union's internal environmental policy have provided a foundation for its leading role in global action on climate change. Despite the handicap of mixed Union and member state competences in that field, it was the Union that secured agreement in the Kyoto Protocol for a modest but significant start to the reduction of carbon emissions, which is a first step towards avoiding catastrophe in the second half of this century. It was moreover the Union which, against active American opposition, ensured the Protocol's ratification by enough states; and the external trade policy was a decisive instrument in this context too, as the essential Russian ratification was ensured by making it a condition of EU agreement to Russia's coveted entry into the WTO. The European Council has now adopted as its target the cutting of carbon emissions in half by the middle of this century; and if this is not to be a quixotic gesture, the Union will have to persuade enough other states to do the same.

Nearly half a century after the failure of the EDC Treaty, the Union returned to the field of defence, where it has recently taken significant steps: for example the creation of its military staff nucleus in the Council Secretariat; peace-keeping operations in Macedonia and the Congo; the creation of the Rapid Reaction Force and of a number of more quickly available smaller battle groups; and the establishment of the European Defence Agency. The Union can continue to build its capacity and to strengthen its institutions to the point where it can undertake almost any peace-keeping operation. But the US, to be joined perhaps by China, will continue to possess unrivalled military power.

The EU has, however, the potential to be the world's principal power in most fields of external policy save the military, where the US and probably China will continue to predominate; and the Union has so far failed to realise its potential, which is to become the predominant power in 'soft security', i.e. in all fields of external policy save the military, thus enabling it to make its full contribution to the building of an effective multilateral system. It is the process of progressively introducing more federal elements in the powers and institutions for the common foreign and security policy, encompassing its external policies as a whole, as has been done internally, which would enable the Union to achieve its aim in the world.

Completing the federal process in Europe and beginning it in the world

Surely enough of the Union's citizens and governments can be moved to support appropriate reform of the Union's instruments and institutions for external action, through understanding what it could do to enable Europeans to play their full part as prime movers of an effective multilateralism to avert the perils which confront the world; and through realising that this would not only ensure that the Union emerges from its present dangerous hiatus to engage citizens and governments in a great project, but can at the same time lead to the completion of its own federal process. Given previous experience since the Maastricht Treaty, it may well be that not all the twenty five member states would support such a development. But a core group, building on Joschka Fischer's suggestion, could agree to move ahead in the field of external relations, remaining open to the others to join them later. This would doubtless present many technical difficulties; but given the political importance of the project, they would not be insuperable. Nor should it be assumed that the British would automatically be incapable of taking part. The dissipation of prewar British enthusiasm for the federal idea which resulted from Britain's particular experience of the war was the primary cause of the lack of support for Monnet's pragmatic method of federal steps applied to the Union's internal affairs. But the British are as much concerned as other Europeans about the dangers facing the world; and British citizens, if not yet the government, may be increasingly ready to prefer a genuine

Euro-American partnership, with the Union strengthened through the application of federal principles, to American hegemony for dealing with them.

It is of course not only in the context of the European Union that the federal idea is relevant. The structure of an 'effective multilateral system' must, if it is to have real substance, contain a growing proportion of federal elements. That is the full implication of the strengthening of the United Nations which is an important aspect of the Union's external policy.

But while existing forms of cooperation can be further improved with states that are far from being liberal democracies, an increasingly federal relationship, with more promise for the future, can be developed among those that are ready and willing, as the European experience has demonstrated. An example of the concept is the proposal for a global climate community with appropriate institutions, for which the EU would take the initiative, and which, together with others from the North and the South of the world, most importantly India among the latter, could combine commitments for deep cuts in carbon emissions with mutual support for sustainable development.[4] As in Europe, the intention would be to deepen the relationship and enlarge the membership, and, in this case, to extend the process of federal development to the United Nations as a whole.

As Tommaso Padoa-Schioppa has observed, in his book on the subject, such a process will take a long time[5]. It is over half a century since the European. Community was founded and the EU is still not a federation. The world will almost certainly take longer. But the relations between member states changed for the better from the time when the European process began. War among them became unthinkable and they were able to accomplish major projects together. Federalists must do everything possible to ensure that Europeans apply their federal experience for the benefit both of themselves and of the rest of the world.

---

4 See Christopher Layton, *A Climate Community: A European initiative with the South,* European Essay No. 15 (London: Federal Trust, 2003, 1st ed. 2001).

5 Tommaso Padoa-Schioppa, *Dodici settembre: Il mondo non è al punto zero* (Milano: Rizzoli, 2002).

Multi-level Governance and Federalism*

Lucio LEVI

The globalization process is characterized by a tension between unification and fragmentation. The global and local do not exclude each other. On the contrary, they are two aspects of a single process. The move towards globalization and world unification coexists with decentralization and localization. Nor is the nation-state destined to disappear.

Ronald Robertson coined the word "glocalization" to describe this process, for while globalization brings with it the unification of markets, civil society, cultural models, life styles and political institutions, it also fosters a need to preserve existing differences, local cultures and institutions. In fact, the moves to equalize and level social patterns simultaneously generate a need to maintain and develop more traditional local cultures and identities.

The trend towards fragmentation, takes two different forms. The first is a type of ethnic nationalism which not only resists globalization, but also can often result in the disintegration of established nation-states, thus leading to the transformation of the world into a collection of closed communities divided by tribal hatred. The second, alternative, scenario foresees the redistribution of governmental powers to different levels ranging from sub-national to supra-national through a structure of local and regional self-government designed to be compatible with supranational powers and institutions.

Thus the erosion of state sovereignty stimulates the need for new forms of governance based on a division of competences between the national and the higher and lower levels of government. The architectural articulation of authority structures which has occurred in the globalization era has much in common with medieval political organization, as Hedley Bull pointed out in his book *The Anarchical Society* written in 1977 at the time when the word *globalization* was just beginning to come into use. His theory of a "new medievalism" underlines the analogy between the reorganization of the national and international political space, in progress during the last phase of the Cold War, and the overlapping of

* Published in Issue 3/2010.

different levels of government from the local to the universal community which was typical of medieval times.

Whereas the formation of the modern state was characterized by the assertion of the concept of sovereignty – i.e. the progressive centralization of power on the military, fiscal, administrative, legislative and judiciary plane – globalization on the other hand triggers a process which is developing in the opposite direction, namely that of the decentralization of political power and legal systems. A growing number of power centers are escaping state control and thereby undermining state sovereignty.

Observation of the effects of the globalization process shows the old sovereign states' diminishing authority, the wider spread of political power and the weakening of legal certainties. Clashes between ill-defined rights pave the way to abuse. Encroachment by the strongest powers and groups against the weakest, the assertion of new privileges, the limitation of individual liberties, the spread of violence: all these aspects of the globalization process represent a serious danger to the values and institutions on which our civilization rests.

The 'state' is an invaluable heritage and a building bloc of the civilization process. On it depends the supremacy of the common good over the private interests. The problem, therefore, is to rethink and reorganize the state, not to abolish it.

In contemporary political science literature, this reorganization of political power at different territorial levels has been called "multi-level governance." This expression echoes the federalist vision of political institutions and enables us to rethink and question the traditional model of the unitary state. It is worth recalling that Kenneth C. Wheare defines the federal government "that system of power sharing that allows the central government and the regional governments to be, each in its own sphere, coordinated and independent." It is appropriate to call this institutional arrangement "multi-level government."

It is simply a delusion to imagine that the destruction of the nation-state alone could prove to be the vehicle towards more elevated forms of solidarity. It is true that the nation-state has led to the deepest political divisions and the strongest concentrations of power that the world has ever experienced. However, the well-known examples of Yugoslavia and Somalia show how the collapse of the state has meant a return to primitive barbarism, to ferocious, selfish tribalism and a return to obsolete forms of solidarity based on ethnic or religious ties.

Faced with these phenomena, one can appreciate the positive aspects of national solidarity in overcoming local, regional and class self-interests and the great role that nation-states have played in our history. France, Spain, Italy and Germany have unified populations with a variety of cultural, ethnic, linguistic and religious backgrounds. To be sure, this unity was achieved by means of centralization, i.e. by sacrificing pluralism. It is what the federalists of the past century, from Proudhon to Frantz and Cattaneo, untiringly denounced even if the federalist political proposal, historically, had no chance of influencing states such as France, Germany and Italy. In fact, the strong political and military pressure that these states underwent on their borders and the radical nature assumed by the class struggle created a drive towards power centralization that no force could oppose. The fact is that democratic centralism has been a stage in the construction of democracy, of its extension to mixed populations with equal rights as citizens; and a means of overcoming old political and economic institutions in which the privileges of the feudal guilds were concealed.

Federalism's contribution to understanding, and therefore to identifying, the limitations of national experience lies in the denunciation of the exclusive character assumed by the ties of national solidarity, which do not tolerate any loyalty towards communities that are smaller or larger than the nation itself. However, national solidarity does not have to be abandoned in the globalization era. It should rather be considered as a necessary step towards wider forms of solidarity shared between nations within regional federations which will themselves be bound together in a worldwide federation. At the same time, national solidarity does not exclude other forms of solidarity within regional and local communities, but can coexist with them.

The federal model is therefore an institutional formula that allows for the coexistence of solidarity between territorial communities of varying sizes ranging where necessary from small local communities to – through UN reform – the entire world.

Evidence shows that the federalizing process is now increasingly widespread. It will eventually embrace entire continents and potentially the whole of the planet. At the same time, certain unitary states have also been influenced by federalism leading to some of them transferring of power towards smaller territorial communities. As a result of this process developing in two directions, one towards the top of the federal hierarchy and the other towards the bottom, it has become necessary to organize federations with more than two levels of government and so to supersede the traditional model that shared power only between federal government and the federated states.

To these two levels of government must now be added (with equal standing within the state) the regional, county or province (i.e. the intermediate community between the region and town), and local community levels, i.e. the borough of a large city or the town. Then, above the continental federation, there is the worldwide level. Of course, in each of these territorial areas, institutions already exist that are a clear expression of governmental and organizational requirements. These are not, however, usually autonomous centers of power but are subordinate to the nation-state. Their institutional reorganization according to the federal pattern allows every level of government to be given an independent power. This implies full freedom for each level of government to have relationships within the framework of its own authority with all the other corresponding or different levels without being subjected to control (except for those of a constitutional nature) of the higher levels of government. For example, Region-European Union relationships, or links between bordering regions, and so on.

The federal model should be seen not as destroying the national model but as superseding it. It is a change in two directions: towards the top and towards the bottom. In fact, the federalist design improves on the limitations of national democracy which is in decline owing to its excessive concentration of power in the hands of national governments. This improvement is achieved by adding new levels of government, popular participation and citizenship, both above and within the nations.

On the other hand, the decline of power politics and the ever closer interdependence between peoples have weakened not only the incentives towards centralization. It has also changed the traditional concept of border. This used to give states the unchangeable shape of a closed society with homogeneous characteristics. The new forms of federal organization link the coexistence of different levels of government with openness and the overlapping of the individual territorial communities.

As an example, the removal of military and economic divisions within the European Union has brought to light the artificial character of nation-states. It is now possible for border populations to develop new forms of association with their neighbors in the European regions such as in the Basque countries, Tyrol, Catalonia and Roussillon, Alsace and Baden, or the region where the French and English face each other across the Channel. Possibly there will be in the future an institutionalization of these regions that goes beyond mere cross-frontier cooperation. This would constitute a new aspect of contemporary federalism and point the way to overcome the obsolete formula of the nation-state.

Democratic Decisions vs. Diplomatic Decisions*

Ludo DIERICKX

The chasm dividing the citizen from the political world is today denounced as a major problem. Because of its increasing complexity and its more and more international and supranational peculiarity, politics is moving away from the citizen, who is, among laws and decrees, subject to European rules: treaties, directives, regulations, which have the fundamental and constitutional force of law as well.

The reason of the deepening of this chasm must be found in the citizen's loss of influence towards the legislator; he cannot either stimulate or sanction him. He is the victim of this increasing democratic deficit. This happens both at a European level and at the level of the Belgian federal state.

First Question

First difference: in a democratic system, citizens are the first subjects of right; in a diplomatic one, this is the role of the states.

A democratic system creates laws, decrees, constitutions, and laws which enforce diplomatic decisions. The diplomatic decision-making system produces texts having the force of law (or constitutional force): treaties, pacts, protocols and in our country, Belgium, co-operation agreements among the state, the communities and the regions. In the first case, legal texts are voted into effect after a public debate in a Parliamentary Assembly plenary session, and facing the media, public opinion and with the participation of the opposition parties. The citizens can follow the debate and intervene directly or indirectly. In the other case, legal texts are established in sittings in closed session, without the participation of the political parties representing the majority and obviously the opposition; media and public opinion are excluded as well. How is it possible to warn and inform citizens promptly? In a diplomatic system, the texts come from negotiations among governmental representatives who speak with "one voice" in the name of the states, member states, and regions.

* Published in Issue 2/2000.

The opposition is always excluded and not considered at all. In contrast, a democratic system allows and gives the right to every party to discuss and amend the texts, to control their application, to sanction their non-execution and to propose alternative law proposals. In a diplomatic system, a person elected from the people cannot make use of this possibility.

For treaties, protocols, European directives, and cooperation agreements, the choice in the best case is between taking or leaving them. The deputy who tries to modify texts by proposing an amendment is considered ridiculous. The diplomatic system leaves to the parliaments a "*fait accompli*". The legislative assemblies can of course refuse ratification, but with high risks. In this case, however, it is necessary to begin the negotiations again which are often very laborious.

The negotiators who conduct the negotiations, of course, are rarely sanctioned. The EU Council of Ministers, which deliberates on regulations and many directives, and the Belgian "Interministerial" Conferences, which elaborate the co-operation agreements among the communities and the regions, cannot be reversed by anybody, not by the European Parliament, nor by the Belgian one, nor by the Councils of the Communities or the Regions. The democratic deficit is even weightier than in a situation of the exercise of Executive powers. Indeed, a government which wields such powers can, in turn, be overturn by a majority of the Chamber.

The diplomatic system certainly has its advantages, especially for the decision-makers. It is often easier to come to an agreement between partners on the basis of give and take, far from prying eyes, and to agree on a package deal than to spread out the problems in a public session of the Parliament. Apart from the institutional aspect, in a diplomatic system (confederation or union of states) there is another problem concerning political parties which do not intervene because they do not exist. It is useless to talk about a Belgian and European citizenship worth the name without political parties at a European and Belgian level. One cannot be a complete citizen if he or she cannot participate in political life by expressing at least one vote against some parties. Without political parties acting at an adequate level, there is no space for political programmes sustainable by the citizens, nor any awareness, nor educational participation.

The democratic deficit resulting from a diplomatic decision (which is however difficult to avoid) can degenerate into a minority dictatorship if the states, the member states, the regions or communities make use of the right of veto they have, thanks to treaties, constitutions, or de facto. This is the case of decisions requiring unanimity or consensus, as it frequently happens in the EU and the Belgian Federal state. The people who hold the political responsibility could be tempted to renounce the diplomatic system (confederal) and to prefer self-determination and pure national sovereignty, which nowadays is becoming however a utopian desire. Furthermore, apart from this relationship between states and nations, there is another conflictual point not considered here.

Second Question

The second question must be addressed to those conditions which allow the transition of pure self-determination towards diplomatic relationships, democratic relationships or vice-versa. Which are the necessary acting centripetal, unifying or centrifugal, regionalist or nationalist forces? Which is the way to turn on their motor? Essential condition: political forces showing firmness, resistance or at least patience. There are several reasons which provide for union or separation. They have been interchangeable in the course of history. Religious, dynastic, linguistic, cultural, economic, social, geopolitical (natural frontiers), ideological (political intentions and visions), and historical (common life memories, cruelties, humiliations) questions are capable of bringing differences or convergences in mentality, cultural identity, habits, life standards… in South Africa, Switzerland, the European Union, differences are not obstacles; in the Balkans, Corsica, ex-Czechoslovakia, Pays Basque, North Italy, Belgium, differences are exploited to force separation and to replace democratic relationships among men with diplomatic relationships among states.

History teaches that democracy, and above all federal democracy, if supported by the will of politicians, is the instrument capable of assembling every difference among human beings. Democracy teaches us that differences can be exploited to divide, create new centres of power, sow the seeds of discord and cause hostilities which could come to the worst extremes.

If human beings agreed on the way of discovering values and truth, they could live together in states of right. Democracy has been invented because people are different: if they were identical, if they wanted the same things, we would not need democratic systems, decisional systems or whatever. Belgium and Europe can be considered as grounds for reflection and experimentation. They have a global responsibility and they cannot allow the triumph of centrifugal and nationalist forces to menace democracy and solidarity.

States Vote, People Do Not*

Tommaso Padoa-Schioppa

When the United States Senate failed to ratify the Comprehensive Test Ban Treaty (CTBT), various ills that have poisoned this century suddenly returned to the blindness of democracy, the fragility of peace, the threat of nuclear destruction. For the most part, these ills stem from the absence of limitations to the sovereignty for states.

The CTBT is intended to ban all nuclear testing (including subterranean) required to develop nuclear arsenals. Such a ban would not ensure peace. But it would diminish the risk that humans will one day destroy themselves in war, since it would impede or prevent the uncontrolled proliferation of nuclear arms among the planet almost 200 nations. It was precisely because many countries with nuclear capabilities – including India, Pakistan and North Korea – did not sign the Treaty that its ratification by the stronger military powers was fundamental. And it is precisely because two of these powers – China and Russia – remained undecided, that the U.S. ratification of the Treaty was indispensable.

Following the "no" vote of the leading superpower – which did the most to work out the Treaty in the first place – the Treaty's implementation has become problematic and unlikely. Many Americans are angry that nuclear peace has been placed in serious jeopardy by their country – the same country that, through its military might and political freedoms, has saved the contemporary world from catastrophe.

The twentieth century might have been more peaceful had the U.S. Senate not twice failed to ratify the Treaty for Versailles – 1919 and 1920 – and, therefore, the entry of the U.S. into the League of Nations. Similarly, the political union for Europe might have come about earlier had the French Parliament supported, in 1954, the establishment of a European defense community. By the same token, world economic relations might have developed more rapidly and in a more organized fashion had, in 1947, the United States ratified the Havana Treaty, which was to establish international authorities in this field. We would have neither the euro nor monetary union had the Danish repeated their "no" vote when called to a second referendum.

* Published in Issue 1/2000.

International treaties on issues vital for the wellbeing, and even survival, of the human race stem from the exercising of the legal-political rights of the sovereign people, either directly or through the assemblies elected by them. This is true of treaties carefully drawn up and negotiated in full view of the public by legitimate, democratically elected governments, but not of secret treaties, such as those of Czarist Russia, which were brought to light only after Lenin came to power.

Is there too much democracy? On the contrary, in the case of the CTBT, there was a lack of democracy. In the first place, while only 48 out of 100 senators voted for the Treaty, it was supported by 80 percent of Americans. In the second place, and more importantly, the case of the CTBT shows the broadening gap between the domain of democracy (the states) and the domain of the general interest (that is, the world).

There are real technical and political issues that concern the whole world – issues therefore, in which any attempt to address the interests of all can only be meaningful if the "all" is interpreted as the entire human race. Greenhouse gasses, the pollution of our oceans, and, of course, the threat of nuclear war are all examples. There are issues relating to security and human rights in which our political and civil conscience regards all human beings as fellows and denies the absoluteness of the sovereignty of states, even if these states act in a weak or contradictory fashion. In some case the "generality" of interests is not global but still goes far beyond state borders. In pursuing general interests that go beyond state borders, however, neither organized representation nor democracy exist.

When nation-states first came into being, their subjects or citizens saw their boundaries as veritably endless as regards culture and the material conditions of life. For some time, achieving political freedoms and civil rights, and eventually introducing universal suffrage, within these boundaries meant granting liberty, rights, the vote, and security to people as such. The American and French Bills of Rights speak of people, and not of Americans or French. But today the survival of the human race has no form of organized representation. There are no forums in which the rights of humans are represented as such. International cooperation does not expressly require democracy; even in Europe, the process is incomplete. In the slow and fickle formation of international authorities and rules that extend as far as the phenomena they are intended to regulate, it will become increasingly important to introduce means for representing both people and governments. The institutions and organization of a world democracy are yet to be invented. When they are introduced they will most likely be different from those experimented with to date – as different, in fact, as the processes used by a handful of residents in some Swiss valley and the millions of citizens that make up the United States.

But these processes must be envisaged and implemented. Partly because of regressive steps such as the U.S. Senate's recent decision, it will become increasingly obvious that democracies within individual states do not satisfy the need for an international democracy. The expression of general will is not a monopoly of the states; it belongs to all people. It will become increasingly clear that without legitimization through democratic processes, international authorities and rules will either not be established or will not be accepted.

Proposals for Europe: a Political and Moral Essay*

Robert LAFONT

The theses which follow will appear utopian as, indeed they are. But utopia becomes a necessity when change is a matter of urgency.

This is because:

- the dangers which threaten men and citizens at the start of a new millennium can't allow the political conscience to remain half-asleep any longer;
- societies' problems must be faced and tackled at a world-wide level due to the globalization of the economy and the worldwide spread of cultural information;
- a new historical subject is now emerging: Europe as a regional ensemble, and this in spite of the obstacles which a raised by the Nation-States, which themselves control the project.

Europe must become our hope now, and this hope must be realized in the future.

It will certainly be remarked, and it may or may not shock some readers, that form the radical viewpoint the nation-state has already been eliminated from our perspectives. But for the clarity of our thesis this was necessary. A true vision of the new Europe cannot be reached if a general and stubborn blindness to fast changing realities persists: among these realities, at the turn of the century, are, the erosion of decision-making powers, the condemnation for historical crimes and the loss of political pertinence of the State – this State which emerged between the 13th and 16th centuries and hardened by and authoritative rule and centralization between the 17th and 20th century and reached its own frontiers through inexpiable wars.

As far as the Nation is concerned we will take it at the time when it as created in France after the American model between 1789 and 1793 before it degenerated into imperialism and centralization. Today, Europe can, in its turn, become such a Nation – and it seems there is no other model.

* Published in Issue 1/2001.

It is a negotiation of history – and all history is made by negotiations – which will tell how the State can become a mediator towards this indispensable mutation, and how the guarantees it offers, in spite of its functional tyranny, to man and the citizen, can be safeguarded under the seal of a new historical subject.

According to what has become more and more obvious in recent years "re-founding the Republic" cannot be seriously envisaged. In Europe the days of the Republic are over. Only a European Constitution can help us to get out of four kinds of dead ends or deadlocks that appeared at the end of the century and which are the final phases of previous evolutions which have suddenly accelerated.

The dead end of State-nationalism

At the same time that the globalization of the economy and stock-exchanges put an end to "national markets" which had promoted and supported the building of nation-states in the period of history which goes from the 16th century to the 1960s, these Nation-States lived on in their shape, structure and nominal sovereignty.

In the Balkans we have seen a return of nationalism in the forms of cruelty and savagery we thought had disappeared once and for all with nazism. The remedies that the international community found to this series of savage conflicts, after two local wars (Bosnia and Kosovo) are merely local partitions which are nothing but a return to the sources of the trouble i.e. State-nationalism – and serve a protection to war criminals and show everything their impotence to alleviate ethnic tensions.

The American military air intervention in Serbia was carried out practically out the limits of legality sanctioned by the U.N. This operation, after the war against Iraq, has proved that this organization of Nations to safeguard peace was but a Club of States where force prevails – in both cases the force of a self-proclaimed "world policeman". It has renewed the scandal of the great bombing raids of the Second World War: the punishing of civil populations for the crimes committed by their oppressors.

However two principles have emerged which will stand as hand marks in the history of humanity:

- first: the right and duty to intervene in the defense of oppressed communities on condition that the strategies of great powers do not choose arbitrarily between groups (why Albanians and not Kurds?) and that a clear distinction be made between peoples and their oppressors;
- second: a supra-national responsibility in peace-keeping and protection of freedoms. If in this respect Europe has been conspicuous

by absent or has lagged behind, the idea of a European military force of intervention has, at least, taken shape.

But can these two principles be acted upon this other Club of States which is Europe in its present form?

The dead end of Territory

National markets were organized in the capitalist phase of the 19th century as the regency of a central power over territory; within its borders, coupling this, at time, with a free-trade policy as conditions required, which seem somewhat hypocritical!

In the case of a hyper-centralized State, of which France has been the model, the capitalist power as applied to its territory a strategy of regular exploitation of its peripheries which looked rather like than of "internal colonialism" and was very strong between 1860 and approximately 1970.

Stop-gap measures generally known as "*aménagement du territoire*" (i.e. town and country planning) taken in a final period (1950-1970) very closely followed the process of territorial imbalance. At the same time the weight of the Common Market worsened the imbalance at the periphery, making this "internal colonialism" more visible (cf. coal crisis and pit closures) by the end of the period.

In their turn the advances in the constitution of this Common Market which have led to the marginalizing of the strong areas of the national territory and the increasing globalization of the economy, have, since about 1980, created a new economic situation. The French center – the Paris area – is far from the center of Europe and cannot protect itself any longer except by means of a massive national investment in the "inescapable Capital" and a perverse use of regionalization towards a further growth of the Ile de France region. "*L'aménagement du territoire*" is, in practice, forgotten.

On the contrary the French regions, like all those of Europe and in spite of the handicap of a biased process of regionalization have begun to "feel the space", that is to say to discover the natural relations of their geographic situation which the artifice of a territory drawn by ancient wars and power diplomacy had blurred for centuries.

At the same time European contracts, credits and subsidies at the outset controlled by the States tend today to be freed from the supervision (cf. the Interreg Programs). The Europe of areas and regions is in the process of being created as the limits and constraints imposed by States are weakening or fading out.

It is the very concept of "territory", a political boundary-marking imposed on socio-economic conditions which has become outmoded and practically useless. It covers a reality which already belongs to things past.

The dead ends of globalization

Runaway globalization accelerated during the last five or six years of the 20th century, this was largely a consequence of the collapse of state-socialism (here communism). It seems to be reaching a climax without serious obstacles in its path. But its triumph seems to beget its own deadlocks.

We see three of them:

- By suppressing or erasing national borders it allows the competition of large interstate regions which take shape on a global scale and whose chances suddenly look unequal. This unequal development that pertains to the very nature of capitalism, accelerated by the stock-exchange driven economies encompasses the whole planet. It renews and carries to its highest level of colonialism of the ancient colonialist powers, but also on a smaller regional scale, for example in Europe it revives the internal colonialism of centralized States. Since globalization obeys no strict rules or laws it cannot but produce inter-regional social conflicts of which the current structuring of Europe between South and North, West and East seems to announce.
- As the whole world is covered by the global market it makes traditional means of production obsolete and it disrupts ways of life and social-cultural habits which must fall into the melting-pot of a unified consumer society. This has already produced a kind of backlash. The fundamental cultural claims which emerged thirty years ago in Occitania (South of France) on the Larzac plateau have now manifested themselves in the demonstrations of Seattle and Davos in all their humanist impetus and picturesque riotousness. Thus all that was local is being molded into the planetary. The conflict cannot but deepen.
- Finally the collusion between the political classes, the illegal fringe and the criminal classes which was commonplace but relatively unusual in the old days has just taken unheard of dimensions. It has developed, with the most dangerous traffics (such as drugs and arms deals) at the very heart of the Wall Street stock exchange power. It has seized the substantial influence over some national governments. In Russia, for example, it has resulted in a paradoxical situation where a reinforced state-nationalism serves in its shape a Mafia-state as a screen or shield for international criminals. The danger has become huge.

The nuclear dead end

During the last half-century, atomic energy has supplied the club of powers who had the means with an arsenal of destruction capable of condemning the planet to death several time over. The equilibrium of terror has undoubtedly prevented a world-wide conflict. But this has now resulted in a deadlock from which we find no exit. It is obvious that this deadly arsenal must be destroyed (which is much more difficult than building it) but due to the weight and persistence of state sovereignties there is no world authority capable to take this decision. A stark paradox: planetary development has escaped from the hands of the States but the destruction of the planet remains in their hands and at the mercy of their petty quarrels and rivalries.

Civil nuclear power poses a danger as well. *Chernobyl* has proved and continues to prove that the gain in productivity brought about by atomic energy is paid back through a threat to the planet. A contest has now been undertaken between the maintenance of atomic power plants and the fight against the dangers they involve (which cannot be reduced to zero). Germany has first made the first move, although insufficient so far, in order to deal with this dilemma.

France is coming to a turning point: its "all nuclear strategy", once a subject of great national pride, despite the destruction without pity of regional resources such as coal, cannot be reversed without a negotiation with its electricity consumers and European clients. Either France keeps its nuclear electricity supply and poses unacceptable threats to Europe or it joins a European plan to replace atomic energy with a mix of new energies and the use of other former non-renewable fuels.

In order to escape from these dead ends the proposal of European democracy, according to me, should have three dimensions.

The European government

There is no mystery about that Europe needs a unified government fully responsible to an Assembly elected by universal suffrage on a non-national list system, with regional modulations necessary to equalize chances, if needed.

Her chief innovation would be the affirmation of a political subject of a new kind: the moral political subject. But if we look at things properly this is what the Nation meant in 1789. In order to reach this goal the laying out of democratic European institutions ought to be accompanied by four solemn declarations.

Declaration to renounce nuclear power and such industries destructive of the biosphere, within the framework of a European comprehensive plan of conversion spread over twenty years (Europe of ecology).

Declaration of acknowledgement of a right to self-organization by national communities, regional or immigrated, in particular linguistic and cultural terms (Europe of Cultural Rights).

Declaration about power, which in a democracy cannot be but ascendant, which means that a decisional pyramid is established from the civic-base unit (municipality or country) up to the European top, passing through the level of regional government (Federal Europe).

Declaration of acknowledgement of social solidarity, that is to say to replace the particular and ineffective fights against unemployment with a periodic revaluation of employment distribution and financial supports (Social Europe).

Such an organization propped up by such important pledges does not solve the world's problems but it defines a privileged area for civic experimentation and establishes at a planetary scale a pole of training and impulse for "universal peace making".

European Territorial Organization

The anarchy which the centralized State maintains in the development of regions and the recent intervention of globalization must be replaced by a rational organization, which poses three questions.

The question of the "civic area" of Europe.

Currently the enlargement of Europe is defined on the basis of the application of Nation-States without any consideration of geographic, historical or cultural coherence. Originating in a local and conjunctural agreement at the world scale, between a group of occidental States the European area runs the risk of becoming a territorial monster brutally and carelessly traversed by insuperable contradictions. A debate must be established between the fifteen member States in order to decide a transition period during which a sound procedure for enlargement will be defined according to a strategy of internal complementarities and external links and connections.

The question of the basic organic unit.

It will be necessary to balance globalization and the territorial weight inherited from States with a manageable from of local democracy which will lead everywhere to the promotion of the relational geographic unit either traditional or post-modern which is known as *pays* in France, *kreis* in Germany, *comarca* in Spain, etc. But we must give this system a well-defined ecological function to protect and organize the local environment, together with a social function of resource equilibrium and work-distribution. It should be given a civic statute, *i.e.* an Assembly with concrete powers elected by universal ballot.

The question of strategic space organization.

It must be clearly stated that it cannot be the State which has deliberately shown that it preserved territorial dysfunctions, the tyranny of center and isolationism. The basic founding unit must be the "European Region" as much as possible with a well-defined historical and cultural identity and with equal powers within the whole concerned area. The region being open by contract to inter-regional relations on the European scale but also to the outside world (for example on the Mediterranean). The setting up of institutions and the joint development of the Senate and a European Economic and Social Committee operating in close cooperation with the European Assembly. Regional autonomy must be guaranteed at its own level by a Parliament elected by universal suffrage based on the countries.

The creation of a European Area to regulate globalization

It has two basic aspects.

The economic aspect.

We need to create at the European level what the States by betraying their proclaimed sovereignty, have not been able to create and which does not exist in the Europe we have built so far: a tool for the control of global mobility of capital. This does not constitute an archaic form of protectionism. It actually consists in letting produced resources flow upward and investment flow downward through a European Development Bank controlled by Civic Power at its three levels and which would implement the fundamental choices made by these assemblies. This is the present dynamic form which suits the functioning of a liberal economy of "regional ownership", which was formulated in the old days to correct "internal colonialism". This might be the beginning of a "third way" between dead socialism and a capitalism which has reached its dead end.

The cultural aspect.

It is first of all linguistic. There is no example in the linguistic history of mankind when the market of goods has not been accompanied by a market of language. Globalization sustained by Internet, has resulted in a surprisingly fast world-wide spreading of English. One can regret this new form of imperialism but it is vain to think opposing it. The game has already been lost. From this point of view the refusal of the French which has a tint of imperial nostalgia is only a series of ineffective and sometimes ludicrous diversions. In this field Europe has a positive choice to make whose economical aspect cannot escape anyone. But this choice of a practical tool for universal communication leaves intact the statement of a right, also universal, recently strongly put forward: the right of any language and any culture to its free development and the right of those who are in danger to the object of rescue operations. This way another dimension of globalization has been defined which we shall call cultural plurality. Of this plurality where French, in the same was as German, Dutch, Italian, Spanish but also Breton, Occitan, Gaelic, Welsh, Catalan, Frisian etc. have a chance to keep a place in the modern world, a European Bureau of Cultural rights should be responsible.

All these options not only would tune Europe up to the evolution of the world in its most positive aspects, but would constitute an example for others, or as the Nations, at a stage of power and self-celebration like to say of themselves in bygone days, Europe would become a "lighthouse" for the world.

Towards a Federal United Kingdom*

Ernest WISTRICH

The election of a Labour government in 1997 signalled the start of major constitutional reform. Until then the United Kingdom had operated one of Europe's most centralised systems of government. The constitutional changes proposed in the Labour party manifesto ranged from the incorporation into domestic law of the European Convention of Human Rights to the adoption of referendums to approve the various constitutional changes. It included the abolition of the hereditary element in the composition of the unelected second parliamentary chamber, the House of Lords, and the introduction of proportional representation in place of the traditional 'first past of the post' system of voting in European elections and in the newly created devolved levels of government.

The purpose of this article is to concentrate on the measures which aim to devolve power from the centre and put the United Kingdom on the road towards a federal structure of government.

Although not a unitary state, like France for instance, the U.K. had operated a unitary system of government over a union composed of several nations who became part of it on different terms and at different times. Furthermore, the union is highly asymmetrical with 48 million living in England, 5 million in Scotland, 3 million in Wales and 1.5 million in the northern part of Ireland. Past pressure for devolution from the centre has varied: strongest in Scotland and Northern Ireland, less so in Wales and minimally in the English regions.

In its first year of office the Labour government took five separate initiatives towards devolution, each with a different dynamic but all aimed at transforming the U.K. into a multi-national and multi-regional state. These have dealt with devolution to Scotland, Wales, Northern Ireland, the English regions and London government. To take account of the varying circumstances there has been no uniformity in the system of devolution applied in each part of the country.

* Published in Issue 1/2001.

Scotland

Scotland united with England voluntarily some 400 years ago under a single monarch, James the First. Whilst government was centralised in London, the Scottish judicial and educational systems remained distinct from those operated in the rest of the union. By a substantial majority, in a referendum held in 1997, proposals for a Scottish parliament and government were approved. Considerable powers had been devolved and the parliament can now legislate extensively. Powers reserved to the U.K. government include constitutional changes, foreign policy, defence and security, immigration and nationality, macro-economic policies and social security. Furthermore, Scotland's tax raising powers are limited to a small variation in the level of income tax. The Scottish parliament is elected from regional lists and is based on proportionality. Thus the first Scottish government had to be formed by an alliance between Labour and Liberal Democrats, as no single party gained an overall majority.

Wales

Wales was conquered by the English and incorporated into the Union in the middle ages. They had no history as a separate integrated political unit and, therefore, demand for devolution has been much weaker than in Scotland. Indeed proposals for a Welsh assembly were defeated in a referendum in 1979 by a 4 to 1 majority. The referendum held in 1997 approved the proposed devolution by the slimmest majority of 50.6% on a turnout of just over half of the electorate. The Government of Wales Act of 1998 created a national assembly with 40 constituency members elected by 'first past the post' and 20 additional members by proportional representation. It has limited executive powers confined to secondary legislation, with powers to enact primary legislation remaining with the UK government and parliament. The first elections resulted in a minority Labour administration which is trying to establish its *raison d'être* amongst an often indifferent Welsh population.

Northern Ireland

The turbulent Irish history has had quite distinct motivations for the devolution of power in that part of the U.K. Ireland was first conquered by the Normans in the 12th century. The Scots invaded it in the 14th century. The English conquered it in the 16th century at the time of the reformation and establishment of the protestant church in England. After the catholic Stuart monarchy was briefly re-established, during the reign of James the Second war broke out in Ireland between James's forces and those of his successor the protestant William of Orange. The latter defeated James in Northern Ireland and occupied the rest of the island. The 19th century was dominated by parliamentary debates on devolution of power under a system of home rule for Ireland. The failure of the British to grant it led to a nationalist struggle for complete separation. Independence was finally granted in 1922 but this excluded six northern counties with protestant majorities who threatened civil war if they were separated from the U.K.

Thus Northern Ireland emerged with its own government and assembly in which the protestants enjoyed permanent dominance over a catholic minority whose rights were unprotected and who were severely discriminated against and disadvantaged. Frequent violent conflicts exploded leading to suspensions of the devolved institutions and their powers. The last suspension occurred nearly 30 years ago. It ended with the power-sharing British-Irish "Good Friday" agreement in 1998. This brought about fundamental changes to accommodate both communities. The Northern Ireland assembly is elected in six-member constituencies by the fully proportional single transferable voting system. All sections of the community are represented in the assembly, on its committees and on the executive. The governing executive must contain representatives of the minority community and key decisions are taken on a cross-community basis by qualified majority voting. Its powers are similar to those devolved to the Scottish parliament, but exclude the right to raise or vary taxation.

English Regions

In its 1997 election manifesto the Labour party proposed to establish indirectly elected regional chambers consisting of local authority representatives. Subject to demand and by regional referendums, these could move to directly elected regional assemblies. Alongside these proposals a Regional Policy Commission was to be established which would create regional development agencies that would be directly accountable to the regional chambers. As demand for devolved and elected regional government varies widely across England, imposing a uniform system at the same time for all was judged to be wrong. The legislation introduced has concentrated on the regional development agencies, leaving the directly elected regional assemblies until later, when demand for them manifests itself. The agencies have limited budgets and limited powers, but it is likely that the greater authority and democratic legitimacy given to Scotland, Wales and London government will lead to growing demand for devolved and elected government in the English regions, especially in the North of England.

London government

The Conservative government of Mrs. Thatcher abolished the Greater London Council in 1986, depriving the capital of 8 million inhabitants of an elected government for London as a whole. Coordination of policies for London was transferred to joint committees of the lower tier of 32 London Borough Councils and to the central government. Following a referendum a new Greater London Authority has been established under the leadership of a directly elected mayor and an elected regional assembly. The mayor exercises all the executive powers of the new authority but is accountable to the 25 members of the assembly of whom 14 have been elected by area and the rest as additional members to ensure proportionality. The mayor's powers include the appointment of a London Development Agency, on the lines of the English regional development agencies, running a new transport authority and controlling the Metropolitan police force. In other spheres the mayor's powers are limited, but his influence is considerable as the spokesman for the whole of London. The authority does not however have any tax raising powers.

Other reforms under consideration have implications for devolution. For instance the House of Lords, which has had its hereditary element abolished, is due for further reform. Recommendations have been made for part of its membership to be directly elected from the U.K.'s regions. Local government is also subject to reform which could lead to greater autonomy and less dependence on central government resources and control than in the past 25 years.

Conclusion

The lack of uniformity in the reforms for devolution are due to historical differences. The system that is emerging is a quasi-federalist one, within which powers of the devolved levels of government are likely to increase over time. The newly empowered parts of the U.K. will surely call for greater autonomy and increased powers, once conflicts develop between central government and the devolved authorities. Demand for regional government in England is also likely to grow as their citizens look enviously at the growing autonomy and self-government in Scotland, Wales and London. The process of reform will, however, take many years, as it has in France and Spain, but its movement towards a more federal system of government is unlikely to be reversed.

Meade's Social Dividend

From Debt to Public Patrimony*

Alfonso Iozzo

The cycle of the industrial revolution is finished and the era of scientific and technological revolution and of a sustainable economy has started. This is a trend that spreads from the center of the world economic system to the areas of more recent industrialization. The Gross Domestic Product (GDP) has been the measure of economic development in the period of industrialization: profit is in fact determined as the difference between earnings and the cost of goods and services used to produce them. The measurement takes into consideration, through amortization, also the use of capital, but it concerns essentially the goods in the possession of the enterprise, and not all the public goods utilized (as the air, for example).

A sustainable economy, instead, requires that also the value of non-renewable resources utilized for production should be considered among the costs. In the Middle Ages, the inventor of the accounting system, Father Luca Pacioli, was calculating profit as the difference between the initial and the final patrimony, while only in the last century did the idea of profit as the difference of earnings and costs spread[1]. The return to the medieval patrimonial method is the real alternative for new definitions of GDP about which people now openly discuss in both academic and political quarters, trying to measure happiness through elements like education, health, longevity and so on[2]. The essence of the patrimonial method lies in the fact that it allows to realize inter-generational solidarity, because it measures the patrimony, and thus one can see whether to new generations a greater or lesser capital is left than the one we received by previous generations. That is an historic change that did not get encoded

* Published in Issue 3/2011.

1 Fra Luca Bartolomeo de Pacioli, *Summa de aritmetica, proporzioni e proporzionalità*, Venice, 1494. In the Chapter *Tractatus de comptibus et scripturis* he presented for the first time the "double entry" accounting system, known later in Europe as the "Venetian method".

2 The search for new definitions of GDP is a widely discussed problem in economics. Recently the French President Sarkozy charged two Nobel Prize laureates, Stiglitz and Sen, to formulate alternative proposals.

yet, except in rare cases, in behaviors and laws. In particular, it is a matter of constitutional impact, because it does not concern the policies to be implemented, but the general norms that must continue to exist even after a change of contingent political majorities.

The most significant change occurred in this field is the Maastricht Treaty, which imposes not to burden future generations with debts contracted by the present generation for getting some goods without paying taxes and duties for them. The problem is more general: given that the quantity of natural goods available to the new generations (water, air, energy, etc.) is continuously reduced, it is necessary to compensate for that by leaving to young people credits and not debts (both public and private).

The Property

In the last century the presence of "pension funds" has appeared alongside the traditional private, public and cooperative property; this phenomenon has been particularly significant in the United States and in Great Britain, and has been expanding in the last years in Europe too. The capital-increasing pension funds are based on the principle that the citizen must save in the first part of his life, when he can carry out a working activity, in order to assure to himself an income in the old age; the scope of the fund is to administer the annual installments in a profitable way so as to get the necessary resources to pay a pension. They are long-term investments, often more than 30 years long, for which monetary stability is essential (otherwise inflation can cut down the accumulated capital).

The capital endowment

The new generations found themselves, at the beginning of the third millennium, in a difficult situation:

- the social capital has been reduced very much due to the indiscriminate use of natural, non-renewable resources carried out by the industrial revolution;
- the States ran into public debts that shall be paid back by future generations;
- in some cases, in particular in the United States, families ran into heavy debts.

The demographic situation of Western countries, in addition, makes the youngsters' situation worse, because, due to the progressive aging of the population, they cannot count on the new generations to pay for their entire pension, even if immigration may alleviate the impact, but cannot change the basic trend. It is necessary, therefore, to greatly change the structure of the welfare system that requires contributions from the young to support the elderly: it is not possible to load the new generations with payments to pay the pensions to the elderly (according to the principle governing social security in the "contributive" system) and simultaneously pay the installments of their capital-increasing pension funds. It is the new generations, instead, that are in need, in the new economic cycle, of the solidarity that in the industrial revolution phase had to be assured, rightly, to the workers who were doing wearing-down jobs and had to be protected in the second part of their life, when they will no longer be able to work. The necessity to turn that trend around is obvious, but it is difficult for political leaders who want to be re-elected to propose and implement the required policies.

A partial exception occurred in Europe, where the new Community institutions were capable, in the last thirty years, to propose policies of inter-generational solidarity, like in the case of the Maastricht Treaty or of the EU environmental and consumer-protection policies: the member States willingly accepted the European constraints, but later they laid the blame and the responsibility of the costs on Brussels, with populist and nationalistic arguments, the outcome of which has been the spreading of euro-skepticism. The deleterious action of the member States made weaker the European instrument, which instead had allowed them to undertake virtuous policies. The dialectics inherent in the federal mechanism, similarly to what occurred with the separation of powers advocated by Montesquieu, is one of the few available means for introducing in the institutional system a balancing of weights and counterweights allowing to generate decisions aimed to the "common good" and not to short-term or sectorial interests.

The social capital

Meade's[3] proposals of a participative economy would allow to outline a path leading towards the endowment of social capital to the new generations. The essence of Meade's proposals is the creation, alongside and partially replacing the pension funds, of a "social fund" capable for distributing a social dividend to all the citizens, independently of the installments paid, differently from the pension funds, and hence of providing a support to the young in particular. Meade contemplates also social services in favor of all the citizens in education and health-care, subsidies for the poor, and measures aimed to encourage a more equitable distribution of property. The social dividend should allow to:

---

3 James E. Meade, *Liberty, Equality, and Efficiency*, (NYU Press, March 1993). Meade's other proposals, in particular the "partnership society", are forerunners of an economic system based on knowledge and scientific development.

- reduce inequalities;
- provide an incentive for risk-taking;
- alleviate the impact of low salaries;
- simplify the social security system.

To make the distribution of such a dividend possible, it is necessary to socialize the beneficiary title-ownership (without the right to administer) of a significant share of the economic assets of a country: Meade suggests as an objective 50% of total assets.

The Norwegian case

A partial realization of Meade's proposal has actually taken place in Norway. Since the wealth of oil and gas which Norway found itself to be in possession of will be consumed with its extraction and will eventually dry up, a pension fund has been instituted where the proceeds are deposited. Only 4% of the returns of that fund can be used annually by the Government to support public expenditure, thus leaving a capital available to the citizens in the future too, when the patrimony of oil and gas will be exhausted[4]. The norms of the pension fund, however, have not been given yet a constitutional force, therefore it cannot be ruled out that in the future some not-so-clever government could be tempted to dissipate the accumulated capital in quest of electoral approval. Also other "sovereign funds" seem inclined today to follow Meade's suggestions, in particular those instituted by the State of Singapore.

The Transition

The real problem that all political projects have to face is the transition from the existing situation to the final goal. How to make the turnabout from public "debt" to public "credit" actually happen?

The international financial crisis gives us an opportunity, if we have the will and the capacity to initiate that transition: the States, in order to combat the confidence crisis, had to take the place of private investors and finance and buy in particular banks and insurances, and in some cases also industries (the automotive one in the United States). The governments' official position is that those interventions are temporary and those activities are to be resold on the market as soon as possible. It will not be easy, however, to sell such big businesses at their real value in a market

4 One can estimate that each Norwegian is presently the virtual owner through the Fund of about 100,000 euros, in contrast with a share of public debt burdening each Italian amounting to 25,000 euros.

that will still be in difficulties, and with the pension funds that have seen a great part of their assets melt away with the stock-exchange devaluations caused by the financial crisis, and with the workers' reduced financial capacity (due to unemployment, devaluation of real estate values, salary reductions) to underwrite new social-security installments.

Using the remuneration of the investments made by the States to institute a "social dividend" may turn out to be a good choice for the political leaders in power. In the United States, a social dividend, if available for use, could be utilized, in a first phase, to alleviate the burdens coming from the introduction of the national health-care service and to make it easier to adopt a "social market economy" and/or the "Rhine" model, which the crisis of the Anglo-Saxon system is putting now on the agenda[5]. Another factor that may allow for the creation of "social capital" is the passage of many goods from the state of *res nullius* (a thing belonging to nobody) to that of *res communis omnium* (a thing belonging to all), which can generate usage rights: a typical case is water and, more recently, air itself.

An example of creation of social capital at the local level can be found in Italy, in the transformation of the Casse di Risparmio (Savings Banks) in public-law-based Credit Institutions, with their capital assigned to "Bank Foundations" with the obligation to use dividends for social purposes. A delicate aspect regards the management of the ownership rights awarded to the State, which, if directly managed by the political class, could lead to abuse of power and clientism, bringing the enterprises become public to ruin, as many experiences in the past have shown. The solution lies in the introduction of norms with constitutional force that award the managing power, as happened in Europe for the currency with the creation of the ECB, to bodies responsible to institutions but autonomous from the governments temporarily in power. Appointments that last longer than electoral cycles, qualified majorities for the parliamentary approval of designations, transparency of managing policies before public opinion are a few of the recent experiences that make it possible to proceed towards Meade's model. However, in order for the Meade's system to work, it is essential that the managers of social patrimonies shall pay the "social dividend" to the citizens directly, without having to pass through the public budget, which shall limit itself to the management of the revenues collected by taxes.

Big crises often produce a profound evolution of the economic systems and of the role of enterprises. A particularly meaningful precedent can be found in the crisis of the 1930s, which transformed the property of family enterprises into big joint-stock companies, in which the decisive

---

5 Michel Albert in his book *Capitalism against Capitalism* (Wiley Blackwell, 1992) had forecasted the present challenge.

role is played by managers; such a model has characterized the American economy until the recent Enron crisis, later made even more serious by the events that battered big banks and insurances[6].

The competences of the various institutional levels

Meade's proposal presupposes, in practice, a "closed" economic and institutional system, and in fact the property of the goods from which to draw the social dividend is assigned, although not explicitly, to the national State. There are, instead, two aspects that must be carefully considered:

- whether the dividend must be given to the "natives" or to the "residents";
- that the political system is evolving towards federalism, with the presence of several institutional levels.

To answer to those points it is necessary to single out the prime responsibilities of the various government levels, because although it is acceptable that, up to a certain extent, property be distributed at the various levels, the utilization of its returns should take different routes depending on the tasks assigned to each level. One can in a first instance assume that the division of responsibilities should be:

- to the world and the continental (*e.g.* the EU) level, the governance of currency, peace (the sword), the maintenance of ecological balance, the big infrastructures (in particular telecommunications, the Internet, etc.), the oceans, the space;
- to the national level, the physical infrastructures for telecommunications, and in particular the handling of solidarity among citizens, which takes the form of financial transfers (first of all the pension system);
- to the regional level, the provision of social services to be delivered on the territory, of which the most significant example is the health-care system, as there must be, for example, easily reachable hospitals;
- to the local level, the solidarity that directly concerns single individuals (care of the elderly, the children, the marginalized).

---

6 Berle and Means, *The modern corporation and private property* (MacMillan, 1932). Berle and Means were already calling long ago for big businesses to take responsibility for the community, lest they be subject to the absolute power of the managers ("neither the claims of ownership nor those of control can stand against the paramount interest of the community. It only remains for the claim of the community to be put forward with clarity and force").

If such a scheme is valid, the delivering of the social dividend would have to be given to the federation's member-States: Mario Albertini did show years ago how the level that handles the currency shall not have also the responsibility for "welfare", and impose the choice of the actual sources for its financing (presently taxes, and in Meade's proposal patrimonies), as there is to avoid the temptation to resort to printing currency, thus triggering dangerous inflationary downturns. The provision of a social dividend, with which the patients' out-of-pocket payments could be paid, would also give more freedom to the citizens in the choice of medical centers, fostering managerial efficiency criteria at the regional level. The social dividend should be given to all residents on the territory who contribute with their work and tax payments to the common well-being.

An evolution of the economic and social system in the direction proposed by Meade would represent a new significant role for the member-States of a federation (as well as for the regional and local levels), although they lost their traditional attributes of the currency and the sword. A truly federal system would thus be realized, which will obviously evolve its internal balances in the course of time, but which for a long time could count on a virtuous, federal division of powers.

Re-inventing the Welfare State*

Barbara SPINELLI

Sometimes we forget that the thought of unifying Europe in a Federation – born as a concrete project, as opposed to utopia, in the Second World War – does not aim at a simple ceasefire among countries that for centuries have fought each other, disseminating death. It is a project that has its roots in our collective crimes: totalitarianisms and wars. It searches for the reason why people reduce themselves to such a misery that they lose all hope, yearn for an astounding earthly Redeemer and imagine salvation crushing the neighbours: the weakest, most often. It is said that the reasons which pushed Europeans to unify in the 1950s have now vanished because the aim has been accomplished: war among them is nowadays unthinkable. This should explain the reason why there are no more statesmen of the likes of Jean Monnet, Altiero Spinelli, Alcide De Gasperi, Konrad Adenauer: men branded by the Thirty Years' War which inaugurated the first half of the twentieth century.

Those who talk this way neglect a fundamental aspiration of the founding fathers, and its extreme relevance to the present: the aspiration to look with an inquiring eye on the question of misery. They also neglect what the united Europe has tried to do, in order to create not only political but also social and economic institutions. In 1946 we left behind us the twentieth century's crimes with a pact of mutual assistance among citizens. It is called *Welfare* because it was shaped in England thanks to the plan conceived during the war – on mandate of the British government – by William Beveridge, one of Federal Union's founders: the Welfare State keeps the indigent, the outsider, the elderly, the pariah in a safety status. This is the reason why it is such a serious oversight, to think that Europe accomplished its mission, that the heroic times are over, that the Union should nowadays only be the strict guardian of public accounts. As after the war, we need today Founding fathers and heroic Inventors: if today's crisis is a kind of war, it is urgent to imagine long lasting institutions, so that the troubles coming back (misery, inequality) will not generate again social despair, resentment and that hate of the neighbour which is only extinguished when a scapegoat is found (yesterday Jews, today immigrants, in the future maybe elderly people who "die so late"...).

* Published in Issue 2/2012.

Abolishing Misery: this was the title of the book that the economist Ernesto Rossi – co-author of the *Ventotene Manifesto* with Altiero Spinelli and Eugenio Colorni – wrote in prison in 1942 and published in 1946: "It is necessary to unite all of our forces to fight misery, for the same reasons that in the past gave rise to the fight against smallpox and plague: in order to avoid contagion of the whole social body". The challenge today is the same, and it is a responsibility that national and European public institutions should take on. Leaving it to religious groups or to philanthropists would mean slip back to the times when charity was the only relief. In many Arab countries Islamic extremists provide for the Welfare, transforming it in a confessional institution. This is really not the model to emulate: the European states replaced the Church since the thirteenth century, creating secular institutions open to everybody. Also united Europe invests on common bodies because – as Jean Monnet said – "individuals are necessary to obtain the change, but institutions are necessary to safeguard it". And he adds, citing the Swiss philosopher Henri-Frédéric Amiel: "Every human's experience has always a new beginning; only institutions become wiser: they accumulate collective experience, and from this experience and wisdom, individuals submitted to the same rules will see their behaviour, not their nature, transformed". This is also secular: the will to change behaviours, not humankind's nature.

It is important to remember how Welfare State was born, because future electoral campaigns will develop on these issues – in Italy as in Europe – and on the defendant desk we'll find the medicine itself which we decided to take after 1945, in the hope of abolish both war and misery. It is not improbable, for instance, that the Italian right wing parties – not yet amended – will transform Europe in a target: the rules that impoverish and humiliate us would stem from Europe itself, and its "external interference".

Today, providing Europe with a new foundation and concentrating on the battle against misery means understanding why the Union requires from us both things: the respect of certain common rules, and at the same time the invention of new institutions designed to give more confidence to the ever growing army of people who are unemployed or trapped in temporary jobs. It means understanding that the battle against public debt is not an obsession nor an axe: it is the generational pact that the Union asks us to sign, given the fact that the single states, afraid as they were of electoral results, did not do the job. The Treaty of Maastricht forbids to charge future generations with the debts that the present generation made in order to have some goods without paying the respective taxes, writes Alfonso Iozzo, economist and European federalist, in a paper on the re-invention of Welfare State (*The Federalist Debate*, 3/2011)[1].

---

1 See above pp. 143-149.

It would be worth reading this paper, which rests on James Meade's studies, Nobel for economics, about the way to guarantee a minimum citizens' wage to the whole society. The necessary condition is to extinguish public debts, and to transform it into public credits: this patrimony – often not only undervalued but also disliked – would be kept for itself by the foreseeing state, and its destination would be the Welfare State's financing, rather than the current expenses. Mr Iozzo is convinced, just as the liberal Mr Meade, that the nations' or Europe's wealth (GDP) should be calculated with new means – Meade called this state Agathotopia, i.e. the Good place where to live. The criterion is no more the difference between the cost of manufactured goods and their revenue, but the state's patrimony and the way it is managed: the aim is to know if future generations will be left a higher or lower capital than the one we received from past generations. The Maastricht rules use this method, prescribing as first step the extinction of public debt.

The second step is still to be taken: the transformation of debt into credit, which would protect citizens in times of crisis. Not everybody has the Norwegian oil as patrimony, but Oslo is a model and every state has water, wind, and possibly new energy sources, and also public goods consumed by individuals. Since sooner or later Norway will run out of oil and gas, it created a pension Fund with the energy revenues, which is safe from market hazard. Only 4% of the Fund can be used annually for public expenditure, leaving to the citizens a capital at disposal for the future, when the patrimony will be exhausted (through the Fund, every Norwegian is the virtual owner of around 100,000 euros, while every Italian has a share of public debt of around 30,000 euros).

After fighting public debts, Europe could think about similar initiatives, pushing states toward the guarantee of a new social security. Even more, it could make everyone understand that wasted water and polluted air should now be included into the costs of Welfare: they are non-renewable goods, just like Norwegian oil. There is much talking about the need to relaunch the economic growth. But it will not be the growth of yesterday, and this truth should be told: because industrialised countries will not have the same growth rate as Asia or South America, and because our growth will be at the forefront only if it will be ecologically sustainable. Here lies the importance of the electoral rendezvous in different countries of the Union: not only the national ones, but also the 2014 election of the European Parliament. Those who will cry against taxes and against a Europe too grim and severe to be obeyed, promise a fictitious world, a Cockaigne-land where every day is Sunday, but with a fraud. Better knowing it beforehand, than too late. Better rediscover heroism, which we always need.

What Future for Federalism?*

Fernando A. IGLESIAS

> "As soon as headed towards home I mentally said good-bye to all my different politically orientated fellows. Their intimate pride relied in knowing that they were coming back to their battle-place in their political organizations, which did exist, were well known, were expecting for them and were now prepared to celebrate them for their firm loyalty. My unique pride was completely different in nature, as no political organization was neither waiting for me nor preparing a celebration in my honor, or even awaiting for my presence in their ranges. I had to be the one to create a new and different movement for a new and different battle; a battle that only I was to consider – beyond its current inexistence – more important than those in which all my fellows were going to engage in. By then, I had with me only myself, a manifesto, some thesis, and three or four friends who were waiting for me to finally know if the action to which I had been referring so much would really start".
>
> Altiero Spinelli (coming back from Ventotene)

I was in Ventotene, the beautiful island where Altiero Spinelli wrote the famous *Manifesto for a Free and United Europe*, and I was there to participate for the sixth time at the Federalist seminar. Everything looked fine until the woman beside me got nervous. As soon as she realized who we were, as soon as she heard all those young enthusiasts speaking in favor of the European Union, she cried: Europe is destroying everything! The Euro is destroying our economy! Stop the European Union, do me a favor!

She didn't look as a fascist or a reactionary, and her three Vietnamese adopted children seemed to me a good argument in favor of her cosmopolitanism. And then she insisted: Europe is devil! May be she was not aware enough of the fact that the Europe of nations used to solve its financial crisis not by 10% of unemployment but by a 10% of deaths. Maybe she was too busy studying and comparing the History of the first and the second part of the 20th European Century, as well as too young to remember genocide and war. But as many of the youth people that were there for the seminar have a slight chance to get a decent job in the next years, she surely had a point. Then the seminar started and things

* Published in Issue 3/2014.

got business-as-usual. Everybody, including me, agreed on the need of a new plan for overcoming austerity, reinforcing federal instruments of economic policy and re-launching the European productive system. Carbon tax, Tobin tax, defense of wages and pensions, reinforcement of the Central Bank capacities and the Eurozone, more investment on research and infrastructure and a more green economy were proposed as the recipes for the future. Who could be against them? But the scream of the cosmopolitan mother was still echoing in my ears…

In each and every meeting of the seminar the hidden assumption was more or less the same: European problems are – indeed – European, and can, should and must be solved at the European level. But, are they? Can they? Can anyone (nations or regions) establish a carbon and a Tobin tax and change a significant part of its productive system into alternative energies without damaging its global competitiveness? Can a regional entity adopt a Keynesian stimulus to the demand without suffering the same kind of "drains" that Keynes described about nations almost eighty years ago? Are the stop of climate change, the reduction of international conflicts, the management of migrations, the regulation of financial markets, and each and any of the basic troubles Europe faces today solvable at the European level? And if the answer is NO, if the answer is "All the main problems that Europe is facing are global ones, and they can only be solved at a global level", despite which we insist in solving them at the European level: can we still consider ourselves federalists? Was not federalism about solving different problems at the different scale they occur?

I asked that, and then I had an answer. First, I was told, we can intervene at the European level as there are regional institutions able to deliver active policies, but we cannot do the same at a global level. Therefore, the rational choice is intervening at a regional level, avoiding any kind of world utopianism, as there is nothing similar to the EU structure at a global level. Secondly, I was instructed, the rational strategy must be building a truly federal Europe first, and only once the process is fully completed, start thinking about the world. It does sound rational, does it not? Maybe. But, is it federalist?

Let me put it like this: if Spinelli, a Mussolini's prisoner who had already spent ten years in prison, had though this way, if he had considered that by those times there were not European but national institutions, if he had proposed "Let's build a democratic Italy, and a democratic Germany, and a democratic Spain, and then we start to think about a united and democratic Europe", would have the European Union ever existed? Was not this the basic dissidence between Spinelli and the many Italian and European political forces that were in favor of the unity of Europe but wanted to postpone it till the moment in which the democratic rebuilding of European nations happened? How many were the democratic nations in Europe before the start of the unification process? How many the democratic leaders? Were not national democracies in Europe the daughters of the regional integration and not their mothers? Was not the *Ventotene Manifesto*, and the foundation of the European Federalist Movement, and every act of Spinelli's life a denial of the strategy of working through the existing institutions, of the "step-to-step" strategy and of the principle of "first, focus on the smaller and easier thing, and only then on the rest"?

May be Spinelli was wrong, but we can however consider current realities and make some questions about them. Is there any hope of solving European unemployment without raising the global demand and, in order to do so, without a better global distribution of wealth? Is there any possibility of stopping global warming by switching the European economy into a green one, or this goal supposes a global policy and therefore, some kind of world democratic institutions able to overcome national egoisms and delivering it by legitimate means? Is there any future for the Euro as long as the dollar continues to be the global currency, allowing the United States to swarm with dollars the global market without paying the price of inflation, meanwhile the proposal made by the director of the Chinese Bank about creating a world currency based on a basket of the main currencies of the world sleeps in the fridge? What about the increasing incapacity of the United Nations in the management and reduction of international conflicts, the raising uncontrolled movement of people through frontiers, the raising number and dimension of fiscal paradises, the lack of regulation of global financial markets, the increased risk of a catastrophic global pandemic and so on? It seems only to me that all these are global troubles and that any policy that a national or regional structure delivers about each of them could be necessary and urgent (nobody denies it) but in the long term, at the end of the day, they are only temporary palliatives.

Finally: how could regional policies applied to global issues be the main task, the priority, if not the exclusive goal, of any federalist strategy? Are not European parties more proper organizations in order to deliver them at the European level? Is not precisely the existence of European parties and EU institutions the living prove of the success of the past work done by Spinelli and the European federalist organizations, as well as the incontrastable evidence about the necessity of looking forward for new federal goals? Should not a truly federalist strategy leave European policies to European parties, EU institutions and other non-federalist organizations? Should not they prioritize the building of institutions at the global level in which they are – at the same time – more decisive and less existent?

Whatever we think about all this, we must agree on this simple fact: the two branches of the federalist movement – the Europeans' and the wordlist ones – will not be remembered because of their interventions at existing institutions but because of their decisive contribution to the creation of new ones: the European Union and the European Parliament (which overcame the European Economic Community) and the International Criminal Court (ICC), the truly seed of a global system of Justice. Both of them were the fruit of decades of hard efforts made by federalists, and extraordinary achievements, and a great contribution to the international community. Who could possibly put it in doubt? But the moment to recognize that they are also children who have already escaped from the hands of their funding fathers and have their own life has come. Some advices here and there is OK. But when the lives of the fathers continue to rotate around their children nothing good can ever occur.

A world federalism focused on the managing of the ICC, as well as a European federalism focused on the European Union's policies, constitute an alteration of the federalist practice, which is and always was about the development of new institutions able to cope with the new scale of problems that the globalization of social processes enacts. They are also the best recipe for we federalist become a sect of old nostalgic people, proud of a glorious past but unable to face and to cope with new challenges. If this is not wrong, the reform of the UN and the international financial institutions (World Bank and IMF), and the creation of a UN Parliamentary Assembly as the embryo of a future World Parliament must be the priority for a true federalist strategy, as well as regional campaigns focused on institutional building such as the transformation of the parliamentary assembly we call "European Parliament" into a true parliament and the development of a Latin-American Criminal Court against Transnational Organized Crime, among others.

Without a global perspective, all sort of regional federalisms – such as the European one – are condemned to turn into an expression of nationalism applied to a enlarged scale. Unless they believe in some ethnic or cultural superiority of Europeans over Americans (which should be even worst), the European Federalists who are so critical about the role played by the United States of America and propose the United States of Europe as the solution of every global trouble are in flagrant contradiction. Seven decades after the *Ventotene Manifesto*, the elementary truth is that its most famous paragraph, which starts by marking the emergence of a new "dividing line" between "progressive and reactionary forces" and finishes by defining the latter by their decision of giving priority to the "international unity" over any other consideration, must be applied to the European unity itself. The *Ventotene Manifesto* defined the unity of Europe not as the ultimate goal but as the first and necessary step towards a world federation. And the time for taking it seriously has come. Of course, a world federation here and now is a utopia, but the time for putting its constitution in the international agenda is now. Before global crises kill the dream of a European Federation, or democracy inside the national states of the world, or the world…

How do we know that this time has come? How could we know that the time to change the successful "Europe-first" strategy that was rational at the end of the Second World War and constituted the base of the most amazing progressive process in the History of human kind has arrived? Well, the fact that any basic problem of Europe is only a local expression of a global one that cannot be solved at the regional level is the proof. But, unfortunately, the European Union has been so successful at evolving its internal structure according to the new situations created by its own evolution as a complete disaster in the "external" front. No matter how insufficient are the European "internal" institutions there is no possible paragon with the complete lack of a common European Union foreign policy, with the failure of the European support to the processes of regional integration in other continents, with the disagreement among national members of the EU on UN Security Council reform, with the absence of any European strategy on UN reform, and with the inexhaustible incapacity of the European Union to have a voice in every international conflict. This has converted the EU into a mere witness of what real powers decide over the world, which, of course, includes Europe.

The transformation of the European Union into a federation is becoming, therefore, a necessary but defensive goal; not the roof but the floor of any truly federalist strategy, supposing, but not admitting, that a European Federation could be reached without a strong change in the global political structure. Thinking that the internal dynamic of Europe, a continent in which just 6% of the world population live in, will prevail over the global winds of History is the kind of naive mirages that use to lead towards wild catastrophes. A fully developed European Federation in a tyrannical and anarchic world ruled by big national powers, global financial markets and intergovernmental undemocratic organizations such as the UN Security Council, the G20 and the IMF is, here a now, a utopian project, and the difficulties that the European Union is facing at this very moment are the best example of that.

Are these words against European federalist organizations? Is this a vindication of the World Federalist Movement? Not at all, as the WFM has also fallen into the same trap as the European federalist organizations: being seduced by the temptation of focusing on the management of the institution to which they "gave birth" – the International Criminal Court

– instead of moving toward the construction of new institutions that the accelerating globalization of social processes requires.

Federalism is one thing. European nationalism is another. The dream of a democratic, wealthy, pacific and fair Europe within an undemocratic, poor, warlike and unfair world is getting as unrealistic and reactionary as the dream of democratic nations within the frame of the WWII was at Spinelli's times. Europe, which has been so successful in building internal institutions as unsuccessful in the development of a common foreign policy, the support to the constitution of other regional integrations, the federal and democratic reform of the United Nations and so on, must be a leading force for a global change. Otherwise, European policies will continue to fail, regional separatism and national populism will continue to raise, and cosmopolitan mothers and other European citizens will continue to shout against Altiero Spinelli's dream.

Part Two

European Unification: an Unaccomplished Project

Giampiero Bordino

Europe's unification process is experiencing in recent years a period of great difficulties. The global economic and financial crisis, started in 2007-2008 and still not overcome, at least in Europe, and the worsening of civil and inter-state conflicts in the Caucasus area and most of all in the broader Mediterranean area, from the Near and Middle East to the Horn of Africa and to the Sub-Saharan area, have dramatically highlighted the limits and contradictions of an unaccomplished political-unification process. The Europe of national States and of an ever more inter-governmental European Union (practically paralyzed by national vetoes and lacking popular legitimation) is today, as testified by facts much more than mere opinions, absolutely impotent in the face of global and trans-national challenges, like, lately, the massive flows of migrants and refugees from the Mediterranean area that have been sweeping it.

If this is the situation we are in, it seems to be particularly useful and appropriate to re-consider the interpretative keys through which *The Federalist Debate*, in the years from 1999 to the present, has tried to explain, in the frame of the ongoing globalization process, the events and the various phases of the continent's integration process that led to the current outcome: from the failure of the constitutional project to the prevailing of the inter-governmental method, dominated by the relations of force between national States and by their mutual vetoes in the years following the Treaty of Lisbon and particularly in facing the crises both inside and outside of the Union. What comes out is a series of challenges only partially met, of missed opportunities, of proposals and projects more or less pursued and carried out, of old and new problems never completely solved. The Union, ultimately, was never able to adequately solve either the problem of the efficacy of its policies (which contributed to make the level of popular consensus towards the unitary project decline more and more), or the problem of a fully-developed democratic legitimation. A decisive critical moment from this viewpoint has been that between the years 2002 and 2005, when it was attempted to endow Europe, through the Convention, with a common Constitution, although in the form of a Treaty of constitutional nature. Indeed, during the Convention phase the necessity was strongly stated to build a true European government. But in the end, as well known, to that challenge no adequate answer was given, neither by the national leading classes nor, and this is the worst aspect, by the EU public opinions, as shown in 2005 by the failed ratification referenda in France and in The Netherlands.

On the occasion of the 50th Anniversary of the birth of the European Community, the review, with an Editorial by its Editor, offered a comprehensive balance of the EU integration process as accomplished till then. On the one hand, the integration process has been indeed a great success. It led from 6 to 27 member States; in 1979 the great political feat of a common Parliament directly elected by the citizen took place; in 1999 the monetary unification was started, and was concluded in 2002 with the introduction of the European single currency. But the fundamental, historic achievement of that great project has been in the first place the guarantee of peace in Europe through "the extension of law to the sphere of international relations", in accordance with the Kantian model. In the federalist perspective, it could be a possible model for the entire world. But on the other hand, the integration process remains dangerously unaccomplished so far, and the Union lacks both the capability to act (due most of all to the right of veto that its member States still keep over fundamental areas, like fiscal and budgetary policies, and foreign and security policy), and an adequate democratic legitimation. Europe cannot be only a market and currency union, and the lack or weakness of the policies just mentioned jeopardizes, as was made evident after the start of the global economic and financial crisis of 2008, the very survival of the single currency and, more in general, the possibility of maintaining and developing the "European social model" which is, to some extent, the peculiar "identity card" of the European civilization in the world. As Joseph Borrell writes in his recent analysis of the limits of inter-governmental policies and the perspective of a new legitimation of the Union in a federal horizon, "the only political project that can give legitimacy to integration, and mobilize the European citizens is the survival of the 'social model' and the European way of life in the face of globalization". It is on these grounds, at the same time social and identity-related, i.e. implying the awareness of a common belonging, that we can defeat the new nationalisms, populisms, the dangers of xenophobia and racism which, at the beginning of the 21st century, are increasingly threatening Europe and more in general the world.

Rules, institutions, a shared sense of belonging are, together, the pivots of every community, and the foundations of its stability and cohesion. From this viewpoint, it is essential, in order to further the ends of the unitary and federal European project, to introduce the European citizenship of residence. As Paul Oriol observes in a note presenting the ongoing, grassroots initiatives to promote in Europe that kind of citizenship, "Nationality is not the only criterion for awarding rights. More and more, residence is playing that role". There is to remark, in the light of the most recent events, that such a choice may allow us to deal with the problem, become by now explosive, of the inclusion of refugees and migrants, guaranteeing to all, whatever their national origins, the exercise of the same rights and duties and, at the same time, promoting in the hosting communities an adequate level of social cohesion. To cite the European Union's motto, there is to realize "unity in diversity"; namely, Europe is confronted, in our global century, with a decisive challenge: how to promote and ensure a peaceful and consensual living together, sharing the same territory with human groups which are more diverse and much more mobile than ever before.

To realize the European federal project, a crucial role, in the analyses and proposals appeared in *The Federalist Debate*, is that of political parties and more in general of civil society movements. In other words, a strong "democratic infrastructure" is necessary to promote and build the European federal project. Instead, as Jo Leinen observes, "European parties have had little influence on shaping the political program of the Union until today". To that effect, it is necessary to set up some kind of regulation, a statute of the European political parties. But in any case "A first prerequisite for stronger European political parties is the continuing constitutionalization of the European Union". In that direction, in order to strengthen the Union's democratic legitimation through the role of parties and civil society movements, a great opportunity is provided by the Lisbon Treaty, which in Art. 11 introduced the European Citizens Initiative (ECI), an institution of participatory and direct democracy. It is an opportunity not adequately exploited so far, but which poses, as Sylvia-Yvonne Kaufmann writes in analyzing its content, origins and motives, "A great responsibility on Federalists".

A recurring theme in the European debate between the end of the 20th century and the beginning of the 21st on which *The Federalist Debate* has returned several times is that concerning the relation between the EU's "enlargement" in the geographic territorial sense, and "consolidation" in a political and institutional sense. Can Europe, that passed from 6 to 27 member States, with other candidate States in the waiting, withstand and develop further without a proper institutional strengthening in the perspective of a federal-type state? As Heinz Timmermann observes in his article, "three ideally typical scenarios" can be outlined: a strong constitutionalization process in the federal direction; an "erosion scenario" with a substantial regression of the Union towards a mere free-exchange area; and a more complex and articulated scenario of a "flexible integration", in other words a variable-geometry integration characterized by a core of States more advanced in their unification process, open to subsequent adhesions. Each one of these scenarios implies different possibilities of realizing the integration process: as experience can teach, only a strong, federal-type institutional structure can make old and new enlargement paths really sustainable. In the perspective of a "flexible integration", the role of the countries belonging to the common-currency area is crucial. The euro-zone can consider itself to be the natural candidate for the dynamic core of the flexible-integration project, and in essence of the project of a fully-fledged federal Europe. Actually, it may well be stated that there is "An urgent need for the Franco-German couple to take the lead, backed by Italy and with the support of the Commission and the European Parliament" (Dusan Sidjanski).

Another recurring theme in the reflections carried out in *The Federalist Debate* in the course of the years is the role of Europe in the world. Europe and the world are indeed the review's two fundamental poles of interest since the beginning. As written with great clarity in the Editor's Editorial mentioned above, "In future the EU will exist only if it is able to become a global actor". In the face of the global dimension of the challenges Europe has to answer, no European national State is by now in the position to exert its influence on them on its own. The pathetic illusion to be able to count on one's own in the world drives the national leading classes to impotence. For these reasons, and to make two meaningful examples, Europe is not present as such neither in the International Monetary Fund (Daniel Gros observes that should the euro-zone instead be present, it would have the relative-majority quota, hence the decisional power, in lieu of the United States) nor in the UN Security Council. In the absence of a common foreign, defense and security policy, Europe has still no voice in practice in the world. A Europe with no voice in a globalized world with no government, dominated by the relations of force between big, continent-wide States and new global actors of a non-State nature (terrorist groups, organized crime, trans-national economic and financial organizations, etc.): this is the dramatic picture which it is necessary for us to try to leave behind as soon as possible. The national leading classes do not want to cede power and transfer it partly, in a federal perspective, to a supra-national European level, sharing it in order to be really able to cope with the global challenges threatening European societies. Shall a world war (the third, probably a kind of permanent "global civil war", of which many signals can already be seen today) be once again necessary to drive them to do so, as after 1945? Maybe there is still some hope, as Tzvetan Todorov writes: "After all, Nelson Mandela succeeded in persuading the South African government to peacefully cede him its power..."

Back to the Dream[*]

Barbara SPINELLI

It was one of those works – the unity between the Europeans built after the war – that men undertake when they approach the brink of the abyss, and decide at this moment to take a look at themselves: when they see the disasters they were capable of, and explore the reasons of a fallibility too callous to be fruitful. And yet, they are not *blasé* enough, not overwhelmed by the indolence that according to Paul Valéry was the sickness of the European spirit after the 1914-1918 war: the "*tedium* of rehearsing the past and the folly of always trying to innovate", the unfitness to recover and learn once again.

The Nobel Peace Prize was given last October to that re-start of history, and to the turning point that was the reconciliation between France and Germany, two countries that in just 70 years had fought three wars. From the pooling of resources vital for both of them – coal and steel, sources of wealth and death – was born the Union we have today. Never before was the link between peace, democracy and rule of law so clear in the awarding of the Nobel Prize. It was as if the invention of Europe were the living proof that signing a ceasefire is not making peace. That to hold together on a continental scale the three goals – peace, democracy, rule of law – we need to go beyond the treaties between States, beyond the non-belligerence between sovereigns that do not recognize any power, nor law, above them.

When Jean Monnet proposed and created the Coal and Steel Community, he explained the reasoning that inspired him: "When we look at the past and become aware of the enormous disaster that Europeans have brought about to themselves in the last two centuries, we are literally annihilated. The reason is very simple: each one has tried to fulfil his destiny, or what he thought his destiny was, applying his own rules". It was thanks to this awareness that the unity of the Europeans became a model, and for a large part of the world it still is: from the ethnic massacres, from the clashes between cultures and religions, the only way out for the nation-States consist in getting rid of the illusion of being self-sufficient – of the fiction of absolute sovereignty – and in creating common political institutions whose purpose is to fulfil the fate of several associated countries, not

* Published in Issue 1/2013.

of just one. In Asia, in the Middle East, the supranational community method remains the golden path to overcome nationalisms: much more than the solitary American power.

It was a kind of conversion, the one experienced by the Europeans. Instead of the national gaze, the cosmopolitan gaze; instead of treaties between States, a partially-federal union since the beginning, to which the old absolute sovereignties were delegated. Europe is an old dream, but in the 20th century it becomes a practical project, a necessity, giving birth to an institution with state features. An institution that lives side by side with nation-States that admit not only their fallibility, but even their dangerousness for themselves, if they yield to nationalist frenzies. Only after its own Thirty-Year War (the one that goes from 1914 to 1945) did the continent find out that it is not enough to lay down the arms: the most urgent endeavour is to understand why such bloody conflicts arise. "They arise because of the easiness with which the States bring the functioning of their institutions into question", said Monnet. Better to watch out since the start: wars devour democracies, but it is the degradation of democracies and their institutions that throws peoples with no helmsman into wars.

This was at stake, after 1945: stop the wars, and at the same time give new strength to the institutions, make them less discontinuous. Unity arises by saying no to nationalism, but also to what drives them crazy: poverty, corruption of democracy, and the fading of the rule of law, even before that of human rights. Awarding the Prize in these days is peculiar indeed. Its intent is probably a stern warning but in some way it sounds like a mockery, though we can hardly imagine an ironic jury. It stamps a seal on a progress, but indicates how we risk to fail it. It shows what Europe wanted to be, but it is not yet or any longer. The clashes on the euro, Greece transformed into a scapegoat, the abnormal weight of a single State (Germany): it is not the union we aspired to for decades, but a construction which is de-constructing itself and going backwards rather than complete itself. It is as if the jury were telling us, between the lines: "You Europeans have invented something great, but you are not up to the prize we are awarding today. You are a promised land, but you still live in the desert as the Jews who fled from Egypt". If Europe will be pleased with the award, it means that it sees only the celebratory surface of the event, not the chaos that seethes beneath.

Such prizes are not simply "received". They must be meditated, questioned, as ancient Greece used to question the oracle of Delphi. The response does not change over the millennia: know thyself (*gnōthi seautón*), it repeats. Know the betrayal of your initial promises and the ridicule of your apotheosis. Try to understand why the Union does not arouse hopes any more, but distrust, fear, and sometimes disgust. Left halfway, Europe is not yet the supranational institution that preserves democracy and the welfare State. It is identified with one of its means – the euro – as if the currency and the economic therapies so far devised were its final aim, its horizon of civilization. The obsession with the financial rescue plans and the refusal of any alternative obscured and reduced our concern for democracy and solidarity, and for the project of a Europe that, united, can become a power in the world.

The ideal thing would have been for the Union not to go and receive the prize, but to convey the following message to the Nobel Committee: Europe's *citizens* (not the States and not even the common institutions, much less meritorious) will pick it up when the task will be really carried on and accomplished. When we will finally have a Constitution that – as in the American Federation – begins with the words "We, the citizens …" When we will go back to work, and will shed the *tedium* of re-starting our history. Technical subterfuges do not last: only institutions last. The turning point is political, mental, and, just like in 1945, it is St. Augustine's maxim that we need to adopt: *Factum eram ipse mihi magna quaestio* – I had become to myself a big problem, and a big enigma.

From War to Peace

The Achievement and the Danger*

Tommaso Padoa-Schioppa

The euro has come into our everyday life. Its first days have been marked by the changes in our little habits; the anecdotes about its start will be many and they will linger on the inevitable mishaps and on what went wrong, rather than on the great economic and political changes of which the euro constitutes just one episode. What are these big changes?

Professional economists and central bankers believe that the most significant change occurred three years ago, when in Rome, Paris, and Amsterdam the national Central Banks (venerable, often several-centuries-old institutions) ceased to rule their countries' currency, to determine its value by fixing the level of money supply, and to be able to trigger or to avert inflation. As far as the central banker's main functions are concerned, it is then that the national currencies ceased to be real and became just a proxy. Since then, liras, francs, guilders have been only, as somebody said, the national names of the euro, which in fact was already in existence.

Although true, all this looks to the average citizen almost irrelevant compared with the change brought about by the euro coming into their everyday habits. Indeed politicians and normal citizens understood the reality much better than central bankers when, fifteen or twenty years ago, they were able to understand what monetary union really meant, when it was explained to them that banknotes and coins in liras, marks, and pesetas will be replaced by a single banknote or coin, with a single name.

Margaret Thatcher was right when she used as an argument for opposing the single currency her desire to maintain the picture of the Queen of England on banknotes. The plurality of currencies in Europe started just in this same way, when, a couple of centuries after the deposition of the last Western Roman Emperor, the kings – whom we call barbarian – dared take the emperor's image off the face of coins and put theirs in its place. That act signified that they no longer recognized any authority above them, as they were, exactly, "sovereign". And "sovereign"

* Published in Issue 1/2002.

was the name given to one of the coins in the course of European history, while others were called louis, real, napoleon, and carlin. Today, those sovereigns go back in the ranks. It has a certain poignancy to see the heads of King Albert of Belgium, Juan Carlos of Spain, and Beatrix of the Netherlands happily established on the back of the one-euro coin, aware of stepping back, after almost fifteen centuries, to the status of mere rulers of a province of the empire.

In the meantime those kings and those sovereign powers have made quite a long journey. A journey of progress in civilization. Sovereigns have relinquished paganism, given peace and security to their territories, unified language, emancipated politics from religion, promoted art and science, administered justice, expanded trade, and set sail for the discovery of the world. They have also learned how to moderate their power, acknowledging respect for parliaments and ministers. They were taught, sometimes only after having lost their head, that people were not subjects, but citizens, and that people did not belong to them, but they to the people. Some of those sovereign powers even became republics, no longer passed on by hereditary right. But as well as being a journey of progress in civilization, it was also a journey of blood and barbarism. Pacification inside the boundaries, but war, pillage, conquest, and oppression outside. Colonial exploitation, forced conversions, unfair taxation, currency counterfeiting, and torture. The progressive moderation of sovereign power took place inside their kingdoms, not outside. The original act of arrogance, by which sovereigns had dispossessed the emperor of the currency, was not reversed. Indeed the sovereigns remained barbarians in not acknowledging any power above themselves. And barbaric was the last apotheosis of unbounded sovereignty, when (in two World Wars) the whole hard-won progress in civilization was disavowed and a return to paganism was attempted.

For those in their thirties this is past history, told them by their grandparents and great-grandparents. But while Europe was still in the darkness of the Second World War and nobody knew how it could get out of it, those grandparents and great-grand-parents, often in exile, in jail or in the underground struggle, acting in France, Italy, Germany, Switzerland independently of each other, were working out an interpretation of the tragedy which was taking place, were thinking of how to avoid it repeating itself, and were trying to prepare a different future. Monnet, Spinelli, Maritain, von Moltke, and Einaudi are some of their names. Only by putting an end to the claim of the States to unbounded power, only by subjecting the sovereigns themselves to a higher power that would regulate them in some well-defined areas of politics and economy would it become possible to put an end to the continuous alternation between wars and precarious truces, which had scarred European history for more than three centuries, until the final tragedy of the World Wars.

The road chosen for building peace was that of the economy. Gradually a space was created in which goods, capitals, services, and people could move freely – even more freely than they could move within any one state before the European Union was born. In order for those liberties to be guaranteed and regulated at the same time, and in order for every citizen and every business in every country to rest assured they could enjoy them with no risk that another country could prevent them from doing so, a power was instituted superior to that of any one state: the power to make laws binding for all, to ensure their enforcement and to prosecute violators. They did not create a European State; but in the economic sphere powers were established at the European level which are typical of a State.

For approximately fifteen years the currency of such a European "State" was the dollar; later, for almost twenty-five years, the mark; now, the euro. The world outside has watched this evolution with astonishment. Scholars and specialists have debated and doubted. It was the first time that there was no coincidence between currency and state; that the project was to give a single currency and a single central bank to a "body" which did not have proper state apparatus, its own army, its own foreign policy, and its own police force. So deeply rooted was the habit of the coincidence between currencies and states, that for the "country of the euro" the name 'Euroland' was swiftly coined.

The euro is a step in this long journey, a change of centuries-old habits, which go much deeper in our culture and our identity than the simple acts of making payment, or counting. What specialists do not always understand, is understood by politicians with vision and courage. "The euro is a matter of peace and war", Kohl said many times to his fellow citizens and to Europeans. "If it had been done before, many wars would have been avoided", I have been told several times by strangers in different European countries that I have met by chance and asked them what the euro meant to them.

Why is it a matter of peace and war? Printing a note of one hundred euro costs a little more than ten euro-cents. Why then when a stranger gives it to us are we ready to give him in exchange something real, worth not the ten euro-cents, but one hundred euro? We will never meet that stranger again, and yet we trust him and that piece of paper he hands over to us. We trust him because his note is our note, his sovereign is our sovereign, we are part of the same society, we abide by the same laws; in sum, we are fellow citizens. This is what the barbarian kings wanted to reject by dividing the empire and throwing out the emperor; this is what their present-day descendants want to affirm, for reunifying Europe, by taking their place on the back of the one-euro coins.

The change of habits that the euro marks and promotes concerns the boundaries of our society, the perception of who is and who is not our fellow citizen. Day by day the definition of the society we feel we are part of will change. Here lies the most significant change to our habits brought about by the euro; but here lies too the danger. The danger is to think that the euro is the last step, that a united Europe is already accomplished. Those who wanted the single currency most passionately wanted it so that it could help us take further steps, not that it be the last one. The barbarian sovereign is not claiming any longer unbounded power, but there is no emperor yet. The inscription "1 euro" on the face of a coin cannot rise to the rank of emperor. If we want the habit of regarding the man who uses the same coin as us as our fellow citizen not to be an illusion and, in the end, false, then on that habit we must build more.

European Democracy is Valuable Too, not Just the Monetary Union*

Amartya Sen

When in 1941 Altiero Spinelli, along with Eugenio Colorni and Ernesto Rossi, signed the famous *Ventotene Manifesto*, they were fighting "for a free and united Europe". The Milan declaration that followed in 1943, establishing the European Federalist Movement, reaffirmed the commitment to a united democratic Europe. This was a natural extension of Europe's quest for democracy led by the European Enlightenment, which in turn inspired the whole world. It is, therefore, particularly distressing that the danger to democratic governance in Europe today, coming through the back door of financial priority, is not receiving anything like the concern that it should generate. The tradition of democratic public discussion is being undermined by the unregulated power of rating agencies to command, in effect, what democratic governments should do, often supported by further commands by international financial institutions.

Two distinct issues need to be separated out. The first concerns what Walter Bagehot and John Stuart Mill saw as the need for "government by discussion". If the financial guardians have a realistic understanding of what needs to be done, their voices should get serious attention in democratic public dialogue. But this is not the same thing as allowing them the ultimate effective power to command democratically elected governments, without any general resistance from democratic Europe. The power of rating agencies can be restrained and moderated only by the power of coordinated political voices in Europe, which is missing.

Second, it is, in fact, quite hard to see that the sacrifices that the financial commanders have been demanding from precarious countries would deliver the ultimate viability of these economies and guarantee the continuation of the Euro within an unreformed pattern of financial amalgamation and an unchanged membership of the Euro club. The diagnosis of economic problems by rating agencies is not quite the voice of verity that these agencies pretend. It is worth remembering that the record of the rating agencies in certifying financial and business institutions preceding the 2008 economic crisis was so abysmal that the

* Published in Issue 3/2011.

US Congress seriously debated whether they should not be prosecuted.

Since much of Europe is now engaged in achieving quick reduction of public deficits through drastic public expenditure reduction, it is crucial to scrutinize realistically what the likely impact of the chosen policies may be, both on the lives of the people and on the generating of public revenue through economic growth. In addition to a bigger political vision, there is also the need for clearer economic thinking on the effects and effectiveness of the "blood, sweat and tears" strategy of maximal deficit reduction.

The high morals of "sacrifice" do, of course, have an intoxicating effect. This is the philosophy of the "right" corset: "if madam is at all comfortable in it, then madam certainly needs a smaller size". But if the demands of financial appropriateness are linked too mechanically to immediate and drastic cuts, the result could not only be more than necessary hardship, but also the killing of the goose that lays the golden egg of economic growth. The tendency to ignore the importance of economic growth in generating public revenue should be a major item for critical scrutiny – from Britain to Greece. In Britain the questions to ask concern only the wisdom of the policies freely chosen by the government (without much encouragement to public discussion), rather than what is being imposed from outside, as it is in Greece, which has little option to defy the commands of the financial bosses.

Maximal cuts may reduce public expenditure as well as private spending, but if that leads also to reduced incentives for growth, this can make public revenue go down sharply. The strong connection of growth and public revenue has been widely observed in many countries, from China and India to the United States and Brazil. There are lessons from history here, too. The big public debts of many countries when the Second World War ended caused huge anxieties, but the burden dwindled rapidly thanks to fast economic growth. Similarly, the huge deficits that President Clinton faced when he came to office in 1992 melted away during his presidency, greatly aided by speedy economic growth.

How did some of the Euro countries get into this mess? The oddity of going for a united currency, the Euro, without more political and economic integration has certainly played a part in causing this crisis, even after taking note of financial transgressions that have undoubtedly been committed by a country like Greece or Portugal (and even after noting Mario Monti's important point that a culture of "excessive deference" in the European Union has allowed these transgressions to go unchecked). It is to the huge credit of the present Greek government – Prime Minister George Papandreou in particular – that they are doing what they can, despite political resistance, and it is also a good cause for the Greek government to try to get Greece out of the culture of corruption that overwhelms Greek business and economic relations.

However, neither the long-run benefits of far-reaching Greek reforms, nor the pained willingness of Athens to comply with the demands of international financial commanders, eliminates the European need to examine critically the wisdom of the requirements – and of the timing – that are being imposed on Greece. Austerity has an immediate appeal to the financial guardians today, but it is not at all obvious that these guardians have anything like a clear understanding of how economic growth would re-emerge in Greece, which is currently shrinking quite rapidly. Aside from the dampening economic effects of maximal cuts in the cause of saving Greek's membership of the Euro zone, the restrictions of Euro itself make the international prices of Greek goods and services high and often uncompetitive.

It is no consolation for me to recollect that I was firmly opposed to the Euro, despite being very strongly in favour of European unity, for reasons that Altiero Spinelli had outlined so powerfully. My worry about the Euro was partly connected with each country's giving up the freedom of monetary policy and of exchange rate adjustments, which have greatly helped countries in difficulty in the past, and prevented the need for massive destabilization of human lives in frantic efforts to stabilize the financial markets. That monetary freedom could be given up when there is also political and fiscal integration, as the states in the U.S. have.

The wonderful political idea of a united democratic Europe has been transformed over the years to make democratic politics seem subsidiary to complete fidelity to a programme of incoherent financial amalgamation. Rearranging the Euro zone now would have many problems, but difficult issues have to be intelligently discussed – with a European democratic commitment to do so – taking realistic empirical note of the different circumstances that apply to different countries. The last thing that Europe needs today is to drift in financial winds fed by narrow-minded and severely incomplete economic thinking, often coming from agencies with a terrible track record of anticipation and assessment. Stopping the marginalization of the democratic tradition of Europe has an importance that is hard to exaggerate.

Europe Needs a Government*

Fernand HERMAN

Mr President, ladies, gentlemen, honourable members of the Convention, you have heard at length from diverse members of civil society who have expectations of Europe.

Those expectations are many and pressing. For the most part, we share them, but the organisations I represent today are concerned principally with the capacity of the institutions to meet these expectations. Because nothing is more harmful than the repeated declaration of elevated ambitions which are never realised.

If the institutional triangle – Commission, Council, Parliament – has so far been able, in its current configuration, to create the customs union, the single market and finally the monetary union, it is because they worked above all to create common rules, that is to say to carry out legislative and regulatory work. With monetary union and, above all, political union, we need less legislation and more action. So it is the function of the executive that must be reinforced. In other words, Europe needs a government. The citizens have that aspiration, if not that right.

This government cannot be the Council for four simple reasons:

1. To govern one of the largest commercial and financial powers in the world is a full time job, and cannot be carried out in the spare time of people who are already completely absorbed by the management of their own countries.
2. The members of the Council are elected or appointed to defend their national interests and not the European interest. That is why they are always ready to haggle and concede over this or that proposal, something which they demonstrate every day.
3. Being accountable only to their national parliaments, they will never be punished for failing to serve the common interest well. They can never be held to account by the elected representatives of the citizens of Europe. They will be democratically unaccountable.

* Published in Issue 3/2002. This speech was given at a plenary session of the European constitutional Convention on 24 June 2002. The author was representing the Federalist Voice network of federalist and pro-European organisations lobbying the Convention.

4. Even though it composed of the strongest figures from their respective countries, the Council is the weakest of the European institutions because it is divided over most issues. A team of strong and vigorous horses pulling in different directions will travel less far than a team of half-starved nags pulling in the same direction.

Because it is legally independent of the national governments and politically accountable to the European Parliament, the Commission should become the government of Europe. But in order to be able to act effectively and decide efficiently, there should be no more Commissioners than there are portfolios, between twelve and a maximum of fifteen. A system of rotation giving each member state an equal right to nominate a Commissioner would maintain the principle of the equality of states. The interests of the small states would be better defended by a strong and independent Commission, guardian of the general interest, than by a Commissioner swamped by a vast Commission downgraded to the level of a second Coreper.

The legitimacy of this executive would be strengthened still further by the election of its president by the European Parliament acting, in the introductory period at least, as an electoral college. Perhaps in the future one might envisage the introduction of a direct election.

It would be suitable that the legislative function should be carried out on the basis of co-decision between the Parliament and the Council, which itself should always vote by double majority (a majority of states representing a majority of the citizens).

We would support the *Lamassoure report* regarding the division of competences, and the proposals of the Commission regarding foreign policy.

For the simplification and the transparency of the system, it would be wise to bring together the three pillars into one, with the single exception for defence matters where the intergovernmental method and flexibility should remain for the time being.

Since its foundation in 1957, the EEC has had a legal personality at the international level. It is an aberration that the Union, which was supposed to take European integration a step further, is deprived of one. This means it is unable to act properly in the fields covered by the second and third pillars in its dealing with third countries.

Finally, we should review the procedure for amending the constitutional treaty. In a real democracy, it is unthinkable, indeed insupportable, that the will of the representatives of three hundred or even four hundred million people can be obstructed by a country with no more than three hundred thousand inhabitants.

Must the results of the Convention be put to a European referendum, even though some member states do not permit this? The organisations I represent are divided on this question, but all agree that Europe must be built not only by consultation but also by involving citizens and representatives of civil society in the formulation of European principles and decisions.

A Democratic Constitution for the European Union*

Romano PRODI

First of all let me express my warm thanks to all members of the Convention, and to you, Mr Giscard d'Estaing, for the dedication and intelligence you have shown in those long months of hard work that went into this phase of the constitution-building process. The Convention's success has brought a lasting change in democratic life in the European Union. A great job well done and an unhoped-for result. The draft prepared by the Convention thus provides the basis – an excellent basis – for drawing up the final version of the Constitution. This is a good thing because above all the text has great symbolic value: this is the first time the Union's foundations have been debated in an open, democratic forum representing the peoples and States of Europe.

Second, the draft Constitution resolutely tackles the issues of institutional balance and the complex nature of the Union. The debate has been intense and thorough, and it has allowed all the fundamental issues put forward to be dealt with coherently, namely:

- finding a new and more effective way of reconciling the two tracks of European integration – the Community and the intergovernmental;
- striking a balance between the States' political representation and that of the people, and the resulting roles of Parliament and the Council;
- devising a way to organise the representation of the Union's general interest and the legitimate interests of the individual Member States.

Third and lastly, the Convention has laid the basis for the essential job of bringing the Union's policies up to date.

The Intergovernmental Conference that is to finalise and formalise the work of the Convention is now commencing. I see two extreme standpoints emerging and I believe we need to discuss this frankly:

* Published in Issue 3/2003. Speech made at the European Parliament, Strasbourg, 3 September 2003.

First there are those who believe the Convention's draft should be left unaltered because it represents the only compromise that could be reached and the one with the greatest legitimacy.

Then there are those who would like to throw everything up for discussion because sovereignty is ultimately vested in the States and the last word should be theirs.

However understandable those standpoints might be, I believe both are open to criticism. From the start, ever since we advocated the Convention approach at Nice, we in the Commission have always said that the Intergovernmental Conference should be a short, focused, conclusive phase. But this does not mean it should just be a rubber stamp, because that would deprive the Intergovernmental Conference of its political responsibility. Clearly this Intergovernmental Conference cannot be compared with any other that has gone before, since it will be working on the basis of the excellent work of the Convention. But it still has its primary function, which is to allow the heads of State and government to exercise their political responsibility and present the definitive text for approval to the institutions and the people in their Member States. So it involves a new phase of political ownership. And that does not, of course, demand a lengthy Intergovernmental Conference, but it does call for a proper period of reflection.

There are aspects of the draft Constitution that bear clear witness to the fact that the compromise reached is incomplete or does not go far enough and that the result achieved to date is not the end of the line, as we had originally hoped. So the Member States, in whom sovereignty is ultimately vested, should be able to discuss it once more and see whether there are areas where it can be improved.

It is the Commission's duty to point out such areas. As it stands, the draft Constitution still calls for unanimous decision-making in over 50 sectors, including some key areas of life in the Union. In such sectors we risk trusting our future to an unconstructive approach involving doing nothing and putting the brakes on, rather than to a positive approach entailing making proposals and building alliances with a view to shared goals.

Everyone agrees, moreover, that one of the shortcomings in the current situation is the lack of a proper instrument for coordination of Member States' budget policies. But I wonder how people think such coordination can be achieved if the 25 future member countries can continue to exercise a power of veto freely in the area of indirect and company taxation.

Then there is the central problem of the future balance of powers between the Commission, the Council and Parliament. The draft Constitution proposes a Commission made up in a way that will – in my opinion and that of the whole College – make the institution representing the Union's general interest less able to do its work effectively and credibly. The solution put forward creates a distinction between Commissioners by creating, unnecessarily lesser category. No people of the Union deserves to be represented by a second-class Commissioner. The consequence would be to split the College, where the link with the Member States has been the Commission's driving force for the last 50 years. More progress is needed to make sure every member country has a full Commissioner.

At the same time, the present draft Constitution leaves choices open on crucial points, such as the way the Councils are to work and responsibilities in the field of external relations. But the task of the Intergovernmental Conference is to make the work of the institutions more transparent and more effective and to prevent duplication and halfway solutions that may breed future conflicts.

Lastly, the Convention did not have time to update the current wording on the Community policies. In some cases this dates back to the 1950s and has been partly superseded.

It will obviously be difficult to settle all the issues still outstanding. But it is our duty to take a step back from the current political circumstances and give careful thought to those points where changes are necessary and can still be made now, so the constitutional structure is even more capable of meeting the challenges ahead. We need to see whether the political will exists. Is there no such will or is it a sense of realism that is inducing us to refrain from tackling these issues and to leave the text to stand?

If this is the case, the Commission is willing to take note of this calmly and realistically, mindful of the fact that significant progress has in any case been made. Essentially this has been the case every time the treaties were amended. It was true for the Single European Act and for the Maastricht and Amsterdam Treaties. It will be true here too. But we must realise we will need to be ready to cope with further crises and agree further changes and adaptations. This is what European integration has always entailed – a mixture of vision and reaction to unfolding crises. It is the history we have lived through and we know it well, even if there are times when we need to move forward more quickly. And this is definitely one of those times. At all events, if we want to capitalise on our experience and really draft a Constitution to last, we must provide for mechanisms that allow decisions to be taken tomorrow where they cannot be taken today.

We must look at more realistic procedures for amending the Constitution to allow us to act quickly and effectively – under pressure of crises – where the arrangements we are setting out today turn out to be insufficient. The worst-case scenario would be to find ourselves with ill-adapted constitutional provisions that simply cannot be amended because this would call for unanimity among at least 25 Member States. This is true as regards decisions calling for unanimity, which applies even today in so many sectors, and it is also true as regards bringing policies up to date, which even now we are unable to tackle. A Constitution set in stone for all time, incapable of providing the solution to future crises, would be not only a Constitution with something lacking, it would be the negation of the whole history of European integration. And that we must avoid at all costs if we want to perform our historic task responsibly.

In our work we need to keep a clear vision of the direction the Union should continue to follow. Peace, freedom and solidarity must continue to be our goals in the day-to-day work of the institutions. To do this, we must give the Union the practical tools to attain and hold to those goals. The Union must speak with a single voice in the world – a strong, authoritative, peaceable voice. Internally and externally it must be able to uphold the force of law which imposes duties but also protects the individuals, safeguarding their freedom to act in an ordered, creative society. Lastly, the Union must have the means to show solidarity. This takes the form of support for the poorest, in an inclusive society. It is expressed through joint action to provide assistance in the event of natural disasters. Lastly, it is based on the duty of mutual defence, in the conviction that the defence of each and every Member State is the best way to show we belong to a single family.

A new phase has now started: we must finish the good work done by the Convention – wisely, resolutely and with courage. Of course it needs to be finished quickly. But above all it needs to be finished properly. The Commission will continue to do its part to help achieve that aim.

Europe Needs to Renew its Vows for Federal Union*

Guy VERHOFSTADT

Euro-sceptics are shamelessly exploiting the current economic crisis to misrepresent and undermine the European Union, its history, its institutions, its goals and its working methods. Like a marital union, the EU requires constant attention, support and belief that it can work in difficult as well as good times or else it risks separation and divorce. It is time now for a renewal of vows; to recommit to a federal union that is more stable, more efficient and more accountable.

The economic and financial crisis has showed up the key weaknesses in economic governance at EU level where a monetary policy was introduced without a parallel fiscal policy. Unlike other global currencies like the dollar or yen, the Euro still depends on 17 different economic strategies and bond markets, no common treasury, no common debt issuance and no common banking supervisor. This explains, to a large extent, why the bond markets extort far higher interest rates from Eurozone countries than from the US or Japan despite lower levels of public debt. Some of these lacunae are currently being addressed but progress is painfully slow and consensus on a common vision remains as elusive as ever.

This vision, we believe, should be based on a federal structure, defined and agreed in a new, concise constitutional document to be drawn up by the next European Parliament in conjunction with the Council and submitted to a referendum across the EU. The 'f' word has been much maligned in recent years, yet many Member States are themselves federal structures. It is perfectly possible, for example, to be Flemish, Belgian and European all at the same time. Indeed, in an increasingly post-national world, where the global economy is driven by major trading blocs and emerging markets, the European nation states of the 19th century lack economic and political weight. The G8 group of wealthy industrialised nations in 2030 will likely look quite different from that of today. In this context, sovereignty is better pooled at European level than lost at the global level.

* Published in Issue 3/2013.

However, the European Union struggles to win the hearts and minds of the public. Although the European Parliament has legitimacy through direct elections it still lacks credibility in the minds of many voters who don't feel motivated to vote for their MEPs. The five-yearly European elections are treated largely as national referendums on the government in office rather than a chance to really debate the political choices to deal with transnational issues like climate change, terrorism, immigration or globalisation and national governments have a predilection for blaming Brussels for everything that goes wrong whilst claiming credit for everything that goes right. There needs to be a sea-change at all levels of public consciousness: European political parties must make a real effort to mount EU-wide campaigns and address the challenges we face together as a Union of 500 million citizens rather than just as 27 separate national entities whilst the prospect of electing the European Commission President from Party lists would be an incentive to improve turn-out so that voting is seen to have tangible consequences.

The next European Parliament, to be elected in June 2014, should become a Constituent Assembly whose chief responsibility would be to draw up a draft Constitution, in agreement with the Council of Ministers. The text should be short and concise (unlike the last attempt) and confine itself to genuinely constitutional aspects of EU governance and be submitted to a referendum simultaneously across all countries of the Union. Individual States could then also determine if they wish to be part of it. That is not only democratic but would force all countries to confront the issue of Europe head on and no longer hide in the shadows. Some countries may wish to forge ahead with closer integration whilst others may prefer a slower lane. There should be no compulsion, nor exclusion from the club. But the current state of muddling along is only creating friction (even animosity) and failing to deal with very real and pressing policy matters that require decisive action.

The European Union was intended to bring together the peoples of Europe after the devastation of two world wars, fuelled by nationalism on the back of economic depression. If we allow these forces to gain a foothold once again on our continent we will have wasted a century of building closer ties and condemned history to repeat itself. Federalism is our bulwark against nationalism. It is the right model for addressing the supranational challenges of the 21st century.

The Unaccomplished Way Toward the European Unity*

Lucio LEVI

This year is the 50th anniversary of the establishment of the European Community. This event represents an opportunity for reflection on the historical meaning of the European unification.

At the beginning, the EC was a union of six countries. Now it stretches from Lapland to the Mediterranean and from Poland to the Canaries and includes 27 countries. It is a Community of 487 million inhabitants where 23 official languages are spoken, and includes approximately 100 ancient ethnic minorities. It has an executive commission, a parliament, an upper house, a court of justice, a central bank, a currency, a citizenship, a flag, an anthem, a passport. National borders have been abolished.

The unification process has developed with the ups and downs characteristic of a difficult undertaking such as the overcoming of the sovereignty of an increasing number of states which joined the original core of the founding states.

It is worth recollecting two dates which represent milestones in the history of European unification. The first is 10 June 1979, when the European Parliament was first elected by universal suffrage. This represented a qualitative leap in the construction of European unity with the European Parliament becoming the first supranational parliament in history. It is an innovation that could change the world history. Democracy, which usually stops at state borders, has become international. In future it could become global with the transformation of the UN General Assembly into a World Parliament.

The second date is the 1st of January 1999 when the European Central bank was established, thus opening the way to the circulation of the euro in 2002. It was a historic step on the road toward the construction of a European sovereignty. The euro has been a great success. The share of euros in the global official reserves amounts to 25%. Since December 2006, the quantity of euro notes in circulation in the world has overtaken the dollar. This is an extraordinary performance considering that it is only five years since the euro was launched. At the same time, the euro is the

* Published in Issue 1/2007.

starting point of a transition toward a polycentric international monetary system and, as an integrated global market cannot work with many competing currencies, towards a world currency.

What is the historical significance of the grand design of European unification? The most important achievement of the EU is undoubtedly peace. After centuries of warfare, Europe has never before lived so long in peace as it now has in the post-2nd world war period, which coincides with the beginning of the process of European unification.

What is peace? It is not simply the absence of war. This is the negative notion of peace which Kant called "truce" and placed in the same category as war. Instead, positive peace, requires a political organization which prevents war through entrusting the power to settle conflicts among states to a federal authority acting on the basis of law. According to Kant's philosophy, the foundation-stone of peace is law and – more precisely – the extension of law to the sphere of international relations.

"War appears to be as old as mankind, but peace is a modern invention", said Henry Maine. War has always been considered a normal event in political life, the vehicle for settling conflicts unsolvable through diplomacy. The novelty of the EU lies in the fact that it represents the most successful attempt so far to build a new form of statehood at international level, even though its pace has been slow and hesitant.

The EU is the most intensively regulated region of the world. Its political institutions impose restraints on what sovereign states may do in their relations with each other, and in this it shows the way to what the UN could become in the future: namely, the guardian of international law and the framework of a process of constitutionalization of international relations. The European integration process weakens national governments and compels them to co-operate in order to solve together the problems they are unable to cope with separately. It creates a European civil society side by side with national civil societies, and establishes European institutions that represent a decision-making mechanism which progressively depletes national institutions. The process has advanced to such a stage that war among European Union member states has become inconceivable. The current political debate on the Constitution shows how far the process of unification in Europe has advanced. In other words, slowly and imperfectly something like a European Federation is taking shape.

It is wholly unrealistic to plan fusion among nation-states; that is, among forms of political organization based on power centralization and international antagonism. The EU represents a rejection of such nationalism which knows no other way to pursue unification but imperialism. The EU is not and will never be a state in the traditional meaning of the word. It will rather be a Federation of states. The nascent

European Federation is facing the task of promoting mutual toleration and solidarity among nations. The vitality of the European unification experience springs from the attempt to reconcile unity on the one hand with the Old Continent's diversity of peoples on the other. It relies on the principle that the result of any attempt to suppress differences will be worse than accepting them. The experience of the European Community brings ample evidence that the epoch of World Wars has passed. The enlarged EU, which now includes most Central and Eastern European Countries, represents the overcoming of the Cold War.

In spite of this success, the mood of the Europeans towards celebrating the birth of the European Community is one of indifference. As Pope Benedict XVI, drawing up a balance of 2006, has stated: "Europe seems to be tired, or rather seems to be inclined to take leave of history." By blocking the European Constitution, the French and Dutch electorates have suddenly made the future uncertain.

It is a fact that the European unification project is as yet unaccomplished. The EU still has only a limited capacity for action. The budget is only 1% of the European GDP. The proposed rapid reaction force agreed in 1999 has not yet been established. Moreover, widening the Union without first strengthening it threatens the cohesion of its political institutions and carries with it the hidden danger of the EU regressing to the status of a free trade area.

During the past half century the construction of the EU was based essentially on economic integration under the protection of the US. In future the EU will exist only if it is able to become a global actor. The growing role of the euro and the mission to Lebanon can be judged as positive steps in the right direction.

Another weakness of the EU lies in the right of veto, which continues to be the rule in such crucial areas as foreign, security and fiscal policies, and constitutional revision. It is a dream to imagine that the 27 member states can all proceed at the same speed. Unanimous ratification of the Constitution was an illusory expectation. True, 18 countries have now ratified the full document, but the rejection of the Constitution in France and the Netherlands has meant that – following the current rules which are at variance with the democratic principle – the will of a small minority can in the end prevail over that of the majority.

The only way out of this deadlock is to entrust EU citizens with the power to express their decision through a European constitutional referendum. This method will oblige governments to recognize the sovereignty of the European people and comply with the majority rule. An EU-wide referendum will mark the birth of the European people who will appear on the stage of political life as the holders of the constituent power.

In conclusion, it seems that Europe's destiny can be to define global models. If the EU becomes able to speak with one voice, it will unify its representation in the IMF, the World Bank and the Security Council and will therefore become the vehicle for UN reform.

A European Government to Get out of the Crisis*

Andrew DUFF

Five years ago you had the temerity to elect me, at our Congress in Paris, as your President. What a five years this has been. It has been, first and foremost, the five years of the Great Crash, in which our banking system almost collapsed, our standard of living declined, and any complacency we may have had about the rise of Europe in the world stakes was dispelled. It has been five years of asymmetric shock which has tested to destruction the EMU settlement of the Treaty of Maastricht. It has been five years of hectic crisis management by the leaders and institutions of the European Union – making some mistakes, learning by doing (often too little, too late). After the first great crash in 1929, Europe fell apart and went back to the battlefield and descended into the worst depravities ever known to man. This time it has indeed been different. European unity has survived intact – not covered in glory, not making great strides to the federal constitutional settlement which we at UEF want to see, not without social hardship, particularly among the young, not without losing out in international affairs – but nevertheless the semblance of unity and the basic structure of the European Union has survived.

I promised when I accepted the post of UEF President in 2008 to try to keep the federal option on the agenda. That has not always been easy. The European Parliament in which I serve has not been at its most progressive or coherent. The rise of nationalist forces, and so-called 'eurosceptics' who march to the beat of the nationalist drum, has continued. The leadership of the mainly 'pro-European' groups has sometimes seemed intimidated by the hard pounding of the crisis. That is why we have created the Spinelli intergroup of federalist MEPs. The nascent European political parties, on whom so much rests, have remained fairly weak. Parliament has not accepted the bolder proposals to reform the EU (such as the election in a pan-European constituency of a certain number of MEPs from transnational lists). The negotiations on the new MFF, lasting for an age until 2021, have been depressingly familiar to all those who

* Published in Issue 1/2014. Keynote speech held at the XXIV Congress of the Union of European Federalists, Berlin, 16 November 2013.

remember Mrs Thatcher. National governments simply transpose their own templates for fiscal tightening, even rigid austerity, on to the EU without stopping to consider for one moment the real added value and cost efficiencies which could be gained by a genuine transfer of some public spending from the national to the European budget and treasury.

In foreign policy, quite frankly, far too little has been achieved. There has been progress in some parts of the Western Balkans (notably Kosovo and Serbia) but other countries (Bosnia, Macedonia) are going backwards. Cyprus remains a large, sad frozen conflict where, scandalously, the *acquis communautaire* does not apply. Turkey is as far off as ever from finding a durable and intelligent relationship with the EU. President Putin has not learned to respect the new norms which the EU has tried spasmodically to inject into East-West relations. Terrorism continues to stalk us at home and frustrate us abroad. NATO departs its long and costly Afghan campaign in a fairly sorry state and with little accomplished. The Middle East continues to boil, especially in Syria, while the European response to the Arab revolutions has lacked strategic confidence and direction. And we have found no answer to the problem of immigration, legal or illegal.

It is all too tempting to cast around to lay blame. Many, of course, blame what they simply understand as '*Brussels*' – a culture of blame which those of us who are 'Bruxellois' are not, frankly, very good at combatting. Some love to blame the Treaty of Lisbon, that new settlement which crept into life late (and bound with reservations, qualifications and derogations) only on 1 December 2009. From our point of view, Lisbon was a large step forward in the governance of the EU, and the UEF was right to campaign for its successful ratification.

The implementation of the new treaty, however, has not been smooth. The financial crisis and economic recession have provided the worst possible circumstances in which to try out the new institutional system. The rule book has not always been respected. The heads of state and government, in particular, have arrogated powers to the European Council in response to the crisis, a process which has stretched the Lisbon treaty close to breaking point. The role of the Commission, once the motor of integration, has been diminished. National parliaments have adopted a more truculent mood, while many national political parties have ceased to maintain support for European integration. Constitutional courts, including the European Court of Justice in Luxembourg and the *Bundesverfassungsgericht* in Karlsruhe, are increasingly raising their judicial eyebrows at some of the goings-on.

Undeniably, the time has come to consider again a general revision of the EU treaties in order to restore full democratic legitimacy to the project of building a united Europe. There has been much talk for many years of democratic deficit, not least among federalists, but not really enough talk about the deficit of government. We, who know better, must adhere equally to the governmental legacy of Jean Monnet and Robert Schuman as well as to the parliamentary legacy of Altiero Spinelli. In my view, there is nothing inherently undemocratic about any of the institutions of the European Union and nothing particularly malevolent about those who run them. The greater problem is the absence of government – by which I mean an efficacious executive authority with the capacity to act across the wide range of topics which today's challenges throw up, and an executive authority possessing an armoury of instruments sufficient to deal with the complex challenge of integration. This is not the usual discourse of the bland, centrist 'pro-European'. Federalists are radicals, but we must not fall into the trap of being simplistic. As H.L. Mencken said: "There is always an easy solution to every human problem – neat, plausible, and wrong".

Federalists are criticised – sometimes with justification – for being too convoluted. It is not easy to correct such a deficiency of European government, and surely not quickly. It takes time and persuasion to convince those who hold the reins of national power to realise their relative impotence. It is not straightforward to reform the opaque and diffuse exercise of executive authority at EU level – strung out as it is between European Council, European Commission, Ecofin, Eurogroup, European Central Bank, European Stability Mechanism, the EU regulatory authorities of the financial sector, and the troika including the IMF. It is not easy to persuade national governments or parliaments of the democratic need to centralise power not in themselves but in people to govern at the EU level who can be sacked by the European Parliament when they get it wrong. Government is a pretty thankless task at the best of times, and it would be naive for those of us who wish to strengthen the firepower of the EU to expect to be loved for what we do and say. But there is a strong story to be told about how political disorganisation and institutional weakness contributes to sub-optimal economic performance, the poor delivery of public goods and democratic failure.

Unfortunately, the crisis has had the effect of accentuating some of the worst aspects of EU governance: the tight coordination of national economic policies is very technocratic and not liable to parliamentary accountability at either EU or national level. Where national governments, as in Greece, are forced by the EU to devalue internally at a time of deflation there is certain to be social hardship and fierce political protest. And the resolution of the banking crisis has only just started. Imagine the political reaction when 'Brussels' starts to punish share-holders and depositors by closing down banks not just in Cyprus but also here in Germany. Is the EU robust enough to take the tough decisions which are long promised but still outstanding to separate sovereign from private debt? Does everyone realise the magnitude of the transfer of national sovereignty implicit in European banking union? Are we ready politically to make the case for the progressive mutualisation of sovereign debt across the internal borders of the Union? Is the fact that fiscal union must be run by a federal government generally recognised?

I ask these questions not to doubt that, as ECB board member Jörg Asmussen says, 'federal institutions can prevent local crises from becoming systemic', or to question the federalist logic of the actions of Mario Draghi. But the federalist argument has to be won not just in academic and official circles, and with the markets, but also democratically, even on the streets.

In May 2014, in the European Parliamentary elections, we have a chance to campaign for the federal Europe which we espouse. Such campaigning will never happen at national level: see how the recent election campaign for the Bundestag was about everything other than Europe, which is seen as too complex, too distant and too problematic. See how national leaders, if left to their own devices, prefer to dissemble about the scale and scope and pace of European integration: if the EU has done nothing else well, it excels at procrastination – in that over-used but nevertheless rather good American metaphor, at 'kicking the can down the road'.

Next year, however, is crunch time. Banking union now is critical if the euro is to be salvaged. If the euro does not survive and prosper, the European Union itself will fall apart, and fall apart quite quickly. Already the temptation to disintegrate, to dismantle what has been achieved over the last decades, risks overwhelming the United Kingdom. Let us never underestimate how quickly 'destiny henceforward shared' can turn into '*sauve qui peut*'.

The UEF has a proud history of refining federalist thought in Europe. We do it well. We are a rich intellectual family with strong historical ties. Yet we must now speak more boldly outside the family circle. The Fundamental Law drafted by our colleagues in the Spinelli Group and published by the *Bertelsmann Stiftung* is a good start because it shows what a federal union would really be like, as well as how it can be done.[1]

David Cameron may be able to peddle his defeatist prospectus of a weaker, looser confederation of nation states; but in the Fundamental Law we now have our own optimistic prospectus of a strong, democratic

[1] The Spinelli Group, *A Fundamental Law of the European Union*, (Bertelsmann Stiftung, 2013). Also in eBook version via www.spinelligroup.eu.

federal union of states and citizens. The UEF manifesto which we will vote on tomorrow is the next big step: once passed it will be promoted to all the European political parties, including their champions, the *Spitzenkandidaten*, whom they will elect to lead their electoral campaigns into the May fight and beyond.

The Crisis and the Weakness of the European Demos[*]

Josep BORRELL

All the changes that have come about in Europe because of the crisis, particularly those that still need to be implemented, imply a transfer of sovereignty to a supranational level that should be accompanied by the necessary democratic control at that same level. This has not been the case until now, and the crisis itself can explain it. But for the future, we must consider the political model the EU is going to adopt. This may be, as is well known, intergovernmental or communitarian. It is not clear which of the two paths is easier, and it is even less evident which enjoys more support from the European public. We have already learnt the risks brought about by the elites' wilfulness when they propose rushing headlong toward political integration. Those of us who were members of the Convention believed that the idea of a constitution would awaken the pro-European enthusiasm of the people. But suspicions about the construction of a super-European state were more important, and the project was rejected. The change brought about by the crisis has not gone in the direction of federalism. The intergovernmental logic of assistance in exchange for budgetary discipline has predominated without increasing fiscal harmonization.

Since 2010, when a Eurozone member state needs financial assistance it is not the communitarian budget that offers it. It is financed by the other governments in proportion to their own resources and controlled by their national parliaments. It could have been done differently, by giving resources to the communitarian fund that gives financial assistance to EU countries outside of the Eurozone that have problems with their balance of payments. But there was a preference for an intergovernmental system, of which the ESM is the most elaborate expression.

In this way, the problems with the democratic legitimacy of EU decisions have been aggravated. Quoting Pisani-Ferry the problem with this system is that general European interests are not well represented, the role of the Commission is limited and the EP plays almost no role at all.

* Published in Issue 3/2015.

The member states, through the European Council, have been in charge of making decisions under Germany's predominant role. Politics continue to be national, and decisions to contribute with resources or to make adjustments belong to national parliaments. Each one of them responds to its national interest. They should not be blamed for that, because that is their role. As we have already stated, national interest is perceived very differently if one is standing in Berlin or in Nicosia.

The intergovernmental model seems to agree more with the weakness of the European demos and strong differences of identity among European people. But guaranteeing legitimacy and political control in an intergovernmental model requires complex institutional changes and difficult modifications to the Treaties.

A serious development of federalization requires giving the EU, or the Eurozone alone, enough fiscal capability to finance European public goods and stabilize transfers. To increase the legitimacy of the EU, the EU must appear as an agent that manages 'its' own resources instead of a part of the resources of the states. The EP should be able to vote to create European taxes. This would greatly increase the perception of its importance. If 'no taxation without representation' was once the claim, Europe must now say 'no representation without taxation.'

This would be the opportunity for the EU to create truly European taxes based on the wealth generated by the very process of integration through the development of the single market. Or by taxing the type of phenomena that respect no borders but that we want to control, such as financial transactions, or that we want to combat, like CO_2 emissions.

At the basis of the EU legitimacy problems, and particularly the Eurozone's, we find the weakness of its social dimension. The crisis has made this lack of legitimacy worse because it has required more discipline and more solidarity. Both dynamics require institutions that have the legitimacy to make decisions that affect fundamental political questions. It will be necessary to combine the two sources of legitimacy that converge in the structure of Europe, the legitimacy of states and the legitimacy of citizens, evolving toward a bicameral system in which the EP fully assumes the representation of the people and the EU Council assumes territorial representation. The Commission should be an executive power supported by a parliamentary majority. Its president should be elected based on the results of the European elections and should be able to name the commissioners. The number of commissioners should be reduced. The European Parliament should have legislative initiative.

The "federal" budget for the Eurozone, notably greater than the current 1%, should be based on expenses of transfers and investments of a countercyclical nature, such as the unemployment insurance on a European scale recently proposed by the IMF. This would imply breaking another taboo: that the EU cannot intervene in interpersonal transfers. It would imply a harmonization of labour policies. The mechanisms of interpersonal solidarity would relocate asymmetrical shocks, sharing costs among the entire EU. The interpersonal solidarity mechanisms are produced in consolidated political communities such as those found in national communities – or discussed communities, such as Cataluña today, when the national community is not perceived as such. And this is not the case of the EU. Moving from a limited and conditioned solidarity among states to a solidarity among citizens requires a shared *ethos*. But while this is a utopic idea, that is what we should address when in the construction of a political union. It makes sense to have a single currency that demands the coordination of economic and fiscal policies in order to set up the Eurozone as a federation similar to the American model. In reality, the United States was born as a federation when Hamilton converted state debt into federal debt, which would in part be the effect of eurobonds. But I doubt that we are living a Hamiltonian moment in Europe at this time. Hamilton could do it because states' debts had been generated in the fight against a common enemy, colonial England, and Europe lacks today a common enemy to make us consolidate our goals.

Instead, we as Europeans should consolidate our goals around a common objective that can no longer be based on avoiding a repetition of the horrors of the past, but on achieving future benefits that can be perceived in daily life. As Habermas says, the only political project that can give legitimacy to integration and mobilize European citizens is the survival of the "social model", the European way of life in the face of globalization. But we must be conscious that nowadays the citizens of many countries think that the EU project, particularly its economic project, has done no good in this regard and even threatens the social norms they want to defend.

Europe and the World*

John PINDER

The European Union has moved quite far towards a federal system for its internal affairs, and the Constitution takes it significantly farther, though with notable exceptions in fields such as macroeconomic policy, the ceiling for the Union's budget expenditure and the opt outs from the euro and from Schengen. But the institutional system for external relations remains predominantly confederal: intergovernmental and subject to the veto for foreign, security and defence policy; and with a variety of federal mixed with intergovernmental elements in other fields, mainly economic and environmental. The Union Minister for Foreign Affairs, as President of the Foreign Affairs Council, which is responsible for the former, and Vice President of the Commission, in which he is responsible for the latter, will have to ride simultaneously two quite different horses.

Examination of the causes of the sharp difference between the quasi federal character of the Union's internal polity and the confederal character of governance of its external affairs may throw some light on the significance of existing federal elements and the potential for their further development. There are grounds to believe that the incremental creation of the internal polity has been driven by the response to the existential challenge that had been posed by World War Two, which made the founder members ready to share some sovereignty in order to ensure that the Westphalian system of sovereign nation states would never again lead to war among them. This fundamental motive has been largely ignored in much of the academic literature, because it kills the sacred cow of the realist and related schools, while the neofunctionalists were so fascinated by their spillover clockwork that they neglect the original motive which wound it up, as well as largely contributing to keep it in motion; while since their glory days, before the Second World War War crowded them out, the English speaking federalists failed to achieve substantial academic respectability.

It happened that the sharing of sovereignty also enabled the Community's member states to manage their growing economic interdependence to their mutual benefit; and that led Britain, among others, to join. But the original motive remained powerful enough to drive member states through the phases

---

* Published in Issue 3/2004.

of common market, single market and single currency, accompanied by the development of institutions in a federal direction all of which impinged significantly on sovereignty.

That motive, however, did not generally extend to the sharing of sovereignty with respect to the Union's external policies, which were not seen as an essential element in ensuring peace among the member states. Nor, until recently, did merging that aspect of sovereignty seem necessary for their security, for the only apparent existential threat came from the Soviet Union; and the United States, leading the Atlantic Alliance, was able to look after that.

Now, however, global threats have intensified, involving the spread of weapons of mass destruction, wars, failed states, terrorism, global warming, monetary instability, mass poverty and mass migration. The US as the sole superpower cannot cope with them. The US and China as the only superpowers in the not too distant future would be an unstable, unpredictable combination. The EU, with its economic weight, experience of creating its own peace system, worldwide relationships and capacity for partnership with the US and other major states, has the potential to be the world's principal peace building, and prosperity generating, power. The member states and citizens are predisposed towards strengthening the global multilateral system, with third world countries, some of which are fast becoming major world powers, fully on board. Already in 1954, Jean Monnet envisaged that the Community could show how mankind could work together for a more peaceful and prosperous future[1]. Surely the Union could, half a century later, and faced with global existential challenges, apply its institutions and instruments of external policy to help move the world in that direction. That is the perspective in which the following outline of federal and intergovernmental elements in its present arrangements for external policy, including provisions of the Constitution, is presented.

Trade, money, aid, climate change

The EEC Treaty provided effective federal elements for the Community's commercial policy, with the common external tariff as its principal instrument and the Commission as its negotiator, responsible to the Council which was to move to qualified majority voting. Already in the Kennedy round of trade negotiations in the mid 1960s, this had a remarkable effect, with the Community proving itself an equal partner of the United States, which had hitherto been able to determine the results of previous rounds virtually

---

1 Jean Monnet, *Les Etats Unis d'Europe ont commencé. La Communauté Européenne du Charbon et de l'Acier: discours et allocutions 1952-1954* (Paris: Robert Laffont, 1955, p. 128).

unilaterally[2]. The EU and the US have remained more or less equal partners in subsequent rounds as well as in the establishment of the World Trade Organisation, with its potential to bring the rule of law into the heart of the international economy. While the results have been generally liberalising for the advanced industrial countries, the Union has not yet used this federal power to bring third world states into the system as whole hearted participants.

Four decades later the lesson that a federal trade applied by institutions with essential federal elements can change the balance of power in the world has still not been learnt, for although the euro has the potential to outweigh the dollar as an international currency, the US still dominates the international monetary system and in particular the International Monetary Fund. Yet if the states participating in the euro were to combine their IMF quotas, and hence voting rights, as the existing Treaty and Article III-90 of the Constitution allow, and as some other groups of states in the IMF already do, the resulting federal instrument would give it greater voting power than the US. Both would have the right of veto, so would have to arrive at mutual accommodations, as they have done in the field of trade. In doing so, the EU is likely to be more inclined than the US to work towards a just and stable world monetary system, taking full account of the interests of third world countries.

Development aid is also particularly important in that, in addition to combating poverty, it can contribute to the development of pluralist democracies and market economies under the rule of law and thus help countries to become full participants with due influence in the world's economic and political system. The EU provides some 55 per cent of the world's aid, about one fifth of which is a federal instrument from the Union budget and four fifths comes from the member states. The Union's aid to emergent market economies and democracies, particularly in the Central and East European accession states, has given it much useful experience; and the annual budget of over 100 million through the European Initiative for Democracy and Human Rights is particularly relevant, in contributing to an essential basis for an eventual global community. But the target of 0.7 per cent of Union GDP for development aid is far from being achieved; and the Union's share may not be substantially increased so long as the decision on the size of its budget remains subject to the unanimity rule, with a financial perspective probably not much above 1 per cent of GDP until 2012.

Despite the complication of mixed competences, with the Union having substantial powers in the field of the environment and the member states retaining them in crucial aspects of energy policy, the Union managed to

---

2 Lawrence B. Krause, *European Integration and the United States* (Washington, DC: The Brookings Institution, 1968, pp. 224-5).

lead a critical mass of states towards agreement on the Kyoto Protocol, embodying a significant, even if inadequate, measure to control emissions of greenhouse gases and hence to make a start in counteracting climate change and in particular global warming, which may well be the gravest of the existential threats facing humanity. But American opposition has weakened the Protocol's effectiveness and prevented, so far, its entry into force. This has led to a proposal for a global climate community, which would bring together countries from North and South of the world to establish a group committed to reduce emissions by more than half by the middle of this century, with institutions embodying principles akin to those of the European Community in its early days and with substantial support for the technological adaptation of third world countries in order to ensure sustainable development[3]. The initiative would have to come from the EU, with partners such as India, Brazil, South Africa, Japan and Canada as well as many others; and the intention would be to encourage those remaining outside to join the founder members, as has happened in the EU, which could be one way of approaching a global community system. Like Britain in relation to the European Community, the United States would be apt to join once the global climate community had been seen to work. Here again, the Union would surely need a more federal system, including for its financial resources, in order to be able to put such a policy into full effect.

The United Nations, Nato and European defence

The strengthening of the United Nations and its institutions is an objective shared by the Union's member states, although a satisfactory reform of the Security Council to enable the Union to be properly represented doubtless remains a long way off. This reflects, of course, the refusal of Britain and France to renounce their status as permanent members, but also the early stage of the Union's defence cooperation, with some steps being taken, but on a strictly intergovernmental basis.

If the Union's policies in matters of soft security are to be fully credible, however, it will have to be able to undertake substantial military operations in fields such as crisis management, peace keeping and peace-making, starting with the rapid reaction force. Nor, while it is unrealistic to envisage developing military power that could rival that of the United States, should the Union be inhibited from further incremental development of its own defence capacity, seen as complementary to the US in the Atlantic Alliance. This process will, in order to be effective, have to be facilitated in future constitutional reforms by introducing federal

3 Christopher Layton, *A Climate Community: A European Initiative with the South, European Essay N. 15* (London: Federal Trust, Revised Second Edition, 2003).

elements into the institutions relating to armed forces. If enough political will is generated, this would lead eventually to the integration of armed forces within a federal state.

Federal reform of the system for external policy

Thus the Union could develop an impressive external policy in the major fields of soft security and a certain capacity in hard security, even before any further constitutional reform. The European Foreign Minister should have significant influence, both as a Vice President of the Commission, 'responsible there for handling foreign affairs and for coordinating other aspects of the Union's external action', and, as President of the Foreign Affairs Council, contributing to 'the development of' and being required to 'carry out' the common foreign policy' (Art. I-27).

Such evidence of the Union's ability to work effectively for improvement of the world's political and economic system could attract very substantial support for the vision of the Union as the world's principal peace building power. Eurobarometer surveys have repeatedly shown that a substantial majority of citizens favour a common foreign policy; and the strength of feeling about such matters was shown by the millions throughout the Union who demonstrated in 2003 against the war in Iraq. So there is potential support for radical action to counter the global threats, which could provide a political basis for further constitutional reform.

The Constitution opens the way to this by giving the European Parliament the opportunity to secure the calling of a Convention to consider constitutional amendments (Art. IV-7); and the provisions for enhanced and structured cooperation offer a way for a core of states to put relevant arrangements into effect, even if others prefer to stand aside and reserve their right to join later. Thus Europeans have the opportunity to respond to the global existential challenges by developing federal structures to deal with the Union's external policy, as they did in the 1950s with their response to Europe's own existential challenge by developing an increasingly federal structure for its internal polity.

The Union of the Peoples of Europe and the Example of Mandela*

Tzvetan TODOROV

The Union of the peoples of Europe commenced as a reaction against the wars which had devastated the continent in the 20th century, or against the menace of totalitarian regimes. Paradoxically, the politicians who contributed most to its birth were the worst enemies of those peoples: first Hitler, then Stalin. The overcoming of national divergences was possible as a result of the perils threatening the continent: the return of war, the imposition of a Communist regime. On the one hand, the constitution of (unified) European politics is a success: wars have become impossible between member-States and attempts to overthrow democratic governments have failed.

On the other hand, the implausibility of inter-State wars in Europe is at the heart of a tragic illusion: that of automatic invulnerability, extended also to the extra-European world. It is shown by the exiguity of military expenditures in the majority of European States. Truth be told, Europeans chose a different solution: to delegate their own defense to a loyal ally, the United States, while obtaining security advantages without taking on the relative costs. Nonetheless, this free-ride policy has its drawbacks. In fact, from the moment Europeans rely on others they give up effective control on the security measures taken by the latter. Consequently, they cannot protest against the use of such measures without losing face: in case they do not approve them, why does not the European Union directly provide for its own security? To mention recent examples, how can it denounce the torture of enemy prisoners, legalized by a previous US administration? How can it dissociate itself from the massive use of drones, destined to execute faraway suspects, never brought to justice in court?

How can Europeans protest against the general surveillance of all means of communication throughout entire segments of their population, and even of allied Heads of State? In all these cases, we should expect an incontrovertible reply: these measures – they would say – are indispensable not only for our own security but also for yours.

Hence, Europe would do better if it assumed on itself its own security, in order to establish a better balance between efficacy and legality while

* Published in Issue 2/2014.

escaping from the temptation of excesses – what ancient Greeks referred to as *hubris*. This attitude of moderation, able to preserve and keep together different policy principles, may become the EU's trademark also in other fields related to public policies. In particular, the one regarding relations between politics and economics. In Soviet-style dictatorships, economic needs were entirely subjugated to political diktat. The consequences are known: empty store shelves, chronic shortages, populations turning to ingenious measures to satisfy their needs.

However, in the contemporary state of world economy another peril has emerged: the globalized economy, free from any constraint by politics, tends to even subdue the latter. The term "democracy" has lost its significance: power does not belong to the people any more, but to multinational corporations. To sum up this last point, only a very limited number of individuals (those whose power derives from their wealth) determines peoples' destiny. In principle, the European Union would have the capacity to propose, and even impose, more balanced relations among different powers, in order to avoid that the pursuance of economic efficiency leads necessarily to the destruction of any social protection and legal control – in a few words, of life quality, that is the ultimate goal of our institutions.

In the defense sector, as well as in the economic one, the EU would succeed where single States are destined to fail: military self-protection without legalizing torture and obviating the problems of a globalized economy. But in order to face these challenges and thus become a world player, it is imperative for the EU to strengthen its own unity. This evolution must proceed hand in hand with a democratization implying the transfer of powers from the European Council – which brings together the EU Heads of State and Government – to the EU Parliament, whose members are elected by EU citizens. It should be the parliament to elect the executive body, the Commission, presided by a President who would also be the President of the European Union (a function now absurdly divided between different people). For the time being, this desirable course of European institutions meets with a considerable obstacle: the attitude of the political elites in each country, fearful of losing at the European level the prerogatives they enjoy at the national level (according to the principle: "half a loaf is better than no bread"). How can we convince them to give up voluntarily their power? Maybe the endeavor is not so impossible. After all, Nelson Mandela succeeded in persuading the South African government to peacefully cede him its power…

Until that happy day comes (for the European Union), every measure aimed at strengthening the EU Parliament is a step forward in the right direction. The higher the participation in the EU elections, the greater the legitimacy of the Parliament will be.

Europe's Place in the World in the 21st Century*

Peter D. SUTHERLAND

In light of probable increasing threats to Europe during the 21st century, we need a more coherent and effective EU as an actor on the international stage. None of the 25 nation states of the EU (even the most powerful) can be truly effective or sometimes even relevant acting alone. Our publics seem to grasp this point better than our politicians. Eurobarometer polls across Europe highlight strong support for "more Europe" in foreign and security policy. There is an expectation among our international partners also that Europe should assume greater global responsibilities. On some global issue such as Kyoto and the international criminal court, the EU has already provided leadership, showing what can be done when we are united and speaking with one voice. There remains, as Christopher Hill wrote some years ago, an "expectation-capabilities gap" in EU foreign policy.

The world is likely to become more dangerous for Europe. The security, economic and demographic trends are not encouraging. Europe will continue to grow modestly – in GDP and perhaps membership – but such technological advantage as it may have in areas as information technology, biotechnology, and nanotechnology will be eroded. Europeans will by 2025 comprise a mere 6% of the world population, while Africa and the Middle East will see a high population growth. The prognosis is for tensions and strong migratory pressures in the regions around Europe, at a time when Europe is becoming increasingly dependent on the rest of the world, especially for energy. It is forecast that by 2030 Europe will be externally dependent for 90% of its oil and 65% of its gas. China and India will drive global energy demand, and seek new sources in Central Asia, Africa and the Middle East. In this and other ways, European security interests may be directly or indirectly challenged by tensions arising not only in the near neighbourhood but also further afield.

Europe has the potential to rise to these challenges and to share in the new opportunities created by emerging markets and globalisation more generally but can only do so by continuing to adapt and develop institutionally.

---

* Published in Issue 2/2007. Excerpts from the Charlemagne Lecture – 22nd November 2006.

From the very beginning the Treaty of Rome recognized that there could be no internal market without a customs union that, in turn, could not survive without a common trade policy. Today it is even more clear that internal and external policies are interdependent, especially in a world of open markets and free capital movements. Economic and monetary union has led to the emergence of the euro as the world's second most important international reserve and trade currency, giving increased influence to the EU globally.

Most of the internal policies of the EU have substantive international implications. For example, the completion of the internal market has led to the adoption of EU standards in key technologies around the world (China's motor industry, food safety, mobile communications and so on). EU competition policy not merely provides an important internal regulatory instrument, but addresses issues such as international cartels or abuses by dominant undertakings that may affect global markets. There are also strong demands from third countries to cooperate with EU programmes like research policy, education and transport. The fast development of EU policy in the area of justice and home affairs is reflected in the external dimensions of these issues.

In many of these areas policy is a shared responsibility between the EU and the Member States and this presents particular challenges in achieving coherence. The inaccurately named constitutional treaty tried to deal with these problems. In part this was by proposing a new position of EU foreign minister that would have given the EU – so it was hoped – more coherence, more consistency and more visibility. These were and remain good proposals. I deeply regret the lack of progress on them during the current *pause for reflection*. It seems to me that we have too much pause, and too little reflection. However cautiously, we must continue a process of giving responsibility to the Commission to develop policies in the common interest rather than relying purely on dialogue between capitals. We should recognise that intergovernmentalism has generally not worked in the past and is not the answer for the future. The euphemism used for this intergovernmentalism is often the word "cooperation", but co-operation between sovereign states is not enough. This is essentially the failed model that gave rise to the need for the EU in the first place.

One of the main reasons for the EU's success has been adherence to the rule of law. This fact of supranational law at its base distinguishes the EU from all other intergovernmental associations of states. Member States have accepted that they will sometimes be outvoted in the Council in some vital economic and social matters because the EU is a community of law. All Member States are equal before the law. Governments may protest and procrastinate, but in the end the system works because all members accept the primacy of Community law. This law-based approach also characterises the EU's approach to foreign policy. It is sometimes excessively obsessed with agreements, rules and regulations. But I think there is great merit in the EU championing a rules-based approach to the international system.

From its inception, the EU has worked for the gradual opening of global markets and a rules-based international trading system. Had there been no EU there would be no WTO and Europe today would consist of a number of fragmented and protectionist areas totally incapable of contributing to globalisation.

The reason for our success in international trade is that we have adopted a supranational approach to decision-taking. We have a corps of highly professional and coherent officials in Brussels that produce timely and relevant policies taking into account a genuine EU perspective on issues. This allows the Commissioner to speak with the full authority of 25 member states in trade negotiations. Our partners may on occasion not like our policies but they do respect us as a major player.

There are important lessons we can learn from how we operate in the trade field that are equally applicable to foreign policy. The Union could be as effective in other policy areas if it wanted to, simply by providing for a single representation. The aim must be for the future EU foreign minister to speak under a similar mandate in the CFSP field where there is an agreed policy or common strategy. Member States would thus continue to enjoy bilateral relations with third countries but they would not discuss EU policy towards them in areas of agreed EU policy. Solana is already accepted as a spokesman in some key areas of foreign policy, for example in the recent nuclear talks over Iran, but the situation is complicated by the fact that the 'big three' EU Member States tend to operate separately in fields such as this. Other Member States are suspicious of this model, which resembles a *directoire* rather than a real common policy. I see nothing wrong with smaller task forces being established, under a Council mandate, to deal with particular issues. However, these groups should be under strict reporting requirements to the whole Council and be subject to its ultimate authority when acting on behalf of the EU.

The foreign policy machinery works badly at present. European foreign policy has always been overly bureaucratic. There are numerous squabbles over issues of competence and too many actors involved – the Member States, the Council, the High Representative, the Special Representatives, the Commission, the Parliament, each with their bureaucracies, interests and ambitions. Some improvements have been made as a result of Solana's appointment, yet he operates with woefully inadequate resources. The situation is further confused by the six-monthly rotating Presidency, often setting its own (national) priorities. A plethora of different legal bases for external action in different fields further complicates the picture, as does the fact that the EU itself has no clear legal personality, which would have been remedied by the Constitution.

In light of the challenges facing Europe we cannot continue to allow all decisions to be taken on the basis of the lowest common denominator. I recognise that you cannot have Qualified Majority Vote for military action, but for the vast majority of foreign policy issues there should be no insuperable problem in introducing majority voting. This could be done in stages. First, with an 'emergency brake' to provide for consultations at the European Council in the event of a major disagreement; second, moving to a super qualified majority; and then, some day, in a third stage, to the normal QMV procedures. I understand the *Quai d'Orsay* carried out a survey last year seeking decisions since 2000 where France would have been outvoted in foreign policy. With the notable exception of Iraq (and here military action was involved) there were no cases. I rather suspect there would be a similar result if the same assessment was made in the United Kingdom or Germany.

Whilst I believe we must move steadily towards QMV in foreign policy, I also recognise that this itself is not a panacea for an improved foreign policy and will take time to achieve. This is why I think there has to be action on a number of other issues. These include the designation of an EU foreign minister (combining the roles of High Representative and Vice President of the Commission), the creation of a European diplomatic service, legal personality for the EU, and the end of the rotating Presidency role in foreign affairs. Some of these improvements require changes in existing Treaty provisions. That may take time. If necessary, I think we can make the first two of these improvements without a new Treaty. These proposals were all in the constitutional treaty and I do not wish to underestimate that fact.

We need to go much further and consider what could be done even before any new treaty is ratified. One priority must be to enhance the complementarity of various policies and to reconcile different objectives (for example in trade, agriculture, development, environment or migration). There is already a high level of consensus on the broad framework of the EU's external objectives. What is missing is a more systematic approach to setting strategic objectives and political priorities at both geographical and thematic level so that policy objectives guide the choice of policy instruments (rather than the reverse). There should also be improved upstream co-ordination to promote consensus on issues of EU relevance that are subject to discussions in multilateral organisations, for of global governance, and regional organisations.

Even when the EU has clear objectives and an agreed course of action, the impact and effectiveness of our action is often hampered by mixed messages as well as slow and complex implementing procedures. The EU therefore needs to ensure that once a policy decision has been taken by the EU, all actors integrate this into their diplomatic and public messages as well as in their own policy development. This implies reinforced coordination in Brussels as well as better use of the EU's diplomatic capacities to convey clear, single messages to partners.

There is considerable scope for Member States to co-operate more effectively in third countries. Jointly the EU and the Member States dispose by far the largest diplomatic machinery in the world. The EU has ten times more missions and three times more personnel at its disposal than the US. But is Europe as effective as the US in foreign policy? Are we using the human and material resources which we collectively invest in foreign policy in the most effective way?

If foreign ministries do not ask the question, finance ministries will certainly ask why there needs to be 25 separate EU Member State missions, plus a Commission delegation, in countries x, y and z, when the EU is supposed to operate a common foreign policy. We must also ask ourselves what kind of people should we be recruiting to serve Europe's interests. European diplomacy needs more experts on climate change, inward investment, migration and terrorism.

There is also much that could be done to improve co-operation between Council and Commission. There should be increased sharing of intelligence and a greater exchange of diplomats and officials between the Member States and the EU institutions. A major increase in the tiny CFSP budget is also necessary if the EU is to make any progress towards fulfilling its global ambitions. At the same time, there needs to be clarity as to responsibility for different budget lines. Defence ministers also need to become more involved in EU affairs. It is surely time that there was a European defence white paper rather than 25 separate papers. Finally, I am convinced that it will be important to enlist the support of the European public, through the involvement of the European Parliament and national parliaments as well as the media and NGOs, for the goals of the EU in foreign policy.

In conclusion, the EU has developed steadily as an international actor during the past decade. Much has been achieved but the record could have been better if we had acted quicker through strengthened institutions. The proposals I have outlined would be seen in some capitals as being at the modest end of the spectrum, but if implemented they could lead to a significant improvement in the EU's external performance. Of course, foreign policy remains a sensitive area and Member States are keen to retain their historic prerogatives and traditional links. Foreign ministries are also reluctant to negotiate themselves into a reduced role while there remain unanswered questions about legitimacy and significant differences of foreign policy culture, experiences and expectations. But if we are to meet the challenges of the 21st century we have to recognise that the adoption of the Community method would bring significant advantages. In the short-term, individual actors and institutions may see advantages in the freedom of manoeuvre that comes from exercising their responsibilities in an autonomous way, but in the medium and long term, the global influence of the EU will depend upon the ability of the Member States to speak with one voice – and to take the necessary decisions in a timely manner.

The Search for a European Identity: Who Are We?*

Giampiero BORDINO

In the long constitutional process towards Europe's political unity the issue of the European demos, of its identity, has often been regarded, and above all dealt with, as secondary with respect to the issue of the political order and the institutional arrangement required for the Union. But the issue of the demos and its identity – Who are we Europeans? What is the meaning of being Europeans? How can we be simultaneously European and Italian, or French or German and so on? – cannot be dodged. The lack of an identity and of a feeling of belonging can in fact turn against the on-going institutional processes, as the negative outcome of the referenda on the ratification of the European Constitution shows. If we are not adequately conscious and convinced of "belonging" to a common European space, there is the risk, as there are identity-related urges to satisfy, that other and different spaces of belonging (localist, ethnic, national at best) will be cultivated to a hypertrophic degree, and that in between these spaces attitudes tending to exclusion and the generation of conflicts will be primed, as our common, even recent (Yugoslavia, the Balkans) European history tragically reminds us.

To this end, some reflection on European identity looks necessary. But first, a more general and preliminary reflection would be appropriate on what identity means today in the globalized world of the 21st century we have just entered. As our individual experience may tell us, identity never is – and never has been, not even before this global age – solely or simply a "given". It is "a process", the result of a more or less conscious elaboration of identity construction which is the result, on the one hand, of our past, and on the other hand of our future. Our identity, in other words, depends upon what we have been and also upon what we plan to become. With respect to the past (the history behind us) we all – both as individuals and as human groups – inevitably make choices and selections: we pick up the fragments that are more effective for our present and for our future projects. Over the rest we draw a veil and forget them. Hence not even the past is a given, for it too is a process and a construction. History, as Benedetto Croce said, is always "contemporary", because it is

* Published in Issue 3/2006.

always revisited at the light of the trends of today and the intentions for the future.

To understand this, it is sufficient to think of how national identities in Europe have been built over the past centuries. In all cases, during the course of national unification processes, on the one hand fragments of the past (those functional to the unification process, considered useful for legitimizing it) have been picked up, and, on the other hand, projects for the future have been made. One convenient interpretation of the past legitimized the unification process, and that in turn brought people to look at the past in a different way. National identity – ethnic, linguistic, cultural – was used by the States and their ruling classes as a "symbolic umbrella" for legitimizing political unification (and it also legitimized, with tragic results, the wars always waged in the name of one's own identity against the others') as if it were a natural given. In reality, a national identity was never "a given", but has always been a construct: for example, Italian national identity, above all linguistic, is the result of mass schooling, of mandatory conscription, of the unifying action of State bureaucracy, of the internal migration processes that have hybridized peoples and cultures, and lastly of the mass communication media, with television taking the first place.

In the 21st century, with globalization, this evident process-related and constructed character of identity has, so to speak, collapsed. In fact, today both individual and collective identities increasingly depend on and are built through processes of transnational mobility which affect all societies and territories with ever greater intensity. The mobility of goods, people and "signs" (news, images, values) nurture every day people's imagination, offer a growing variety of identity options, make new life choices possible. As anthropological and sociological studies have highlighted in the last years, identity therefore appears ever more mobile, composite, plural, even "floating". This applies in the first place to the hundred millions of people of various transnational *Diasporas* (American-Indians, Anglo-Pakistanis, French-Moroccans, Italian-Americans, etc.: the new "hyphenated" identities) that dot the world and originate from mobility and migrations, but it applies also to some extent to all those who with globalization are experiencing ever more various and articulated social relations in their local context, and those who are themselves mobile and travel to different countries, surf transnational and global media networks (Satellite TV's and the Internet), watch and become acquainted with different and distant images and life-models.

If we now, as is necessary, reflect on European identity, we are faced with a new aspect of 21st century identity. European identity cannot be conceived or searched for as if it were a "natural fact" which even the present national or local identities were not; instead, it must be constructed both by looking to the past and at the same time making plans for the future. The path to follow for identity-building is to rethink history and at the same time plan and realize the new *polis*. This is exactly what the Founding Fathers of the European Community from Schumann to Monnet, from Einaudi to Spinelli did in their day, when they critically reconsidered Europe's wars and at the same time devised and proposed a new project for the Europe of peace.

European identity, in this perspective, is unlike what happened in the past with national identities. It can be neither univocal, nor exclusive. Being European must by necessity mean having a plural identity open to differences, facing the world, and hence cosmopolitan. It is not an "ethnic" identity – for that has not been true even of national identities – but "ethical" in the etymological meaning of the word: namely, of custom, of life-style, of values. It must be able to face both the complex and composite character of European history and society, and the new transnational dimension of the globalized world in which we are living.

European history presents, for this purpose, many historical experiences and cultural contributions that can be singled out and placed among our roots: Greek philosophy, Christian universalism, the Jewish culture of the *Diaspora*, the multicultural and tolerant experience of Islamic Spain, Humanism and the Renaissance, the Enlightenment, liberal political thought, the theories and practices in the 19th century of the social State and of inclusive democracy, and so on. In European history, as in that of the other continental civilizations, there is everything and its contrary too: peace and war, solidarity and massacres, the Christianity of the Crusades and the Wars of Religion, and the Franciscan and ecumenical one, the culture of equality and that of biological and racial inequality, liberal democracy and the Fascist and Stalinist totalitarianism, the nationalist culture and that of supra-national federalism. Europe, in retrospect, appears as a great depository of many possible and diverse identities, often not mutually reconcilable, among which it is necessary for us to make choices according to the values of the present day and the projects for the future.

As to identity and belonging, Europe is confronted, in our global century, with a decisive challenge: how to promote and ensure a peaceful and consensual living together, sharing the same territory with human groups which are much more diverse (because of origin, language, culture of reference, etc., besides social status) and much more mobile (because of migration, work, etc.) than ever before. How can we make possible and construct institutions adapted to such pluri-identity (the "hyphenated" identity): that is, the pluri-belonging, pluri-languagespeaking, pluri-citizenship of such human groups? Already today we are simultaneously citizens of a particular nation and of Europe; and tomorrow, hopefully, of the world too.

I believe it is evident that in order to realize a coexistence of such a kind it is necessary to promote the idea of a plural identity open to diversity, mild, cosmopolitan, for the alternative would be the totalitarian State and the ethnic cleansing that we have already experienced. This is a challenge with which other civilizations and other continents are also confronted. If we are to avert the "clash of civilizations" which some are actively trying to fuel and of which others passively complain, it is necessary to call on all civilizations to become mutually committed to such an identity model. In this respect, we need "more Europe", not less. Europe must put herself in a position to propose to the world "a pact of civilizations" (a new global *foedus*) that may in time defuse the permanent worldwide civil war that seems to have started. It may well lie right here, in this perspective and in this new European identity project for the 21st century.

Where Do the Boundaries of European Integration Lie?*

Heinz TIMMERMANN

The nature of the EU

Where do the boundaries of European integration lie? On such an issue a lively political and scientific debate and controversial discussions are currently taking place within the European Union. This applies to both aspects of EU integration to which I want to refer here also against the background of cultural identities: the inner deepening of such integration and the geographical enlargement of the Union towards its neighbouring States. The two aspects are intertwined since the enlargement of the EU is in the end premised on its deepening, if we intend to provide the Union with both internal and external capacity of action. Conversely, the deepening has however often given impulse to the enlargement.

Against this background, the EU with its 480 million citizens has become highly attractive and the number of its Member States has risen in the meantime to 27, while the possibilities of further growth are still open. It has gained global political capacity of action and, increasingly, military power too; it has become the most powerful commercial area in the world and the most important donor of international development aid; the Euro has emerged as a leading currency in the international financial architecture, together with the dollar. Thanks to the CFSP/ESDP[1] the EU is present in 13 areas of conflict all over the world, whereby due to her extensive engagement it resorts to military means only as an *extrema ratio*. The EU can make use of an impressive range of instruments, from diplomacy to trade policies, development policies, and the means of justice and police as well.

Furthermore, the gain in power and influence has so far boosted the internal capacity of action only in a limited way. Decisions require the unanimity of the Member States, a fact which limits deeper integration. The willingness to a further enlargement clashes against the internal differences especially in the light of Turkey's approach at its borders. A symptom of all this is the breakdown of the 2005 Constitutional Treaty,

---

* Published in issue 2/2009.

1 Common Foreign and Security Policy / European Security and Defence Policy.

even if 18 of its then 25 Members have already ratified it. Whether the EU Reform Treaty of Lisbon, which is similar to it in its contents, will be ratified by all its Members or not, has yet to be seen. Where do the causes of the limits of the EU integration capacity within and without lie? Here are some suggestions:

a. The EU has no clear representations of its final aims as points of reference for future developments. The limits of its integration are rooted in its nature: it is a League of closely-cooperating States with divided and shared sovereignty; in other words, a *sui generis* actor with a multilayered system of supranational, national, and regional competences, but it is no sovereign superstate in the sense of the centralized model of the 'United States of Europe'. In this sense we can understand the idea and project of the Union as postnational rather than antinational. From this, it follows that the mandatory recognition of common universal values, based on the cultural, religious, and humanistic legacy of Europe, values which are the bases of EU membership: Liberty, Democracy, Rule of Law, Social Rights, and Attention to Human Rights. However, the functional aspects of co-operation are differently shaped in the light of the depth of the integration and are an object of debate among the Members. They extend from the minimal level of the willingness to participate to economic integration in the form of the internal market to a maximum of commonality with regard to Foreign and Security Policy. It is within this range that the clear boundaries of a deepened EU integration do emerge.

b. The problems of deepening integration derive not only from the different interests of the Member States, but also from their different historical and cultural identities. The Berlin Declaration issued in March 2007, on the occasion of the fiftieth anniversary of the Rome Treaties, openly refers to the EU decision to guarantee the various traditions of its Members and the multiplicity of its Languages, Cultures, and Religions. With the exception of Turkey, the historical and cultural differences that limit the integration are in fact less, once a largely accepted formulation has been introduced in the Reform Treaty with a general reference to God, instead of a specific link to Christianity. Many more are the differences in the respective political cultures and identities which set limits to the process of integration. In particular, this has to do with the understanding of national sovereignty: some countries want to stick to it – see Britain, the Czech Republic, Poland – while others – such as Germany, Italy, and Belgium – are clearly willing to share further slices of their sovereignty also in delicate matters. In this sense, the apparently paradoxical phenomenon becomes clear, according to which Euro skeptic Members tend to support further accessions since they see them as a means to weaken the degree of integration. Pro-integration States, by contrast, have a skeptical position towards excessive enlargement.

c. Divergences as to renouncing sovereignty are particularly linked to the Foreign and Security Policies of the Union. In December 2003 the EU adopted a 'European Security Strategy', in which its aims in the field are stated – security is understood in its military and civilian aspects. It's then up to the Member States to take part in well-defined common actions in application of the principle of 'enhanced cooperation' on what has already been achieved. The limits of the convergence of interests and integration proved to be particularly extreme in the wake of the Iraq war, when – to say it with Rumsfeld – the 'Old Europeans' such as the Germans and French refused their participation to an initiative which they deemed contrary to international law, while the 'New Europeans' of Central and Eastern Europe have engaged on the side of the US. They expected to gain security from Washington rather than from Brussels, as also highlighted by the controversies over the envisaged positioning of elements of a missilistic system in Poland and the Czech Republic.

d. Another problem on the road to further integration is constituted by the different cultures of memory between 'old' Western Europeans on the one hand and 'new' Central and Eastern Europeans on the other. They fully leave their mark on the current Foreign Policy and in particular on the relations between the EU and Russia and in this way they undermine the possibility of a common political line within the Union. The 'traumas and experiences of those for which the Cold War was a synonym of oppression and dictatorship' are here opposed to the lasting and positive experiences of peace and wealth in the West – as Günter Verheugen, the German Vice president of the EU-Commission did put it. Fears of Russian 'imperialism' are living part of the culture of memory of Poland and the Baltic States. On the grounds of a particular collective memory also in the future such fears will unfold their effects and set limits to the deepening of EU-integration. The strength of the resistance of different cultures of memory in current politics in general, their impact on the dynamic of integration in particular, and the urgency to find a common debate ground on the past, are clearly demonstrated by an appropriate plea of the German Foreign Secretary Steinmeier. In it he calls for an open and frank dialogue on the grievances of the past and wonders, 'Haven't we reached a point when historians from Russia, Poland, Germany, and the Baltic countries can elaborate a common critical and self-critical effort to balance the different national viewpoints, with which we still interpret our common history?'. This is at the moment a sort of concrete utopia. The way towards a common memory, a common understanding of history – briefly, a common European memory – is still a long one.

e. The European public sphere is characterized by an extreme mismatch between the importance of the integration process and the relevance the media attribute to it. Here the EU-integration is mostly interpreted as an elite project with a strong democratic deficit, whose causes can in particular be traced back to the intergovernmental and bureaucratic nature of the Union. This is not that correct since the competences of the European Parliament are enhanced in the Reform Treaty and national parliaments in the future would be consulted in the case of bill proposals on the part of the European Commission. The number of EU-employees is smaller than the corresponding figure in Cologne. In the same manner the overall lack of interest in the developments of the Union constitutes an obstacle towards further integration. This nourishes fears that an expanding and stronger bureaucracy in Brussels might more and more subtract competences to the national interests. A European citizenship as instrument of control and balance against integral European statehood is in the earliest stages of its development.

Scenarios of a deeper EU-integration and its boundaries

The following scenarios should not be understood as a way to belittle the astonishing results of EU-integration in terms of peace and welfare. Not least, the attractiveness of the Union to its Neighbours in Eastern Europe, the Balkans, Turkey, and the Mediterranean countries underlines the success of the EU-integration project. Also, the resumption of central elements of the abandoned Constitutional Treaty in the Reform Treaty of Lisbon shows the willingness of the 27 Members to continue the integration process and not to flow into stagnation, devolution, and disintegration.

There is agreement on the following mandatory key aspects: the inclusion of the Charter of fundamental rights in the Treaty; the extension of the co-decision procedure for the European Parliament in the form of the right of co-decision on fully-fledged European laws; the extension of the procedure of qualified majority voting in the Council; the possibility of a stronger, flexible, and different co-operation between single Members in some fields; mandatory proposals in the areas of labour laws and basic social rights; the provision of a 'High Representative for the Foreign and Security Policy', who in the person of Solana would borrow continuity and effectiveness to European foreign policy in his double function as President of the Council of Foreign Ministers and Vice President of the EU-Commission. So far in the Union three people from different institutions have been in charge of international relations.

However, as to the future steps of the integration process, many questions are still open and constitute possible sources of conflict, so that at least in the medium term the limits of integration are clear. Among them: the range of political cultures in the countries of the Union with regard to the different visions of sovereignty; the lack of a link between an effective central government and democratic participation; divergences on the question of majority voting and the development of a common political line, for example with regard to energy security as a nucleus of European politics; the international role of the EU with its alternative choices, extremely visible in the Iraq war: strong links with the USA or critical confrontation with it. From this mix of positive and problematic processes we can single out (in the wake of Johannes Varwick) three ideal typical scenarios, which give account of the integration capacity of the EU and at the same time of its limits.

a. With a great leap in the direction of a federal state, the Members are willing to further give up sovereignty; the EU develops into a supranational federation with its own Constitution, strong common institutions and procedures of control and legitimation. In this sense, it would also gain power in terms of external intervention and integration, and it would be in the condition to bring its integration potential further afield. However, the emergence of such a federal state, which would be endowed with an effective vertical power and would gradually incorporate the political and cultural identities of its Members is unlikely, and, after the early hour's idealism, currently finds less and less supporters in the political and scientific circles.

b. The 'erosion' scenario is based on the assumption that the EU would sooner or later fall apart or that it would be creepingly eroded and develop back into a free trade area. As to the causes, we can mention among others: the resurrection of power politics rivalries among the Members after the end of the East-West conflict, which had enhanced their cohesion; the growing appeal of the return to national historical/cultural roots as a reaction to the processes of Europeanization and globalization and their perceived threat to identities; the effect of a 'permanent' enlargement on national interests and political/cultural identities. However, this scenario which would rather reduce the boundaries of EU-integration and its attractiveness to candidate States is unlikely too, as all Members know, regardless of their preferences in the integration matters; in the light of increasing globalization, national 'ways' remain in fact without chances of success and would thus become counterproductive. National States are no longer in the condition to solve alone problems in such sectors as economy, energy, and international relations. A conflictual competition would again trigger historical instability in the EU-space and export it to its neighbours as well.

c. The most likely scenario is that of the already-tested praxis of the 'muddling through'. From a middle term perspective the EU remains what it is according to the Lisbon reforms: 'an incomplete and complicated sui generis political model in need of reforms, that is still indispensable for its Members and citizens and the stability of the continent', (Varwick) and at the same time does not touch on the various cultural identities, as long as they do not harm the basic European values. Even if for some time to come there won't be any deep reform or further steps towards integration, it is generally accepted that without the EU effective governance of the space it encompasses is no longer possible.

Within this framework we can think of a further deepening of what is already possible now under the current treaties, that is, a sort of 'flexible integration' whereby in a two speed model a group of States in the form of a 'nucleus' go ahead with some policies; such core remains open to the rest of the national-orientated Members who have chosen to stay behind. Examples of that are the Schengen Agreements, which have been so far adopted by 25 States, and the introduction of the Euro, which is the single currency in 16 States. Following this scenario, which is very intensively debated among the elite, the specialists, and the European public, the perspectives of domestic EU integration and that towards its neighbours are absolutely open. Since neither the EU-documents nor EU citizens show a clarity of purposes as to the integration process, it is difficult to forecast the geographical boundaries of further EU enlargements.

Geographical boundaries of EU-integration

According to Art. 49 of the 1992 Maastricht Treaty, theoretically any 'European State' has the right to apply to join the EU. Membership to the Council of Europe (a European regional organization which closely co-operates with the EU and, with its 47 Members – including Turkey – aims to defend human rights) can be seen as a criterion for qualification as a 'European State'. Hence, cultural, religious, or spiritual aspects are no requirements at all in order to join the EU and do not play any role in the decisions of the Commission and the Council. Decisive elements in joining the EU are, together with the latter's absorption capacity, the so-called three *Copenhagen criteria*: the implementation of universal human rights, the development of an efficient market economy, and the application of EU law (the *acquis communautaire*). In this sense, it sounds logical that the EU openly negotiates the accession of Islamic Turkey, that the Balkan States with their different historical and cultural legacies and religious shaping are in the list of accession candidates, while the new neighbours in Eastern Europe – the Ukraine, Moldova, and a democratized Belarus – as well as the South Caucasian countries – can nurture hopes to become Union Members.

Admittedly: while the basic possibilities of the geographical expansion of the EU are clearly circumscribed, it is difficult to forecast now the geographical limits of the EU with regard to time and space. The Lisbon

Treaty re-formulates the legal and institutional premises according to which the EU remains in principle open to new Members. Moreover, all Member States must agree on the membership application, a fact which is becoming increasingly difficult in consideration of the tension between divergent interests and an increasing number of States.

In relation to the three scenarios, we have referred to the different consequences for possibilities and boundaries of the enlargement. In the 'federal State' scenario accession would still be possible, even if the high demand of radical processes of transformation would be difficult to fulfill. On the other hand, the 'erosion scenario' would exercise a minimal pressure on neighbours, since it wouldn't require any qualitative jump. Finally, the 'muddling through' scenario puts the EU in front of the existential problem of defining its future boundaries, without jeopardizing its own identity. It calls for a well-defined balance between the absorption capacity and the maintenance of the integration dynamics on the one hand, and the maturity of the candidates on the other. In the past, the two aspects have positively influenced each other, as the combination of the enlargement to new countries and the deepening of the integration foreseen in the Treaties of Maastricht, Amsterdam, and Nice demonstrate. We don't know yet whether this could work with 30 or more Members.

Against this background, the European Neighbourhood Policy offers no membership perspective to the States in Eastern Europe and South Caucasus. By contrast, many see it as a substitute for or even a protection against such a perspective. Others see such a policy as a model in the direction of a gradual approaching of the States of the two regions to the EU, as well as the early stages of a future membership in the sense of the States of Central and Eastern Europe. Russia too, with its vision of a 'Greater Europe', would take advantage of such a flexibility of the EU Eastern borders – provided that the envisaged Treaty of Strategic Partnership between the EU and Russia with its four Common European Spaces would come into existence.

The Eurozone, the Dynamic Core of a European Federation*

Dusan SIDJANSKI

The European elections will allow us to take stock of the European Union, to assess the progress made in combating the financial crisis and the extent of the damage to the economy and European society. The sluggish revival of economic growth is not triggering a clear drop in unemployment; companies going bankrupt, poverty and a general sense of depression amongst the population are all factors which have sapped European drive. Jean Monnet's strategy of integration sector by sector ultimately leading to a political Union has reached the end of the line. Worse still, the spillover has been reversed due to the shock of the crisis and the negative effect of austerity.

Admittedly an arsenal of measures have been taken to avoid the disintegration of the Eurozone, but certain crucial questions have not yet been answered: can the euro survive in the long term without the implementation of a real economic union and in the absence of fiscal and budgetary federalism? Moreover, can the 18-member Eurozone survive and grow without a political Union and strong social cohesion? It is more and more obvious that the Member States of the Eurozone have a decisive choice to make: either they must embark on the path towards a federal political Union or accept the demise of the euro in the long run. Since coins were first invented thousands of years ago, we know that minting money is a sovereign act, a symbol of political power. No currency has survived without a political armature, in the form of a City or a State. Consequently, the Eurozone urgently needs to be strengthened by placing it within the framework of a federal Union.

Increased Economic Union

Ironically the 18 members of the pioneer federative core continue to function according to the intergovernmental method, whilst being part of a Union within which the community method is becoming widespread in the areas of the "economic community" component. Therefore the Eurozone must urgently be converted to the community method by including the

* Published in Issue 1/2014.

Commission and European Parliament, in an 18-member configuration, in the decision-making process according to qualified majority. A step has already been taken in this direction by the establishment of the Eurozone Summit. In turn the ECB, which has increased its responsibilities, could in future be given competences as regards debt, growth and employment. Proposals abound concerning the European Stability Mechanism (ESM), the economic stimulus fund, the adoption of a budget of 3% of GDP within the Eurozone. The debate about macro-economic policy is in full swing, completely unintelligible for the vast majority of citizens. For them, their main concern is job insecurity, the high cost of living for a family, in a nutshell everyday worries which seem so far removed from the realms of high politics of our European leaders. European citizens are directly affected by the repercussions of austerity, spending cuts in the field of welfare and education, along with salary cuts and reduced purchasing power. The dream of prosperity promised by a United Europe has turned into a nightmare, with no hope in sight. Hasn't the time come to launch a European Project?

Austerity is a breeding ground for the re-emergence of nationalism, together with the rise of extremist parties and movements supported by the despair of those social classes which have been sacrificed. As a result, there has been an alarming increase in the number of extreme right-wing parties such as the National Front in France and its Dutch ally, or extreme left-wing movements, anti-European protestors who use the Union and Brussels as a scapegoat. The political situation in Greece is dramatic, with the coalition government majority hanging by a thread. According to polls *Syriza*[1], a party of a rather dubious nature, is in the lead, followed by New Democracy, and in third position there looms the threat of the neo-Nazi movement "Golden Dawn"! The latter is characterised by its racism and its violence, which is counterbalanced by the assistance it provides to the most disadvantaged classes of the population.

Increased Political Union

The cradle of democracy is in danger, yet we choose to ignore this by allowing the *Troïka* to carry on with its austerity policies. The case of Greece is far from unique. The recent election of a neo-Nazi at the head of *Slovakia's Banská Bystrica* region is a shocking reminder that xenophobia and europhobia in the guise of an anti-Roma campaign is threatening Europe's fundamental values. Added to this is an abundance of populist movements. Spreading like wildfire via the social networks, they all seem to concentrate on undermining political systems and, to an

1 Alexis Tsipras, leader of Syriza, is the head of the European Left in the European Parliament.

even larger extent, the economic and social fabric. So many concurrent dangers which are darkening the European sky and in the light of which the proposed measures are likely to prove ineffectual.

Centripetal forces are at work within several European countries. In the United Kingdom, while Scotland is preparing for a referendum on its independence, Prime Minister Cameron has promised to organise a referendum on membership of the European Union under pressure from the UKIP and from a group within his own party. At the same time, the Flemish Region of Belgium is demanding its autonomy, while the government of Catalonia is putting pressure on Madrid to launch a referendum on its independence. Added to this resurgence of nationalism, we find an increasing number of regional independence movements. In order to satisfy at least some of these demands which would lead to a proliferation of micro-States, wouldn't it be wise to establish a "Senate of the Regions" within the political Union, along the lines of what was proposed by the German Länder during the negotiations on the Maastricht Treaty? This would be a means of reinforcing the autonomy of Regions and large Cities, and at the same time guaranteeing their participation in the legislative process.

The fact that the crisis is threatening democracy within the European Union is a wake-up call for European leaders and citizens. There is an urgent need to take Chancellor Merkel's warnings seriously concerning the dangers which not only the euro but also the whole Union are exposed to for lack of a political Union which makes provision for a government and a Second Chamber. These cautionary words are relayed by President Hollande's speeches in favour of an economic government and a global strategy, including a real common foreign and defence policy for a Europe speaking with one voice. France's military interventions in Mali and the Central African Republic are just such examples of actions and initiatives which in future should fall within a global strategy.

Daring to commit to a European Federation

On a global scale, the new balance of power and the challenges posed by the emerging powers such as China, India and Brazil, Russia's resurgence, require a common response if the Union aims to hold sway within the G20 and on the global playing field. The violent nature of the conflicts in the immediate surroundings of the Union, as well as the threats made by terrorist groups and criminal organisations all plead the case for the creation of a European Federation. It goes to show that there is an urgent need for the Franco-German couple to take the lead, backed by Italy and with the support of the Commission and the European Parliament. Even if it may be difficult to imagine a 28-strong political Union, it is nevertheless imperative to start with the Eurozone while allowing other Member States the possibility of joining. History has taught us that those federations which survived were constituted around a federative core.

A political Union would enable European cohesion and solidarity to be restored. It would allow the introduction of eurobonds in support of the European New Deal, which would include the financing of large-scale projects in the areas of infrastructure, communication, research and innovation, which would imply renewed impetus for education and training; a package of immediate measures providing a strong boost to employment and to the structure of small and medium-sized companies, the main employment providers. This would result in a revival of the dynamics of integration within the Eurozone and, consequently, within the European Union. Let's hope that the coming European electoral campaign will concentrate on presenting concise and intelligible proposals for a European Federation, for the European New Deal. These are the major topics likely to rekindle hope amongst the citizens of the European Union.

The Eurozone in the IMF*

Daniel Gros

Europe's leaders never tire of reminding their constituencies, almost like a mantra, that the major emerging-market countries are overturning the existing global economic order. But when it comes to recognizing that reality in the world's international financial institutions, they adopt a different tune. This is particularly true of the eurozone.

The eurozone as such has no representation in the international financial institutions. Instead, 12 eurozone countries are represented on the board of the International Monetary Fund via six different "constituencies", or country groups. The two largest, Germany and France, have a constituency all their own. Ten other eurozone members are part of four other constituencies headed by Belgium, the Netherlands, Spain and Italy. However, these four constituencies also contain more than 20 other countries, most of which are not even EU members.

Together with the Scandinavian and British constituencies, there are thus eight EU representatives on the IMF's executive board. Given that the IMF's Articles of Agreement stipulate that there can be only 20 board members, this means that 40% of all the IMF's executive directors are Europeans, with one-third coming from the eurozone.

The IMF is a prime example of the over-representation of Europeans in international fora. Counter-intuitively, however, the excessive number of Europeans actually diminishes Europe's influence, because they usually defend national interests, which are often divergent. The net effect is that common European interests are not represented at all.

Contrast this current condition of extended misery with the only sensible long-term solution: a pooling of IMF quotas by all eurozone countries. The eurozone would then have one constituency, or seat, on the Fund's executive board, filled by a candidate nominated by the eurozone group of finance ministers.

The European Central Bank could also, perhaps, be involved, nominating the deputy of the eurozone executive director at the Fund. In this way, Europe's fiscal and monetary authorities would be forced to cooperate

* Published in Issue 1/2011.

in shaping their input into IMF decisions. Many countries (including Germany) already follow this "double-headed" approach.

The eurozone representative would be very influential, because he would represent an even larger quota than that of the US. Indeed, the US Treasury's *de facto* dominance within the IMF would become a thing of the past.

But, given the scant interest of European Union members in transferring further competences (and juicy international positions) to the EU level, the chances that this solution will prevail seem remote. Germany, in particular, feels that it has no reason to share its IMF representation with other, fiscally weaker eurozone members. And the French seems scared of contagion: once France agrees to a common eurozone seat at the IMF, others could cite it as a precedent to be applied to the United Nations Security Council, where France would then risk losing its permanent seat to a common EU representative.

Until now, the rest of world could only grumble at Europe's obstinate refusal to recognize its relative decline. Since no European country would agree to give up its seat on the IMF's executive board, the only way out was to add more and more temporary seats for the dynamic and underrepresented emerging economies.

Such a process, however, cannot go on forever, because with each increase in size the IMF's board becomes less and less effective. This is why the US has now decided to throw a cat among the European pigeons.

The US (which has veto power) has now taken the stance that it will no longer approve the current higher number of executive directors (24 at present). This has confronted the Europeans with a quandary: if they do not agree to give up some seats on the IMF board, some emerging countries, such as Argentina, Brazil, and perhaps even India, would lose theirs. The EU does not want to be held responsible for this. The pigeons are thus fighting among themselves over who should be sacrificed.

Until now, it could be argued that the eurozone did not have a common fiscal agency that could represent common eurozone interests. But this has changed with the creation of a European rescue fund in the form of the European Financial Stability Facility (EFSF).

Funding the next intra-eurozone rescue will be rather cumbersome and costly, because financial markets distrust complicated structures like the one set up to finance the EFSF. This suggests a golden opportunity for Europe to make a virtue of necessity by pooling its access to much-cheaper IMF funding.

If, for example, Ireland (or Spain) needed emergency support, the other eurozone countries could simply agree to lend it their IMF quotas.

The troubled country could then rapidly obtain a large IMF loan, given that the eurozone countries' quotas total about €60 billion – and that IMF loans can easily reach multiples of the quota.

Creditor countries like Germany would also gain, because they would not need to extend vast sums in guarantees to the EFSF while still safeguarding their interests within the EFSF's existing structure. All eurozone members, then, have an interest in concentrating in a smaller number of constituencies, with the EFSF representing their collective interests within the IMF.

A Federal Europe for Promoting a New Model of Growth[*]

Alberto MAJOCCHI

"Those of us wanting a unified Europe, the European integrationists, must leave behind the half-measures and pragmatic false compromises and learn again what really matters to us. The United States of Europe. Nothing more and nothing less. The current crisis has shown us that half-measures cannot withstand harsh realities, nor can false compromises. It has also shown that European visionaries were the true realists. And that only the path towards the United States of Europe can provide a real alternative to failure".

J. Fischer[1]

1. During the last two years a deep crisis has ravaged the world economy. The main industrialised countries have been heavily hit; less the new emerging economies. The governments have tried to face the crisis with the traditional instruments of expansionary fiscal and monetary policies. A full recession has been avoided, but rich countries are not completely out of the crisis. This dramatic experience has shown that there is an urgent need for change. In the past century, the main objective of economic policy has been to promote GDP increases, that were identified with a rising welfare. But this is no longer the case in the new world economy. In many countries GDP increases, but the quality of life is not improving at the same rate. The pressure on natural resources is unsustainable. Looking for more and more energy sources, natural disasters follow, as the oil spill in the Gulf of Mexico shows. Globalisation and the ensuing increased worldwide competition apparently oblige many countries to dismantle their welfare system and to trim down environmental protection. Thus the time seems ripe for moving urgently from uncontrolled growth towards sustainable development and a better quality of life.

While the crisis of the world economy has been originated in the financial sector, it has been rapidly spreading into the real economy. It has arisen out of a fundamental disequilibrium within the American economy, where demand has for many years outstripped the value of output, with

* Published in Issue 1/2011.

1 Joschka Fischer, *The United States of Europe*, Lecture to the Heinrich Heine University, Dusseldorf, June 1, 2010.

an ensuing permanent deficit in the trade balance, twinned to a budgetary deficit in continuous expansion and to a growing indebtedness of the private sector. From 1976 to 2007, the richest 1% of the American households seized 58% of the total increase in real income. As a consequence of this growing inequality in income distribution, in the US the banking system has been largely involved in supporting the demand either of houses (and other durable goods) or consumption goods, disregarding the over-use of natural and material resources, and thus favouring the emergence of the twin deficits and the worsening of the global environment.

2. The uninterrupted growth of the world economy has been supported during the last two decades by a spectacular increase in productivity, ensuing from a worldwide expansion of a huge wave of technological development, following the implementation of the ICT revolution originated in the US. But the model of growth prevailing in the United States is now obsolete since it is largely based on a resource-exhausting, consumption-oriented demand, and the American economy remains the most energy-intensive in the industrialised world. Furthermore, the increase in consumption for the American households is largely satisfied through cheap imports coming from industrialising countries. It is true that this US demand supports exports from these areas, but in this way real resources move from the less rich countries of the world towards the richest one.

The balancing role played by the US in supporting the growth of world economy in the period after the 2nd World War – with a surplus in the trade balance funding the deficit in capital accounts – is now totally absent. After the adoption of the Marshall Plan, European states were obliged to import consumption goods from the US, since domestic production was totally disrupted as a consequence of the war and these imports were paid through the inflow of American funds. But in this way were supported at the same time both the conversion of the US economy from military production to the production of civil goods and the recovery of the European economy. Now the twin deficits in the US are financed through capital imports from the rest of the world.

Unfortunately, all over the world the American model of growth has been largely followed. This model – that is still generally prevailing – has characterised the second half of the last century, but should now be radically changed. For most countries, the main factor determining the growth rate was a technological development of an imitative kind. It was sufficient to import the best technologies from the most advanced countries to raise productivity and to increase the standard of living. But many countries have now reached the technological frontier and are unable to restart growth through import of technologies from abroad.

If a new phase of growth has to be kicked off, a renewed capacity of innovating must be promoted and the production of new kinds of goods and different production processes should be envisaged.

3. A better quality of life is the main objective of the new model of growth, but the achievement of this goal requires as a first step a deep change in the pattern of consumption. In rich countries, goods should be purchased, in greater quantity than today, that satisfy real human needs and improve welfare. Many of these goods are immaterial – for instance, personal services, cultural goods, natural resources, environmental quality. Furthermore, in the post-industrial world, following the ICT revolution and the ensuing increase in labour productivity, working time could diminish, thus creating space for more leisure. Consequently, demand for enjoying cultural and natural goods could increase. At the same time, a larger quantity of material goods should be made available for satisfying basic human needs in the poor countries of the world. This is the first step for starting an endogenous process of growth in those countries as well.

Production processes too should be modified in depth. Environmental protection should be considered side-by-side with profit-maximisation and competitiveness in evaluating the effectiveness of the methods of production adopted by firms. In this evaluation, energy-saving and the trimming down of the use of natural resources should be considered as important parameters. More efficient capital goods could increase productivity, thus providing room for higher wages and better conditions of life for the workers.

4. In rich countries production processes are largely energy-intensive. This is particularly true for the United States that consumes a quarter of the world oil production even though it has only one-twentieth of the global population. As President Obama has recently remarked, the time for clean energy is now and the use of so much energy for unit of GDP should be decreased.

As it is well known, climate change is linked, to a great extent, to the burning of fossil fuels. To fight global warming the use of fossil fuels should be largely cut down. A carbon-energy tax could be effective in promoting both energy-saving through the higher prices of energy brought about by the energy share of the tax, and fuel-switching, since the carbon share of the tax favours the use of fuels with less carbon content. Hence the tax could promote a curbing of CO_2 emissions and a conversion of the productive structure along the path towards a low-carbon economy. Part of the revenue flowing from the energy-carbon tax could be used to promote innovation in the field of renewable energy or in exploiting new energy sources, while competitiveness of the countries implementing the tax could be protected by introducing custom tax adjustments, that is burdening imported foreign goods with the same tax levied on domestic production.

5. At the world level, the pattern of growth followed in the past is now unsustainable since the global environment is unable to support the enormously increased pressure on natural resources. The foreseen expansion of world population from 6 to 9 billion will intensify global competition for natural resources and put a further pressure on the environment. The world was ecologically in equilibrium when only one billion people were rich and energy-consuming. Now, luckily, the ratio between rich and poor is reversed and a new equilibrium could be reached only if the consumption of natural resources and the exploitation of energy sources are decreased in the rich countries since, from the point of view of equity, it is more and more unacceptable that more than one billion of the bottom poor be excluded from a reasonable standard of living.

Furthermore, it is true that, while the availability of consumption goods has been continuously increasing, even in the affluent societies many essential needs are not adequately satisfied. Hence, policy measures supporting across-the-board consumption demand are not an effective way out from the current crisis. More selective policy measures are needed and a process targeted to the promotion of a sustainable development – from an economic, social and environmental point of view – must be started as soon as possible.

6. A policy promoting the recovery of the economic activity worldwide is the unavoidable first step to be adopted to favour the kick off of a process achieving sustainable growth. In the affluent societies this policy should not be targeted to a further increase in consumption demand, but to the strengthening of a new and more balanced economic and social model, environment-friendly. Investments are essential to achieve this goal, as well as a redistribution policy aimed to cutting down existing inequalities in income distribution, with the ensuing negative economic and social effects. But consumption should be supported in the poor countries through a Keynesian policy at the world level targeted to the achievement of the Millennium Development Goals spelled out in the Millennium Declaration adopted in September 2000 by the United Nations, committing Member States to a new global partnership to reduce extreme poverty and setting out a series of time-bound targets with the deadline of 2015.

The transition to a sustainable development pattern requires the implementation of a plan including expenditure projects in different areas:

- research and development expenditures and promotion of higher education, to strengthen the competitiveness of domestic production;

- public and private investments in advanced technologies and support to champions in the new leading industries;
- financing projects to improve the quality of life for the citizens (water and air quality, sustainable mobility, renewable energy, urban renewal, efficient personal services, especially for weak people – babies, old people, the disabled);
- investments to promote conservation and to enlarge utilisation of cultural goods and natural resources;
- investments for completing worldwide the existing network in the fields of transport, energy and telecommunications.

7. In the traditional economy, growth depends on unceasing increases in demand and enhanced production-efficiency through market incentives. Prices reflect the balance between demand and supply and provide the right incentives for an efficient allocation of the production factors. But in the new economy, the external costs of production and consumption activities due to pollution and to the use of natural resources should be internalised into prices to avoid market failures and to maximise welfare. This outcome could be achieved through the use of economic instruments (environmental taxes, emission trading system) and of command-and-control measures. But the costs of an environmental policy are translated into higher prices, either with taxes or with command and control measures, and these higher prices curb demand increases of goods and services. Hence, the question follows: is economic growth hampered by an environmental policy?

In the literature about environmental policies an important role is played by the Porter hypothesis that the constraints deriving from environmental policy oblige firms to promote technological innovation and, consequently, prop up economic growth. Porter suggests that innovation concerns product and production processes, but also new management practices, with an ensuing decrease in production costs. As a matter of fact, countries with rigid environmental constraints show higher rates of productivity increases: Germany, the most performing export country worldwide, is one of the most advanced in environmental protection as well. Hence, it seems justified to draw the conclusion that in the long run there is no trade-off between economic growth and environmental protection.

8. In the old model of growth, GDP changes are widely used to evaluate the effectiveness of an economic policy: but GDP by itself is not an efficient indicator of welfare. Environmental damages are not computed in GDP, while expenditures caused by environmental degradation increase GDP. If an efficient policy of prevention of diseases is implemented,

health expenditures decrease and welfare apparently is worsened. This example shows that a new set of indicators is needed to measure welfare. The overall aim of this set is to favour policy measures able to improve the quality of life, both for current and future generations, through the creation of sustainable communities able to manage and use resources efficiently, and to tap the ecological and social innovation potential of the economy, ensuring prosperity, environmental protection and social cohesion. The conclusions of the Stiglitz-Sen-Fitoussi Commission promoted by the French President Sarkozy represent a useful first step in the right direction.

9. The condition of life in urban areas represents an essential feature of the quality of life. Everywhere in the world, progress is generally taking place within the cities and people concentrate in these areas, in the developing countries too. But congestion and pollution are endemic in urban areas, with external costs that bring about a worsening in the quality of life. Furthermore, given the increasing ratio between urban population and means of transport, urban mobility is not guaranteed to everybody. Urban life is particularly poor for the weak layers of the population, especially babies and old people.

Then, a first problem that must be urgently addressed is ensuring mobility to all the urban population, while simultaneously promoting a progressive reduction in the use of private vehicles. An unavoidable pre-requisite to achieve both these goals is to carry out a policy providing a coherent planning of urban development, that takes care – as a relevant priority – of environmental needs. As a second step, the growth of an efficient network of different kinds of public transport should be ensured and funded. But the implementation of this plan requires a lot of money and a long period of time. It follows that, if the final goal has to be achieved, during the transition period the use of private vehicle should contribute to the funding of the mobility plan through a system of road pricing, like that already implemented in London, Singapore and, with different characteristics and objectives, in Milan; a system that is able to reduce progressively the use of private vehicles and to provide at the same time the money to fund the investments needed to develop the public transport network or alternatives modes of transport.

10. One of the worst effect of urbanisation is the difficulty to guarantee a sufficient food production to feed the population in the poor countries as well as in the rich ones. In developing countries, a large part of the population is fed through self-production of consumption goods, that becomes impossible when people are urbanised. A green revolution aiming to productivity-improvements in the agricultural sector is quite important. But agricultural-policy measures *per se* are not sufficient. The rate of population growth should be checked and this demographic policy

should be backed by measures targeted to supporting a process of decentralisation of economic activities, so that the agglomeration effect pushing people to move to the most congested urban areas could be balanced.

11. Some conclusions could be drawn from this analysis. The transition to an environment-friendly world is in march. But it has to be recognised that the process of changing the current economic model at the world level requires a multilateral effort. No single country could reach this outcome acting alone. But, if it will be able to reach a political unity through a federal link, Europe has the possibility to play an important role in this process, showing that it is possible to overcome the national dimensions, that are totally inadequate in the modern world to achieve a sustainable development.

A federal Europe could adopt a new set of indicators of welfare, as it has been suggested by the Stiglitz-Sen-Fitoussi Commission, and advance along the path already pointed out in Article 3 of the Treaty of Lisbon on European Union stating that "the Union's aim is to promote [...] the well-being of its peoples". The investment program needed to kick-off a new phase of growth could be funded with the emission of Union bonds. In this way, while member states should be obliged to comply with the Maastricht constraints, guaranteeing financial stability, a growth policy could be implemented by the federal government, adopting the golden rule of public finance that debt is only allowed when funding expenditures for investments – and not consumption. Hence, with such virtuous behaviours the existing trade-off between stability and growth could be dismissed.

At the federal level, the transition to a low-carbon economy could be funded by a carbon-energy tax, while at the urban level road pricing could guarantee the transition to a sustainable mobility model. If Europe succeeds, this could be a strong incentive for other countries to follow the same path. But the success of the European policy requires a radical change in the existing institutional structure. Only a federal Europe could play this role, implementing an effective economic policy backed by an external policy promoting a positive European role in the transition to a multilateral world.

12. This positive evolution of the economic perspectives of the world economy has been supported by technological growth, and globalisation has given the possibility to new countries to be included in the industrialised world. But a global effort is required to include in the process the bottom poor countries as well. The African continent represents the black hole in this process of balanced growth. As a matter of fact, not only equity, but also efficiency requires that income distribution should be improved between and within the different countries. This is a difficult,

but decisive task, and in this area too Europe – with its past experience in the promotion of income growth in the new countries joining the Union – could show that a positive outcome is possible. Combining the promotion of environmental protection and a better quality of life with a fair distribution of income within the European continent and all over the world, a federal Europe could show that a policy aiming to raise welfare for human beings everywhere in the world is possible.

Now it is up to the European people to promote the building up of an effective federal Constitution, overcoming the dramatic limits of the existing European Union, confirmed with overwhelming evidence by the economic slowdown of the last two years that has shown how the current European crisis is only superficially a financial crisis. As Krugman rightly remarked, "to make the euro work, Europe needs to move much further toward political union, so that European nations start to function more like American states"[2]. Fischer also has recently reminded us that the recent European meltdown "in essence is a political crisis caused by the political weakness of the EU and the euro area". And he added that "if the EU is unable to act as one, then the euro area can and must act as its vanguard, firstly within the Treaty and, if that brings no results, or they prove too slow, outside the Treaty, but in its spirit and in the interests of the Union".

It is up to the governments to take this decision, but it is the role – and the duty – of the federalist movement to promote an initiative mobilising the public opinion and pushing European governments to act urgently.

---

2 Paul Krugman, "The Making of a Euromess", in *The New York Times*, February 15, 2010.

Europe by the People*

Carsten BERG

The demand of greater and more effective involvement of EU-citizens is not new. Before the founding of the EU's predecessor and the recently abolished Coal and Steel Union, Charles de Gaulle declared in 1949: "I think that the organisation of Europe has to proceed from Europe itself. I consider that the start shall be given by a referendum of all free Europeans."

A referendum as the definitive founding act of a political Europe! This is what the Italian European federalist Altiero Spinelli imagined, when in 1984 he proposed the creation of an EU constitution which would have to be ratified by the people in a Europe-wide referendum. The supporters of this federal idea were already a generation ahead and had to wait patiently until the time was ripe for more democracy in the EU: and that did not happen until recently.

After half a century of European integration it has become common sense that Europe needs to overcome its democratic deficit. The Laeken Declaration laid the foundation of the Convention which among other things is charged with examining: 1) how Europe can be more democratic, more efficient and more transparent, and 2) what might be the route to a European constitution. This concrete task has inspired the creative thinking and the courage of many Europeans. Many members of the Convention have spoken in support of a Europe-wide referendum on the results of the Convention's work: Convention President Giscard d'Estaing stated at the opening of the assembly at the end of February that treaties should be concluded by countries, but constitutions by peoples – and that he therefore approved the idea of a European referendum. Giscard's deputy Amato has declared his support for an "informal referendum". Another vice-president, Dehaene, has emphasized that he is in favour of a "European constitutional referendum" as long as this is held all throughout Europe.

Both within and on the fringes of the Convention, many members have spoken in favour of the Europe-wide referendum including the British House of Commons MP David Heathcoat Amory, the German Bundestag representative Meyer, and Austria's former transport minister Einem. The idea of a referendum is especially strong among members of the

* Published in Issue 1/2003.

European Parliament delegation to the Convention: Lamassoure, Duff, Timmermans, Brok, Voggenhuber, Kaufmann and Garett have explicitly expressed their support for a European referendum.

People of all European Countries value their freedom of choice and feel the need to have a say in decisions affecting their lives. A European Constitution will most positively influence European people's lives and it will be the best way to reach a common basic agreement as it codifies the way we want to live together in Europe tomorrow. A Europe-wide referendum is an explicit recognition of the principle of the sovereignty of the people which ought to underpin the construction of a federal Europe. It connects the two principles of individual freedom and common agreement.

In addition the following aspects are worth considering:

1. A proper European Constitution with a whole set of new institutional arrangements and legal personality requires a broader legitimacy than only the signatures of some heads of state. Today we are not talking about another treaty change but about the creation of something close to a new state. Citizens will accept this new kind of statehood from day one only if they have been asked to endorse it.
2. Opening the perspective of a Europe-wide referendum makes a new dialogue possible. It will integrate EU-citizens in the drafting process. With the prospective plebiscit on the Conventions's result, its members are "forced" to draft a comprehensible text which is so simple and openly democratic that it will receive the citizens' vote. Given the necessarily quick decision to put the new Constitution to the people, broader public communication between the Convention members should be expected.
3. The discussion around the referendum will be stimulated by the media and politicians. The exchange of arguments will make the citizens more competent, more motivated and more ready to learn the way in which Europe works. Thus, the role of citizens will be strengthened.

A classic argument against the Europe-wide referendum is that there is no such thing as a "European public" and a "European People". The European referendum is an ideal means of creating a European debate across the national borders. European politics will only become relevant to the citizens of Europe when they have the opportunity of real participation in this very essential decision. If this does not happen, they will continue to feel alienated and apathetic and the EU will remain a bureaucratic, elitist organisation. In the words of de Gaulle: "Europe will be born the day on which the different people, in their depth, decide to join. It will not suffice that members of parliaments vote the ratification. It requires popular referenda, preferably held on the same day in all countries concerned". Legal technocrats argue that we cannot have a European referendum because a European Constitution providing for that has not yet been implemented. Obviously, this very conservative argument can be refuted if there is the political will for a referendum. It would be no problem for national parliaments – given the political will – to implement ways to make it possible for every country to hold a political referendum on one day all over Europe.

If one really wants to appreciate and grasp the potential impact of the referendum-idea it will be important to focus on the communication process across Europe that is triggered during the conventional drafting process and also in the months leading up to the vote, which is forecast for June 2004 along with the EP elections, and not exclusively on referendum day.

The immense historical challenge for federalists is to intensify the dynamic communication process explaining the need for a federal constitution. Our ideas are convincing, thus there is no reason to hide. First steps were initiated by JEF on the 9th of November 2002, with the successful organisation of "referendum-action" in Lyon, Florence and Frankfurt simultaneously. Courageous actions like these are carried by the European idea that Federalists have been cultivating for decades. This European spirit releases the necessary energy to overcome the fears of the sceptics and to win the referendum challenge fulfilling the dream of Europe as made by the people and for the people.

In summary: the trend towards the federal idea of a European referendum has received massive support from the most varied sources in recent months. The advantages of this process detailed above are capable of reducing some of the greatest deficiencies in European democracy: participation, legitimacy, transparency and efficiency. Faced with the monumental significance of a European constitution we can expect already today that there will be at least a number of national referenda in EU-countries. Therefore our specific federalist responsibility is to further show evidence for a Europe-wide referendum that is to be fought as a European rather than a national contest. Let's face it and become active.

European Citizenship to Residents*

Paul ORIOL

In democratic countries everybody has rights that make him, in some ways, a citizen: social, cultural, labour rights. But almost everywhere the political citizenship is reserved to nationals.

According to the European Charter of Fundamental Rights (*the Charter*): "Everyone is equal before the law" (Art. 20) and: "Within the scope of application of the Treaty establishing the European Community, and without prejudice to the special provisions thereof, any discrimination on grounds of nationality shall be prohibited" (Art. 21 (2)). Equality is the rule, inequality the exception. Exceptions will have to become rarer according to the Tampere Summit Conclusions: "The legal status of third country nationals should be approximated to that of Member States' nationals. A person, who has resided legally in a Member State for a period of time to be determined and who holds a long-term residence permit, should be granted in that Member State a set of uniform rights which are as near as possible to those enjoyed by EU citizens".

The Treaties

The EU citizenship has been instituted by the Maastricht Treaty (the Treaty): "Every person holding the nationality of a Member State shall be a citizen of the Union" (Art. 8-1). The Treaty lists the rights attached to this citizenship: "the right to move and reside freely within the territory of the Member States" (Art. 8A-1), "protection by the diplomatic or consular authorities of any Member State" (Art. 8C), "right to address a petition to the European Parliament" and "to apply to the Ombusdam" (Art. 8D), "right to vote and to stand as a candidate at municipal elections in the Member State where he resides, under the same conditions as nationals of that State" (Art. 8B-1) and "at elections to the European Parliament" (Art. 8B-2).

These rights are of a very different nature. The right to move and to reside can be referred to the Rights of Man: "Every person has the right to move freely and to choose his residence in the territory of a State" (Art. 13-1 of the Universal Declaration of the Rights of Man) and "Every

* Published in Issue 2/2004.

person has the right to leave any country, including his own, and to return to his country" (Art. 13-2). This freedom, called for since the Rome Treaty, is not yet fully recognized, even for citizens of the EU. Its extension to nationals of third countries is provided for by the Charter: "The freedom of movement and residence can be granted [...] to nationals of third countries legally residing in the territory of a Member State" (Art. 44-2).

The diplomatic and consular protection is a right of the national. "The State must give its protection to its nationals which translates into diplomatic and consular protection to be given to nationals being abroad ..." (European Convention on the reduction of cases of multi-nationality and on military duties in cases of multi-nationality, François Julien-Laferrière, *Migrations Société*, No. 80, March-April 2002).

The right to petition and to apply to the Ombusdam is a right of any administered person. The Treaty grants it to "any natural or legal person residing or having its registered office in a Member State" (Art. 138D) and the Ombusdam is "empowered to receive complaints from any citizen of the Union or any natural or legal person residing or having its registered office in a Member State" (Art. 138E).

The right to vote and to stand as a candidate at municipal and European elections is reserved to EU citizens.

The Treaty makes of a citizen, in turn, a person-citizen, a consumer-citizen, a national-citizen or a citizen-citizen. Of course, the Rights of Man or those of consumers are also a form of citizenship. But the core of citizenship is indeed the participation in political decisions. The Charter goes further than the Treaty: "Everyone has the right to freedom of peaceful assembly and to freedom of association at all levels, in particular in political, trade union and civic matters..." (Art. 12-1). It grants to everybody, hence to nationals of third countries, the right of participation, "in particular in political ...matters". Nationals of third countries may be members of a political party "at all levels", may preside over them, but they cannot vote in any political election.

Present situation

Because of the Treaty, over the same territory people having the same duties are enclosed in castes of citizenship with different rights:

- national citizens living in their national territory (365 million people) have the right to vote and to stand as a candidate in any election
- EU citizens being in a EU country other than that they are nationals of (5 millions) have only the right to vote and to stand as a candidate in municipal and European elections

- nationals of third countries (15 millions) have (in Belgium[1], Denmark, Finland, Ireland, Luxemburg, Netherlands, Sweden) or do not have (in Germany, Austria, France, Greece, Italy) the right to vote and to stand as a candidate in certain local elections, depending on the laws of the country of residence and on peculiar norms of some countries (Spain, Portugal, United Kingdom) and in all of the States, there are outcastes, as the *sans-papiers*.

The EU citizenship adds a legal discrimination to the many already (ill)suffered, and in a way legitimizes them. In order to suppress such a political discrimination, could the residence be taken as the criterion for awarding citizenship, just as nationality is?

It is obvious that, according to the subsidiarity principle, it is a State that awards its nationality. It would be obvious likewise that it is the EU that awards the EU citizenship. But the EU citizenship is based on nationality, so the States are awarding it indirectly. Hence an inconsistency. Two brothers, Turks, establish themselves in the EU, Ali in Belgium, Umit in Germany. After 7 years, Ali gets the Belgian nationality and becomes an EU citizen. Umit cannot do that. But, as he is perfectly integrated, his business prospers. He calls Ali to live with him. Since his arrival, he, a Belgian and hence an EU citizen, has the right to vote and to stand as a candidate in municipal and European elections. He does not know Germany, does not speak German… Umit cannot vote, but could help him in that task!!!

The Treaty has shown that the arguments against the right to vote for foreign residents are weak in the face of a determined political will. The EU citizens enjoy their rights deriving from the EU citizenship whatever their degree of integration, the length of their residence, the language they speak.

There remains to speak of the reciprocity principle: no fundamental principle requires reciprocity for awarding new rights. It is never claimed for opening citizenship to Norwegians or New Zealanders. Such requirement would make the quality of democracy within the EU dependent on the States that the foreigners have left for escaping corruption, bad management or oppression. The countries that have given the right to vote before the Treaty have done so with the intention of democratizing their society. They have given it to all residents whatever their nationality.

Extending citizenship is the conclusion of the slow but progressive process of bringing the rights of foreigners in line with the nationals', of extending the right to vote towards a real universal suffrage (from the

[1] In Belgium, nationals of third countries do not have the right to stand as candidates.

wealth-based vote to suffrage reserved to men, then to women, then to the young).

Nationality vs. Citizenship

The link Nationality-Citizenship is just an historical one, albeit it is made sacred by the notion of nationality, which can be felt as essential, uncreated. However, laws on nationality vary a great deal depending on traditions and real or alleged interests of the moment.

According to the 1999 census of population, there were 3,260,000 foreigners in France. Demographer Hervé Le Bras could write: "If France had the same laws as the United States, the 510,000 foreigners born in France would be French. And if we had the laws of Latin American countries, residents for more than 10 years would have acquired the nationality of the host country. We would count then 638,000 foreigners only!" (*Coup de Soleil*, No. 21) And we could also add: with the German laws, before the last reform, or the Swiss laws they would be 6 or 7 million! So, depending on which legislation is applied, the "foreign" population can vary from 600,000 to 6 million! That relativizes the notion of foreigner and that of national.

The Belgian law of 2000 has made easier the acquiring of nationality, determining a significant reduction of the number of foreigners in Belgium without any real change in the composition of that population! Actually, there have been "61,980 naturalizations in 2000, 62,982 in 2001 and 46.417 in 2002. Before that, the country was registering between 25,000 and 35,000 naturalizations a year" (*Le Soir*, 21/06/2003).

Nationality is not the only criterion for awarding rights. More and more, residence is playing that role. From the rights of the sans-papiers to the right to get the nationality, passing through the social, labour, cultural, political rights. Rights that were considered political yesterday are recognized today, in democracy, to foreign residents: right of association, expression, manifestation, to join trade-unions…

The link nationality-citizenship appears so "natural" that often the two words, citizenship and nationality, are used interchangeably. However, they do not answer the same question.

Nationality answers the question "Who are we?", and the answers are several, because people's allegiances are several: nationality, but also family situation, profession, religion, gender, age, and to a little extent citizenship… There is no point in negating the links which exist among people of the same nationality, even if such links make often reference to common ancestors and such attachment is explained by the right of blood. This story is mythical at the national level, and it is even more so at the European level. There is no European people, there is diversity of peoples, of cultures, of religions…

Citizenship answers the question: “How to construct a common future in diversity?” A citizen is one who takes in his hands his situation respecting the common good and, in democracy, with no exclusion. Citizenship implies a relation with others, conflicting but egalitarian.

The European Commission could say that “the nationals of other Member States integrate themselves in the economic and social activity of their hosting country, all the more so as they already enjoy the same rights as the local nationals… It is more logical, if not fully justified, to take part in the elections organized in their town of residence, even if they have the nationality of another Member State, rather than to continue to participate in the elections of a town where they no longer reside, which they have the nationality of”. (Proposal for a Council directive on the right to vote of nationals of another Member State in the municipal elections in the Member State of residence, COM (88) 371, 24/06/1988). If the awarding of political rights is a factor of integration and they are awarded to some and not to others, does it mean that there is an intention to integrate some and not others?

Everybody must be in a position to participate in the construction of a common future, by his professional, sporting, artistic, demographic contribution; but also to participate in the moment when decisions are made. Citizenship is a factor of social cohesion. Can one imagine a true equality in the enforcement of law without equality in drafting it? The right to vote and the EU citizenship would legitimize actions which often are performed already when one participates in the life of his neighborhood, his company, his church, his sporting club or his association of school parents. To this *de facto* citizenship there must correspond a *de jure* citizenship, lest frustrations are generated.

Europe cannot but be based on universal values. Moreover, it must really accept both the variety of cultures and universalism. It cannot be content with a petty multi-culturalism and universalism without, one day or the other, paying the consequences. Nation-States have often been created before citizenship, before the institution of democratic systems; and they are not there even for the EU: there is no European people, there is no European nation-State. The EU citizenship is a citizenship without State. Diversity is congenital in Europe. Why not to base “Europeanship” on citizenship, on adhesion to principles, on participation? Why shouldn’t Europe be a creation by its citizens, by all those who declare their will to participate? Such desire of egalitarian citizenship will constitute the European identity, that cannot be a national identity. Adhesion by naturalization is an adhesion to an already-constituted mythical community. Adhesion by citizenship is an adhesion to a project, to an identity in the process of being built, which rests on a political plan, on reason.

Practical considerations

On the occasion of the European Social Forum, the campaign and a petition[2] "One Million Signatures in favour of European Citizenship for all Residents" has been launched. It is supported by more than 250 organizations from 12 out of the 15 EU countries. One million signatures for asking the Commission a proposal on this matter, related to the project of the European Constitution. In order to bring this political discrimination in the European political space in the making. At the moment of European elections, of the discussion on the project of the Constitution, of the out-bound enlargement, which should not make us forget the in-bound enlargement and the 15 to 20 million people living on the EU territory without having its citizenship. Its goal is to modify the criteria for awarding the EU citizenship, which should be: "Every person residing in, and every national of, a Member State shall be a citizen of the Union". Such a wording would be closer to the values declared in other places.

2 The text of the petition is available in 11 languages of the EU on the website: http://fidh-ae.org/petition-million.htm.

Strong European Political Parties for a Democratic EU*

Jo Leinen

On the eve of the 50th anniversary of the Rome-Treaty, the process of European Integration is in danger to come to a halt. Citizens, media, academics and politicians alike, criticize the democratic deficit. However, the ratification of the European Constitution, which would have lessened this deficit, is blocked. The referenda in France and the Netherlands as well as the missing public debate on the Future of Europe have shown that the EU is still lacking the democratic infrastructure to conduct a truly pan-European debate. A key role in providing this infrastructure is to be played by European political parties.

One of the main reasons for the EU's democratic deficit is the missing link between the European institutions and the citizens. On the national level the link between citizens and decision makers as well as the link between political debate and political decisions is provided by political parties. European political parties as a tie between the Union's citizens and EU policies are hardly developed. Only recently, European political parties have emerged and begun to improve the debate about the challenges for Europe.

European democracy needs strong European political parties

The political system of the Union does not yet stimulate sufficiently pan-European debates. Although the European Parliament, the Commission and some NGO-umbrellas can be seen as supranational actors, the view of citizens on European issues still follows merely the positions of national politicians. National governments use "Brussels" as a scapegoat for unpopular decisions, although the same governments are responsible for these very decisions in the European Council and the Council of Ministers. Combined with the often anti-European reporting in the purely national tabloid media, this leads to a rising gap between the citizens and the European decision makers. Debates in which the benefits

* Published in Issue 1/2007.

and costs of political decisions on the EU level are discussed, hardly take place outside Brussels.

In federal systems such as Germany, Austria and Switzerland, political parties play an important role in linking national, regional and local levels. Party members from the different levels are involved in party decisions and follow the ideological line of the party. On the European level such link is missing. The parties have hardly succeeded in agreeing on a clear overarching political line, nor is the loyalty to the European party position very strong. Not only do leaders of the national parties hesitate to follow a European party line. Also positions of European parliamentarians, government representatives in the Council and Commissioners from the same party often differ fundamentally.

Obstacles to strong European political parties

One of the reasons for European parties being weak is that they cannot yet fulfil their tasks. On the national level, parties have clearly defined functions: the elaboration of a political program for the future government, the recruitment of political personnel and the feedback of legislative decisions to the voters. In the EU, these functions have been partly taken over by other institutions.

The political programme for the EU is drawn up by the European Parliament, the European Council and the Commission. While the work of the Parliament is dependent on the positions of the strongest party groups, the European Council and the Commission are made up of members of all big parties. Decisions on the political program in the latter two institutions are taken by unanimity, not allowing any of the parties to establish a high political profile. Furthermore the governments in the European Council are supposed to take decisions in the interest of the entire country, not only their voters. The contrary applies to the Commission, whose members are supposed to act in the interest of the entire Union, but have therefore similar difficulties to follow a party line. European parties have had little influence on shaping the political program of the Union until today.

Also on choosing the future leadership of the Union, European political parties have had so far not much influence. Indeed the party membership of the candidate matters, which is shown by the fact that after the election victory of the conservatives in 2004, Manuel Barroso, a conservative politician, was made President of the Commission and not the better qualified but liberal Guy Verhofstadt. But the nomination of the candidates is not done by the standing bodies of the European parties, but by all EU heads of state and government. Furthermore the Commission Presidents until today had little loyalty to the European parties. As previous Prime Ministers, they have gained their European experience in

European Council meetings and are more likely to respect the wishes of member state governments, than those of the European party leaders.

To date, European political parties have not been able to sufficiently connect the European level with the citizens. Contrary to the national parties, European political parties are not made up of individual members. The statute of the European socialist party limits the party membership to national parties. Indeed, the statute of the European people's party allows individual membership. Nevertheless, just as with the greens and the liberals, individual members account only for a very small percentage of the entire membership. Thus, the European political parties still have to rely on the national structures of the member parties to communicate the European political programme and European politics. However, in the local branches of the national parties, European policy does not yet play an important role. Party members consider the discussion of European issues not as their priority; European decisions seem to be far from the reality of the local work. If the European political parties wish to fulfil their role as link between decisions taken at the European level and citizens at the local level, they have to either build up a direct membership or develop new instruments to reach out also to the local level.

The Party of European Socialists has established a new tool called "PES @ctivists". These "activists" are not individual members of the party, but function as ambassadors of the European party at the local level and participate in pan-European political discussions on a wide range of topics. This could serve as a role model also for other parties.

The future of European political parties

Although more than fifty years of European integration had to pass before European parties gained their independence, a lot of progress has been made since the regulation on the financing of European parties has been passed in 2003. Before European parties can play the same strong role in European democracy, which they play at the national level, still many reforms of the structures of the EU as well as of the running of the parties need to be done.

A first prerequisite for stronger European political parties is the continuing constitutionalisation of the European Union. The institutional reforms foreseen by the European Constitution will bring Europe closer to a full democratic design: with their votes in the European elections the citizens will not only decide on the political programme of the European Union, but also influence the choice of the political leadership. Furthermore the European Constitution strengthens the European Parliament by introducing the co-decision procedure as the rule for European legislation, and by only allowing for a limited number of exceptions. Also on budgetary decisions the parliament will be strengthened. On the other hand, the President of the European Commission will be elected by the European Parliament and the Commissioners will need approval of the Parliament, once the European Constitution enters into force.

Besides institutional reforms, there is also the need for more specific regulations on the functioning of European political parties. These need to be laid down in a truly European statute for European political parties. On May 23rd, 2006 the European Parliament has adopted a resolution stressing the need for such a statute[1]. It needs to establish the rights and obligations of European political parties and lay down rules on their internal functioning, such as guidelines for the democratic nature of parties (regular elections and nomination of candidates). To date, the European political parties are registered as associations, mostly under Belgium law. One of the aims of establishing a European statute is to enable European political parties to obtain a genuine European legal personality. This would give them the same obligations and rights in all member states. Even if the participation of European political parties in European electoral campaigns, referenda and other campaigns seems to be self-evident, this is not clearly foreseen by the *acquis communautaire*. The statute needs to bring clarity in this perspective and needs to allow European political parties to do their work.

Experiences in some member states have shown that political foundations can be an important element of the democratic infrastructure. They provide political education by organising seminars, conferences and directly supporting students through grants. Since political foundations are close to the respective political families but independent from them, they provide an important space for politicians and academics to brainstorm on upcoming political challenges, without having to be accountable for their statements in front of political bodies. Thus they represent important think tanks for the political parties. In order to develop European democracy, political foundations also need to be developed at the European level. They can play a leading role in organising Europe-wide political discourses.

Also the role of political youth organisations must be strengthened. They play an important role in the formation and education of future political leaders in Europe. The already existing youth party organisations arrange numerous activities at the European level, which helps to sensitise future national politicians on the importance of European politics. Steps

---

1 European Parliament resolution on European political parties (A6-0042/2006), 23.03.2006, rapporteur Jo Leinen.

should be taken to recognise the role European youth organisations play and to ensure sufficient financial support to their activities.

The gap between citizens and the EU institutions must be bridged with the help of European political parties. In their short existence, the ten European parties have matured considerably. However, much needs to be done before the structures of the EU allow for European political parties to play a leading role in the EU political system and before the parties are strong enough to do so. In the near future a statute for European parties needs to be established and the European Constitution needs to be ratified. Also, the parties need to implement brave reforms which will enable them to adopt strong European manifestoes, decide on top candidates for elections and provide a link between citizens' interests and European decisions. The first results of these reforms need to come into effect before the next European elections in June 2009, in order to improve the voters' participation and therefore reduce the democratic deficit.

The European Citizens' Initiative

A Great Responsibility for Federalists*

Sylvia-Yvonne KAUFMANN

On April 1st, 2012, Europe will break new ground: from then on one of the most important innovations in the EU, the European Citizens' Initiative (ECI), will be in force and for the first time in history direct transnational democracy will become reality. Thinking about this breaking event, it is worth having a short look back at a long way full of stones.

A short look back: ECI, a child of the European Convention

Almost a decade has gone since the idea of ECI was developed within the European convention in 2002/2003. For me, as well as for the great majority of colleagues in the Convention, it was clear that the European Union needed a comprehensive reform, a reform that will ultimately overcome its democratic deficit. The debates were consequently focused on institutional reforms, especially on strengthening the power of the European Parliament as the direct representation of Europe's citizens and on giving the national parliaments a better say in European politics. But, at the same time, it was clear that democracy in Europe needed more to bring the citizens onto the political centre stage.

Shortly after the opening of the Convention, a first meeting took place between some parliamentarians in the convention – such as Alain Lamassoure (EPP-ED, France), Johannes Voggenhuber (Greens/EFA, Austria), Josep Borell Fontelles (PES, Spain), Casper Einem (PES, Austria), Jürgen Meyer (PES, Germany) and me – and *Initiative & Referendum Institute, IRI Europe* (a network of activists engaged for direct democracy, brought together by the Initiative & Referendum Institute, IRI Europe). This meeting on March 20th, 2002, marked the start of an intense debate between NGO-activists and members of the first constitutional assembly in the history of the EU to develop ideas and concepts as to how direct-democracy elements could be included into the forthcoming treaties. That was far from being easy. There was no existing

* Published in Issue 2/2011.

prototype which could somehow be taken up as a basis of reference. And a closer look at the situation and experiences in Member states showed, on the one hand, that the existing national models were very different and, on the other hand, that a majority of Member states didn't have any rules for any kind of direct democracy instruments and consequently no political culture in this respect at all.

In the beginning of 2003, an informal common working group of NGO-activists and convention members began to discuss detailed proposals, which were to be presented to the Constitutional Convention. At that time, within the convention as well as within civil society the debates strongly focused on the question whether the new treaties proposed by the convention should finally be adopted by referendum, by referendum in all Member states or by a Pan-European one. There was a growing public pressure in favour of the referendum idea from different parts of our societies, and more than 120 NGOs were intensively campaigning for it. So, different convention Members started to present individual proposals and on March 31st, 2003, a contribution (CONV 658/03) in favour of a European-wide referendum on the EU Constitution was presented to the Presidium of the Convention. It was introduced by Alain Lamassoure and signed by 38 Convention members, alternate members and observers.

However, the idea of a European-wide referendum was confronted with strong opposition, coming especially from national governments and from the main political forces. They were against for principle reasons and based their arguments on legal difficulties and problems. So, in the end there was unfortunately no chance to convince the presidium of the convention to take up this proposal.

But our working group followed from the beginning a two-track approach. When it became clear that the referendum idea won't be successful, we intensified our work on a different question: the idea to strengthen democracy and citizens rights by introducing a new tool into the treaties, the right of initiative for citizens. In spring 2003, the presidium of the convention published its first draft for a chapter on "democratic life in the European Union", which contained also a draft-text for an article on the principle of participatory democracy. But there was a big disappointment: besides the formula of structural dialogues with the representative organisations and civil society, there was no mentioning of direct democracy at all.

After dramatic weeks with intense debates and lobbying, a proposal by Prof. Jürgen Meyer finally made it through. The proposal (CONV 724/03) entirely focused on the Citizens' Initiative dimension, and was based on the approach of equalising the role of the citizens (when it comes to influencing the European Commission) with the initiative rights of the Parliament and the Council. About 70 members and alternate members of the Convention supported it. With common efforts from MEPs and national parliamentarians in the Convention, we managed to break down the last resistances in the Convention Presidium: on the eve of the last Convention session, the citizens' initiative right was included in the draft constitutional treaty, giving citizens for the very first time in history a direct-democracy tool at the transnational level. With the adoption of a key demand by many people and NGOs, the Convention opened a window to transnational agenda-setting from below.

This proposal built the foundation for the final text in the draft constitutional treaty, presented by the Convention Chairman Valéry Giscard d'Estaing on June 13th: "A significant number of citizens, not less than one million, coming from a significant number of Member States, may invite the Commission to submit any appropriate proposal on matters where citizens consider that a legal act of the Union is required for the purpose of implementing this Constitution. A European law shall determine the provisions regarding the specific procedures and conditions required for such a citizens' request" (Art. I-46, p. 4). As with a lot of other promising elements in the Convention's draft constitutional treaty, such as the incorporation of the Charter of Fundamental Rights, the European Citizens' Initiative right symbolised a departure from the old-style European Union.

But after the adoption of the "Treaty establishing a Constitution for Europe" by the Heads of State and Government in Rome on October 29th, 2004, the ratification-process failed after the No-Votes in France and in the Netherlands in 2005. Extraordinary efforts were necessary to rescue the substance of the Constitutional Treaty and it took another three years until the ECI – now Article 11-4 TEU – came into the focus of political debates again. It was – by no surprise – the Committee on Constitutional Affairs of the European Parliament (AFCO) which took the lead in summer 2008. Although being confronted with the still ongoing ratification-process of the Lisbon-Treaty, it insisted on an early start of a broad and detailed debate on the implementation of the ECI. It was the main intention for a majority of parliamentarians to give a political signal to the citizens before the European elections in June 2009, namely that it is the Parliament the institution paving the way for a simple and user-friendly ECI-regulation and which in the interest of the people strives to put it into practice as soon as possible.

With the adoption of my report on ECI in May 2009, the Parliament has indeed managed to prepare the ground in that respect. So, it defined the Lisbon-Treaty formula of "a significant number of Member States" to be ¼, or seven Member States; it called on the Commission to receive the organizers of an ECI in order to allow them to explain in detail the matters raised by a successful ECI with more than one million signatures, and it demanded public hearings with the organizers of a successful ECI. In 2010 – thanks to the excellent work of co-rapporteurs Zita Gurmai (S&D, Hungary) and Alain Lamassoure (EPP, France) –, it was possible to embody these essential points in the regulation and to drop, for example, the original bureaucratic proposal by the Commission to check the admissibility of an ECI only after 300,000 signatures have been collected. So, it was the Parliament again which provided proof of being the guarantor of the intentions of the Constitutional Convention.

Looking ahead: Let's make the ECI a success story

With the approval of the ECI-regulation by the Parliament and the Council at the beginning of 2011, there is now about one year of time left for citizens and for organized civil society to discuss and consider how to use this new instrument. As we all know, within a lot of different political forces and NGOs the debate started already. And who else if not us, the European federalists, should examine whether to launch a European Citizens' Initiative too or to be prepared, at least, to support one.

From my point of view, the European federalists do have a high responsibility for the ECI becoming a success story. We as federalists have to do our utmost in order that people in Europe feel and see that their wishes and ideas are taken seriously by the European institutions; that Europe is not a project of the elites, and that there is the political will to build up Europe together with its citizens. One thing is sure: if the first ECI projects won't succeed, it will mean an extraordinary damage to democracy.

The steady decline in participation in European elections and the extremely low participation in the 2009 elections were already alarming. But having a look at the figures of recent opinion polls in Germany, for example, one should be even more alarmed. The figures of a representative opinion poll issued on January 26th, 2011, by the "Frankfurter Allgemeine Zeitung" show that in Germany the support towards the EU is declining dramatically. To the question "Do you think Europe is our future?" only 41% of Germans answered with a Yes. The answers to the question: "How quick should the development towards a united Europe proceed? Quicker or more slowly?" showed that since the 1990s the percentage of those in favour of a quicker move towards a united Europe is constantly going down. At the beginning of 2011 only 12% of the consulted persons were in favour of quicker integration. The same negative trend was reflected by the answers to the question "How much do you trust the European Union?". In the last five years, about 50% of Germans said that they have little or almost no trust in the EU, while 1/3 of the people said that their trust in the EU is high. But at the beginning of this year the figures were even worse – there were only 26% of the people left saying "I trust in the EU".

So, thinking at how to make the ECI a success story, federalists should take these wide-spread public opinions in our Member states very seriously. But it is not only this background which must be taken into close consideration. Two other elements will have a great importance: which topic and the time-table. Concerning the topic that the UEF and its national branches shall choose to be engaged in, it is sure that only a pro-European issue aiming at deepening European integration and taking up a widespread need or common public interest in our different member-states should have all our support. Concerning the time-table, one should keep in mind the times required. With the ECI starting on 1st April, 2012, it will take more than one and half years – from the submission to the Commission, the collecting of the minimum one million signatures in seven Member states, the process of verification of the collected signatures, until the date of the Commission's decision on how it will proceed with the ECI –, it will be actually on the table around November 2013. Only then will we know what the Commission intends to do, whether it wants to pick up the citizens request or reject it. That will be just on the eve of the next European election!

Therefore, an ECI that we as UEF may decide to be in favour of should be considered in view of the European elections of 2014. It must be successful – to encourage people to get involved in European affairs and to encourage them to take part in the EP elections. European unification will only last if a Europe of the citizens is built up. The new instrument, the European Citizens Initiative, gives us the chance to go ahead in this direction and to follow the spirit of Jean Monnet, who said that the aim is not to unify States, but peoples.

Part Three

The Integration Processes at the Regional Level

Giampiero BORDINO

One of the recurring, important themes which *The Federalist Debate* has been focusing its attention on in the course of the years is that of the regional integration processes taking place in the world, from Europe (the most advanced institutional process) to Asia, Africa and the Americas. In the context of globalization, the effects of which have spread all over the planet and are interconnecting its various parts, regional integration processes have been started in different forms and times, and had different outcomes; they have often taken as a model, at least in their intentions, the European experience developed after the end of the Second World War. With regard to the global challenges that all the peoples and the States of the world have to cope with, the integration processes of great regional areas of a continental dimension look particularly important. Globalization, which interconnects and makes all the societies and the territories of the world mutually dependent, is today without a government. It is to some extent controlled and regulated by inadequate and precarious forms of governance, providing only negotiation tables for public actors (states, international organizations, etc.) and also private actors (economic and financial bodies, trans-national organizations of various types, even illegal and criminal, etc.), which do not guarantee either peace and stability or development, or the social and environmental sustainability of that development. Hence, in such a context, the economic, institutional and cultural integration processes at the regional level, aiming at a more adequate governance first, and at an efficient government at the world level later, do present a fundamental importance. They are, in short, the *tesserae* of a multi-level, federal-type political architecture that should prospectively make a new civilization path possible and, given the mortal risks that all of us are running today (wars, human and environmental catastrophes, etc.) due to the absence of a shared order based on law, should ensure the very survival of the world.

As far as Europe is concerned, in addition to the integration regarding the countries inside the Union (treated specifically in Chapter 2 of this book), its current regionalization process is challenged on the outside from two directions: from the East, the Caucasus and Russia, and from the South, the Mediterranean basin. Two areas, as is well-known, with increasing instability and recent crises, where initiatives of regional integration should be put in place even within their own borders. In the analyses in *The Federalist Debate*, the first direction, that to the East of the Union, is burdened by the negative consequences of the failure of the idea of a "Common European Home" proposed by Gorbachev in the years of the collapse of the Soviet empire and the post-communist reshaping of Central-Eastern Europe. The absence of a true European government and of a common foreign and security policy has *de facto* prevented Europe from playing a role of its own, in a dialectical way *vis-à-vis* the choices of the American super-power, in the project of a "Common European Home". As a consequence, the enlargement to the East, with the entry of former communist countries into the European Union, has certainly been a necessary and altogether successful route, but in some aspects it was problematic, and did not solve the primary problem of a security and stability system agreed with post-Soviet Russia (that has remained in any case a big nuclear power); it did not tackle the problem of setting up a new Euro-Asian order, participated and guaranteed by all the concerned actors. As Antonio Mosconi (1999) writes in analyzing the complexity of these issues, "Only a European Union government would have the necessary authority to draw up, along with Russia itself and the United States, a strategy based on the sequence defence-euro-plan-market to prevent a grand collapse on our eastern frontiers". Bringing the eastern post-communist countries into the market-economy and the western defence system, the offspring of the cold-war, without dealing with the problem of a new, shared security system at the Euro-Asian level: this was the mistake that is still impinging on the future of Europe and, more in general, of the world. At the base of all this there are on the one hand, as we already said, the absence of an autonomous voice of the European community, and on the other the policy of isolating Russia pursued by the United States and NATO, with the consequence of dangerously fueling, as a defensive reaction, the new nationalism of the Moscow government. As Ira Strauss observes, "They played a game of renewing geopolitical competition *vis-à-vis* Russia...The aim of the game was to deprive Russia of its influence in the Caucasus and Central Asia...As part of this game, the Talibans were welcomed by the US where they were coming to power..."

As for the problems and challenges of the Euro-Mediterranean area, once again the absence of a common foreign and security policy has contributed to produce a worsening of instability, crises and conflicts, which came to a climax in recent times with the political and humanitarian catastrophe of hundreds of thousands (prospectively millions) of refugees fleeing to Europe. The Euro-Mediterranean integration projects, although pursued to some degree and even realized, did not reach a fully operational status, and no great Euro-Mediterranean community was ever established that could promote peace, security and development in that area. At the heart of that challenge there has been and there is the unresolved knot of the Middle East and its conflicts, to which *The Federalist Debate* has devoted for years a particular attention. In the perspective outlined on several occasions by the review, solutions of some federal type are necessary to bring peace to the area. To that aim, it is required first of all to foster "as a transitional stage, the setting up of a joint Mediterranean framework, shared by all Mid-Eastern and North African countries, together with European countries located along the Mediterranean basin" (Yossi Amitai). More specifically, every prospect of bringing peace and stabilizing the area passes through a reconciliation between the Arab world and Israel. It is a very difficult route, which seems today, looking at the hard facts, almost unthinkable. But, as John Parry writes using a historical comparison, "Who in the Europe of 1941 would have dreamed that, within ten years, six of the combatant states would agree to place fundamental sectors of their economies under common control?". The route to pursue passes through the peaceful coexistence of two separate States, the Israeli and the Palestinian, with the prospect of a wider regional federation. In concrete terms, a Palestinian-Jordanian federation, in turn confederated with the State of Israel. More in general, solutions of a federal/confederal type can be proposed and pursued all across the Arab world. As Hazem Hanafi writes, a regional integration project is necessary for the whole greater Arab region, that is, for 22 countries and 530 million inhabitants. The regional cooperation forms realized so far, from the League of Arab States onwards, have all failed, hence there is to conceive and propose a form of "asymmetrical federalism" that guarantees diversity and pluralism.

A similar route can be also proposed to cope with the Balkanization process that has hit Sub-Saharan Africa, due to both the heritage of colonialism, and the mistakes of the local leading classes (these factors are analyzed in this book in Jean-Francis Billion's article). In this area, the regional integration projects, although not realized, of Léopold Sédar Senghor and of the Ghanian Kwame N'Krumah (of the same year 1958), presented at the pan-African conference in Accra, remain in any case a cultural and ideal patrimony that can be made fruitful.

In Asia, economic and political regionalization processes, documented and analyzed in the articles by W. Arputharaj and Ken Endo, are in progress in different forms and among different countries, in a context of a strong economic growth and of an ever greater interdependence. Given the important role that Asia has been progressively playing in world economy and politics, the success of the integration processes in this area represent a decisive added value for the entire world.

Finally, regional integration processes are in progress, as is well-known, also in Latin America, where a significant influence, at least cultural or political and cultural, is exerted by both the North-American historical federal model, and the model of regional integration developed after 1945 in Europe. The difficulties and contradictions of the many already-initiated integration processes, from Mercosur to the Andean Community to the more recent UNASUR and CELAC, highlight on the one hand the existing resistances to schemes involving the sharing of fundamental aspects of sovereignty, and on the other the persisting and recurring reemergence of thrusts and movements in favor of supra-national answers to problems that cannot be tackled at the national level alone. A meaningful example, testified in Fernando A. Iglesias' article, is given by the recent project of a "Regional Criminal Court Against Organized Crime", which prospectively may lead later, "through the establishment of similar courts in other world regions", to a "World Criminal Court Against Transnational Organized Crime". As shown by the experience of the International Criminal Court and, in Europe, the Court of Justice in Luxembourg (a body of the European Union), and the European Court of Human Rights (a body of the Council of Europe), the route of establishing regional or global jurisdictional bodies is a strategic, fundamental course of action; it requires to gather actors and interests of many countries of the world around shared projects, and allows sometimes to anticipate and foreshadow, as happened with the Charter of Fundamental Rights in the European Union, even their legislative regulation. In this case too, a *tessera* of that multi-level institutional architecture which the world is in desperate need of for trying to escape the chaos that is threatening us.

Rethinking the “European Common Home”*

Antonio Mosconi

The solution of Russia’s grave economic crisis and the consolidation of its recent and fragile democratic institutions represent the prime objectives for European security today. Consider the population and income of the various zones of Europe compared to those of the United States[1]: turning from the Union to the nineteen countries of Central and Eastern Europe, one cannot help feeling concern and scepticism over the uncertain prospects of enlargement. These countries have an average *per capita* income of three thousand dollars (something like that of China), but the quota of resources they allocate to defence is more than twice that of the EU. Their foreign trade with the EU and developing countries is growing rapidly compared to the traditional relations of integration between Central and Eastern European countries. These include Catholic, Protestant, Orthodox and Moslem countries, whereas the Christian religions are predominant in the EU; they aspire to a lay concept of the state which, as in the EU, allows the separation of the political from the religious sphere, but some of them are still threatened by the complex links between religious fundamentalism and political nationalism. The acceleration of the entry procedure for the principal countries of the former Eastern bloc, in contrast to the postponed consideration of

* Published in Issue 1/1999.

1 1996 statistics. Population in millions. GDP in billions of $ at the current rate of exchange (World Bank method). *Per capita* GDP in thousands of purchasing power parity $ (PPP$, UN method). The figures in parentheses are on a scale of 1 – 100, where the corresponding US figure equals 100. The nineteen Eastern European countries are: Albania, Bosnia-Herzegovina, Bulgaria, Czech Republic, Cyprus, Croatia, Estonia, Iceland, Federal Republic of Yugoslavia, Latvia, Lithuania, Macedonia, Malta, Poland, Romania, Slovak Republic, Slovenia, Turkey and Hungary. The four European republics which previously belonged to the former USSR are: Byelorussia, Moldavia, the Russian Federation and Ukraine.

	Population Current	GDP	Current GDP	P.C.	PPP	GDP
United States	270	(100)	7.263	(100)	27.358	(100)
European Union	372	(138)	8.586	(118)	23.064	(84)
Swiss and Norway	11	(4)	451	(6)	24.733	(90)
Eastern European Countries	189	(70)	549	(7)	3.093	(9)
Former Soviet Republics	214	(79)	441	(6)	2.060	(8)
Europe	786	(291)	10.027	(138)	12.690	(46)

Turkey's admission, delineates an alarming scenario, aggravated by the lack of implementation of the Common Foreign and Security Policy[2].

If one then looks further to the East, where the *per capita* income of the four European republics which used to belong to the former Soviet Union has fallen to two thousand dollars, it is hard even to imagine how the geographical, historical and cultural unity of Europe can ever be crowned by its political unity. And yet the prime trading partner of these four states, apart from the CIS itself, is the EU. Like "the Nineteen", "the Four" too allocate twice the proportion of resources to defence that the EU does. The Orthodox Church, which is predominant in "the Four", is not in harmony with the Catholic Church; the former had to learn to live with communism, while the latter celebrated its funeral rites, while taking exclusive credit for its demise. The contribution which Christian unity could make to the chances of peace is important, but in reality we have so far witnessed the identification of the various churches with opposing nationalist movements, not only at diplomatic level, but also in local wars.

With the end of Gorbachev's political project, which had aimed to transform the Soviet Union into a federation capable of gradually steering the transition from soviet socialism to the social market, and thus to start a process of development through opening up to the world market and co-operation with the EU and the USA, most of the Eastern European countries have looked towards the European Union and towards NATO to rebuild prospects of development in a framework of security. Those who have studied the theory of *raison d'état* cannot fail to see how all this feeds Greater Russian nationalism and could re-kindle the flames of power politics. To prevent such a regression, which could cast the region back into darkness, even the most enlightened American plan[3] is inadequate. The latter tries to hypothesise Europe as an "American outpost in Eurasia", capable of attracting into its own orbit Ukraine too, which is already pro-western, (unlike Byelorussia and Moldova, both pro-Russian), detaching it from Moscow. Such a manoeuvre, however, could not but increase Moscow's sense of insecurity and frustration, already dangerously high, reinforcing its most nationalist, revanchist and antidemocratic tendencies. The chance of peace cannot be seized if Russia itself cannot find its own ambit of freedom and security by securing its own links with the EU until they can be genuinely institutionalised. Whether the result is reached by a political strengthening of the OSCE, or by establishing a federation

2 So far eleven countries which have applied for membership of the Union, eight of which previously belonged to the Eastern bloc (Estonia, Latvia, Lithuania, Poland, Czech Republic, Slovak Republic, Slovenia and Hungary), and the other three are situated on the fringes of the Arab-Moslem world (Cyprus, Malta and Turkey).

3 Zbigniew Brzezinski, *The Grand Chessboard* (New York: Basic Books, 1998).

among federations, or even by setting a date, however distant, for Russian membership of the EU, is an important question, since the choice of means influences the realisation of the ends. For now however, and until the EU implements the CFSP, it is crucial to be aware of the strategic priority of avoiding the collapse of Russia.

A first reflection must be made on the strategy of enlargement. To us Europeans it appears that, for the building of the Union, the method adopted started with the market and will arrive, via the currency, at foreign and security policy. But this is not the case. First came defence and the currency (NATO and the dollar), provided by the Americans, then the market. The opposite course only concerned the winning of independence from the United States. This optical illusion could prompt us to propose the "community method", i.e. the order market-currency defence, as the strategy for enlargement. I believe that one could not make a more serious mistake. An excessive faith in the capacity of self-regulation of the market in countries where this is lacking, and the extension of the logic of the "Maastricht parameters" to economies which can hardly call themselves monetary, would increase the probability of a profound and prolonged de-stabilisation of the former Soviet empire. The situation demands that references are sought rather in the mix of policies put in place by the Americans immediately following the Second World War: a Marshall Plan, then a defence community. This means turning upside down the order of priorities of the "Community method". Defence and foreign policy must once more assume first place, so that on the one hand, Russia can feel secure both in the western sphere and in relation to the Asian powers whose economic and military strength is rapidly rising; and on the other, the United States can be reassured by the Russia's entry (in whatever form) into NATO and not only into the European Union.

The currency, i.e. the euro, must precede the market and enable its completion, just as the adoption of the dollar as European currency preceded the formation of the Common Market. Only the economic and financial reform of Russia, which will be made possible by a "Marshall Plan" supported mainly by the EU, particularly considering the American incapacity to support a further burden on the already enormous foreign debt, can finally allow the largest European country to enter the continental single market and the global market. Only then will Schumpeter's *entrepreneurs* become the protagonists of Russian economic progress instead of the *buccaneers* evoked by Keynes.

A second reflection concerns the formulation of the plan. Russian-produced consumer goods will for some years yet prove inadequate to the sophisticated demands dictated by global competition. The theory and practice of five-year plans allowed industrialisation by forced stages and the production of the tanks and airplanes necessary to stop Hitler at Stalingrad, but they had catastrophic results when applied to the production of consumer goods. However, in order for Russia to put itself in a condition to present itself on the world markets, one cannot simply trust to the market. The resources on which Russia can draw to finance the immense investments necessary for *perestroika* essentially consist of energy, raw materials and the military industry, all sectors in which the American success too owes more to planning than to the market[4]. The exploitation of these resources requires strategic security and political stability (consider the vulnerability of oil and gas pipelines many thousands of kilometres long), an adequate financial plan and investments in the most advanced technologies; without forgetting the need to ensure the availability of food and other consumer goods in sufficient measure to prevent the development of a Weimar scenario. Only a European Union government would have the necessary authority to draw up, along with Russia itself and with the United States, a strategy based on the sequence defence-europlan-market to prevent a grand collapse on our eastern "frontiers".

4 John Kenneth Galbraith, *The New Industrial State* (Boston: Houghton-Mifflin, 1967).

New Myths about Russia and NATO*

Ira Straus

One welcomes any prospects for improved NATO-Russia relations, but there is cause for scepticism in face of a new spate of myths being promulgated by Western diplomats in the last couple of days. One myth is that Russia does not want to join NATO. The other is that Russia might also get a *veto* if NATO starts consulting seriously with it, and that every NATO member has a right to veto decisions in the alliance.

Let me start with the second point, since it is the psychological basis of the fear of Russian membership. Do NATO members in fact have a right to veto decisions in NATO? No. The North Atlantic Treaty – which anyone can easily find and read, it is only two pages – leaves the NATO Council free to set its own procedures. It did this deliberately, so that members would have no right of veto. This has been attested by the late Amb. Theodore Achilles, the main author of the Treaty. It has been attested by Dirk Stikker, the third Secretary General of NATO, who devoted several pages of his memoirs to explaining why there is no right of veto in NATO. It has been attested by many, many other authorities.

It is another matter if the Council often extends to its participants a *de facto* privilege of veto. This is a matter of diplomatic courtesy, not of right; and if we may speak plainly to one another, not in the ingrown language of certain diplomatic circles, we should say that it is often a mistake, a problem of too much self-indulgence and mutual indulgence on the part of NATO diplomats, with the result of obstructing important work and undermining both the strength and the flexibility of the alliance. As to the fear of Russia getting a right of veto, it is impossible under the North Atlantic Treaty. As to the prospect of Russia getting a *de facto veto*, it all depends on what is meant by this phrase. If it means that NATO would let Russia repeatedly obstruct decisions, then it is highly implausible, but if it were to happen, it would be due to foolish behavior on the part of the other diplomats sitting around the table, not because of any veto rights on the part of Russia. If it means that NATO might sometimes compromise with Russia's view rather than ignore it, and might give Russia's voice as much weight as it gives to, say, Luxembourg or Hungary, then it is highly desirable. Russophobes within NATO have been complaining of a

* Published in Issue 1/2002.

"*de facto* Russian veto" for years, every time there was a hint that NATO might compromise with Russia's views on some subject. Their idea of cooperation is, it would seem, that Russia should give its view and then NATO should make sure to do the exact opposite.

To avoid this kind of malicious treatment of Russia's valid concerns, it is extremely important that Russia's voice should come with a real weight attached to it, something that makes it hard to ignore. The present proposals do not yet seem to provide for this. Western officials have mostly spoken as if the only way to do that would be to give Russia a right of veto, which they justifiably oppose although they unjustifiably speak of it as a real issue. Sergei Ivanov, the Russia Defense Minister, has said much more realistically that Russia's voice can be given real weight by giving it a vote: "Russia would have the right to vote, the right to take decisions ditching the present form of cooperation within the Russia-NATO Permanent Joint Council where such a mechanism does not work". Somewhat surprisingly, his comments have been more democratic, as well as more constructive and more realistic, than those of Western commentators, who have almost invariably focused on the undemocratic idea of a *veto* and then proceeded to complain about it. However, there has been one report – in the Russian press (*Interfax*, Nov. 23), not the Western press – that has Lord Robertson also speaking of a vote for Russia: "A Russian envoy or ambassador to Brussels could periodically attend the council's meetings on certain issues and have the right to vote at them", he said. When asked what issues Russia could vote on, Robertson said that these include fighting terrorism and possibly nonproliferation of nuclear weapons and setting up of a nonstrategic missile defense system in Europe. Ironically, Vladimir Lukin, former Ambassador to the U.S. and vice-speaker of the Duma, said that the Blair proposals are not as good as membership, not because he wants a veto but because he wants a vote: "It is better for Russia to become a NATO member, to receive a voting right and a veto right at that organisation."

The talk of a veto, then, is misleading on all counts. It is misleading in all its myriad forms, forms so contradictory that they should have given reporters a clue that there was something wrong with it. Yet it has spread widely in the last few days in the Western media. Why? To begin with, it built on many previous years of mythmaking on this subject. In the current round, however, it seems to have started with a question from Reuters about whether Russia wouldn't be getting a veto power. This brought a careless answer from Lord Robertson that maybe it would be so. And that answer brought a spate of fearful reactions in European capitals, reactions that verged on a hysteria. The fears grew rapidly to the point of threatening even the meager improvements in Russia-NATO arrangements that Tony Blair has been proposing. Russian officials had to deny that they have any wish to get a right of veto. This in turn was mistaken as confirmation that the issue is real.

As to the myth that Russia does not want to join NATO: the Russian elite has explained for years that they would like very much to join the alliance as an equal member, but Mr. Putin has already stated clearly that Russia does not intend to "stand in queue to join NATO" like all the other small countries of Central and Eastern Europe. The meaning of his comment is that Russia does not intend to put itself through the humiliation of going through a beauty contest like the other countries, get judged on whether it meets the standards, face a series of report cards, jump through hoops demanded by the West and then find that the bar gets raised and new hoops are put out for some new jumps, and so forth. If Russia is to join NATO, it will not be by standing in queue, nor by sneaking in through a hidden entrance, but by a mutual decision in which both sides agree on terms that make it something that is in the mutual interest.

This is the plain meaning of Mr. Putin's comments. I might underline the accuracy of this interpretation, by mentioning that, several days before Mr. Putin made his comment about "not standing in queue" to join NATO, I had heard the exact same formulation quoted from a figure in Mr. Putin's Administration, and the meaning of the formulation was to support, not oppose, preparations for Russia's joining NATO. Specifically, the meaning was to say that it was necessary to go ahead with unofficial discussions between Russians and Westerners about how Russia could join NATO, to prepare public and elite opinion for Russia's joining, and to arrive at some plans for doing this in a way that would be in the interest of both sides, so that in the end Russia and NATO could proceed in a dignified manner to agree on a plan for Russia joining and carry it out.

The mass terrorist murders of September 11 could have never occurred, if America and NATO had followed the natural course in the 1990s of forming an alliance with Russia. Instead, they played a game of renewing geopolitical competition *vis-à-vis* Russia, what they called "the Great Game". The aim of the game was to deprive Russia of its influence in the Caucasus and Central Asia. It was a drunken game, a kind of cold war hangover. As a part of this game, the Taliban were welcomed by the U.S. when they were coming to power; it was only afterwards that America gradually turned against the Talibs. But it never could agree to actually being wholeheartedly on the same side of Russia against the Taliban – not until the massacres of September 11.Then we paid the price for our drunken elite games *vis-à-vis* Russia.

Are we finally cured of the hangover? On the level of the people, yes. But then, we always were cured on that level. It is the elite level that counts. We have, as everyone in the elites from Sergei Ivanov to Lord Robertson has stated, a historic second chance, now when we are united against a common enemy, to build the kind of relationship that we ought to have built in the 1990s. But are the elites ready to build a workable framework for this relation, or to let it slip through the fingers in this period, which is the period of greatest openness and opportunity for doing something new?

The Blair proposals offer some hope. It is, however, a half-way hope, the hope of a first step that would need to be built on as a launching pad, not treated as an institutional landing point. The hysteria and retreats already surrounding the Blair proposals offer cause for concern that they will be whittled down and the space for growth cut out of them, just as happened to the NATO-Russia Permanent Joint Council four years ago. A historic opportunity is a terrible thing to waste.

For a Euro-Mediterranean Community*

Pier Virgilio DASTOLI

No one had expected the Arab Spring!

Nowadays it makes us wonder how Arabs will be able to build a State subject to the rule of law and sustainable economies. Diplomacy, economy and society must be rethought to meet the aspirations of this young Arab generation to a new model of development, a strong legal system, a strong regional integration, all in a revamped context. Meanwhile, the Europeans deal with internal and external challenges and with an extremely difficult decade just begun, where peace, democracy, citizenship, economic prosperity and social development may be called into question.

Faced with the events of the Arab Spring, we shall stay far away from fear, bad advisors, and choose innovation, peace, citizenship, democracy and prosperity in a new framework that meets the challenges of the twenty-first century. These are enormous challenges. For the European Union and for the Arab countries the issue of a new architecture for their cooperation gives us the opportunity to find a double positive response to our internal and external challenges and to the aspirations of the Arab world, on the basis of a true dialogue with each other.

To find this double hit, must we go beyond partnerships as the Union for the Mediterranean or the Neighborhood Policy provided by the European Commission Communication on 10 May 2011?

The Italian Council of the European Movement proposes something new, that is, building the "Euro-Mediterranean Community (EUMED)" – in addition to the partnerships, "according to the different forms", proposed by the European Union to the Union for the Mediterranean, Euro-Mediterranean Parliamentary Assembly and Anna Lindh Foundation.

This community is not intended to replace the EU enlargement process towards the Balkans (Croatia and then Serbia, Montenegro, Bosnia-Herzegovina, the former Yugoslav Federation of Macedonia, Kosovo, Albania) and Turkey. We propose that this community be initially limited to countries going on the way of constitutional reform and with a new strong institutional, legal and democratic regional framework, opened to all North Africa people and to the dialogue with Sub-Saharan African

* Published in Issue 3/2011.

countries. It is going to be like a new ring involving the European Union and its neighbours, showing an innovative approach inspired by the beginning of the CZECH 50s and the Helsinki process of the mid-1970s.

Do not forget that the European Communities were instruments of peace and prosperity because they were equipped with institutions and common law (which are not insured or provided by partnerships). For this historical reason, we think that a "community" formed from the expectations of the civil societies of the South and North shores of the Mediterranean and inspired by the historical experience of the CZECH could represent a new point in the Euro-Mediterranean relations.

For the Italian Council of the European Movement, the objective of the next proposals is to extend to the Neighbourhood Policy – planned by the Prodi Commission in 2003 – the EU instruments of peace, which are: eliminating State violence (Democratic Governance), eliminating class violence and corruption (social solidarity), associating the southern Mediterranean countries, which is a key to prosperity, and promoting the European and Mediterranean Sea security in the Twenty-First Century. Prosperity and security are related to the shock that might occur over the next decade because of problems such as the "rarefaction" in the energy, environment, food, water and raw materials sectors. These concern a set of common goods that the nation states are no more able to guarantee to their citizens.

The double positive solution proposed and the ability to recover from the crisis, with a long-term vision, must consider the nationalist tendencies and the "every man for himself" approach growing in the European Union. Populism, which spreads like a metastasis in our political classes, is feeding on hate and, at the same time, it influences the political parties during the national and local elections.

To oppose nationalism and populism we must produce prosperity in a new way. To achieve it, we need a new vision of the European social pact. It has involved many stages and formulas: the project for peace (the CZECH and Common Market), the project for economic growth and free movement of goods, capital, people and services, the single currency (the domestic market, the Euro, the Lisbon Strategy, and Europe 2020), a project for a Europe of citizens, the public space of democracy (the election by direct universal suffrage of the European Parliament, the right of citizens' initiative), of freedom, justice and security, fundamental rights (the Charter of Nice, the Copenhagen criteria, the freedom of movement of persons in the Schengen Agreement, and in particular the mobility of students, teachers and researchers). The European agreement has thus provided the four pillars (peace, prosperity, democracy and citizenship), each of which must be consolidated and strengthened in a more integrated and inclusive Union. In this spirit, the Italian Council of the European Movement considers that the project, the method and the agenda should be discussed to continue the journey to the United States of Europe – as envisaged in the *Ventotene Manifesto* by Spinelli. A "Euro-Mediterranean Community" could revitalize the process of European integration because it would be a new way to deal with vital issues that have an impact on peace, prosperity, democracy and citizenship. These are the challenges of the economy, the environment, migration and the enlargement of the EU borders. The Euro-Med Community would have four 'baskets' to address:

- Peace and Human Rights, access to information, freedom of expression, participation and justice
- Green Economy[1], water, energy, food, green and connected cities
- Integrated Economic Region[2]
- Youth.

The Helsinki process (which contributed to end the Soviet empire) had three baskets as well: security in Europe, cooperation in economy, in science, in technology, in environment and in the humanitarian field, which was a prelude to the broader field of protection of human rights.

The first goal is peace and democracy. Peace is the area where European integration has reached its major successes. Peace at the external borders and domestic civil peace are two valuable public goods that must be safeguarded. Nowadays new crises (financial, resources, climate) have replaced a set of various crises that have marked the history of humanity, aimed to conquer spaces and territories.

They could lead humanity to war for energy or water, and resume the conquest of space, especially agricultural. The desert of North Africa is going to play a key role in the energy supply for Europe, starting from the solar energy. Peace and democracy both presuppose a rule of law, and judges whom citizens can have access to. The respect of fundamental rights can be enforced against the states, which shall accept to respect the mechanisms of humanitarian intervention and mediation.

From the European point of view, it is essential for us to include in the budget adequate resources to enable the EU to be equipped with the necessary tools for "peace keeping" and "peace building". In this context, one might imagine to give the Union exclusive competence in the areas of cooperation to development and humanitarian aid, which today are considered by the Treaty of Lisbon a shared competence. On the contrary,

---

1 *Rio +20 Agenda*. See UNEP's Green Economy Report.

2 As proposed by the European Roundtable of Industrialists (ERT) and by professor Mario Monti.

the Spinelli's draft of 1984 stipulated that they would become a Union's exclusive competence in a ten-year transitional period, respecting the international agreements in force. Following the same principle, relations with neighbouring countries – considered privileged under Article 8 of the Treaty of Lisbon – could become an exclusive competence of the European Union after a ten-year transitional period.

The second basket is the big market, as it was provided for in the objectives of the Euro-Mediterranean Partnership in 1995. Today, while Asia goes on to become the planet's most powerful economic area and China emerges in the role of the main world nation, the same that it had been from the year 1000 (70% of the world GDP) until the Industrial Revolution (14% of GDP in 1880, but 5% in 1950), the Arab countries are facing a much more open chance with China, ever more present in the Mediterranean and African areas.

We must be conscious that things are moving very quickly on two floors: on the one hand, the EU is no more the obligated economic partner of the Arab countries. On the other hand, Europe's soft power in the world will become increasingly dependent on our ability to propose to the Mediterranean countries to participate in a big market. It must be capable of responding to the challenges of energy, environment and agriculture, as it has been recently proposed by Professor Mario Monti. In this context, we believe that the EU should have the tools to help Mediterranean countries to establish and develop an intra-regional trade among them, now virtually non-existent.

With the Euro-Mediterranean Community, we could have an extraordinary opportunity to make effective and efficient the UN program called "green economy in the sustainable development context and the fight against poverty," which would thus become the third basket of the Community. It could establish itself in the world because slow economic growth and demographic constraints on the use of resources will not leave us other choice but to innovate in terms of technology and society.

This third basket would concern energy, water, food, including the common agricultural policy, commodities, the green cities connected to each other by an ecologically-sustainable transport infrastructure.

We believe it is time to conceive a new dream and give new impetus to progress. Our strategic interest is to plan and realize it with the other Mediterranean Basin countries. However, we should not do it against the others but with the others: the United States, China, Japan, Russia, India, along with the African Union and the Arab League, and talking with other forms of regional integration like Mercosur.

Don't forget that this year we celebrate the fiftieth anniversary of the interdependence declaration given in July 1961 by John F. Kennedy. The

European Union is now facing a triple choice (the European "trilemma") which appears as a vital challenge: financial stringency, investment in green infrastructures and maintenance of the welfare state and public services in the context of an ageing population.

In this spirit, the European Union must define an inter-generational pact that will consider this triple choice and the impact on the young generations in the EU and outside, as we are told by the young people of Puerta del Sol and the young people of Tunis.

The European Union has lived successive and spectacular enlargements. They have found their *raison d'être* in many aims: first of all the enlargement seen as an extension of the single market and as a lever for growth. It could be also a tool for strengthening peace (think of the Balkans) and the geo-political role of the European Union (Turkey). But these enlargements have also led to a Europe in which populism and the contempt for the other are growing, and where the construction of the European Union becomes more and more an intergovernmental process, therefore weak and undemocratic.

Here is the project of the Euro-Mediterranean Community that we intend to submit to a public debate:

"It is the European Union as such that should have a seat in the Euro-Mediterranean Community.

The European Union would keep its institutions, if necessary reinforced in their supra-national dimension, and its center of gravity would remain in the triangle Brussels-Luxembourg-Strasbourg, while the Euro-Mediterranean Community could endow itself with institutions of its own partly inspired by the ECSC experience:

- a High Authority composed of three men and three women would be based in Istanbul;
- a Senate composed of 2 representatives for each country would be based in Tunis;
- a Court of Justice would be based in Strasbourg;
- in due course, an Inter-Parliamentary Conference will be based in Gaza.

Its center of gravity will be delimited in a first phase by the square Istanbul-Strasbourg-Tunis-Gaza. The European Union shall declare itself in favor of the entry in this Community of an Israel-Palestine Confederation or Federation, as proposed by Professor Jo Weiler. And when this will happen, Jerusalem could become the capital city of the Euro-Mediterranean Community".

Would it be foolish to expect to see the European Union represent the 27 within the Euro-Mediterranean Community? A mad project to envisage progress and prosperity in the Euro-Mediterranean area? A folly to imagine a new architecture to exit permanently from the Israeli-Palestinian conflict?

Before declaring as madness all these proposals, let's hear what the citizens want to say about freedom, peace, democracy, prosperity, solidarity, cultures and religions. Let's listen to what they think of these issues: the four baskets and the charter of a Euro-Mediterranean Community.

A Diplomatic Conference on the establishment of a Euro-Mediterranean Community involving, in addition to the European Union and the Arab countries on their way to democracy, the representatives of the African Union and the Arab League, should be preceded by a Conference of the Euro-Mediterranean Civil Society – as happened in 1948 at The Hague on the eve of the European integration process, or as happened in the early 1990s at the Helsinki Citizens Assembly. This conference should bring together leaders of the social-networks revolution, professors of law, history, economy, sociology, architecture and new technologies, coming from both sides of the Mediterranean and working in projects for the green economy, young people and migrants organizations, voluntary organizations and development experts. The conference should be organized by the European International Movement and the Council of Europe in collaboration with the European Commission and the Economic and Social Council, in the framework of the international network of economic and social committees. It would be appropriate to involve also the Committee of Regions.

We propose to organize that conference in Tunis in 2012, as was suggested by the board of the European Movement International, and to start the project on 25 September 2011 on the occasion of the 50th anniversary of the Perugia-Assisi March. Similarly, the diplomatic conference should be preceded by a financial conference on the mobilization of public (EIB, EBRD, World Bank) and private (banks, pension funds, foundations, European and Arab groups) capitals, to support a financial project such as a "Marshall Plan for the Mediterranean" (in its historic meaning), as proposed by the Spanish Prime Minister Zapatero and now revived by President Obama, who talked, on the same occasion, about institutional building. An important signal in the right direction has been given by the European Bank for Reconstruction and Development (EBRD), set up after the end of the Soviet system, which gave 2.5 billion euros to the countries involved in the "Arab Spring", which add up to those of the World Bank and the Gulf Co-operation Council.

The peoples of the Southern Mediterranean countries and the Europeans must reflect on all these issues, becoming aware of the fact that, like it or not, we are on the eve of a great change of the planet and humanity. This change will soon be imposed by the shock linked to the problems of energy, raw materials, water and environment. The Europeans and the peoples of the Southern Mediterranean countries have the opportunity to be an example and see how the Mediterranean, cradle of our civilization, can contribute to a big transition, building a new community of values and rights, beyond cultural differences, to ensure prosperity and to let humanity take a new step towards peace and democracy.

The Arab Spring, Federalism and Euro-Arab Relations[*]

Hazem HANAFI

Democracy and Federalism

The push towards democracy in the Arab World is a push towards federalism, and *vice versa*. Federalism, especially asymmetric federalism, has been gaining increasing attention for its ability to manage, moderate or resolve conflicts, and to accommodate different levels of diversity (*de facto*) and forms of government (*de jure*) without sacrificing the unity of the polity. Asymmetric federalism could be translated into asymmetrical representation, different rights and functions, veto powers, opt-in or opt-out options or time-bound restrictions.

The Arab World, 22 countries, 330 million people, larger in size than the US, Canada, Europe or China, has an overall GDP of almost two trillion US dollars in 2010, and has such strong common ties as language, history, culture, ethnicity and religion. Yet, not only they failed to achieve a modest level of cooperation, integration and development, but have also become a battleground for widespread inter-state and intra-state conflicts, have been subjected to occupation or foreign domination and have fallen behind in major human-development indexes.

Motives for Union and motives for Autonomy continue to co-exist in the Arab World. The study of the application of federalism in the Arab world is important for four reasons:

- On a pan-Arab level, it may be able to open a new path for regional cooperation and integration that has traditionally been scattered between two extreme poles: a unitary and centralized system on the one hand, and a loose confederacy on the other;
- Federalism is being currently proposed in three Arab states: Iraq, Sudan and Somalia. Many local and international observers think that the solution to the chronic problems facing these countries is in adopting federal arrangements to ensure healthy power sharing, decentralization and more respect for human rights and democratization;

[*] Published in Issue 3/2011.

- Half of the Arab countries, those who are in Africa, are members of the African Union, an emerging federal system since 2000;
- Because federalism is being forcefully proposed by the "West", especially in Iraq under occupation and Sudan under sanctions, there is the danger that it becomes stigmatized as "imperial" and "foreign", turning it into another unneeded conflict issue like democracy did. Federalism in the Arab world should not become another missed opportunity due to lack of proper consideration or misunderstanding.

Two models for regional cooperation and integration have been tried in the Arab world. The first was envisaged in the writings of Arab nationalist thinkers[1], and it centered on creating a united Arab state, with one center of political power and a centralized state machinery. Several micro attempts involving two, three or four states have failed during the 1950s and 1960s, but the dream of Arab unity has managed to survive these failures, which were blamed on conflicts of interests and attitudes, incompatibility of political and socio-economic conditions, and the role of external factors not favourable to the creation of one large united Arab state.

The second model of loose confederacy is reflected in the creation of the League of Arab States in March 1945 by the seven independent Arab states at the time. The objectives of the League were to enhance cooperation among Arab states in all fields:

- Economic and financial affairs – including commercial relations, customs, currency, and questions of agriculture and industry;
- Communications – this includes railroads, roads, aviation, navigation, telegraphs and posts;
- Cultural affairs;
- Nationality, Passports, visas, execution of judgments and extradition of criminals;
- Social affairs;
- Health affairs.

Against such objectives, the Arab League has failed in achieving any meaningful results (the League moved to Tunisia after Egypt's peace treaty with Israel in 1979), but political disputes and distrust among members are frequent; several regional groupings have been created, among them: the Gulf Cooperation Council (1981), the Arab Maghreb Union (1989),

[1] Rio Abd al-Rahman al-Kawakibi's *Characters of Authoritarianism* (1854-1902), Sati Al-Hussary's *Language and History* (1879-1967), Constantin Zureiq's *Arab Mission* (1909-2000), Michel Aflaq's *Bathism* (1910-1989).

and the Arab Cooperation Council (1989). The Arab league, however, is too weak to enforce its decisions, as the Arab Court of Justice, per Article 19 of its Statute, has no clear jurisdiction. The continuous failure of these two models, largely blamed on the bad execution of policies, not on the suitability of the models themselves, opens the way to examine whether federalism could be an alternative model, more appropriate for Arab regional cooperation, integration and conflict management.

Federalism and Conflict Management

The Arab-Israeli conflict

Palestine is one land, two peoples, with no shared identity or agreement on the polity. "Division" of the land is offered as a solution, whilst the federal principle of "sharing" may be more useful. With each community wanting the "whole", each is dissatisfied with the half it gets and looks at the half it lost. The most obvious and viable federal option would be to establish a bi-national, bi-lingual, bi-communal and bi-state federation composed of an Israeli state/province and a Palestinian state/province, with Jerusalem as the seat of the federal government. A Union of Israel and Palestine, a parliamentary federation, with features like those in the UK, Belgium, Canada and the EU. Principles of asymmetrical and non-territorial federalism would apply.

Regional integration

Disparities in wealth or power among states didn't hinder federal solutions in other federations. Coordination and sharing lead to better economic management, as one can read in *The Federalist Papers* in the American experience or see in the EU. Federalism is the political framework to implement plans for cooperation and integration.

Diversity and Pluralism

There are diverse minorities in the Arab world, with variables of language, ethnicity and religion; some minorities differ only in one aspect, some differ in multiple.

Some question the legitimacy of the state (as the Kurds in Iraq), while others only question the legitimacy of the regime or the government in power. Some have had civil wars (Lebanon, Sudan) while others experienced frictions and civil strife. Some were always ruled by the majority, while others who were the minority ruled over an absolute majority (as the Alawites in Syria), and there are cases where there was no clear majority. There are some who refuse to be labelled as a minority, or are a minority in one setting but a majority in a different setting (as the

Arabs in Israel and the Sunnis in Iraq). Some have received more external help than others: the Arabs in Israel have links to the wider Palestinian population in the West Bank, the Shi'ites in the Gulf, Iraq and Lebanon have links to Iran.

The solution to this problem is complex, because it needs to contemplate more than one type of solution (recognition and acceptance, participation and democracy, associative techniques, federalism) to accommodate the different varieties of minorities' demands. Federalism allows and promotes the overlapping of multiple identities to function through unity, and asymmetrical Federalism could be particularly helpful in this regard. For example, language rights could be granted to all minorities, which in practice will benefit mostly the Kurds in Iraq and the Berbers in North Africa, whereas other minorities (the Copts in Egypt, religious minorities in Lebanon and the Gulf) have all accepted Arabic as their mother language. Also, depending on the political demands of minorities, asymmetrical federalism could employ different systems of representation and participation. Federalism, furthermore, allows "experimentation" on different levels. Laws could be tried at the state level before being implemented on the federal level or laws could be passed first on the federal level giving time for states to adapt and adopt them.

The Arab world and the EU

There is nothing new in stating that the European integration project has been unique, a classical example of federalism without federation. Looking back at the original plan of Schuman and Monnet, promoting slow, integrative, functional piecemeal steps to remove the causes of war in the continent, one can only wonder if that plan went too well too fast. Is the EU a model for other regional or continental federations?

The plan envisaged, in simple terms, that as integration increases, the likelihood of war and conflict decreases, till such a time when a federation would be possible. During the process of integrative federalism the absence of war and conflict is due to the rewards and constraints of an existing and potential cooperation, i.e. interlocking states in a web of mutual cooperation and interdependence, that reformulates a situation in which conflict is dominant and strives for aspects of cooperation. As decisions rest primarily with the nation states, they have to see these rewards themselves and accept some related constraints on their decision-making in order not to engage in conflict. It is purely a conscious sovereign decision. However, when a federation is established, central institutions would play a much greater role in maintaining peace, i.e. there would be an element of coercion. It is not difficult to see how this idea of a federation whose central institutions have the upper hand and responsibility in maintaining peace, law and order in Europe, fits within the general trend towards federalism elsewhere in the immediate post-war era.

As each federation is the product of a specific bargain within a suitable variety of federalism that answers a specific question, federal systems are not exportable. Each is designed to work within specific inputs to produce a previously agreed upon output, each is designed to solve a specific problem. Federalism has an intrinsic capacity to adapt and evolve, because it is primarily based on a bargain, the institutional features of a federation that allow, promote and require compromise and the existence of multiple levels of governance, where "experiments" could be made on a trial basis at one level without necessarily affecting another. This natural capacity to adapt to changing circumstances and evolve to accommodate new realities, features and institutions allows federalism to manage, moderate and even resolve conflicts. With the increasing diversity of the federal systems, designs and institutions, federalism provides an ever increasing pool of ideas to accommodate various interests and needs.

Federalism is alive in Europe like in no other place, and is passionately debated among millions of people from dozens of countries. It has served to rebuild European consciousness after centuries of religious reformism, renaissance, rationalism and enlightenment, and after it experienced a crisis in the 20th century. Is federalism the core value Europe is giving to the world in the 21st century? Will the Arab world relations with Europe change after its recent wave of democratization, and allow for more equal relations and mutual appreciation? Will the center-periphery model give way to a more egalitarian model? Will the voice of the people in the Arab world count as in Europe? How this will impact the economic and political cooperation between the two regions?

Federal/Confederal Solutions to the Israeli-Palestinian-Jordanian Conflict*

Daniel J. ELAZAR

Since 1976, the Jerusalem Center for Public Affairs, through its Institute for Federal Studies, has tried to formulate constructive federal arrangements for the parties of the region that will recognize Eretz Israel/Palestine's pluralist and multi-ethnic character and the national aspirations of its peoples. We have developed eleven options designed to accommodate the interests of the involved parties, specifically Israel, the Palestinians and Jordan, by building new political arrangements based on federalist principles.

A solution based on federal principles is one that combines self-rule (or self-government) and shared rule (or federal government) over the territories in dispute. However difficult to achieve this may be, it is the only possible outcome which has a chance of success. A move in this direction requires recognition by all parties of the failure of the exclusive sovereignty model to provide the basis for an acceptable solution to the problem of Judea, Samaria and Gaza.

Any accommodation based on power-sharing and limited autonomy for certain groups must be carefully balanced to at least minimally accommodate the security, nationalist and political interests of the participating parties – without at least minimal satisfaction of vital interests, even the best laid plan is doomed to fail. While Israel, the Palestinians, and Jordan are the parties directly involved in any settlements, the interest of the Great Powers (particularly the United States) and Egypt and the other Arab states must also be taken into account.

For the three principal parties involved, security and national integrity provide the major impetus for their minimal interests:

For Israel:

- Peace secured by formal treaty.
- Security arrangements on its eastern border providing strategic depth, early warning against any possible enemy attack, protected airspace, control of vital roads for defense purposes; and minimum exposure to terrorist infiltration from the east.

---

* Published in Issue 1/2002, excerpt from an article that can be found at the Jerusalem Center for Public Affairs site (www.jcpa.org/dje/articles/fedconfed-sol.htm).

- Maintenance of governance over a united Jerusalem as its capital.
- The continued right of Jews to reside in Judea, Samaria and the Gaza district.

For the Palestinians:

- Recognition of their national identity and practical political expression of that identity.
- Continuation of the special links with Jordan and the Arab world.
- Continuation of economic links with Israel.

For Jordan:

- Survival of Hashemite Jordan, including protection against possible extremist Palestinian factions.
- Formal and practical expression of the bonds between the Palestinians involved and the Hashemite Kingdom.
- Official status, duties and responsibilities in connection with the holy sites of the three.

The following four approaches are commonly viewed as possibilities for solving the conflict in the territories.

- Israel's withdrawal to pre-1967 borders (either fully or with the most minor territorial adjustments) and the establishment of a Palestinian state either separate or linked with Jordan.
- The extension of Israeli sovereignty (annexation) over the territories.
- Repartition of the territories to accommodate Israel's security needs (e.g., the Allon Plan) and allow separate political space for the Palestinians.
- Development of a form of shared rule over the territories by Israel and an Arab partner.

The first two options, involving total withdrawal or total absorption, run completely contrary to the non-negotiable interests of one, another, or all of the concerned parties. The third option, repartition of the territories on terms more favorable for Israel, has been firmly rejected by the Arab parties to the conflict, although it is acceptable to many Israelis. This leaves shared rule as the only viable alternative.

The strength of federalism lies in its flexibility and adaptability. The model focuses on people, not states, as the repositories of political sovereignty and legitimacy, thus shifting the issue of sovereignty to a different plane.

Moreover, proper use of federalism requires the provision of adequate guarantees to each entity through a constitutionalized commitment to shared self-rule. Federalism seeks to encourage unity and diversity together.

Federalism – self-rule/shared rule – involves both structure and process. A federal process must be combined with a federal structure to create a viable federal system or arrangement. A successful federalist process hinges on some sense of partnership among the participating parties based on a commitment to negotiated cooperation on issues and programs. There must be a commitment to open bargaining among all parties to achieve consensus or, at the very least, an accommodation which protects the fundamental integrity of all parties.

Contrary to some widely held opinions, federalism is more than modern federation. There are a number of different federal structures successfully functioning in the world today. In that sense, federalism can be understood as the genus and its various forms, species of the genus…

It is far from certain that the parties to the Israeli-Palestinian-Jordanian conflict have the will to federate. Nevertheless, there is no reason to presuppose that they could not develop the will under the proper circumstances. The objective conditions for federal solutions prevail, although the events of this century make it difficult to achieve. The question remains, however, as to whether there is a sufficient cultural basis for making federalism work among these peoples.

In order to successfully integrate federalism into a given polity, a federal political culture must exist, or be developed, within the constituent population. Among the factors which must be developed are a commitment to democratic government, a willingness to accept pluralism and power-sharing, an agreement to resolve conflict through negotiation, and finally, a sense of self-restraint in pursuing political goals and in the exercise of power which reaches beyond the other tenets of democratic government to include a commitment to power-sharing. Israeli Jews come from a long Jewish political tradition of federalism and a deeply federal political culture. A deep relationship between Jews and federalism can be traced back to the Bible: the first manifestation of God's covenant with Israel was the confederation/federation of the twelve tribes. Their federalism was reflected in the tribal federation and covenants of the Bible and through the federal political structures developed in most diaspora communities. Study of this dimension of the Jewish political tradition indicates how this federalist infrastructure has contributed to the Jews' predisposition toward constitutionalized power-sharing.

For the Arab world it is difficult to generalize. Different parts of the Arab world have had different historical and cultural experiences which have molded their individual political cultures. For example, Egyptian national existence has been based on a strong hierarchy and there is very little historical reason for a predisposition toward power-sharing. The Palestinian experience, on the other hand, has historically been based on a strong village and familial structure, providing for a large degree of institutionalized decentralization. The Bedouin experience has been very open to federalism due to the confederal links which exist among clans and tribes.

Nothing in modern political thought among Arab states resembles a theory of federalism. With the exception of the United Arab Emirates (essentially a Bedouin confederation in modern dress), all twentieth century experiments with federalism in the Arab world have failed. Islam is also a vital force in influencing modern Arab political thought. Muslim political theory emphasizes hierarchical and often personalized rule, with consideration for how to induce justice by hierarchical rulers, rather than how ruling hierarchies can be constitutionally limited. Furthermore, Islamic doctrine seems to almost prevent anything other than a superior-subordinate relationship between Muslims and non-Muslims. As *dhimmi* (protected inferior peoples), Jews and other non-Muslims were respected as "peoples of the book" in Muslim societies, yet they were not considered to be equals or potential partners for governance. Such covenants as there are in Islam are hierarchical, regulating and regularizing the relationships between superior and subordinate.

Some contemporary Muslim thinkers have come to believe that the Arabs might, in fact, be predisposed toward some form of federalism because they are perforce a federal nation divided into peoples and states. This is reflected by such state names as the Egyptian Arab Republic and the Syrian Arab Republic and also by their belief that, like the Bedouin, Arab states wage war against one another without losing their sense of common nationhood (*umma*), even as they preserve their separate people hoods (*wataniya*).

Examination of the historical experience of the Palestinians allows some room for optimism. Traditionally, Palestinian society has been highly decentralized – each village self-contained within the context of whatever external rule was imposed. Rule was shared among the various dominant clans (*hamulot*) and the leadership came from the heads of notable families. Adult males were able to participate in the governance of the village through their activity in the village militia. This system of governance prevailed through 1948 but it was replaced by more formal local government when these villages came under Jordanian, Israeli or Egyptian rule. The Arabs as a whole (including the Palestinians and the Hashemite Jordanians) do not appear to be readily open to federal arrangements with non-Arabs, and especially with non-Muslims. But the

Palestinians do have a history of informal power-sharing between the village and the state and, in view of the range of options and flexibility inherent in the various federalist options, it may be possible to construct an arrangement not in contradiction with Arab political culture, and, moreover, to adapt the Arab political heritage to a federalist solution…

The Best Alternative?

Is there a best solution? There is no single best solution under all circumstances. What is proposed here is what we believe to be at this time the most viable and pragmatic solution with a chance of successful implementation and sufficient fail-safe mechanisms to minimize the risks that must be taken by the parties in question if there is to be any solution.

From Israel's point of view, as has been articulated previously, a proper federal solution would provide the Jewish state with peace, appropriate security guarantees, provide protection for the Jewish settlements in the territories, and a share in the land's common resources (particularly water resources). These are three absolute necessities in the minds of virtually all Israelis, however they interpret the way to achieve them.

For the Palestinians, there remains a strong interest in being linked in some way with their brethren east of the Jordan river, located in territory which, according to the original League of Nations mandate and the PLO platform, should be part of any Palestinian state. When the PNC recognized Israel's right to exist in its statement in Algiers, it made no concessions whatsoever with regard to Jordan's right to exist independently of the proposed Palestinian state. In spite of that, Arafat is reluctant to accept Jordan's offer of federation because the Palestinians know that by accepting even a simple confederation with Jordan they will remain at the mercy of the Hashemite rulers and the Jordan army which has crushed them before and has promised to do so again if necessary. Despite recent developments in Jordan, Hussein (*now Abdullah, Ed.'s Note*) has little or no commitment to republican, not to speak of democratic, ideals. Jordan, indeed, should be even more Palestinian than it is. For Hussein (*now Abdullah, Ed.'s Note*) and his Hashemite Kingdom of Jordan, a federalist solution offers an opportunity to regain a foothold west of the river including a presence in Jerusalem at least (having some connection with the holy sites located there). The advantages of obtaining access to a port directly on the Mediterranean (which would come with Gaza) would also hold great appeal to Jordan.

In the interim, the only way in which a Palestinian link with Jordan would protect the Palestinians is if Israel were involved as a third party. An Israeli counterbalance to the Hashemite ruler would be a powerful guarantee of Palestinian self-government. The Palestinians, to gain a reasonable measure of self-determination, must accept a federal solution and find the appropriate partner or partners for it. Since neither Israel nor Jordan is acceptable alone, perhaps the Palestinians can be brought to realize that what is good for them is a combination of both – just as Israel has come to realize that, since it will not be allowed simply to absorb the territories, such an arrangement would be the lesser of two evils for it. Since Jordan has no other option, it will have to come to the same conclusion. It seems that given the considerations of the minimal absolute needs of each of the parties involved, at this juncture the best solution possible would encompass a Palestinian-Jordanian federation in new boundaries that reflect Israel's security needs, overlaid by a confederation with Israel. A Palestinian-Jordanian federation would mean one overarching general government for all of the Arab-governed territories on the east and west banks of the Jordan river, divided into two or more constituent states, at least one of which would be controlled by the Palestinian Arabs west of the Jordan river. Israel's role would be primarily to act as a guarantor that both sides live up to their federal obligations as determined by the peace settlement and the parallel constitutional negotiations between King Hussein (*now Abdullah, Ed.'s Note*) and the Palestinians. The integrity of the federation will be important because the federation will be viewed as one Arab state (albeit with two or more constituent entities) in the realm of international affairs.

While the Jordanian-Palestinian federation takes hold, Israel (territorially adjusted to include the State of Israel and segments of Judea, Samaria, and Gaza needed for security purposes or so extensively settled as to be appropriately part of the Jewish state) would be integrated into the arrangement through a confederal arrangement with the Jordanian-Palestinian federation. In a confederation, the states that come together can preserve their full political and juridical characters while establishing certain permanent joint bodies to serve their common needs (as opposed to a federation where one overarching general government rules a single polity).

This arrangement would guarantee Israelis access to the territories that they give up and will also give them a share in critical decisions concerning water rights and other common concerns. Among the tasks that could be entrusted to the confederal administration would be security in the former administered territories (other than the local police), control and distribution of water resources, economic and fiscal coordination including the maintenance of an open labor market and the promotion of economic development. The functions of the confederation could be conducted by the confederal governing institutions directly, or they could be assigned temporarily (or permanently) to one state or the other. For example, Israel could be made solely (or principally) responsible for security matters for a set period, after which, if things worked well, security could become a shared function.

Such a confederative structure could be governed through a council whose members would be appointed by the parties involved, either through the two states or, perhaps more effectively, by Israel and each of the federated states of Palestine/Jordan. If the former, voting could be on the basis of parity. In the case of the latter, voting would have to be weighted so that the Israeli vote would equal that of the Arabs. The capital of this confederation would be located in Jerusalem and the Arab presence in Jerusalem could be acknowledged in an appropriate manner. Moreover, any territorial concessions which might be made would be based on an allocation of jurisdiction rather than decisions on ultimate sovereignty, either indefinitely or for an interim period. Such a federation-confederation combination as proposed here would fulfill all of the fundamental concerns of the involved parties. The Palestinians would get their state, albeit a federal state rather than an independent sovereign one, but they would also be guaranteed a share in the governance of the shared Arab state. Jordan would have a continued standing west of the river. Israel would get secure borders, recognition by its Arab neighbors, and a continuing constitutional relationship with those parts of the historic Land of Israel not within its full political jurisdiction. Most of all there would be peace, a concept which by now the vast majority of the people involved seriously want.

What Is Israel's End-Game?*

Seyla BENHABIB

Israel has lost its political vision and military might without a clear political sense dominating its actions. Military power, freed from subordination to political goals, is blind and brutal. No one in the Israeli leadership has a political vision. Many who advocate a two-state solution also know that their future relations with a Palestinian state would be less like those between Italy and Austria and more like those between Tibet and China. But suppose there were a confederation in Israel-Palestine. This confederation could become the kernel of a Middle Eastern Union of Peoples, in which Turkey, Egypt, Saudi Arabia, Jordan and many other states would conjoin much along the model of the European Union.

Israel's military attack on the Gaza Strip, home to a million and a half Palestinians, was launched on December 28, 2008, the last day of *Hanukkah*, the "Festival of Lights". *Hanukkah* tells the story of the revolt of the ancient Hebrews, led by Judah Maccabee, in the second century BC against Antiochus IV Epiphanus. Legend has it that when the Maccabees succeeded in liberating the Temple from Antiochus, they found only enough oil to light the menorah for one night. Yet that oil burned for eight instead.

While the Israeli political echelon and military command had many reasons for timing their attack on Gaza as they did, they certainly knew the heroic resonances the Festival of Lights would have for the Israeli public: once more, Jews were writing a story of resistance against their oppressors: the threat to collective survival was heroically defeated by Defence Minister Ehud Barak, the new Judah Maccabee.

These potent memories of Jewish survival and resistance, together with the post-Holocaust determination that "Never again" will the Jewish people be subject to destruction, are the emotional wellsprings which Israel's leaders tap whenever the country is engaged in a war. Yet the strategic and *Realpolitik* considerations of the present Gaza military action are clear enough: no state, it is said, can accept continuous and unpredictable rocket attacks; it is obliged to defend its borders and inhabitants. Those who look a little deeper, however, point out that the Gaza operation

---

* Published in Issue 2/2009.

is attempting to restore Israel's seeming military invulnerability, lost in the wake of the 2006 Lebanon War.

None of this, though, accounts for the ferocity of the Israeli action, its disproportionality not only to the attacks from the other side but even to any imaginable Israeli goal, and its violation of international humanitarian law, and possible engagement in war crimes. Why?

The true answer is that Israel has lost its political vision and military might and that no clear political sense guides its actions. Military power, freed from subordination to political goals, is blind and brutal. No one in the Israeli leadership has a political vision, and I don't mean a strategy of long-term goals squeezed in between two election cycles and revisable according to the circumstances, but a political vision, the way founders of republics are supposed to have. How will this commonwealth endure? What lasting institutions can it bequeath to its children and grand-children in which they will be free to flourish as individuals and citizens? Who today has this kind of political vision to offer in view of the Israeli-Palestinian conflict? The Israelis have certainly lost it. And the Palestinians, although they have the force of morality and the wind of history at their backs, have been repeatedly defeated and degraded by Israel, and betrayed by Arab nations, always long on rhetoric but short on deeds.

Since the nineteen-sixties, the Palestinians' political vision has been inspired by the "third-worldism" of the "wretched of the earth", a discourse of nationalist and statist modernization, which showed its clear limits during the support by the Palestinian leadership for Saddam Hussein's invasion of Kuwait. I still remember the late Edward Said's extremely moving piece in *The New York Times* of Fall 1992 which admitted this Palestinian foolishness and described clearly the end of Fatah ideology. The vacuum left by the collapse of westernizing and modernizing military bureaucratic ideologies everywhere in the Arab world, was quickly filled by Islamist ideologies represented by Hamas and Hizbollah: the new Islamism is a disciplinarian, purist and moralist outlook, inspired by Ayatollah Khomeini's revolt against the West, and gaining its influence among the Palestinian population as much through its blistering rhetoric about the destruction of the Jewish state as through its programs of solidaristic and redistributionist neighbourhood help and Islamic charity.

Hamas, like other early Islamist movements in Turkey and elsewhere in the Middle East, represents an egalitarian and redistributionist vision of Islamic solidarity that is also deeply authoritarian and anti-liberal. In the 1980s, Hamas was supported by Israel as an alternative to the more secular and militant Fatah, much as the US supported Osama bin Laden and the Mujaheddin against the more secular and socialistically inclined

Fedayyin in Afghanistan. In both cases, the genie flew out of the bottle, and now Israel, as well as the US, are stuck with the shifting of allegiances by Hamas, and the much more formidable Hizbollah, from Islamic social work to Islamist militarism, from Sunni patrons such as Saudi Arabia to Shi'ite ideologues in Iran. There is nothing in this constellation that should give comfort and hope to progressives and Leftists. Our commitment to the equality, self-determination and solidarity of peoples must, therefore, remain a critical principle and must not be sacrificed to blind partisanship for one group or another.

Israel's security in a post-Westphalian world

What, then, is Israel's political end-game? Israel is caught in striving for Westphalian security in a post-Westphalian world, in which borders have become porous, and when germs, news, commodities, money, but the human body, travels more and more quickly and in ever larger numbers. Tunnels have been dug between Egypt and Gaza to smuggle in weapons purchased with Iranian money. Oil money floats into the hands of itinerant preachers and false holy men from corrupt Sheiks and Kingdoms in the Gulf protecting their vulnerable dynasties, as well as from the irredentist and irresponsible regime in Iran. Defunct weapon systems from Russia and from former Soviet Republics such as Kazakhstan, Kyrgyzstan, and Azerbaijan find their ways into the hands of their Muslim brethren. And cynical Chinese weapon merchants and Russian tycoons are only too happy to peddle their goods in the region.

And Israel pretends to be shocked! Shocked that missiles with the capacity to reach Tel-Aviv are now stored in the Gaza strip and in southern Lebanon. Shocked that small groups of Hamas militants launch rockets mounted on mobile carriers while hiding among the hapless civilian population. But this is hypocritical: Whether strategically or normatively, it hardly explains or justifies Israel's massive retaliation. Even Saddam Hussein, during the first Gulf War, fired some lame scud missiles into Tel-Aviv, and children and adults alike went and collected their gas masks and sat in their apartments waiting for the missiles to fall. Israel knows and has known for quite some time that its supposed shield of military might has been pierced by ever new generations of weapons.

There is no perfect security and total invulnerability in this new world at least since September 11, 2001 – if there ever was such a thing as total invulnerability in the political realm. Yet it is Israel's shock at its own vulnerability that is making it act more and more belligerently towards its neighbours. Even having the nuclear bomb provides no security, not because Iran may acquire one, too, but because the use of nuclear weapons against targets in Lebanon, Syria, the Gaza strip, the West Bank and Jordan would make Israel itself unlivable by spreading radioactive clouds throughout the area, contaminating water and vegetation.

Four political visions

Several political discourses in contemporary Israel try to face this situation without offering a new vision of politics:

1. The prospect of perpetual war. Although politically indefensible by any self-respecting politician, this is a psychology taking hold of the souls of many ordinary Israelis. Many believe that war will be a way of life and that there will never be peace in Israel-Palestine.
2. By contrast, Liberals and progressives of all stripes advocate a two-state solution, because they believe in the principle of the equal self-determination of peoples. Yet others accept this because they are concerned with what is called "the ticking demographic bomb" of high Palestinian birth rates and because they do not want to be minority in a majority Palestinian state, whether democratic or not.
3. Then there is the vision of a greater Israel based on religious belief, namely, the view that the ancient lands of Judaea and Samaria belong irrevocably to the Jewish people.
4. This is to be distinguished from the secular vision of a greater Israel, including the Palestinian territories, to be governed by some mutually acceptable economic agreements, combining together free-trade and economic growth zones.

At least since Yitzhak Rabin's peace initiative and the Camp David Accords, the idea of a "two-state solution" is the official policy of Israeli and of the American administrations. But the "two-state solution" has an ambivalent core and every so often its hidden meanings erupt into public consciousness. The two-state solution became widely accepted not only because it guaranteed the right of the Palestinian people to self-determination, but because it promised "demographic disengagement". Suddenly, the demographers, those pseudo-politicians of hidden race thinking, argued that if Israel continued to occupy Gaza, the West Bank, and East Jerusalem, then it would end up exercising military control over 5 million Palestinian Arabs, including those who are Israeli citizens and who live within the 1967 borders of Israel. Given the high Palestinian birth rate, it was felt that the Jewish nature of Israel would be at stake unless it disengaged from Gaza and returned some portion of the territories. Nightmares of being a minority in a state which one had founded to protect oneself from being second class citizens, despised, exploited, maligned and killed *en masse* were revived; suddenly, all the ghosts of the Jewish unconsciousness, from the *pogroms* of the Cossacks to the Nazi extermination camps, came forth and a significant majority of the Israeli population signed on to Camp David and said "two states, side by side" to escape from this nightmare.

Yet many strategists of Israeli *Realpolitik* and many Israeli settlers have never accepted this vision. Since 1967 the settler movement has grown from a group of dreamy fanatics who believed in the sacred "land of Israel" (*Eretz Israel*) as opposed to the "state of Israel" (*Medinat Israel*) into a mixed mass of well-armed and well-funded militants and religious groups. They are the ones who shot Palestinians during Friday prayers in a mosque in Hebron, and the murderer of Yitzhak Rabin, Yigal Amir, came from their ranks. Like the murderers of Anwar Sadat in Egypt, who belonged to the Muslim Brotherhood, these are groups living in another age, hearing the voices of ancient gods, feeling the tremors of ancient wars and obeying ancient myths. They remain an irredentist and dangerous force for Israelis and Palestinians and will try to spoil any lasting peace in the region because their *raison d'être* is a messianic vision of ancient and unending struggle. For them, the revolt of the Maccabees has a special resonance. Their violent potential is also manipulated by politicians on both sides to further their own short-sighted goals.

But just as the plight of the Palestinians has been used by corrupt Arab regimes to shore up their own tattered legitimacy, so too the settler movement has been used by cynical Israeli elites to advance their vision of a secular, greater Israel. Described in unforgettable terms by Amos Oz in his book *In the Land of Israel*, there are the tough Jews attached to the land, who are oddly progressive when it comes to matters of economic cooperation and development with the Palestinians. Reminiscent of the white Rhodesian farmers and the enterprising cattle growers of Australia and the ranchers of South Africa, these are men who want to control and develop the land of Israel/Palestine. By contrast with liberals who are worried about the "soul of the democratic Israel", they are more concerned with the "muscle" of Israel's economic and agricultural reach. The hero of the 1967 war, Moshe Dayan, belonged to this group, as does the now half-living and half-dead Ariel Sharon. For them, as long as the Palestinians are quiescent and thrifty capitalist entrepreneurs, as long as they develop the land rather than ruin it, coexistence is possible. The dreams of this group were shattered in 2005 when angry Palestinian mobs destroyed all those beautiful greenhouses built by Israelis in Gaza to grow and export roses, tomatoes, and avocadoes all over the world. The wrath of the Palestinians that manifested itself in the destruction of property was interpreted by this group, as by many colonial masters before them, as proof of the incompetence of the natives to work hard, guard property, and add value to capital.

The current military operation in Gaza contains elements of all four political discourses – perpetual war; a two-state solution; religious greater Israel and a secular greater Israel – and this is why it is incoherent in its final aims: Does Israel want to occupy Gaza again and build greenhouses which will be destroyed yet again? Does Israel want to destroy Hamas and its military and civilian institutions once and for all and then get out of Gaza in anticipation of a two-state solution which will then be hardly possible? Does Israel want to reoccupy Gaza and put its troops in harm's way as well as commit potential war crimes against the Palestinian population? No one is quite sure.

Like Tibet and China?

Are there then any genuinely political alternatives in the current situation and not just military strategies that are paraded as if they were political visions? Within Israel, there is a movement for dissociating Israeli citizenship and Jewish ethno-religious identity, to enable Israel to become the land of all its citizens. This would involve full or partial repudiation of the Law of Return, which grants the right to Israeli citizenship to every Jew who has been recognized by some rabbinic authority. Until very recently, Israel's law of citizenship had not been reformed and many migrant workers and their children as well as non-Jewish partners and spouses could not obtain Israeli citizenship at all. Ironically, in the last decade it has become easier for Russians who pretend to be Jews to obtain Israeli citizenship than for a Palestinian-Arab, born and raised in East Jerusalem, because s/he will be considered a security risk and because the status of East Jerusalem is up in the air in terms of international agreements. As significant as this vision is, it runs the risk of becoming a kind of benevolent imperialism, particularly when the demand for citizenship is extended to include Palestinians in occupied territories, whose status is unsettled in view of the absence of a comprehensive peace treaty.

Any serious political thinking about Israel and Palestine must be based on the premise that military force is a deterrent only, and an increasingly questionable one, at that, and that it is not arms but humans who conclude peace. Peace is a collective good. Israel is caught in a defunct Westphalian model of sovereignty which assumes that the state is in control of all that is alive and dead within and at the margins of its boundaries. Most advanced democracies know that this is no longer the case, neither normatively nor empirically. Sovereignty is a bundle of state privileges and prerogatives which can be shared, delegated and co-exercised with other groups and powers. Many in the Israeli leadership know that they will never permit full Palestinian sovereignty over air space, be it in Gaza or the West Bank; over the free passage of goods in and out of ports in Gaza, which will be the only form of access to the sea for a future Palestinian state; nor will Israel give up control of the underground water reserves extending on both sides of the 1967 territories. So why does one pretend that a sovereign Palestinian state will be sovereign in the sense in which Israel would like to consider itself sovereign? The sad and simple truth is that such a Palestinian state will be perpetually bullied, controlled, monitored, and occasionally smashed by Israel. Precisely because many who advocate a two-state solution also know that their future relations with the Palestinian state will be less like those between Italy and Austria and more like those between Tibet and China or India and Kashmir, many Israeli politicians pay lip service to this ideal, while making sure on the ground that it becomes less and less likely.

Suppose a confederation

But dream with me for a moment. Suppose there were a confederation in Israel-Palestine. Suppose that the neutralization of groups like Hamas and Hizbollah, which do not recognize the existence of the state of Israel, was a goal common to Palestinians as well as to other Arab nations, but that if Hamas would recognize Israel's right to exist it would have a seat at the table; suppose that there were common air, maritime and water controls jointly exercised by an Israeli-Palestinian authority; suppose that there were a common currency and regulated settlement rights for each ethnic group in certain parts of the common territory. Israel would not have to face a civil war against the fanatic settlers in Hebron and the West Bank, who would then either have to live under a regional municipal Palestinian authority or would have to return to Israel. But Israel would not have to defend their land grabs through incursions into Palestinian territory; the Palestinians would not have to pretend that the Bantustan of Gaza could in any sense be part of a Palestinian state; instead, Gaza would be an autonomous region in a joint Israeli-Palestinian confederation. Gaza and the West Bank would hold elections for municipal and regional administrations and governments, under some clearly defined power-sharing agreement with each other and with Israel.

A confederation would not mean the disappearance of the national collective polity and identity of each people. Within the pre-1967 territories, that is the Green line, Israel would remain a Jewish state, with its language, holy days and elections; but it would share power in military, security, intelligence, currency and trade matters with the Palestinian state. Likewise the Palestinians would have their own language, holy days and elections, but the two peoples would develop some form of joint school curricula, particularly in the teaching of history which did justice to historical truths and to the suffering of both peoples. Children of a new generation would learn to have empathy rather than hatred for each other. There would be some equalization of socio-economic and welfare rights in this confederation, so that everyone would not want to move into the wealthier Israeli provinces; religious pluralism and liberal civil rights would be respected equally for all Jews, Muslims, Christians and all people of other faiths. For the religiously observant who would want to have their personal affairs to be administered by religious authorities, there would be optional religious courts, but there would also be a shared Bill of Rights for all peoples, which would guarantee equal civil and political rights.

If I allow myself to dream further, I imagine that this confederation could become the kernel of a Middle Eastern Union of Peoples, in which Turkey, Egypt, Saudi Arabia, Jordan and many other states would conjoin much along the model of the European Union.

To those who would accuse me of wanting to get rid of the state of Israel, much as they argued against Tony Judt, when he dared raise some of these proposals in the *New York Review of Books* some years ago, I ask: what alternatives do you really have to offer the Israeli and Palestinian peoples besides perpetual war or the imperial project of a secular or religious greater Israel? If you want Israel to retain its soul as a liberal-democratic state and preserve its Jewish identity without racism, discrimination and war against another people, dare to look beyond defunct visions of the Westphalian state. France, Italy, Germany etc., have not disappeared within the European Union; quite to the contrary: their capacities for governance and their ability to provide their own peoples with peace and prosperity have been enhanced. A republican confederation of Israeli and Palestinian polities corresponds both to the realities of increased interdependence developing on the ground between Israel and the Palestinians, as well as offering stability and prosperity in the future. The tragedy of Gaza should bring with it new political visions.

Reflections on Middle Eastern Regional Integration*

Yossi AMITAY

For quite a long while I have been following the debates on issues related to the processes of globalisation and regionalism, of which Europe is the key-player. I must confess I have been observing those discussions with more than a bit of envy. For me, the vision of one, united world system that consists of regional groupings, transcending ethnic, religious or lingual fanaticism, whereby every group or human association be granted optimal self-expression, is a long desired ideal. The EU is but a milestone in this historical process, and is by no means its final destination. But even as it functions nowadays, the EU is supposed to serve as a model for similar processes which, at some given future, will hopefully take place in other regions, including the Middle East. "Hopefully", I said. But do actual processes that have been taking place in the Middle East over the last few decades really substantiate these hopes? Is present-day Middle East really situated at the threshold of regional integration, the major features of which are voluntary reduction of the sovereign authority of individual nation-states in favour of joint regional groupings, and replacement of particularistic local interests by shared regional ones? Are the peoples of the Middle East really ripe for such a transformation?

Let me indicate in advance that there are no ready-made, unequivocal answers to those questions and to many others, related to the issue under discussion. Every direction is possible, be it an optimistic approach, detached from realities on the ground, or a pessimistic approach, reflecting a static perception of current realities, and overlooking interactive dynamics of historical developments. It seems to me that in order to shape a balanced outlook on that issue, a brief survey of relevant developments in our region over the last decades would be appropriate. Many scholars of Middle Eastern studies share the concept that the most significant process that has been taking place in the Region since World War I is the collapse of the Ottoman Empire and the emergence of a new regional order. The most meaningful manifestation of that new order was the birth of particularistic nation-states that replaced what previously used to be a single, all-embracing political entity, namely the Ottoman State. That

* Published in Issue 3/2000.

state was heterogeneous in its ethnocultural composition, and homogenous in its shared dual source of authority: Islamic belief and state-system on one hand, and loyalty to the ruling dynasty on the other hand. While it is true that the Ottoman State collapsed on account of being a member of the defeated coalition in WWI, it is also true, in retrospect, that that collapse came as no surprise, since accumulative domestic and external processes that culminated in that downfall had already been there many decades before.

The emergence of Arab nation-states in the wake of WWI reflected a concept characteristic for the international community at the time, which consisted of liberal and democratic values but also comprised an inherent contradiction. That concept endorsed the right of all peoples to national self-determination, alongside the dominance of the strategic, economic and cultural interests of the colonial superpowers, primarily Great Britain and France. That dualism, in addition to some fundamental contradictions that had been inherent in the Arab societies in the first place, set stumbling blocks on the road to development of the newly born nation-states. To mention some of them: firstly, the traditional leading social groups were considerably weakened, but they were still holding their traditional legitimacy and authority, whereas the alternative groups, representing the liberal and constitutionalist trends, had not yet gained sufficient strength and momentum. Secondly, the very setting-up of those Arab nation-states, the delineation of their border-lines, and the shaping of their domestic power structures, all were products and initiatives of European superpowers that divided between themselves influence zones and areas of direct domination. It took the Arab societies quite a long period of time to adjust themselves to the new reality, which was almost entirely different from any socio-political reality they had ever known. Thirdly, the emergence of social and political institutions in the new nation-states took place concurrently with national liberation struggles against foreign domination, and, to a lesser degree, against local traditional rulers.

Those struggles set for those societies a distinctive agenda and a list of priorities that hindered domestic social struggles and blocked mobility tracks of new social forces. Fourthly, the emergent Arab nation-states were caught, from the very start, in an ongoing debate, between themselves and within themselves, over the issue of pan-arabism versus distinctiveness of each Arab people. This debate is still going on nowadays, though it seems to have lost much of its original intensity. It has bred many internal and inter-Arab tensions. Fifthly, the emergence of the Arab nation-states took place, from its very inception, against the background of the historical confrontation over Palestine, between Jewish and Arab national movements. For quite a long period those two national movements were considered mutually exclusive. This conflict, that culminated in the

Palestinian tragedy of 1948, cast a huge shadow on the socio-political development of the Arab societies for many years. It is not the purpose of this paper to provide a detailed chronicle of the major processes and events that occurred in our region over most of the 20th century. It rather aims at shedding some light on the background of the problems the region is facing nowadays, given the accelerated processes of globalisation and regionalism in other parts of the world, primarily in Europe.

What is the present situation?

Some of the above-mentioned historical realities, which were depicted as obstacles blocking the development of the Middle East Societies, have undergone essential transformations which must not be overlooked. First and foremost, all countries in the region, with the sole exception of the Palestinians, are now free from foreign domination. Those countries have witnessed the growth of new social groups which had been almost negligible in the wake of WWI. Many countries in the region underwent a liberal experiment in the 1920s and 1930s, which, by and large, reached a dead end in the early 1950s and was replaced by radical military regimes. Those regimes entertained messianic nationalist visions, but eventually failed to secure stability and prosperity. It was a frantic historical stage, in which one military regime was soon to be toppled and replaced by another, until some of them ultimately managed to survive long enough, as transitional stage towards the re-emergence of a civil society. Liberal democracy has not been implemented yet in any Arab country, but a long road has been taken towards the emergence and growth of social groups that are possessing both the skills and the desire to push for a broader scope of democracy and human rights. The nation-states in question, in this sensitive stage of transition from military authoritarianism to civil society, have been acutely challenged by radical pan-Arab groups on the one hand, and radical Islamist groups on the other hand. So far the nation-state, as a political structure, has shown a remarkable viability, which for many observers had been unexpected, given the messianic fervour of Islamist and Pan-Arab movements.

Last but not least, over the last decade or so, the Region has undergone a peace-making process, which may eventually terminate the Arab-Israeli conflict. The process is still on the move, and is far from reaching its end. It seems that such a deep-rooted conflict, touching so many sensitive nerves and interrelated issues, cannot be solved instantly. The process can be likened to tango dancing, with dancers moving two steps forward, one step backward. We may witness many ups and downs in the foreseeable future. However, the general direction of the process is very clear. It should be mentioned, though, that completion of the peace-making course between Israel and all her Arab neighbours does not necessarily imply an immediate change of hearts. Peace accords, whenever attained, will be very fragile, and their implementation will face many difficulties on the ground for some years to come. Formal peace agreements, those that have already been reached and those that are about to be, are not a sufficient condition for creating a new fabric of human relations, but they are an indispensable one.

To speak from a very personal perspective, one modest by-product of the peace process, as far as I am concerned, is the fact that I have been privileged to serve as Director of the Israeli Academic Center in Cairo for the last three years. This small achievement, which is not devoid of hardships and obstacles, is for me a dream come true. Over the years I have had many open talks with Egyptian friends and colleagues, and it became evident to me that the often-heard slogan in Cairo and other Arab capitals, that peace for the Arabs is a "strategic choice", does reflect something that is very real and solid. Firstly, peace orientation has made Egypt and other Arab countries an attractive target for massive investments on the part of the international business community. Hence it is certainly a leverage for economic growth, which provides a better setting to cope with traditional evils in those societies, namely poverty, illness and ignorance. Secondly, some circles in Egypt, and probably in other Arab countries as well, do believe that broadening the scope of peace and cooperation in the region will positively contribute to broadening the scope of democracy, political participation and human rights in their respective countries. In turn, these changes will have positive bearings on the development of the economy and human resources, and so on and so forth. This does not necessarily imply an Arab acceptance of Israeli negotiating positions or *vice versa*, but it certainly is an indication of a pragmatic approach to peace, and hence of a good chance of laying foundations for regional cooperation.

I would like to devote my final comments to the prospects of setting up a regionalistic system in the Middle East, in view of what has so far been said. Seven years ago, following the conclusion of the Oslo Declaration of Principles (DOP) between Israel and the PLO, Israeli leader Shimon Peres, the architect of that agreement, voiced the "New Middle East" slogan. Peres was undoubtedly affected by the EU precedent, and by the spirits of globalisation that were then blowing worldwide. The slogan Peres raised was not warmly welcomed, neither in Israel, nor in the Arab world. Although everybody understood that peace and reconciliation are historically inevitable, the immense hardships on the short and medium range have given rise to all kinds of fears and apprehensions regarding what the future has in store.

Is the Middle East region, which is in most part Arab and Islamic, but comprises also entities that are neither Arab nor Islamic, currently heading for a regional setting? The potential is apparently there, but there is still a long way to go. The countries of the Region must first undergo an accumulation of necessary processes in terms of economic accommodation and changes of political culture, both within each of those countries and in relationships between them. The ripeness and viability of the nation-state concept in leading states in the Region lend us some hope. It seems that a certain "critical threshold" has yet to be crossed, regarding levels of economic growth, *per capita* income, rules of the democratic game, collective and individual human rights, etc... I, for one, share the view that the key to such progress lies with the completion of the peace process in our area, and the long-awaited historical reconciliation between the Arab world and Israel. Paradoxically, such a reconciliation may contribute to resolving inter-Arab rivalries, and to placing the entire regional set of relations on a complementary rather than a competitive basis.

One final comment, regarding the possible European role in this process. In view of ongoing and predictable hardships in creating joint regional frameworks for Israel and her Arab neighbours, it seems useful to encourage, as a transitional stage, the setting up of a joint Mediterranean framework, shared by all Mideastern and North African countries, together with European countries located along the Mediterranean basin. Such an interim stage will not only absorb the shock of the reconciliatory encounter between the Arab states and Israel, but will also provide an inspiration for a new political culture shared by all future participants in the new Middle Eastern regional grouping.

Reconciling the Irreconcilable*

John PARRY

When asked to comment in July 2006 on the then current outbreak of hostilities between Israel and Hezbullah forces based in Lebanon, US President George Bush was quoted as saying that the 'root cause' was terrorism. He was wrong. Terrorism was, and is, a symptom of a malaise whose roots lie much deeper: firstly, in the injustice of centuries of anti-Semitism in Europe culminating in Hitler's 'Final Solution' in which certain elements in the occupied European countries also took part; and, secondly, in the injustice suffered by the Palestinian people by the creation without their consent of an immigrant nation state in their midst, plus its consequences. These experiences have shaped the psychology of both Israelis and Palestinians and must be taken into account when discussing a possible future for the region.

Historically Jews were to be found in many parts of the Roman empire, particularly after the fall of Jerusalem in the year 135 AD, and under the emperor Caracalla's constitution of 212 AD they acquired Roman citizenship. Ironically, it was the spread Christianity that brought increasing instances of religious discrimination against them, even leading in the early Middle Ages to forced conversions. But despite these injustices the Jewish faith and religious practices remained intact, reinforced by the emphasis they placed on education. Several were held in high esteem for their scholarship or their skill as physicians or astronomers.

Because many earned a living in commerce, their contacts with fellow Jewish communities across Europe, North Africa and the Middle East enabled a flourishing international trade to develop. Yet anti-Jewish sentiments lurked beneath the surface even in peaceful times. A notorious example occurred in 1096, when thousands of Jews in the Rhineland towns and provinces were slaughtered by the armies of ruffians on their way to seek fame and fortune in the First Crusade, though both the Church and the Emperor condemned this brutality[1]. In fact the Church's attitude, clearly stated by St. Bernard, was that it was 'far better to convince and convert the Jews than to put them to the sword'[2].

* Published in Issue 3/2006.

1 See Stephen Runciman, *History of the Crusades*, Vol. I, Bk. 3.

2 See Letter 393 in *The Letters of St. Bernard*, Edited by Scott-James.

A further example of anti-Jewish hostility occurred in Britain when riots in the city of York in the year 1190 resulted in the massacre of 150 Jewish men, women & children. This was eventually followed by King Edward I's decision to expel all Jews from Britain. They were not legally readmitted till the mid-17th century. Meanwhile, the papal 'Lateran Council' of 1215 ordered that all Jews in Latin Christendom should wear a distinguishing badge and forbad Gentiles either to work for or lodge with them. In a series of staggered expulsions over the next two or three hundred years, Jewish communities were also forced to leave France, certain German states, Spain and Portugal. Many fled to eastern Europe though a substantial number settled in North Africa. Discrimination in the Arab lands was in most cases considerably less severe. There, Jews and Christians – as People of the Book – were required to pay a poll tax but otherwise were mostly free to practise their own religion as they wished.

In western Europe it was not until the late 18th century that tensions began to ease. Works such as Lessing's *Nathan the Wise* – a plea for mutual understanding between Jew, Christian and Muslim – had begun to appear even before the liberal ideas of the French revolution had swept across Europe. But was it possible for Jews and non-Jews to live peacefully together, each respecting the others' views? Today's situation in the 'free' world, in which a person can achieve high political office whatever their religion or origin, was still on the distant horizon. For the philosopher Moses Mendelssohn, a close associate of Lessing's, the first step involved a search for common ground between the communities with the aim of achieving a greater degree of assimilation, although some members of his own family still held at least a nominal conversion to Christianity to be more practical. This became the route followed by a number of talented Jews including the poet Heinrich Heine, the composer Gustav Mahler, and the future British prime minister Benjamin Disraeli.

Moreover, the post-Rousseau, post-Napoleonic rise of national consciousness in 19th century Europe carried with it the danger of a revival of anti-Semitism, as one young Jewish idealist – Theodor Herzl – was to discover. While studying law at Vienna University Herzl joined the Albia *Burschenschaft*[3], an exclusive student club whose members were strong supporters of German nationalism. He had long been an enthusiast for German culture and this seemed a natural thing to do, but within months anti-Semitic elements among Albia members had gained control of the organisation, claiming not only that Jews could never be truly German but also that they should be barred from the professions. Feeling that for him at any rate assimilation had been denied, Herzl was left with no choice but to quit in protest.

---

3 See Steven Beller, *Herzl*, Chap. 1.

The concept of 'nation' and of the nation state had become fashionable in Europe. German unification – at that time just ten years old – was only its most recent expression. Hungary – where Herzl was born – had become semiautonomous within the Hapsburg empire, Italy had unified in 1860, and nationalist movements elsewhere were also developing. If such self-conscious nationalism meant that Jews were to be regarded as aliens, should not they too have their own nation state? Herzl brooded over this idea for some years until, in 1896 and by then a well-known journalist, he decided to publish the proposal as a pamphlet: *The Jewish State*.

The response was immediate[4]. In Vienna the Jewish middle class was scornful. Why should they abandon their comfortable lives to pursue such an unrealistic dream? But Jews in Russia and eastern Europe, living under difficult conditions and still victims of discrimination and occasional pogroms, took the opposite view. For them the proposal offered hope, and their enthusiasm resulted in the birth of the Zionist movement which held its first international Congress the following year in Basel.

Yet where should this Jewish state be situated? With imperialist arrogance, the UK government, busily expanding its own settlements in East Africa, offered land in Uganda. This was considered, and then rejected. Did not all Jews dream of "Next year in Jerusalem" – a phrase repeated every year at Passover? Little thought was given to the fact that Palestine was then part of the Ottoman empire and already had a long-established Arabic-speaking population, mostly Muslim but with Christian and Jewish minorities.

In World War I the Ottoman empire (specifically Turkey) allied itself with Germany and this brought about a radical change in the region. Britain now faced the possibility of losing control over the Suez Canal which was a vital trade route to her empire in the east. To counter this threat, Arab nationalist groups were contacted with offers to assist them in their struggle for independence from the Turks. Moreover, Britain was also hard pressed on the western front in Europe. Help was desperately needed, but could America be persuaded to abandon its neutrality? In an attempt to win over influential Jewish support in the USA, the British promised to permit the establishment of a 'Jewish National Home' in Palestine.

This commitment, confirmed in the Balfour Declaration[5] of November 1917, also contained the sub-clause 'that nothing shall be done which may prejudice the civil and religious rights of existing non-Jewish communities in Palestine, or the rights and political status enjoyed by the

---

4 Beller, *op. cit.*, Chap. 4.

5 A.J.P. Taylor, *England 1914-1945*, Chap. 3.

Jews in any other country'. Despite this 'guarantee' the document caused an uproar among Palestine's Arab population who saw it as a threat to their own national right of self-determination. The Zionist interpretation – that it opened the way to the establishment of a Jewish nation state and that Palestine would become 'as Jewish as England is English' – only served to confirm Arab fears.

In July 1922 Britain formally undertook responsibility for Palestine under the League of Nations mandate. This responsibility Britain could well have done without. Having been freed from the Ottoman administration, Palestinian Arabs were in no mood to submit to British 'colonial rule'. Attempts to agree a constitution were fraught with difficulties. The proposed elected legislative council never got off the ground. Meanwhile, a steady stream of Jewish settlers arrived in the country, establishing successful industries and farming communities, for the most part using only Jewish labour.

Europe too had fundamentally changed. The rise of extreme nationalism, particularly but not exclusively in Germany, led to an increase in anti-Semitism unparalleled since the Middle Ages and with it came a further increase in the number of Jews wishing to settle in Palestine. A proposal to divide Palestine into two states, Jewish and Arab, while keeping Jerusalem and Bethlehem under British mandate[6] had to be abandoned when the partition commission reported that the Jewish and Palestinian communities were so intermingled that no geographical boundaries between them could be established. In trying to be fair to both sides – 'to reconcile the irreconcilable', as the historian A.J.P. Taylor put it[7] – the British were out of their depth.

Twenty-one years after the end of World War I hostilities began in Europe again. Country after country was occupied by National Socialist troops. Often with the collaboration of the local police, Jews were herded into trains and transported to concentration camps. Six million perished in the gas chambers or by other means. A few who managed to escape fought as partisans, but these were exceptions. Once the war had ended thousands of survivors fled towards Palestine by any means possible.

For the British, responsible as the mandatory power for maintaining peaceful relations between the different communities in Palestine, this vast influx of refugees determined to establish the State of Israel caused major problems. Despite the UK's leading role in defeating the Nazis, liberating the camps and hunting down war criminals, their attempts to control this new situation resulted in acts of violence by both Arabs

6 Taylor, *op. cit.*, p. 354.

7 Taylor, *op. cit.*

and Zionists. In July 1946, in an action later denounced by the Jewish National Council, the terrorist group Irgun Zvai Leumi led by Menachim Begin[8] planted a bomb in the King David Hotel in Jerusalem, causing the deaths of almost a hundred British soldiers and civilians. Some days later two young British sergeants were kidnapped and hanged from street lampposts, while in London security services discovered a Stern Gang plot to murder the Foreign Secretary Ernest Bevin[9].

The UK government, its policy in tatters, handed the problem back to the United Nations. Violent clashes between Zionists and Arabs intensified even while the UN debated the issues, finally voting for partition. Despite the continued opposition of the majority indigenous population, British forces left in May 1948 and David Ben-Gurion proclaimed the birth of Israel as an independent nation state. On his orders the recently-formed Israeli Defence Force began to expel the 50,000-strong Arab population in areas such as Lydda and Rammle[10]. In total, well in excess of 500,000 refugees fled the new State of Israel[11].

Neighbouring countries immediately intervened on behalf of their fellow Arabs in the first of the Arab-Israeli wars of which the most recent example is the recent conflict involving Lebanon-based Hezbullah fighters. Any prospect of reaching a just and permanent settlement still looks uncertain. Resentment among the Palestinians remains acute, reinforced since 1967 by the Israeli occupation and/or domination of the rump of what used to be their country. Israel herself, the most heavily armed state in the region and backed by the USA, still sees every conflict as a fight for survival. To an outside observer it seems the only way to move towards a long term solution must be through a modification of attitudes on both sides.

In the view of many immigrants, according to Israeli writer Amos Oz[12], 'The Holocaust convinced many Jews that the cruel game of nations had to be played according to its cruel laws: statehood, a military establishment and a pessimistic concept of the use of military power.' This he rightly regrets. Yet there is another game in town. As Barbara Spinelli has suggested in an article in *La Stampa*[13], no country exists in total isolation. Inevitably Israel and its neighbours are to some extent dependent upon each other. There is therefore a valid case for Israel to move forward from being a Jewish 'nation state' of the traditional kind and to strengthen its

---

8 F. Fernandez-Armesto [Ed.], *England 1945-2000*, Chap. 1.

9 *BBC Radio* 4, 24 July 2006.

10 Benny Morris, *The Road to Jerusalem*, p. 177.

11 Morris, *op. cit.*, p. 190.

12 Amos Oz, *Israel, Palestine and Peace*, p. 12.

13 *La Stampa*, 23 July 2006.

own security by working towards the construction of a regional federation.

Such a move would naturally be long-term and would depend on – and, in fact, contribute to – reaching an accommodation over current problems. A model already exists in the early history of the European Union. Who in Europe in 1941 would have dreamed that, within ten years, six of the combatant states would agree[14] to place fundamental aspects of their economies under common control?

In preparation for the future, Israel must realise that in the eyes of the world her policy towards the Palestinians has so far failed. Responding to every terrorist attack with overwhelming force is understandable, particularly in the light of the barbaric acts suffered by Jews in the past, but it is now counterproductive. To subject Palestinians to terror attacks by helicopter gunships, destroying power stations, houses or cars; to block funds needed to pay doctors and nurses; to set up checkpoints in the West Bank or otherwise preventing farmers reaching their fields, patients getting to hospital or children going to school: all these are actions which lead to despair, and it is despair which recruits terrorists together with those who support them.

Developing an alternative strategy offering the Palestinians some hope for a better future must become a priority. Theodor Herzl's vision of establishing a Jewish state in Palestine assumed a harmonious relationship between the new arrivals and the existing population[15]. Perhaps this was naïve, yet out of the present ruins it must be possible to build a more prosperous and peaceful society. The 'two-state solution' depends upon it, and so too does Israel's security. Going in stages beyond the 'two-state solution' towards a wider, embryonic federation involving several of the neighbouring countries – such as an independent Palestine, with Jordan, Lebanon and perhaps Egypt – could in due course lead to peace in the Middle East.

In this context it is worth recalling some words spoken by Ehud Olmert at a conference in Ireland a few years before he became Israel's prime minister[16]. 'How are fears born?' he asked. 'They are born because of differences in tradition and history, and in emotional, political and national circumstances. If we are to overcome such fears, a credible political process must be developed that does not aim to change the other, nor to overcome differences, but that allows each side to live peacefully in spite of them.'

---

[14] In the Treaty of Paris (1951) establishing the European Coal and Steel Community.

[15] Theodor Herzl, *Briefe und Tagebücher* (Propyläen Verlag, Einführung, p. 12).

[16] Quoted by Brian Keenan, "After the Flood", in *The Guardian newspaper*, 22 July 2006.

Recent Developments of Regionalism in East Asia and Their Implications for Europe*

Ken ENDO

Regionalism in East Asia is in fact a vast subject on a vast area[1]. In dealing with this topic, some would start from the ASEAN and the so-called ASEAN+3 (Japan, China, South Korea) around which, traditionally, the regional organisations in East Asia have been structured[2]. Yet, the ASEAN is, if you will, like the Benelux. One would need bigger powers in constructing a region. In this light, instead of describing the general stuff on those traditional organisations, we may rather be allowed to start from a specific diplomatic initiative by Japanese Prime Minister Yukio Hatoyama in recent months for the East Asian Community (EAC).

As is well known, Japanese politics has – finally – renovated itself with the change of government after the last August general elections. The new premier Hatoyama can be seen as a peculiar person, and barring a financial misconduct he is likely to be in power for some time to come, and may deserve some attention.

He proposed the creation of the EAC as part of the electoral manifesto, and a goal now shared by Chinese and Korean leaders, albeit as a long-term one. On the domestic front, too, he presented local and regional sovereignty as one of his priorities, with which he intends to increase autonomy at those levels. Thus, he is a man of some sort of multi-level governance.

His peculiarity is visible in his opinion to give electoral rights to long-term foreign residents in Japan, not only for local and regional elections but also for national and general ones. Hatoyama was criticised (by right-wingers) for his remark that the soil of Japan does not only belong to the Japanese people, but also to long-term resident foreigners. For the moment, even the local and regional electoral rights for foreigners are stuck in the legislative process, which means no possibility to give those rights for national elections, yet that is the measure of his peculiarity.

---

* Published in Issue 1/2010.

1 This term here covers Northeast as well as Southeast Asia.

2 See for instance Tamio Nakamura ed., *East Asian Regionalism from a Legal Perspective Current features and a vision for the future* (London: Routledge, 2009, chap. 1).

He bases his political stance on the vague philosophy of fraternity, an idea which apparently came from his grand-father, Ichiro Hatoyama, also a Prime Minister, who was influenced by Comte Richard Coudenhove-Kalergi. As some may know, Coudenhove-Kalergi was the leading 'Pan-Europa' proponent and Austrian aristocrat, whose mother, Mitsuko, was Japanese. This Prime Minister Hatoyama reads and knows on the construction of Europe, and explicitly refers to that experience when proposing the EAC[3].

Is this just a dream of a strange man, influenced by an obscure 'founder' of Europe?

While, quite clearly, the Prime Minister's talks on EAC are still at a quite early stage of concrete policy formulation, it should not be dismissed too lightly, as it is founded on a few factors accumulated over the past several years.

Economically speaking, intra-regional trade interdependence in East Asia has risen rapidly: in 1980, the trade figure in East Asia (ASEAN, NIES, China, Japan) represented 33.6%, as opposed to the EC's 52.6%. In 2003 (before the EU's Eastern enlargement), EA with the figure of 54.5% approached quite closely the EU's 58.1%. Also the figures of regional GDP are more or less balanced: NAFTA has 14.3 trillion dollars, the EU 13.3 and EA 10 (with the most rapidly growing economies).

Politically, too, the East Asia Summit has been instituted since 2005, amongst the ASEAN 10 countries plus Japan, China, South Korea, Australia, New Zealand, and India.

Of course, there is a number of differences between Europe and East Asia: the latter has no unified currency, no solid legal institution, a huge gap between the rich and the poor. Yet, something is going on. After pointless confrontations between Japan and its Asian partners under the previous LDP governments, Japan is heading for a pro-Asian diplomacy.

If East Asia is to build a common space, with reference to the European experience, it should do so with a number of cautions.

First, East Asia should maintain good diplomatic relations with the US. Historically, Europe was built in parallel with some military-security arrangements, notably the NATO. European integration was promoted by the US, with which it aimed to run counter to the Communists, inside and outside.

---

3 Part of Hatoyama's political vision can be read in English. See Yukio Hatoyama, "A New Path for Japan", *New York Times*, August 26, 2009. A longer version can be found in "My Political Philosophy", Voice, August 10, 2009, available at http://www.hatoyama.gr.jp/masscomm/090810_e.doc.

Second, while keeping good relations with the US, East Asia should jointly enhance its own three P's: Peace, Prosperity, and Power, just like Europe did. It is not just about reconciliation between Germany and France, but about power and influence.

Finally, this East Asian common space should be equipped with a sort of human-rights umbrella, *à la* CSCE, so that the peoples under oppression by their own government could have recourse to an alternative channel to defend their human rights. Here too, the European experience may well have a referential power. 'Europe' is not only about the European Union. Just as it was long supported militarily by the NATO during the Cold War, it was also sustained by the Council of Europe where human rights and other concerns (such as minority rights) could be jointly discussed. Within such a framework, there has been the European Court of Human Rights, whose role is to safeguard peoples' rights if unprotected by their own national governments. It is hoped here that the vertical division of powers will have something to do with the expansion of human rights, precisely as it pluralises the channels of protecting rights.

It is far from sure that such a regional construction will take place in East Asia in the foreseeable future. The Hatoyama government badly handled its relations with the US, a cornerstone of prosperity and peace in the region. Yet, suppose, for a moment, that a region is in the process to be formed.

Then, we would immediately see that this is not an end in itself, as we might well have to face the possibility of excessive rivalries between the regions. Healthy competitions are fine but, historically, we have witnessed too many examples of territorially-organised units, whether nation-states or ethnic entities, fighting with each other.

Though at the risk of historical over-simplification, Europe can be seen to have once exported the political model of the nation-state to the entire world. It may be that now it is exporting the model of regionalism. We need to ensure that this sort of parallel regionalism will not lead to excessive rivalry.

The doctrine of federalism is still valid here. The federalist project is incomplete, as far as it serves only to strengthen a region, i.e. Europe. It should be kept in mind that Europe is considered as a 'regulatory empire' – a sort of powerful international actor setting global standards and imposing regulations all over the world, often unilaterally, without properly consulting other regions and nations[4].

4 See for instance Kazuto Suzuki, "EU a regulatory empire", Hokkaido Journal of New Global Law and Policy, Vol. 2 (Special issue on the role of the European Union in global standardization processes) (July 2009), available at: http://www.juris.hokudai.ac.jp/gcoe/journal/LPG_vol2/2_7.

Compared to 'integral federalism' *à la* Proudhon (or Alexandre Marc), the Spinellian type of federalism, influenced by Hamilton, looks more prepared to extend the logic of federalism to other regions and to project it to the global stage.

Europe is already an influential entity. Influence means responsibility. As exporter of regionalism, Europe bears a special responsibility.

In this light Europe must use its influence in a constructive manner, to promote region-to-region cooperation, not fierce rivalries. Without a sensitivity for truly mutual, inter-regional and global cooperation, the construction of Europe may end up replacing the exclusivity of the Nation-States with the same exclusivity of the regions. And for that matter, the Spinellian federalism, a current of federalism open to others, has much to contribute to a certain type of Europe, in favour of global cooperation.

The Regional Unification Processes in Asia

James W. ARPUTHARAJ*

Introduction

The European Union is indeed a good model which many of us would like to replicate in other regions of the world. We do not need to reinvent the wheel but rather to learn from the success or failures of the EU. However, the contexts of various regional unification processes are quite different. While history motivated and built the European Union after World War II, motivation for forming other regional unification processes like ASEAN and SAARC are quite different. Further, the relatively homogenous nature of the membership of the EU is an added advantage. The countries in Europe have a long and similar history of democracy. They are equal in size, and the citizens already enjoy a high level of education and humanitarian standards.

In South Asia, on the other hand, the sheer size of India to a large extent prevents regional unification. With regard to literacy, Afghanistan has only 23%, while some states in India have registered >80 % of literacy. Further, there is civil strife in every single country in South Asia, barring Bhutan and Maldives.

It was a liberating decision to break the Berlin wall in Europe, whereas, in South Asia, India recently constructed a border fencing running for 2478 kilometers between India and Bangladesh. Further, 20,000 troops are stationed between the borders of India and Pakistan, on high alert. And the fact remains that two-thirds of the world's poor live in South Asia alone. As far as political stability is concerned, currently low-intensity conflicts exist in Kashmir, Philippines, Indonesia and Thailand, while the effects of major conflicts in Afghanistan and Pakistan are seen everyday. Some countries like Sri Lanka and Myanmar are clearly failed states, while the governments in both Myanmar and North Korea are regarded as repressive. What of Asia's giants – India and China? While the rest of the region is still reeling under recession, the most populous countries in the world, both leading growth-oriented economies, see a growth rate of over 7%. Asia and the Middle East enjoy the distinction of having every major religion in the world originating from these regions. The region is

* Published in Issue 3/2009.

diverse in ethnicity and languages and most of the countries are united in this diversity. Asia does not have a regional organization, but both South Asia and South East Asia have sub-regional organizations. But these associations exclude the second- and third-largest economies in the world – Japan and China. In this paper, we would focus only on ASEAN and SAARC.

The ASEAN

Founded in 1967, the Association of South East Asian Nations (ASEAN) is a political, economic and cultural organization of countries located in South East Asia. The Bangkok declaration initiated ASEAN, the founding countries being Indonesia, Philippines, Singapore and Thailand. The dominating effect of Vietnam communism in the region, and border disputes between some of the countries motivated them to form this regional union. When its members recognized their apparent inability to resolve disputes bilaterally, they formed ASEAN to address the need for a political-cum-security framework of conflict management and resolution. ASEAN aims to foster cooperation and mutual assistance among members. Through dialogue among its members, it fosters democracy and human rights based on regional criteria. The office of the Secretary General is located in Jakarta, Indonesia. Subsequently ASEAN admitted other members – Brunei, Cambodia, Laos, Myanmar and Vietnam. Thus, with its broadened membership ASEAN is quite heterogeneous – from the most repressive Myanmar to liberal democracies like Singapore and Indonesia, and to the communist and socialist Vietnam and Laos. The dialoguing partners of ASEAN are Australia, Canada, China, North Korea, South Korea, New Zealand, Russia and the EU. There are some landmark achievements: The declaration of Bali on 7th October 2003 aims to pursue closer economic integration by 2020. The Plan envisaged a free-trade region with a population of 500 million, with an annual trade of 720 Billion USD. China agreed to foster trade for an amount of 1.7 billion USD with ASEAN countries. Japan agreed to reduce tariff and non-tariff barriers. However, there are some open issues for ASEAN. It could not admit East Timor as one of its members or as an observer because Myanmar has protested against its admission, due to E. Timor's apparent support to the pro-democracy movement in Myanmar. Despite sanctions against Myanmar for its human rights record, it has been impossible so far to make any progress.

SAARC

Founded on December 8th 1985, the South Asian Association for Regional Cooperation (SAARC) was aimed to provide a platform for the people of South Asia to work together in a spirit of friendship, trust and understanding. It was proposed by the then President of Bangladesh, General Zia-ur-Rehman, chiefly to group the countries of the region to confront big brother India. SAARC aims to accelerate the process of economic and social development among member-states. The office of the Secretary General is located in Kathmandu, Nepal. Once a year, normally in January, the SAARC Summit meets in each of the SAARC countries in rotation, with one of them providing the Chairperson. SAARC initially focused only on cultural and tourist exchanges between the SAARC countries. It relaxed travel restrictions for Judges and members of the Parliament within the region. On 14th April, 2007, when the SAARC summit was held in India, the Delhi Declaration underlined that it was vital first to have better connectivity within South Asia and then with the rest of the world. In line with this, they agreed to improve infra-regional connectivity, particularly physical, economic and people to people contacts. They agreed to a vision of South Asia where there is a smooth, reinforced flow of goods, services, people, technologies, knowledge, capital, culture, and ideas. The fact that SAARC did make some notable achievements is without doubt. In 2004 at the Pakistan summit, SAFTA (South Asian Free Trade Agreement) was agreed upon in principle, to integrate the region in services and regional economic cooperation. SAARC also adopted a social charter resembling the UN's MDGs- (Millennium Development Goals). The year 2007 was declared as the Year of Green South Asia. Further, a road map was drawn towards a South Asian Customs Union in a planned and phased manner. Moreover, modalities exist for sharing information on combating terrorism, narcotics, trafficking of women and children and other transnational crimes. The fact that South Asia is the only sub-region in the world to have a regional convention on the trafficking of women and children is noteworthy. However, due to tensions between Pakistan and India most of the time, regional security issues have not been addressed adequately. There is a high proliferation of small arms and light weapons in the region. Despite lobbying by several groups, including South Asian Federalists, SAARC has failed to address this issue.

SAARC and the EU

EU has an observer status since 2006 with SAARC. The EU greatly values cooperation and regional integration in South Asia. It believes that it can help consolidate its ongoing integration process through an economic influence in South Asia. The EU aims to promote harmonization of standards, facilitate trade, raise awareness on the benefits of regional cooperation, and promote business networking in the SAARC region. To this end, EU and SAARC signed an MOU in 1996 on technical assistance on trade matters. In 1999, they both agreed to improve market access for SAARC products into the EU; and technical support for SAFTA.

Issues to ponder on regional unification

There is fear that the regional federations would focus greatly on strengthening themselves rather than contributing towards a world federation.

Though to a large extent regionalism dilutes nationalism, some opine that regionalism may undermine world federalism. From the experience of SAARC and ASEAN, it appears that the regional bodies have functioned merely as inter-Governmental bodies. People to people contacts have not really taken place. Only civil servants are represented at their meetings. While there could be enhanced solidarity among members of this regional federation, this could suppress dissent by marginalized groups in one country. Take the example of Sri Lanka: China, India and Pakistan supported the efforts of the Sri Lankan Government to eliminate the ethnic Tamil group demanding self-determination. There are many unresolved conflicts within each of these regions. In line with the federalist principle, we need to tackle problems at the level at which they occur. Therefore, dialogues need to be initiated with non-state actors in order to resolve the conflicts.

Way Forward

A global federal framework and federal institutions need to be endorsed by regional unions; this should include a world environmental authority, a world economic organization (to revisit the Bretton Woods institutions), a UN Parliamentary Assembly, a UN Rapid Action Force, Responsibility to protect civilians from armed conflict, the Arms Trade Treaty and so on. Some countries are rich in resources but the people are poor. This is because of improper governance and unequal distribution. There is abuse of the skies and of the outer space and there is no monitoring body. Many countries are yet to ratify and implement the Kyoto protocol and to agree to reduce carbon emissions. There needs to be a reform of the WTO, which should be brought into the fold of the UN. Export of arms should also be regulated and brought within the purview of WTO. Similar to the European Union, members of the Parliament could be directly elected to a UN Parliamentary Assembly. Right now, only the civil servants are represented in the General Assembly of the UN. In order that " we the people", as proclaimed in the UN preamble, becomes true, we need to support efforts towards a UNPA. The UN should have its own protection force (UN Rapid Action Force) rather than depending on member states to provide soldiers for its peace keeping tasks, so that within 24 hours the UN could intervene in any conflict zone. Currently we cannot prevent a calamity like the Rwanda genocide from happening anywhere in the world. The UN could devise a mechanism to address this, through a Responsibility to Protect civilians from armed conflicts program. There is no legally binding instrument to control arms globally at the UN. The UN in the next GA could ratify an Arms Trade Treaty (ATT), a comprehensive legislation covering security-sector reforms, marking and tracing, stock pile management and control of sale of arms to non-state actors. Today most of the conflicts are between state and non-state actors. Unless arms sales to non-state actors are banned, the easy and cheap availability of arms would nurture conflicts.

Finally, "Think Globally and act Locally"

Aiming at the federation of the World, we have to ensure unity among nations in a region, fostering friendship and mutual cooperation. Upholding of Democracy, Federalism, Human rights and Humanitarian values is key to any regional unification process. While there would be enough resources in the world for everyone's need, they are not actually enough due to one or a few countries' greed. Global governance under the World Federal Government is therefore a paramount need of the hour.

The Regional Integration Process of Central America*

Giannis F. Papageorgiou

The success of European integration and the stability and prosperity it offers has found followers elsewhere in the world. The majority of these regional integration schemes, however, limit themselves to economic objectives and tend to avoid ambitious political goals. This is particularly true in the American continent where, despite linguistic and cultural affinities, the various regional integration schemes stay within the framework of inter-governmental co-operation, mainly concentrating in areas of customs and economic approximation and integration. A notable exception to this pattern is Central America. Not only is it the most politically advanced integration process of the Americas, but it also presents several unique characteristics that federalists should approach with more interest. The five countries that traditionally compose the Isthmus of Central America (Guatemala, El Salvador, Honduras, Nicaragua and Costa Rica) share many common traits. They formed part of the Mayan cultural area and, following the Spanish conquest, they became a separate administrative unit (the General Captaincy of Guatemala) within the Vice-Royalty of New Spain (Mexico). The region lacked precious metals and was neglected both by the Spanish administration and by immigrants. Throughout the colonial period, it remained an imperial outpost, sparsely populated and with few and difficult communications with the rest of the world. A small minority of *criollos* (merchants or landowners) constituted the local aristocracy ruling over the mass of marginalised Indians.

The independence process of the 1820s was forced upon Central Americans who were relatively satisfied with the status quo but had to adapt to the changing environment. After a brief annexation of the region to the Mexican Empire (1821-23), it declared its independence in the form of a federal state, the United Provinces of Central America. Its Constitution, strongly influenced by the American Constitution and the Spanish Charter of Cadiz of 1812, provided for a federal State, composed of five provinces (the future states of Central America), a two-tier Parliament and a federal President. Although in theory the central government had sufficient power, in practice military might and finances (including

* Published in Issue 3/2001.

tax-raising) remained largely in the hands of the aristocracy of each province; at the federal level, the fight between conservative and liberal factions kept the Federation in a state of permanent warfare and impeded economic progress. At the same time, divisions between provinces were exacerbated. The final blow to the Federation was given by a peasant revolt of 1838 used by the conservatives to oust the established liberal federal government. After 1840, each province declared independence.

Notwithstanding this failure, the vision of a Central American union, "*the patria grande*", remained alive and guided a series of attempts to rebuild the Federation. They all failed for the same reasons the Federation did not survive: local antagonism, lack of communication, absence of democratic traditions, insufficient economic and political development, and foreign intervention. Only after the Second World War did there appear to be a successful integration scheme: the Central American Common Market (C.A.C.M.), founded in 1960, aimed at creating a customs union and, later, a common market while at the same time coordinating the industrialisation and the economic development of the five Member States. Though the C.A.C.M. was one of the most successful examples of economic integration in the 1960s (and thus constituted a prime example of the neofunctionalist theory), its failure to transform the economic performance into genuine prosperity and the unwillingness of Member States to allow for any democratic opening (most of them were openly or covertly authoritarian regimes) led to its demise in the early 1970s, at the same time that the region foundered in a series of civil conflicts.

Almost throughout the 1970s and during the first period of the following decade, Central America came to international attention, as civil wars in El Salvador and Nicaragua and foreign intervention in them brought the region in the centre of the East-West conflict. Amid concerns that the fight would expand gradually and the escalation might lead to a generalised regional war, regional integration came again to the forefront. When all external efforts to reduce tension (mainly those of the Contadora group, formed by neighbouring Latin American states) failed to produce results and with a military stalemate, Presidents Oscar Arias Sanchez of Costa Rica and Vinicio Cerezo of Guatemala proposed a peace plan based on confidence-building, internal democratisation and the holding of free elections; the Esquipulas plan, adopted in the city of Esquipulas in July 1986 during the first meeting of all Central American Presidents for a generation, included the creation of a directly-elected regional Parliament, the Central American Parliament (Parlacen from its Spanish acronym) as a focal point for reconciliation and peace in the region.

It is important to underline the significance of this step in the history of the region: for the first time, Central American leaders recognised the link between pacification and internal and regional democratic consolidation. Breaking with the tradition elsewhere in Latin America, they looked towards a regional tool in order to facilitate and measure democratic progress nationally and admitted that national and international democracy could not be separate. Thus, the renewed Central American integration process immediately followed a political path and appealed to the popular legitimacy, to be achieved through the direct election of members of the Parlacen. However, this process was thwarted by national resistance, stemming essentially from Costa Rica: as the only democratic state in the region, Costa Rica rejected attempts to grant supranational powers to an institution where the majority belonged to less-than-democratic countries. As a result, the treaty establishing the Central American Parliament was an adulterated version of the original aims; it had practically only a consultative role while its few decisive competencies were frozen by the Costa Rican refusal to ratify the Treaty.

Despite this partial failure, the progressive normalisation of the regional situation allowed for a reinstatement of the old integration instruments and the creation of new ones. This revival culminated in the Tegucigalpa Protocol of 1991 that instituted a Central American Integration System (S.I.C.A.), which also included Panama. S.I.C.A.'s objectives are no longer only economic as were those of its predecessor, the C.A.C.M.; it represents the bridge between the traditional intergovernmental Cupertino and supranational democracy, recognising the indivisible character of development, peace, democracy and integration and the use of regional means to achieve them. Among the founding principles of S.I.C.A. are, in fact, the recognition of the Central American identity and the gradual completion of the regional economic integration.

The institutional structure of the S.I.C.A. draws much from the European model. The Meeting of Presidents is the supreme organ of the System; a Council of Ministers represents the political co-ordinating institution and the Executive Committee, a permanent organ, implements the decisions of the former. Alongside these intergovernmental institutions, one also finds the following integrated institutions: the Central American Parliament, the General Secretariat, which is responsible for the daily running of the S.I.C.A., and the Court of Justice, which has jurisdiction on all matters relating to the legal order of the S.I.C.A. The latter is, in fact, the only integrated institution with decision-making powers and a surprising number of competencies. A Consultative Committee, representing the civil society and the organised social forces of Central America, completes the institutional panorama of S.I.C.A.

At the moment, S.I.C.A. can boast of a number of significant successes. They include a common external tariff, an almost complete customs union and substantial advances in the area of free movement of persons, capital and services. The Court of Justice has shaped the embryo of a Community legal order and the General Secretariat has gradually become the System's administrative and political core, with the Secretary General obtaining an internationally recognised political status and role. The six-monthly meetings of the Presidents continue to be the motor of the S.I.C.A. and unanimity remains the rule in the decision-making processes, but a "community" attitude is slowly developing as are the level of popular participation and the concept of Central American identity. The "Managua Declaration", declared in 1997 by the six Member-State Presidents, established the Central American Union, a step forward to the political integration of the Isthmus. Although the Declaration has yet to become a political reality, in part due to national resistance and in part to the backlash following a series of natural disasters in the area, in particular typhoon Mitch, it still remains the political beacon of integration in the region.

Central American integration continues to face formidable obstacles, including the progression of democratisation. Despite significant progress achieved, democracy is still fragile without, at the same time, being accompanied by social equality: the continued existence of mass poverty practically cancels any democratic achievement. Nationalist resistance to integration continues to be a barrier to full integration, as is the "presidential" character of these States. Furthermore, despite the long tradition of unitary efforts, one still notes the absence of an active popular movement for regional integration. More significantly, the prevailing trend in favour of larger regional or continental free-trade areas in the Americas constitutes a major stumbling block to the separate Central American political and economic integration process: the centrifugal forces advocate direct membership of Central American States in these larger units rather than creating a separate Central American union. The European Union, both as a model and as an aid, can make the difference and help shape the future: a Central America that is a regional union or an integral part of larger free-trade areas, or an amassment of powerless States individually trying to establish privileged relations with a larger group of countries.

A Regional Criminal Court Against Transnational Organized Crime[*]

Fernando A. IGLESIAS

The processes of regional integration in Latin America are facing a stalemate, if not a step backwards. Big political problems have been added to the historical difficulties to foster free trade and custom union in the Mercosur, such as the reluctance of governments to respect the agreement, signed by them, to choose the Mercosur Parliament representatives by popular vote, the conflicts arising from Paraguay's suspension as a member of the regional bloc, and at the same time Venezuela's entry, clearly irregular. Moreover, the Latin American Community and its main institutional body, the Latin-American Parliament, continue their eternal impasse and gradually lose capacity and relevance; UNASUR is still reduced to mere occasional meetings of heads of national executive powers, while the newly created CELAC is not able to assert itself as a southern alternative to the OAS, being affected by public disagreements among the leaders of its major member countries. At the same time, the European economic crisis has demonstrated that the functionalist approach to regional integration, that produced such extraordinary outcomes for six decades, has reached its limits, and that the European Union faces a choice between a definitely federal and political deeper integration and the collapse of the eurozone, first, and of the union itself, later.

Together with the frail situation facing the regional integration processes in the world, Latin America suffers from stifling problems of violence, because it added to its sad record of the most socially unequal region that of the planet's most violent region. The terrible situation in northern Mexico, the Central American gangs and increased drugs use, the drug traffic, the traffic of arms and the human trafficking for sexual slavery and forced labour in other countries, make up a huge regional problem, with negative impact on the lives of the citizens of all Latin American countries, besides becoming, slowly but surely, one of the main obstacles to its economic and social development. In this situation, the only ones that are organized with a supranational logic, that makes the national institutional boundaries obsolete, are the criminals. Protected networks hiding fugitives from justice in other countries, collaboration

[*] Published in Issue 1/2014.

systems between criminal organizations of different countries, exchange of information, drugs and weapons, are just some of the many strategies that reduce to impotence the national systems in their prosecution of organized crime.

Faced with the proliferation of regionally structured criminal organizations and the powerful connections with their counterparts in other regions – such as the Sicilian Mafia, the Calabrian mafia and the Russian and Chinese mafias, among many others – the national security mechanisms suffer from a growing obsolescence and are increasingly subordinate and dependent on national political powers, often complicit in criminal networks. Moreover, far from being an advantage in terms of efficiency, the approach of courts, public prosecutors and national security agencies with regard to the places where the crimes are committed, let them vulnerable to corruption and/or to threats by organized crime. For all these reasons, a regional strategy at least is necessary to face up to a crime that is regionally organized, and to create the basis of a regional integration dynamics, necessary to address other challenges that the countries of the region are facing. It is in this context that the proposal to create a regional criminal court against transnational organized crime arises.

The idea is complex and the proposal has to include the discussion of its final working model, as well as the procedure for its creation. While it is impossible to definitely fix all these issues at the beginning of the process, it is necessary and possible to list a number of basic parameters in order to clarify the subject under discussion and establish a framework for further discussion.

1) The Regional Criminal Court Against Transnational Organized Crime should have three branches: a) the Court itself, in charge of the prosecution and punishment of perpetrators of crimes according to the relevant statutes; b) a prosecutor responsible for proposing, initiating and qualifying the processes and submitting lawbreakers to the Court; and c) a police force in charge of investigations and detentions.
2) The Regional Criminal Court Against Transnational Organized Crime should be the offspring of an international treaty signed by countries that so wish, and should enter into force after reaching a minimum set amount of countries, being open to other countries to join later.
3) The promoters of the creation of the Regional Criminal Court Against Transnational Organized Crime should be a network (or coalition) of governmental organizations dealing with these issues – in particular: the fight against human trafficking and human reduction to labor or sexual slavery, and the fight against drug trafficking and drug addiction – and which feel that its creation

is a fundamental step that completes their struggle and represents the only chance to stop the advance of criminal organizations throughout the region, without which their great efforts will be reduced to defeat and impotence.

The first step towards the finalization of these ambitious goals was the discussion in the round table organized by *Democracia Global – Argentina* and the Spinelli Chair of the *Consorcio Universitario Italiano para Argentina*, in the 5th Altiero Spinelli Symposium about regional integration in a globalized world. Michelle Reyes, director of the South American Coalition for the International Criminal Court, Dr. Mario Ganora, representative of the organization Alameda fighting against human trafficking, Dr. Christian Cao, Professor of Law Integration at the University of Buenos Aires, the MC national representative, Fernanda Gil Lozano, and the President of the Council of the World Federalist Movement and director of the Spinelli Chair, Fernando Iglesias, took part in it.

Throughout the year, the members of *Democracia Global* held meetings also with relevant actors who for training or activity could bring their expertise to the setting up of a feasible program. Among them: members of the NGOs involved in these issues; specialized academics and members of the national political system with an interest in these issues; and national governments and their ambassadors; in all cases, receiving interest and appreciation for the initiative. According to what was discussed and developed, the strategy proposed by *Democracia Global* to achieve the creation, as soon as possible, of a Regional Criminal Court Against Transnational Organized Crime (RCC) is divided into five stages.

The first stage involves the setting up of a Coalition of NGOs willing to work with the aim to create the RCC, under the name of Coalition for the Regional Criminal Court Against Transnational Organized Crime with the corresponding development of its juridical personality and a sustainable financial autonomy. Since *Democracia Global* has been the original promoter of the project and most of the contacts have been established in Buenos Aires, it is proposed to give continuity to the activities of *Democracia Global* and use its legal framework. Therefore an office of the Coalition for the RCC is being created in Buenos Aires and it is legally based in Argentina.

This first stage should include among its aims the spread of the proposal from the Coalition for the Regional Criminal Court Against Transnational Organized Crime to all the political actors – Argentinean, Latin American and of the world – who can contribute to its development, including civil society organizations; global and regional institutions; national governments; embassies and academic circles, in particular those specialized in legal and political issues with a focus on the problem of transnational organized crime or regional judicial and political integration. Furthermore, the setup of a group of lawyers in charge of starting the preparation of the necessary legal framework for drafting the statute of the Coalition for the Regional Criminal Court will be encouraged.

The second step envisages the continuity of the tasks of the first stage, and the extension of the Coalition for the Regional Criminal Court to the greatest possible number of countries in Latin America, through the articulation of a network and the establishment of local and national branches, physical or virtual, in all the cities and towns of the region where there are forces of civil society willing to embrace the goal of creating the Regional Criminal Court.

The third stage forecasts the continuity of the work of the first and second stages and the development of contacts with the national governments of the countries of the region, calling them for the common task of creating the Coalition for the Regional Criminal Court. Its ultimate goal will be the implementation of the founding meeting of the Regional Criminal Court, in which its operating procedures and statute will be established. The same should establish its aims, the crimes that will be under its jurisdiction, its working bodies, its financing system and the minimum number of countries necessary for the Coalition for the Regional Criminal Court to really enter into force.

The fourth stage forecasts the continuity of the work of the first, second and third stages and all kinds of political and institutional work for the accession of the greatest possible number of Latin American countries to the Coalition for the Regional Criminal Court.

The fifth and final stage provides the continuity of the work of the first, second, third and fourth stages, the ongoing monitoring of the Coalition for the Regional Criminal Court, the spread of its criminal and legal actions, and the continuation of the campaign in support to the accession to it by all Latin American countries. The globalization of the RCC model, through the establishment of similar courts in other world regions, as well as its global expansion with the aim to create a World Criminal Court Against Transnational Organized Crime will also be promoted.

Of course, this five-step plan is not a procedural handbook but a project, which is flexible and able to adapt to the circumstances. In all cases, the high interest that the proposal has aroused in all those who joined it fosters hopes for its concrete achievement. It would be a great way to show that the supranational institutions are not an utopia in the minds of unrealistic thinkers but, on the contrary, a concrete and effective answer to the challenges posed by globalization and to the need for peace, justice and prosperity of the world citizens.

Federalism and Decolonization in Black Africa*

Jean-Francis BILLON

It is from the thirties that a certain number of black intellectuals raised the problem of the Balkanization of Africa, which, at the end of the Second World War, was aspiring more and more to regain its independence; a number of them evoked the issue of African Unity as a condition for the independence and the future of Africa. Yet, only the future Heads of State Kwame N'Krumah and Julius K. Nyerere and the academic Cheikh Anta Diop really mentioned or raised the question of an African Federal State. It is necessary, here, to point out the differences between English-speaking pan-Africanists (from Africa or the West-Indies) such as N'Krumah, and the French-speaking ones such as Léopold Sédar Senghor or Aimé Césaire; the latter developed the movement of "*négritude*" stressing the values specific to the black man.

According to our federalist friend, a Senegalese World Citizen, Fall Cheikh Bamba, too early deceased, it was in a great ideological confusion that African leaders fought the anti-colonial struggle. They often wished for unity at the same time as independence, but none of them ever mentioned or supported the necessity of a federalist movement for the whole continent, which had to be specifically African and free from the ideologies of the political classes of Europe, as an indispensable engine and vehicle for African unity. Obviously, the feeble attempts of the 5th Panafrican Congress at Manchester, in November 1945, could not create a strong organization and they were the last expression of the Pan African Federation of 1944. In the same way, the journey of N'Krumah to Paris in 1947 to meet Senghor and French-speaking black intellectuals came out to nothing. Some time later, Senghor tried to launch the African Federalist Party, including Senegal and some of its neighbours, but it also led to nothing. Since there was no unique nor coordinated African scheme, the claims were expressed without any order and remained limited within the national borders (often those of the present African States) imposed by colonialism at the arbitrary carving out by the Congress of Berlin, at the end of the 19th century. This posthumous victory of colonialism turned out to be a total disaster for Africa. On the other hand, in a context of nationalistic exaltation, the projects of Eurafrican Federations between

* Published in Issue 1/2011.

some former colonial powers and their colonies are often considered as the last attempts by European States to maintain their domination. The failure of the Federation planned by Senghor in 1958 (Senegal, Sudan, Haute Volta and Dahomey), then the failure of a less ambitious scheme, the Federation of Mali, or the failure of N'Krumah's efforts after the meeting of the Panafrican Conference of Accra in 1958 were, according to Bamba, to be imputed to the lack of organization which was the rule during all the period that preceded African independence. The union of Tanganyika and Zanzibar, today's Tanzania, was for a time the only successful attempt, thanks to the action of Nyerere.

Senghor's federalism was not limited to Africa: he closely collaborated, before independence, with European Federalists, especially as Vice-President of the Federalist Intergroup in the French Parliament during the debates of the European Defence Community in 1954, then at the Council of Europe. He also kept in touch with World Federalists and he remained, to his death, Vice-President of the World Federalist Movement, initially World Movement for World Federal Government, to which he was connected through his adviser at the Presidency of Senegal, Jean Rous, former Secretary General of the Congress of Peoples against Imperialism, founded with the agreement of Mahatma Gandhi by himself and the British Donald Mac Kay, one of the leaders of the British Federal Union at the end of the thirties.

In 1963, at Addis Ababa, in spite of the desperate efforts of N'Krumah, the Heads of African States adopted the Charter of the African Unity Organization (AUO) which was, for tens of years, to define the political principles and the legal rules of African Unity. As a basis of the new Africa, it proclaimed the principles of "the respect of the sovereignty and territorial integrity of the States" and the "inviolability of African frontiers inherited from colonialism". The founding of AUO marks an important stage in the history of Africa: it affirmed and perpetuated the new African States entities constructed according to the European pattern and model of the Nation-State and absolute State sovereignty. As Bamba has written, "the AUO opened a totally new era for the fight of African Federalists. The State nationalism which has been rife in Africa since that date regularly makes more acute and pressing the question of Federalism".

Part Four

The Contradictions of Globalization without Government

Antonio MOSCONI

States and intergovernmental bodies are unable to tackle the global problems, since an adequate government level to do that is still missing. The control of the globalized economy is entrusted to the "invisible hand" of a small elite out of control, and not, as could be expected, to a world government operating through an international democratic process. This issue has been *The Federal Debate*'s leading thread in the years characterized by the expansion of the global financial capitalism and by the explosion of its contradictions. The newly-adopted free-market approach to economic globalization led to the financial catastrophe of 2008, then to the economic and occupational crisis still underway, but only a few admitted the responsibility of that mainstream economic theory. Among them Tommaso Padoa-Schioppa. At the root of the crisis there is the market fundamentalism started with Pinochet (and his court of *Chicago boys*), Thatcher and Reagan. Their *deregulation* is a failure of politics, that devolved the destiny of the world to the market alone; therefore, handling the crisis that it caused and preventing it from repeating itself cannot happen spontaneously, *à la Hayek* but require a political intervention.

The review has tried to provide critical means for correcting an unruled globalization, in order not so much to block its progress, as to ask for a democratic control of the same through several government levels, up to the world one. It has dealt mainly with the global challenges that cannot find a solution by part of the national States: human rights protection, the elimination of the nuclear (both military and civilian) threat, the fight against terrorism, the policies to contain global warming, the reform of the international monetary system, the drafting of a constitution for the world wide web; and, in sum, the political architecture that could support all these policies and actions, i.e. the democratic reform of the United Nations system.

The peace-keeping missions with humanitarian goals have failed in most of the cases, like in Ruanda, with four million people killed due to the delayed timing of the intervention and/or to insufficient training of the personnel, and yet the States oppose the creation of a UN *Emergency Peace Service,* preferring to reach stand-by arrangements between the UN and individual governments. The real reason that impedes to meet such urgent and desperate needs is the protection of national sovereignties. The *global responsibility to protect* (R2P) idea has been accepted since 2005 only, and is explicitly mentioned in the UN Resolution 1973 of 2011, by which for the first time the Security Council authorized a coercive military intervention in Libya. The R2P has the effect of limiting national sovereignties, but the criteria applied in legitimizing an intervention give often rise to differing interpretations. Building a consensus about any such decision requires to leave no room to motives other than the protection of the civilian population. The UN should have more efficient means for implementing R2P: better intelligence and earlier warnings, rapid intervention capacity, a greater number of mediators, more limited veto power in the Security Council when dealing with mass crimes.

In 1968 in New York, the Nuclear Non-Proliferation Treaty (NPT) was signed, with the aim of preventing Germany, Japan and other countries from endowing themselves with nuclear weapons, which should remain the monopoly of the Fives of the Security Council. The other countries would enjoy the "inalienable right" to ask for nuclear disarmament and to carry out research, production and use of nuclear energy for peaceful ends. Since then, many nuclear accidents have occurred, some of them quite serious (Three Mile Island 1979, Chernobyl 1986) and people have begun to reconsider that energy source all over the world. Germany and Belgium are starting to close down some plants and even France is deciding to close down its fast reactors, but Japan is running counter. The very grave accident at the Fukushima plant due to the tsunami highlights the lack of suitable prevention measures, the presence of errors in the service manuals, the failure of the cooling system and a serious delay by the government in acknowledging (one month later and thanks only to Obama's insistence) an Alarm Level 7 (the same as Chernobyl). It is necessary to overcome the dichotomy between civilian and military nuclear energy. Continuing to exploit the existing plants is a crime against humanity, and building new ones is a crime against future generations.

Lucio Levi's editorial after the Twin Towers attack of Sept. 11, 2001, read again today – as I am doing – just after the Paris assaults of November 13, 2015, looks prophetic. The evidence of the US vulnerability, he writes, is changing the course of world politics. Those in the world entrusting their security to the super-power discover that the National Missile Defense (NMD) is powerless against the enemies hiding in our own societies. Globalization erases the differences between domestic and external aspects of security, between crime and war. It lets other actors emerge, like the gigantic multinational companies, the civil society movements and the international crime organizations, which are eroding the States' sovereignty. Terrorist organizations blend the committing of violence by their suicide-bombers with the possession of huge financial resources, and with the support of part of the international public opinion. With such means they challenge the States' monopoly of violence. The war against Afghanistan has been a tragic mistake. The terrorist strategy aims at inflaming desperate Islamic masses and at undermining their moderate governments. The western strategy, instead, should aim at eschewing a clash of civilizations, choosing the road towards a federal world government. To that end, binding force must be given to international laws, and the reform of the United Nations must be started. The International Criminal Court is a first step in that direction.

The most telling instance of a late political response to problems not solvable by individual national States is given by global warming. The first scientific warning dates back to 1820. The UN convened the first World Conference on climate in 1979, but there was to wait until 1990 to issue the first report by the Intergovernmental Panel on Climate Change (IPCC). The first Conference of the Parties (COP, Berlin 1995) rejected the idea of harmonized policies and proposed a list of non-mandatory actions. Only the Kyoto Protocol (1997) fixed objectives for emissions, but for them to enter into force a minimum number of countries had to sign it, which happened only in 2004. But the United States did not ratify it. In 2009, the United States and China caused the failure of the Copenhagen Summit. At the Durban COP (2011), it was decided to prepare a new Protocol within 2015, which should be implemented starting from 2020 (two centuries after the first warning!). There is no guarantee that the countries will not shun their commitments, emissions continue to grow and there are no coercive measures for reducing or stabilizing them. National sovereignty is still the most precious value, to the detriment of the common good. In order to provide public goods, a balanced system of supra-national institutions is necessary. In their absence, one has to rely on bilateral agreements and on the market, with the consequence that emissions and speculation on pollution rights are increasing.

The Paris COP of December 2015 should produce a first agreement between the countries which, together, are causing 56% of global emissions: China (29%), the USA (16%) and the European Union (11%). An initiative from them could make other countries join in a *binding* agreement for a sizable reduction of global emissions. Attaining that objective is made easier by the development of new technologies concerning solar and wind energy, with an ensuing cost reduction. The American proposal to establish each country's objectives on the base of *total emissions* is unacceptable to the emerging and developing countries, since the US *per-capita* emissions are twice those of China and the EU, which are similar. The Paris COP should not produce another international Treaty, but rather reach an agreement for the creation of a World Environment Organization under the aegis of the UN, with the task of implementing a plan for the reduction of greenhouse gases, and with the powers necessary to monitor the polluting States and the financial autonomy, ensured by a global carbon-tax, to provide disincentives to the use of fossil fuels.

Economic globalization cannot be supported by the currency of a single national State. The crisis of the international role of the dollar is progressive and irreversible. On the financial plane, it manifests itself in the unsustainable level of the American foreign debt. On the political plane, in the US inability to provide worldwide public goods in return for its hegemony. All over the world, people are increasingly calling for a multilateral, shared and democratic governance of the globalized economy. A "new Bretton Woods" should be tasked to solve simultaneously to sets of problems: 1) consolidate/extinguish/use up/ convert the US huge foreign debt and introduce a code that prevents the repeat of basic, permanent and cumulative unbalances of any country's balance of payments; 2) guarantee the financing of the provision of public goods necessary to the functioning of a globalized economy. The goal is the creation of a world currency, but we can start with a unit of account referred to a basket of currencies. That basket already exists: with suitable adjustments, the Special Drawing Rights (SDR) could serve the purpose. The SDR basket must be made more representative by including the renmimbi (the decision should be taken by the IMF at the end of November 2015), and perspectively also other currencies. The increase of the renmimbi utilization is phenomenal, and its inclusion in the SDR basket will increase both its stability and its representativity. The four currencies that are in the basket (dollar, euro, yen and British pound) represent 40% of the world GDP; with the renmimbi, it will rise to 55%. It is necessary, in addition, to change the IMF governance, with the objective to reach a composition more attuned to the economic weight of the various countries, and to foster the use of SDRs as reserve currency and in public and private financial issues. A European initiative would be decisive for attaining a success in this direction. But it requires the unitary representation of the euro-zone in the IMF.

The democratic duty to establish juridical rules for the web is faced with two great obstacles: both the national sovereign States and the trans-national companies pretend to be "legislators for themselves". There is a concrete risk of market censorship, all the more unacceptable the more the Internet is used in non-commercial spheres. A good starting point is the European Union's Charter of Fundamental Rights, in the drafting of which Stefano Rodotà was involved, because it contemplates the protection of personal data as a fundamental autonomous right. It is necessary to formally claim as part of a new world citizenship these principles: liberty of access and use, right to know, respect of privacy, recognition of new public goods. Moreover, the "technical" management of the web must pass from the United States to the United Nations. There is to fear, however, that progress in this issue too will suffer a standstill after the Paris attacks, which were helped by the use of encrypted communications in the Internet. The *liberty vs. security* trap has already been set off; now, at least, it must not be left in the hands of the national States.

Whatever "global emergency" is considered, one comes to the same discouraging conclusion: immeasurable human, social and economic sacrifices, that could be avoided with a proper political management, are still paid as an idolatrous tribute to the independence of national States, whilst *global* interdependence should be recognized as prevailing. No one of the classical elements of the State, territory, people and sovereignty, is left unharmed by globalization. Territories are ever more crossed by trans-national flows of goods, capitals, pieces of information and symbols that escape the control of the States. People too are subject to the dynamics of globalization: in the global era politics must correspond to its diversity and complexity (languages, cultures, religions, life experiences). Sovereignty, finally, is eroded by the development of civil society, of regional, local, intergovernmental and supra-national powers. The State is no longer the whole, but one of the parts, it must negotiate its role and power with other parts, in the form of a multi-actor or multi-level governance. While the States, even the bigger ones, are no longer able to ensure that their citizens will get the public goods they were created for, the threats from outside are producing fears and distrust, and bring about an authoritarian deterioration. What answer can politics give?

Not necessarily the question is to be solved through an authoritarian world government or an ineffective world Parliament. To arrive at a democratic federal government there is a third way, indicated by Kelsen, that of the broadening of international laws and of their progressive constitutionalization. In such a perspective, the institution of the International Criminal Court (ICC) is a leap forward of considerable significance, because the Treaty institutes its jurisdiction not only between States, but also over individuals. Bill Pace is reaping the fruits of a long work that marks the first federalist success at the world level. The NGO coalition set up in 1995 and led by the WFM brought about the draft Statute, signed in Rome in 1998 and ratified by a number of countries (sixty six) sufficient for it to enter into force in 2002, despite the formal repeal by George W. Bush, in 2000, of the previous support given to the ICC by Clinton. Pace's comment to Bush's decision was: "It's unrealistic to think that the perpetrators of the most serious crimes of international concern would submit themselves to trial by their own judicial systems".

Ten years on, with 121 participatory States, the ICC is still meeting severe limitations in prosecuting crimes against humanity. The citizens of the countries that did not ratify the Treaty cannot be prosecuted. The most powerful and violent State is thus shielding its leaders and military personnel from international law. In addition to the USA, other countries, perpetrators of violations of human rights or involved in conflicts and civil wars, did not ratify the Treaty. Among them: China, Cuba, Iraq, Iran, Israel, Libya, Pakistan, Russia, Syria. The ICC, according to Iglesias, should pass judgment also on war crimes committed by citizens of States that do not ratify the Treaty, at least as a moral and symbolic impeachment.

It is unacceptable that the four winners of the Second World War and China still maintain the right of veto on every decision, and that only the governments be represented in the UN. The World Parliament, like those of the ECSC (1951) and the European Common Market (1957) in the past, could initially be composed of representatives of national Parliaments, and have consultative functions. Only in 1979 did the UEF, leading a great coalition of forces, obtain the direct election of the EP members, which marked the beginning of a gradual granting of powers. Today, the EP represents the second larger democracy in the world, after the Indian, and is the first supra-national Parliament, a model for the African Union and the Mercosur. It is true that out of 192 UN member States only 117 are democratic, but all of them should be represented in the Parliament, an instrument of world citizenship, an exercise in democracy and a spur to the development of a global civil society. In any case, democracy is spreading: in 1840 only 3.9% of the world population was living in democratic States; in 2000, 57.1% does. As George Modelski observes, democratization is such a persistent and powerful process, despite periods of crisis like in the 1930s, that it cannot be easily countered. It is a slow, long-term trend, but “it shall not be hurried”. We had better devote ourselves to consolidating the existing democracies than to costly military interventions or pre-emptive wars. The right way to consolidate the advance of democracy is to strengthen NATO, the Bretton Woods institutions and the democratic development of the UN.

The inequity of the present UN system is greatest at its summit, the Security Council, where the decisional power is concentrated in the hands of five States out of 191. Lucio Levi observes that the traditionally-proposed solution, namely, to open the doors to States in a prominent position and entrust them with the representation of the smaller States in the same region, is met with the hostility of the countries excluded. The best solution is the creation of regional groups of States in the General Assembly, who in turn express a representation in the Security Council. The EU is the region which is closer to the fulfillment of that goal.

Its weakness within the UN system is due most of all to the fact that foreign policy and defence decisions must be taken unanimously.

This is the obstacle to be removed to make the EU as such sit in the Security Council, in lieu of the hegemony of the stronger States and of the German request to have a seat there for itself. A strong and independent EU constitutes the first pillar for building a new UN system based on regional groupings, and for overcoming the American supremacy, the unfair distinction between permanent and non-permanent members, and the right of veto.

Hamilton, in the *Federalist Papers* (No. 23), writes: "We must abandon the vain project of legislating upon the States in their collective capacities; we must extend the laws of the federal government to the individual citizens of America". Federalism requires to overcome the distinction between domestic and foreign policy. The idea prevailing in the United States is, instead, that the term "world policy" concerns the relations among States, including war and violence. "Calling those things politics – Baratta says indignantly – is like calling love a rape". And yet, the federalist plans for a world government clash against the wall of that conventional wisdom.

The *tesserae* of a new world order exist already, in its moral and juridical paradigms. An ever growing number of people cannot tolerate any longer that human dignity be subordinated to State sovereignty, but the political classes do not have the courage to put the mosaic together. The European method of Conventions could be adopted to gather a universal Convention. The "One State, one vote" criterion is not enough, there must be a direct popular participation in a process that aims to make the Security Council more representative, preferably on regional bases, to institute a UN Parliament and a permanent global civil-society Forum, to strengthen the functions of the Ecosoc for social justice, to establish a permanent UN police force, both civilian and military, to broaden the ICC mandate and strengthen its structure, and to endow the International Court of Justice with the power to pass judgment on the legitimacy of the Security Council's acts.

Who is Controlling Globalisation?*

Peter USTINOV

The theme of this conference is a vital and difficult one. The question is not merely whether or not there will be a process of globalization. Globalization is happening: in commerce, finance, communications, culture, politics, security, human rights, and almost every other aspect of human life. Globalization is ongoing and unstoppable. The central question is who is guiding and controlling this globalization? Is it a small set of political and corporate elites far from public scrutiny and accountability? Or it is a diverse set of actors involved in a democratic process of decision making?

At WFM we are striving toward a more democratic and governed system of international decision making. We have been working in strategic partnerships with other NGOs around the world to bring us closer to this goal, through our work supporting the creation of the International Criminal Court, enhancing the role of non-governmental organizations at the United Nations, strengthening the capacity of the United Nations to deal with civil and inter-state conflicts, advocating a parliamentary assembly at the UN and a reformed Security Council, and promoting regional federations such as the process occurring now in Europe. I am particularly seized of the matter of the globalization of commerce and trade. As I remarked for WFM's 50th anniversary in 1997 in Montreux, Switzerland.

Today with the galloping globalization of commerce when a growing number of conglomerates are already more powerful than and influential than many governments, the creation of a World Criminal Court, brilliantly espoused by our organization, is an urgent necessity, for the simple reason that crime lives on commerce as a cancer lives on flesh and tissue, and there must be generally accepted constraints in the chaos of business opportunity.

World Federalists are not dreamers, we do not imagine these reforms will occur in a day. But we are also not cynics who believe that systems cannot be changed. I prefer to liken us to "practical idealists" who combine high principles with achievable strategies, long-term visions and short term objectives. And I am proud to consider myself among their numbers and honored to serve as their President.

* Published in Issue 1/2000.

September 12: The World is not at Zero-Point*

Reflections on How to Unite the World in Peace and Liberty, Prosperity and Justice

Tommaso Padoa-Schioppa

1. Introduction

In the tragic crescendo of events which unfolded over a few weeks, Gothenburg, Genoa and New York have made evident to the absent-minded a sickness that we could define as follows: the contrast between the things which divide the world and those which unite it. United in terms of trade, of climatic and nuclear risk; divided by the disparities in living conditions, by the absence of instruments to reduce economic, political, religious conflicts. Uniting the world is the key question of a century, which will certainly not be short if we measure it by the time needed to achieve a lasting result.

We do not know exactly the remedy for this sickness; the path ahead of us is a research, not only an effort of realisation. "War is as old as mankind, whereas peace is a recent invention" wrote Henry Maine, an English jurist, in the mid-19th century. And yet we are not at zero-point, we do not lack essential references. Ignoring them would certainly mean condemning the world to ruin. The events of a few weeks ago have in fact reminded us that the forces of destruction are today seemingly more globalised than those of construction.

First of all: peace, liberty, prosperity, justice are truly universal goods. Not everyone was conscious of this, even a few years ago. They are universal not only because they are desired by all, which has always been the case, but also because now it is no longer possible to achieve them "in a single country". Human beings alive today, and even more so those who are yet to be born, are already united today by the fact of depending on each other for achieving those universal goods.

In the second place: mutual dependence makes the attainment of these goods a political question, i.e. concerning the art and science of governing. It demands the exercise of power, methods to assign and control it, rules,

* Published in Issue 2/2002.

administration of justice, coercion. The etymology of the word "political" reminds us that mutual dependence, and with it politics, was born in the city (the Greek *polis*) and remained there for a long time. Today the city is the world.

2. The market is not enough

Of the three main areas of human activity – the economy, politics, culture – it is undoubtedly the economy which has more rapidly crossed national borders. The term "globalization" indicates the emergence of a global market and of global finance. Supporters and opponents of globalisation in effect seem to share the same myth which, born out of the first industrial revolution, seems impervious to reason and to experience: the myth of the economy as the sole pillar of the social order. This myth makes the enemies of globalisation believe that the evil lies in the market-typical quest for profit (what they call capitalistic mode of production). It prevents its advocates from seeing that an economic system cannot replace a political order. The opponents recognise a state of sickness, but are wrong in their diagnosis. The supporters deny the illness. That the illness is not the failure of the market-based economic system is evident from the comparative experience of the countries which have, in various ways, tried to escape from poverty. The many areas where living standards are high are also those in which market principles have been applied, whereas the areas which have chosen central planning have worsened poverty and corruption from which they were already suffering. In the Soviet area, where all market forms were radically suppressed for a very long time, the economic disaster has been complete and continues beyond the end of the USSR. The longer and more persistent the anti-market experiment, the greater its failure. It is therefore a wrong diagnosis the one which interprets the difficulties of globalisation as the final consequence of the so-called contradictions of capitalism.

But from negating the evil, no less serious dangers may derive: the comforting illusion that growth can, like a purifying wind, sweep away all difficulties; the refusal to correct the distortions of the global market and finance; the inability to reform international cooperation; the claim that economy can solve political issues. When they negate the illness, the supporters of globalisation fuel hostility and rebellion more than their adversaries do. The fact is that to create peace, liberty, prosperity, justice, the establishment of the market is a necessary condition but it is not enough. It is not enough for human society in the same way as it is not enough for a village or a state. Three arguments seem to support this thesis.

In the first place, in order for it to function, the market itself needs juridical, social, cultural, political and institutional bases. In the second place, even if it works optimally, the market does not produce all the goods needed by individuals and by society. There are fundamental goods, such as security or peace, the environment or education, monetary stability or respect for contracts, which nobody can individually produce for himself or sell to others. In the third place, the economy is not everything: you don't live by bread alone, either individually or collectively. Peace, liberty, prosperity, justice are necessary for an orderly development of economic life; they are values, human ideals, for which some are ready to sacrifice their own bread. Not only: they are conditions for something else. It becomes possible to deepen one's knowledge, to enjoy and produce the beautiful, to travel, cultivate friendship and culture, *otium* and contemplation.

3. Politics: the golden path

To refute the sufficiency of the market means that no remedy to the misdeeds of globalisation will be appropriate if it does not bring significant progress towards a political order that is also global.

A mind set free to speculate beyond what appears realisable in a short time clearly identifies the golden path to be followed. It is the path which leads to a world government founded on the very same principles which political thought and the experience of centuries have elaborated for other and more confined human communities (cities, countries, continents): proclamation of the fundamental rights of the individual, government instruments capable of protecting them, subjection of those who exercise power to laws and control by the citizens.

After the two wars which stained the past century with blood, these thoughts finally inspired political action itself. Precisely because the conflicts had been worldwide, so was the system of peace and law that started to be built to prevent their repetition. The concept of "citizen of the world" passed from language to reality.

The League of Nations and the United Nations are the two institutions created to set in motion, following the era of the survival of the fittest, the era of peace and the rule of law among all nations. Today we note that the United Nations is not held in high esteem by the public, that it is often ridiculed for its powerlessness, and that it does not appear to be an ideal for which it is worth sacrificing oneself. And this is the case not only for the very many who inattentively look at world events, but also for the many who are driven by anguish, piety and longing for peace to demonstrate against globalisation, against the tyranny of the market, and for peace at any price. It is true that the number of wars fought in the world since 1945 is reckoned to be in the hundreds, and the number of dead is reckoned to be in the millions. It is true that the United Nations has not been able to prevent extermination in countries like the Soviet Union, China, Cambodia, Rwanda, Yugoslavia, Algeria. But it has missed the target not because the inspiring principle has been mistaken, but because its implementation has been inadequate.

However, the progress that has been achieved along the golden path, and the slow but important changes of traditional concepts and instruments are too often forgotten. In the military sector, the armed forces are no longer institutions merely functional to offensive or defensive war, but also to peace-keeping and peace-making, i.e. to separating warring parties, control of territory, prevention of wider conflicts. The United Nations has currently 16 operations of this kind running, involving some 30,000 soldiers.

Steps have been made since 1948 and the Universal Declaration of Human Rights towards defining and protecting values common to humanity. The concept of "crimes against humanity" has been elaborated, crimes which must be accounted for not in the prejudiced environment of a given place and time, but in the universal environment of the human race and in perpetuity. In line with the same principle of criminal law, according to which society in its entirety is offended by the crime and therefore it has the right to judge and punish, it is agreed that in certain cases the offended society is the whole of humanity.

Faced with the extraordinary acceleration of economic interdependence, with the growing threats that only humanity in its entirety can avert (biosphere, terrorism, atomic proliferation), the steps taken along the golden path have certainly been significant, but indeed slow and incomplete. The instruments which today the UN and other international bodies have at their disposal are quite inadequate.

Such inadequacy has provided the impetus to look for alternative paths: improper forms of government, individual humanitarian commitment, protest.

Improper forms of government are the hegemony by one country over the world, the balance of forces, agreements between nations. Today, these are even more difficult to practise than in the past, and even in the past they have never secured peace. It is not peace, but rather a truce, the temporary and precarious absence of open conflicts which has been established between one or more sovereign powers, each one having the interest or ambition to expand its action and to exercise its influence outside the territory in which it is sovereign. The path of humanitarian commitment is that of thousands of persons who, working for organisations or individually, have gone to Sarajevo or Afghanistan at times of great danger, are helping street children in Guatemala, are teaching at the University of Mozambique, are looking after the sick in India. They are seeds of courage, intelligence, professional skill that do not remain without fruit; but the fruit will not be a political order for the world.

Along the path of protest come together tens of thousands of young people moved by compassion, naïvely longing for peace, fearful of an overlarge world; but also highly sophisticated political militants who wish to revive the Marxist-Leninist myth; and finally rioters and hooligans trained in urban guerrilla warfare. The path of protest denounces the sickness, but does not heal it and may even exacerbate it.

Each one of these three paths may have its usefulness, but none is conclusive, and none can take the place of a tiring journey along the golden path.

4. Trying again and again

The condition of the world is therefore at the crossroads between a golden path, of which we know the goal and inspiring principle, but also its uncertainty and difficulty, and paths of the past, which we know to be insecure and ineffective, demonstrations of self-denial or protest which do not suffice to fill the void of government.

The golden path is rough first and foremost because travelling along it means limiting the sovereignty of states. In a constitutional order inspired by the political philosophies mentioned above, powers and rules would be established, certainly with the participation of all, which would be above national powers. It is in the very nature of a social contract that the contracting parties be bound, but to this principle is opposed the idea that a sovereign state does not recognise any power higher than itself; an idea still so rooted in the dominant culture that merely discussing it seems to seek to endanger the survival of the state. But even if one wanted to go down this rough path, it would be necessary to mark it out anew, finding an answer to difficult questions. Which powers to transfer from the state to a world government? How to ensure proper representation? Which instruments to confer on it? The principle of democracy is a single one, but it is achieved through different procedures and institutions for governing a village, a city, a nation-state, a continental federation, or the world. At each of the historical moments in which the social contract was extended (because the community of people who recognised themselves interdependent became broader) the institutions of government had to be reinvented in order to maintain the characteristics of efficacy, legitimacy, balance of powers, which civil thought and conscience judged indispensable.

In the construction of a world political order within which to pursue that part of peace, liberty, prosperity, justice (I say "part" because not all peace, liberty, etc. are dependent on the state of the world: there is one peace in the family and one in the city, a local and a universal justice) which is realisable only on a global scale, the path is steep. But we must know that we are not at zero-point. We sensed and turned onto that path almost a century ago. The same failures endured up to now have something to teach us.

What Altiero Spinelli said on the subject of European unity is valid for the creation of a world political order: the strength of an idea is revealed not by the fact that it imposes itself without friction at its first appearance, but from its capacity to be reborn out of defeat. If an idea contains in itself what I call the beginning of the solution to a question that torments humanity, to that idea people will come back, trying again and again. The failings of repeated attempts will not succeed in erasing it from people's mind and will.

5. Multiculturalism and common culture

At a certain moment in the history of the West the word "union" was used to define a political order. At first, there was personal union of various territories under one crown (in Spain, in the British Isles), then a union of the people located in adjacent provinces (in the Netherlands).

In those times a unity, which was not only political but also cultural, was recognised, or was attempted to be put in place. That culture developed predominantly in the religious sphere, contrary to what happened in the Roman empire, which however abandoned syncretism and practised persecution when it felt itself threatened by Christianity. Only in the modern age and in the states with a Christian tradition did the separation between political and religious powers mature, and with it the emancipation of culture from political power.

We have to ask ourselves if a worldwide political union without any matching point in the field of culture is possible. The answer is no, it is not possible. Just as a production or trading system requires, for its own global functioning, rules and powers which govern it, i.e. one global policy, a global policy in turn presupposes that some of its founding principles are universally shared, consequently a matching point in culture. The social contract of the world can be written in more than one way; but whatever the wording may be, the ideas and the culture that inspire it must be shared by the contracting parties.

Today we see that precisely on the issue of keeping separate culture and politics, religious and political power, the world is divided so sharply as to make blood be shed and to threaten the security of all. In Afghanistan, eight aid workers (doctors devoted to humanitarian aid) risked being condemned to death because they were found with a Bible in Arabic and with crucifixes. The crime is called "proselytizing". What are the true contours of such a crime? Would respecting the liberty of others consist of saying nothing to them about our truth? Or would not such silence be a lack of respect? Commenting on the case, the Afghan Minister of Foreign Affairs, Muttawakil, said: "We believe ourselves to be serving human rights but there is a small difference of definition. We believe in rights according to Islam, and if someone tries to impose his definition he makes a bad mistake, because this is not the world of a single culture or of a single religion".

I have spoken about a matching point in the cultural sphere, not about a common culture. Just as not all the economy is global, in the same way not all politics and all culture can or must be unitary for there to be peace in the world. If it is true that a global political order is not possible without a minimum shared belief in fundamental matters of political philosophy and law, it is also true that the world is and will remain multicultural. That order cannot and must not aim to block the processes of mutual influence, osmosis, contamination that mark history and often connote its highest points. It must prevent forced conversions, not free conversions; it must prevent the suppression of local languages, not their slow decline into disuse; it must prevent the oppression by the strongest, not the support to a better solution. The rules of how to live together that the West has slowly improved upon, often by way of fatal errors, are imperfect and demand vigilant application; but they are the same as those for which Mandela, Sacharov and Gandhi have endured imprisonment, for which Chinese students died in Tienanmen Square, the boat people have fled from Vietnam, Iranian and Algerian women have been stoned. They are not "European" values or, as it was once said, "bourgeois", as opposed to "Asian", "socialist", or "Islamic" values: they are values without an adjective.

6. Entering into history

The bursting of historic tragedy into an individual's life is an experience which almost every human being undergoes at least once in the course of his life, and leaves him permanently marked. It is, usually, experience of war. This experience transforms our lives, makes us see death as an event that concerns not only the circle of our own loved ones, poses new questions: if history invades our life, what must we do in history, how can we, in our own small way, enter into history.

For many of those who live in prosperous, democratic countries, the images of the attack on the Twin Towers have been and remain the dramatic realisation that our house, school, office are not protected from destruction. Vietnam, Iran, Kuwait, Kosovo, Chechnya were distant names. Some weeks ago, unexpectedly, the war, televised so many times from those countries, ceased to be something of remote places and times. Now that war has become a nearby reality, the difficulty and the price of peace present themselves in a new light. In a comparable but opposite way, the war cried out for in squares in 1914, especially by the young, turned out to be, in the space of a few weeks, not a romantic adventure but a terrible massacre. Even a peaceful existence, as we have seen in New York, can unexpectedly become a terrible massacre. It is now understood that the peace enjoyed for decades in Europe is not the fruit of pacifism, it is felt that the grandfathers and great-grandfathers who enlisted in the two world wars at the same age as those who are students today did not love peace any less than their grandchildren do.

And yet it is true that peace is not made either through violence or non-violence. If we want to improve on the modern invention of peace, action must be taken to prevent war, not to evade those wars already being waged. We must take action in politics, not only in the voluntary service. We cannot wait for the regeneration of minds to be completed: the world of peace-loving people will never come if, in the meantime, the violent ones conquer it. Neither can it be hoped that the humanitarian commitment may look after not only the sick and poor, but also fanatics and terrorists. It is not possible to aim at a uniform culture: a minimal matching point must suffice to draw up a global social contract.

To build peace it is necessary to spare no efforts in the political arena. There is no other method than that invented and applied successfully to prevent war within the borders of each country: to substitute the rule of law in place of the survival of the fittest, to put a limit on the absolute power of the states. It is a very long path that will require much more time than the war which broke out on September 11. Those alive today will not see the end, but they must know that we have already set off, that the goal is known and that we have a compass.

How Is the State Changing in the Globalization Process?*

Reflections and Discussion Points for a Federalist Culture in the 21st Century

Giampiero Bordino

According to a widely-shared definition, the State, at least the modern State, consists of three basic elements: a territory, its people, and a sovereign power. If this is true, every analysis of the transformations affecting the State brought about by globalization cannot but take those three elements, which are all present and interact with each other, as subjects for reflection.

The "end of the territories" (according to Bertrand Badie's definition), transnational mobility and hybridization of peoples and their identities, and the erosion of sovereignty are three phenomena we are immersed in, which affect us personally and continuously, and which, therefore, we have to be aware of and interpret. The federalist culture, that deals with the State and its features, and even proposes (being an ideology) both a model of political structure for the world, and a key for interpreting human history, shall not shun such a task. It must propose a theory and a project for the 21st century, globalized by the economy and completely transformed by scientific progress.

In concrete terms, to start with, what about territories, the spaces we live in and in relation to which we traditionally give a "definition" of ourselves? First of all, the territory is not a *datum* but a construction: historically, there is a political power, the State, that gives it boundaries, makes it become the specific area where its rules and obligations affect the people living in it, gives it a name, thus determining an "inside" and an "outside". But globalization and the scientific and technological revolution in transports and communication that made it possible and still fuels it, have started to "de-construct" such territories, conceived in that way. In fact, territories are crossed more and more by transnational streams of goods, capitals, people, information data and signs (images, sounds, values). Such streams – the "outside" entering inside – increasingly escape

* Published in Issue 3/2007.

State's controls, regulations and directives. The spaces for social relations and activities become more and more numerous (think of the communication space on the Web, or that of finance, or that of the communities of the diaspora), break the continuity and unity of State territories, cross their borders, interconnect through transnational networks parts of those territories.

The State's second constitutive element – the people – is also increasingly subject to the dynamics of globalization and scientific and technological revolution. The migration processes of various nature and origin, and transnational mobility of professions and labor are the main factors of change. The real or pretended (by national myths and ideologies) homogeneity and unique identity of peoples (made today more and more hybrid by migration processes, by the presence of transnational diasporas, by old or more recent forms of mobility that run across territories and States), is lost. Many hundreds of millions of people all over the world – an ever increasing number in ever more territories – have hyphenated identities (Anglo-Indians, Chino-Americans, Italo-Australians, etc.) or in any case "floating" identities; they feel as multi-belonging, acquire multiple citizenships, experience the diversity and complexity of languages, cultures, religions, go through several life experiences and models.

De-constructed territories and hybrid, diaspora-experiencing peoples: this is the difficult puzzle politics and States have to deal with in the global era. How to make human groups of different origin, language, culture, religion, live peacefully and profitably together on the same territory – although disarticulated, as we said, into many relational spaces that may even become more and more transnational? How to avoid the risk of identity conflicts and "ethnic cleansing" that such a complexity may imply? Which institutional architecture, which social and cultural policies shall be devised to cope with this? Finally, the third constitutive element of the State: sovereignty. In the traditional definition, it is the power "that does not recognize any other power above itself and is the source of all powers below itself". In practice, there are now many signals and reasons showing on the one hand a change in sovereignty's ways and forms, and on the other its increasing erosion. At the root of sovereign power's mutation and erosion are many factors, not occasional but structural: in a horizontal and functional aspect, the emerging of civil societies, not only national but also global. From below, the rise of regional and local powers; upwards, the development of forms of intergovernmental and, in some significant cases, even supranational power (like the European Union, in the first place). The increasing functional autonomy of civil society – economic actors, intermediate social bodies, associations and so on – is under everybody's eyes, and many of us experience and practice it every day in our work, profession, political or cultural activities, volunteer work. Civil societies, whose actors (not only big companies, but professional associations, representatives of the so-called Third Sector, NGOs, etc.) are more and more capable of negotiating with the State their role and normative domain, and give themselves potentially global horizons. They ignore frontiers and jump over them, create transnational networks, link together the "local" and the "global" much more than what State governments can do. To take a meaningful example, NGOs, according to a UN estimate, are today 44,000, are present all over the world and tie together its various parts. Globalization and the scientific and technological revolution feed the growth of civil society more than that of the States, and let a truly global civil society form and develop, a global public opinion the States are more and more often obliged to come to terms with.

Secondly, as we said, State sovereignty is changed and eroded by the growth of local and regional powers, which claim, negotiate and often conquer in the field their own autonomy. Sovereignty is less and less "the source of all powers below itself", as per the classical definition, because globalization is proposing ever more often to the local levels reasons and opportunities for greater autonomy, if not separation.

Thirdly, sovereignty is eroded from above, both by the increasing number of international treaties and networks, which force the States to explicitly recognize powers above themselves (as in the case of the States which are members of the EU, or of those that have ratified the International Criminal Court). There are today, according to some estimates (see Sabino Cassese, *Beyond the State*), more than 2,000 international organizations (there were only 123 in 1951), more than 100 international courts of various nature and functions, as many quasi-jurisdictional bodies, a very large and growing number of universal norms addressed to both national administrations and individuals. In addition, big processes of regional integration are under way at continental level (the EU, but also the Mercosur, Asean, the African Union, and so on), which may imply processes of reallocation and sharing of State-like (not just economic) powers and functions. As the French political scientist Zaki Laïdi wrote, speaking of a "fractal State", ever more often – in its relations with civil society, local and regional powers, international and supranational bodies – the State is no longer the "Whole", as per the traditional *souverainiste* pretence, but only a "part", and is forced to negotiate its own role and its own power with other "parts" in the form of multi-actor and multi-level governance.

Given this analytical and interpretative framework, and coming to a conclusion, what challenges is facing today such a changing State, eroded in its sovereignty, and grappling, as we saw, with the unprecedented and worrying puzzle of fragmented territories and mobile, diaspora-experiencing peoples? The fact is that traditional States, even the biggest and most powerful ones, are no longer capable of assuring to their citizens, on their own territory, the fundamental "public goods" for providing which they were founded and were, at least in the modern era, legitimized: peace and security, economic development, social cohesion, public welfare, environment protection, education, etc. Those goods, in the globalization era, shall either be produced and assured elsewhere, or can no longer be produced and assured at the level of a single State. In fact, how can good health be assured to one State's citizens, in the presence of a transnational spreading of diseases or the consequences of environmental disasters occurred elsewhere, in any other part of the world? How to assure security inside one State's borders, when they become ever more porous, the "outside" can almost always be found inside, and the enemy could live in our own house? All this, among other things, is feeding a regrettable culture and policy of fear and suspicion, that contributes to bring about an authoritarian degeneration of the State, and a crisis of democracy, both as the system guaranteeing rights, and as a process of participation and inclusion.

We have to acknowledge that today the fundamental "*public* goods", which are – we must always remember – also the necessary condition for acquiring and enjoying *private* goods (this was well understood already in the Middle Ages: how can you make business if outlaws control the roads or plague is spreading through the cities?), must be produced at many levels and in many "places" (laws, institutions), including the world. No country, not even the American superpower, can produce and guarantee them alone. And neither the EU could do that, even if it becomes an accomplished federal State.

In conclusion: in the face of those difficult and complex challenges, which proposals and projects are currently on the table? I believe that, if we bar the undesirable prospect of an hegemonic world empire, imposed and in most cases managed by the use of force, there are today on the scene of political ideas only three main theoretical proposals that most of the conceivable theories and projects can be related to: the possibility of a "global governance"; a "cosmopolitan democracy"; and the proposal of a "federal-type state-like organization".

The first, the perspective of a "global governance", presents unsolved – or somehow removed – questions on two fundamental issues: that of its democratic legitimization, because it entails a governance negotiated between State and non-State actors, where in the end it is not the head-count that leads to a decision, as happens in democracy, but the balancing of organized interests; and that of efficiency, because no "last-resort" power (which also means the possibility of using legal force) is foreseen, and the executive process is essentially left to the actors' goodwill, or, to be more realistic, to their relations of force.

The second, the perspective of a cosmopolitan democracy, rightly stresses the issue of popular participation and consensus, but removes the issue of power and in particular the assurance that norms at global level are decided and decisions are enforced, as it explicitly excludes from its theoretical horizon the necessity of the availability, and eventual use as a last resort, of legal force.

Finally, there is the proposal of a federal-type statehood, the oldest and most experienced: but, paradoxically, this is a proposal that has to be somehow "re-invented". The federalist project, as we know it in its theoretical elaboration, on the one hand, and in the practical experience of the States that adopted it on the other, offers answers to the two fundamental aspects of the problem of statehood: its democratic legitimization at the various levels of federal power, by participation and consensus; and efficiency, with the presence of a government endowed with command powers, including last resort power. This being said, it should however be acknowledged that, since both the context (a globalized world, revolutionized by the science of the 21st century), and the problem (the production of global "public goods", a worldwide democratic statehood) have no precedent, the federal project for the world is to a large extent to be invented. To this end, it is necessary to open ourselves to other cultures and to become available to search for new interpretation categories and new languages. How to re-read the pre-global federalist theoretical elaboration in the light of the changes under way: the end of territories, the diaspora of people, the erosion of sovereign power? What should be kept of the historical experience of federal States, of "real federalism", and what should be dropped? How to re-think today the institutional model of multiple government levels, "independent and coordinated", in the new context of the globalized world? Many questions come to mind, but many answers are not ready yet. There is a big construction yard open in front of us, to which it is worth calling many people, including the "diverse", to work together in such an endeavor.

For a UN Emergency Force*

Sir Brian URQUHART

In 1948, the first Secretary-General of the United Nations, Trygve Lie, proposed during a commencement speech at Harvard the development of a small, dedicated UN force to deal with the violent and chaotic conditions in Jerusalem. Perhaps unwisely, he called it a "United Nations Legion". In any case, the proposal was greeted with thunderous silence from the permanent members of the Security Council; even the United States and the USSR agreed that it was a terrible idea. The violence in Jerusalem continued.

UN peacekeeping came into full bloom with the 1956 Suez crisis and the creation of the first UN Emergency Force (UNEF I). That force was deployed, due to the leadership and determination of Dag Hammarskjold and Ralph Bunche, within eight days of the General Assembly's decision to establish it. The early peacekeeping forces of the Cold War period were put into the field with similar speed, the record being seventeen hours for UNEF II (to preserve a cease-fire between Egypt and Israel) in 1973. Although the political stakes were often very high, those early forces were less complex than the post-Cold-War multifunctional operations that were later deployed within the frontiers of a single disturbed country. Except for the 1960 Congo operation, these early forces had little or no humanitarian responsibilities. Equally important, they dealt only with governments and national forces and were deployed with the agreement of those governments as soon as a cease-fire was in place.

Although in the early days of its existence a standing rapid deployment force was accepted without major criticism from states parties, such a force became really indispensable when, in the 1990s, the Security Council agreed to set up seventeen multifunctional peacekeeping/ humanitarian missions in quick succession. The role of these operations was far more complex than the original peacekeeping operations, and the humanitarian crises facing most of them meant that even a month or two of delay in deployment was devastating not only for the victims, but also to the mission's effectiveness and subsequent authority. Moreover, very few of their contingents were trained in the fundamental tasks of stopping random violence and dealing with chaos and disorder. This was

* Published in Issue 1/2007.

why situations like that in Sierra Leone, where the rebel faction more or less successfully immobilized a UN force, could easily develop.

The failure to deploy forces in emergency situations can start a chain reaction of disaster, loss of life, and misery. However, late deployment of a mission with forces untrained for the tasks at hand can create an equally devastating humanitarian situation. In her recent, remarkable book, *The Turbulent Decade*, Sadako Ogata, the High Commissioner for Refugees in the 1990s, describes vividly what the absence of trained forces can mean for a large refugee population in whose camps there is no one to keep order or stop factional abuse. The post-Rwandan-genocide refugee crisis in the Great Lakes Region led to homicidal chaos that has so far cost over four million lives as well as many millions of dollars in relief aid and general economic loss. Tragedy in the camps continues despite the eventual arrival of a UN peacekeeping force. Much of this might have been avoided if, in the early stages, Ogata's pleas for immediate military assistance had not been ignored.

I have mentioned this one example because it helps address some of the most common objections to a standing rapid deployment force or an Emergency Peace Service. There are several common objections to this idea, as well as one seldom expressed but very important. The first common objection is related to expense. Certainly even a small standing force would be quite expensive by United Nations standards, though it would still be exponentially less costly than prolonged disasters like the continuing tragedy in the Great Lakes region – in lives, in economic and social disruption and in the cost of humanitarian and other assistance year after year, including at present a UN peacekeeping force that shows no sign of leaving any time soon.

Another popular argument against a standing emergency service is grounded in a belief that "standby arrangements" with governments can and should be enlisted to handle these tasks. That, unfortunately, is not always true. In 1994, there were more than twenty standby arrangements with governments for the provision of peacekeeping forces. Not one could be activated successfully when the Security Council belatedly decided that something ought to be done about the Rwandan genocide. Later on, when Sadako Ogata appealed for help in controlling the very large refugee camps set up outside the borders of Rwanda, only one standby agreement could be activated, and that for so short a time that Ogata ended up asking president Mobutu of Zaire, who was about to be overthrown, for assistance from the Zairean army. Any government has a perfect right not to send its troops into disagreeable and dangerous situations, which is more often than not what the UN has to deal with. Only a professional, specially trained, standing UN force at the full disposal of the Security

Council can be absolutely relied on to respond with the necessary speed in such situations. At present, this does not exist. As Kofi Annan once said, the UN is the only fire brigade in the world that has to acquire a fire engine after the fire has started.

However, the most basic objection to a standing UN peace service is seldom expressed publicly. Protection of national sovereignty is a concern that very often limits the ability of the UN to do the right thing in the right way at the right time. Fear of any UN development that may erode national sovereignty has always limited the UN's capacity for intervention. For this same reason, governments have been acutely cautious about expanding the Secretary-General's sphere of authority. A standing emergency peace service would certainly increase the Security Council's capacity to react quickly and effectively in an emergency, rather than go through the pedestrian and often untimely and unsatisfactory process of setting up a traditional peace-keeping force. Nevertheless, it seems as though it will take more disasters and many more debates before the governments that object to a standing UN rapid deployment force can be convinced that saving lives and stopping incipient disasters before they run out of control is more important, and far less dangerous, than any possible threat to national sovereignty.

Meanwhile, it is vitally necessary that the concept and the practical plan for making an emergency peace service a reality be kept alive. The basic proposal begins by stating, "Because governments have not created the necessary UN capability, the responsibility for breathing life into the UN Emergency Peace Service now lies with civil society, working with allies in the UN and interested governments". This venture is of the greatest importance both to the UN as a responsible institution and to the millions as of yet unknown, innocent victims who might, in the future, be saved by this essential addition to the UN's capacity to act on their behalf. Like many visionary ideas, there are several plausible objections to a UN Emergency Peace Service, or whatever it might finally be called. Nevertheless, there is one overwhelming argument for it. It is desperately needed, and it is needed as soon as possible.

Terrorism and World Government*

Lucio LEVI

The terrorist attack launched against the USA on September 11th has changed the course of world politics. All of a sudden the US has lost its invulnerability. It is the first time since the war of 1812 that it has suffered an attack on its territory. The greatest power in the world has found out it is without arms to counter this challenge. For a few hours the United States was without a government. Bush took refuge aboard the presidential airplane and the federal government buildings were evacuated. But the effects of the aggression were not limited to the US. People in the world which had entrusted their security to the American Empire have suddenly realized they do not have any protection from terrorism. The attack goes beyond the traditional schemes of power politics. The threat is not coming from another state (or from a coalition of states) nor from the missiles of rogue states. It is evident that against terrorism the so-called National Missile Defense (NMD) shield is useless. Airplanes, transformed into missiles by the hijackers, took off from American airports, the suicidal pilots were trained in the US. The enemy is hiding inside our societies.

These terrorist acts cannot be charged to a particular state, although the perpetrators belong to an organization that receives protection from Afghanistan and maybe from other states. This means that globalization has erased traditional differences, like the one between the internal and external aspects of security, or between crime and war.

The globalization process is causing new actors to emerge on the international political stage (the giant multinational manufacturing and financial companies, the global civil society movements, the international crime organizations, etc.), which erode states' sovereignty. But what characterizes the international terrorist organizations is the fact that they combine the exercise of violence by militants willing to sacrifice their life, with the possession of big financial resources and the support of a part of the international public opinion. With these power-conferring tools they challenge the force monopoly exercised by the states, which have become unable to protect men against a violent death (the principal task of the state according to Hobbes). All this proves that the states have ceased to be the exclusive players in international politics. So far the states, and

* Published in Issue 3/2001.

above all those at the summit of the world power-hierarchy, have tried to govern the global civil society by co-operating within the international organizations. Now the attack is aimed at the heart of the power apparatus of states. Violence, displaying itself in terrorist attacks, but also in the action of the *Black Blocs* who infiltrate demonstrations of the people of Seattle, no longer held in check by political institutions, is spreading and risks to drive the world into a state of anarchy or into a new Middle Ages, as the supporters of globalization without government maintain.

The terrorist attacks on the American soil mark the decline of the world order based on US hegemony, as the first World War and the crisis of 1929 marked the decline of the British Empire. These two events opened an era of political turmoil which brought to power totalitarian regimes: first the Soviet and the Fascist, and later the Nazi.

Will the 21st century repeat the history of the 20th? If the terrorist threat is not eradicated, trade, transport, tourism and the very liberty of democratic regimes will suffer. In a climate of insecurity the globalization process, upon which development of the whole world is depending, will come to a halt, and the citizens themselves will call for more security and will ask, if necessary, to sacrifice liberty and democracy for it. No other power in the world can nowadays aspire to replace the United States in the role of stabilizer of the world order. And yet it is unthinkable that the globalization process, which expresses mankind's tendency toward unification, can possibly go ahead ignoring politics and its non-eliminable function of providing first of all security and rules, ensuring, if possible, justice, equity and liberty; in short, a civilized social life. With the fall of New York's Twin Towers also the illusion fell that globalization will self-rule, subject only to market laws.

Anyway it is out of the question that a military solution alone will suffice to counter the terrorist threat. Certainly it is not by indiscriminate bombings over Afghanistan, which will create more innocent victims, that bin Laden and his followers can be eliminated. This way of reacting would be an additional proof of US impotence. It would be a tragic mistake to promote a crusade of the Western and Christian world against the Islamic one. Even because it comprises countries, like Egypt, which have been the victims of terror (remember the assassination of President Sadat). The Islamic world is divided between moderate and integralist trends. If a political strategy can be ascribed to terrorists, we can presume its goal is to inflame the hopeless masses of the Islamic world and to topple their moderate governments. On the contrary, the goal of the West and its allies must be to prevent integralism from taking over and the feared "clash of civilizations", which terrorists would like to provoke, from taking place.

In order to check the trend to disperse power and to international disorder, which is bound to bring about new forms of violence and authoritarianism, it is necessary to take the road leading to a world federal government. This is the only formula that can compound the need for political unity, peace and security, necessary for reining in violence and for ruling the world economy, and the safeguard of cultural diversity, which represents mankind's greatest asset. The states' immediate reaction to the crimes in New York and Washington can be interpreted as the first step of a long journey in that direction. In fact the United States has promoted the formation of an international coalition of an amplitude without precedents, ranging from the European Union countries to Russia, China, down to Pakistan and many other Islamic countries, including the Palestinian Authority. The urge to fight the common enemy who has infiltrated every society has pushed the *raisons d'état* of most governments to converge.

This means that the conditions are being laid for increasing the role of the UN. The US decision to unfreeze the funds for settling its outstanding debts with the UN is a signal in this direction.

To fight terrorism, it is necessary to start measures of international policing. It would be wrong to use the word "war", which implies a clash among states and armies. The road to be followed instead is to fill up the ditch separating organized crime, which has become global and has learned how to use the most advanced technologies, and the security systems, which still remain national.

Therefore, the problem to be solved is how to progressively give binding force to international law and how to reform the UN in view of setting up new forms of statehood at world level. A first step in this direction is represented by the International Criminal Court, which will allow (once it will come into force) to apply international law to individuals, and hence to punish crimes against humanity, as those committed in New York and Washington. But the ultimate goal must be to transfer the coercion power monopoly to the UN.

But certainly repressive measures are not sufficient to defuse the bomb of Islamic integralism. It is necessary to build up a just world order. To this effect there is a significant fact to point out: the agreement between the Federal Reserve and the European Central Bank, concerning the injection of liquidity for supporting the world market and staving off a serious financial crisis. It can be the beginning of a deeper entente addressed to govern the world economy, and which may foreshadow a Euro-American equal partnership. Of course this objective will be attained only when Europe will bring to conclusion its process of federal unification, that will allow it to speak with one voice. Lacking a government, Europe could not fill the power vacuum opened by the decline of US influence. So, it was not able to give any contribution to the solution of the conflicts in the Balkans and in the Middle East, nor was it able to rescue the wrecked economies in Africa and the Middle East. Ethnic conflicts, undeveloped economies and social hardship present in those regions are all phenomena which have fostered Islamic integralism. There is no doubt that Europe has a vital interest, much stronger than America's given its geographical contiguity, of promoting political stability and economic development in this region; however it is not doing so because of its political division.

If political cooperation between Europe and North America is not to be limited to promoting only the interests of North-Atlantic countries at the expense of the rest of the world, other subjects must be involved: first of all Japan, but also Russia and little by little all the rest of the world. The world is looking for security beyond the old schemes based on domination and inequality. Security and economic development of any one state can no longer be conceived of as objectives to be pursued at the expense of other states. They have to be founded instead on the participation of all to the global control of economy and security. Governments, political parties, NGOs and public opinion are searching for a model that shows how to govern globalization. The European Union is the most innovative experiment of a process of markets integration governed by a supra-national authority; it regulates competition, is provided with anti-trust powers, and is subject to a vote of approval by a Parliament directly elected by the citizens. In addition, the euro has eliminated speculative capital movements within the Union boundaries, thus showing both the goal (a world currency), if the same final objective is to be reached at the global level, and the intermediate objective (an area of monetary stability among the euro, the dollar and the yen, on the model of the European Monetary System). Despite its democratic deficit due to the concentration of excessive powers in the Council, which decides unanimously in crucial sectors, the European Union represents an important answer to the need of governing globalization.

If the European Union will be able to bring to conclusion the process of federal unification, it will not only represent the example to be followed to get to the democratic transformation of other international organizations. It will also be a valid reason for extending international democracy to other great regions of the world and within the UN. It means it will become the engine for the democratic unification of the world.

World Security through World Law*

Garry Davis

The lesson of today's terrorist attack on the United States is clear. The violence of the nationstate is being devoured by itself. Commentators, as I write, are declaring that "war" is being waged on the US. But they fail to identify the real "enemy". It is the national war system itself which condones a condition of world anarchy from which "terrorism" derives.

The vulnerability of the anachronistic nationstate itself is being dramatically demonstrated by the carnage wrought by only three highjacked planes on the two principal symbols of America's dominance in the world: the Pentagon and the twin World Trade Towers. Chaos results not to mention the human casualties in and near those buildings.

United States so-called security experts from the CIA, the FBI, as well as the various police services have thus been exposed as totally incapable of protecting either the people or the institutions from attacks from unknown sources. The reason is crystal-clear. The global system itself is based on violence despite the naïve claim of an "open society". The impotence is further demonstrated by the evacuations of all personnel from government buildings in Washington, grounding all air traffic throughout the country, all postal services (Burlington main post office is closed until further notice) responding by shutting down the peoples service institutions. In short, the government is proving itself incapable of governing.

From the end of World War II, this writer, who participated in that war as a B-17 bomber pilot, has been an active exponent of world government. Agreeing with Einstein's prophetic statement that "With all my heart, I believe that the world's present system of sovereign nations can only lead to barbarism, war and inhumanity, and that only world law can assure progress towards a civilized peaceful community". I claimed a civic status which alone could address the anarchic condition perpetuated by the nation-state system, that of world citizenship. Millions followed suit.

This status alone reaffirms the sovereignty of the individual human as well as humanity. Today therefore is a day of historic reckoning for Americans, of massive understanding and awakening to reality. No longer

* Published in Issue 3/2001.

will the American people feel secure in their homes, cities or nation. Their government has been exposed as vulnerable to "alien" forces and purposes. The question each citizen must now answer is clear: Given the world community of humans, given the technology which can effectively eliminate the human race from the face of the planet, what kind of social and political order is necessary to protect the inalienable human rights of "life, liberty and the pursuit of happiness"? Each and every human being must address that question. That is the bottom line of the tragic yet inevitable events of today. Human survival depends on the correct answer.

The Global Promise of the Responsibility to Protect in Libya*

Fergus WATT

United Nations Secretary-General Ban Ki-moon has described the wider implications of the UN's involvement in Libya in the following terms: "Security Council Resolution 1973 affirms, clearly and unequivocally, the international community's determination to fulfill its responsibility to protect civilians from violence perpetrated upon them by their own government".

Determined advocacy of the Responsibility to Protect (R2P) has been a hallmark of Ban's first term as Secretary-General. Nevertheless, since 2005 when R2P was formally affirmed as part of a package of measures at the UN Reform World Summit, wider acceptance of the new political norm has been slow in coming. Clearly, Secretary-General Ban hopes that resolution 1973 will change the terms of debate.

The Responsibility to Protect doctrine rests on three pillars: (1) the primary responsibility of states to protect their own populations from the four crimes of genocide, war crimes, ethnic cleansing, and crimes against humanity; (2) the international community's responsibility to assist a state to fulfill its protection obligations; and (3) the international community's responsibility to take timely and decisive action, in accordance with the UN Charter, in cases where the state has manifestly failed to protect its population from one or more of the four crimes.

Prior to Libya, the international community had taken a few limited "R2P actions", in response to other instances of mass atrocity crimes, for example, economic sanctions such as those imposed on the Mugabe regime in Zimbabwe; or referring the Darfur situation to the International Criminal Court. However, Libya and resolution 1973 marks the first time that the Council has authorized coercive military force to protect civilians. It's a new benchmark for utilizing R2P doctrine.

The transformative significance of R2P is its impact on traditional notions of national sovereignty. The ability of sovereign governments to take whatever actions they like, up to and including committing mass atrocity crimes on their own citizens, is constrained under R2P doctrine.

* Published in Issue 2/2011.

The “international community” takes on new responsibility to assist states in preventing these crimes, and to protect civilians when protection measures fail.

A decade ago, the Canadian-sponsored International Commission on Intervention and State Sovereignty that elaborated the idea of a global responsibility to protect spelled out six criteria for deciding whether military action is justified: right authority, just cause, right intention, last resort, proportional means and reasonable prospects. The latter, “reasonable prospects”, is perhaps the most difficult to assess.

Even with these criteria, there can be differing interpretations of just how this doctrine should be applied. In the case of Libya, there are those who would have invoked an “R2P analysis”, and yet prescribed a different course of action. For some, diplomacy should have been given more time. For others, the extent of the alleged crimes against humanity prior to resolution 1973 had not yet risen to a level that warranted military intervention. In Libya it was the imminent threat of slaughter in Benghazi that led to such swift action by the Security Council.

If resolution 1973 brings renewed attention to the Responsibility to Protect, a great deal of the credit should also be given to President Obama. The U.S. administration has elevated R2P as a policy framework, incorporating it in the new National Security Strategy and developing a whole-of-government approach to implementation across the range of agencies and departments of their government. In Libya, protecting civilians trumped traditional geo-strategic analysis. While this is a promising development, UN-sanctioned civilian protection operations such as we are seeing in Libya are still the exception, not the rule.

In Ivory Coast a political crisis is degenerating into armed ethnic conflict. On March 25 ECOWAS, the relevant regional organization, appealed to the Security Council to take “all necessary measures” to assist UNOCI, the UN’s peacekeeping force in the country, in order to protect civilians and prevent a renewed civil war. So far, the Security Council has authorized a slight increase in the size of UNOCI, but this has not been sufficient to prevent a widening civil war.

Military intervention (for humanitarian purposes or otherwise) is always selective, depending on a range of factors including political will, military ability, international legitimacy and practical constraints on the ground.

The international community’s failure to intervene effectively in all instances should not lead us to condemn intervention in those circumstances when it is possible. The task ahead is twofold:

- to ensure that the resolution is not distorted or used for purposes other than the civilian protection objectives for which it was created. Avoid "mission creep".
- to build on the consensus that Libya and Resolution 1973 represents. Now that R2P has demonstrable consequences, governments must do much more to develop the R2P toolbox, as well as learn from previous mistakes. The debate must become more deeply engaged.

At the UN, there is much that can be done to broaden the organization's capacity to operationalize and implement this emerging norm. There is a range of legal, administrative and political measures that would provide the UN with a more robust R2P toolkit in the years ahead. These include:

- developing the UN's information management and early warning capacities;
- developing the ability to deploy peacekeepers rapidly, particularly in the early stages of conflict;
- expanding and strengthening the UN's corps of mediators;
- diminishing the recourse of the Security Council's permanent members to use their veto to block action when mass atrocity crimes are being committed.

In short, the UN's resolution 1973 represents a crucial measure to save lives and help the Libyan people transform their country from an authoritarian to a democratic state. And in doing so, it reinforces a standard that can and should evolve to responsibly protect the human security of citizens elsewhere, when mass atrocities threaten.

From Hiroshima to Fukushima

A New Look at Our Starting Point*

Kenji URATA

What Was Our Starting Point?

My involvement with the concerns of the International Association of Lawyers Against Nuclear Arms (IALANA) started even before its birth. The Chernobyl disaster occurred in April 1986, after which concerned international democratic lawyers began activities on nuclear arms. Unforgettable in this connection is the influence of Sean MacBride, the Irish winner of the Nobel Peace Prize and the Lenin Peace Prize. IALANA was founded in Stockholm in April 1988, and it held its inaugural general assembly in Den Hague in September 1989, which I heard of during my stay in New Zealand. It was in February 1990, when I had gone to Australia for the Science Council of Japan, that IALANA released its important statement about its major project. A lawyers' movement seeking the abolition of nuclear weapons had already started in Japan before the spring of 1988. I was later sent by the Japanese Association of Lawyers Against Nuclear Arms (JALANA) to attend the second general assembly of IALANA (Amsterdam, January 1992). There, IALANA decided that the World Court Movement, which would seek the advisory opinion of the International Court of Justice on the legality of use of nuclear weapons, would be high on its agenda for the time being, and I found out there how the campaign was specifically to be carried out. JALANA narrowed the focus of its campaign objectives to two areas: demanding the abolition of nuclear weapons and supporting the A-bomb survivors: the *hibakusha*.

After Hiroshima and Nagasaki

The nuclear age kicked off with the success of the Manhattan Project, and proceeded with the pursuance of plans for the peaceful use of nuclear energy. Looking back, we see that humanity experienced the unprecedented catastrophes of Hiroshima and Nagasaki in August 1945

* Published in Issue 3/2011.

owing to the grave crime committed by America's leaders. But the US leadership of the time had an extremely over-optimistic awareness of the dangers of artificial radioactive substances (the half-life of Plutonium-239, a byproduct of nuclear reactions, is 24,100 years!).

The US and the Soviet Union entered into a fierce nuclear arms race and created NATO and the Warsaw Pact alliances to protect their allies with "nuclear umbrellas", while the Japan-US Security Treaty likewise was from the outset in fact underpinned by the doctrine of nuclear deterrence. In 1952 and 1953 both the US and the Soviet Union were already testing hydrogen bombs. In the midst of these developments, America's President Eisenhower delivered his "Atoms for Peace" speech to the UN General Assembly out of consideration for the US strategy on nuclear weapons. The idea was that the International Atomic Energy Agency (IAEA) would be created, and all governments – including the Soviet Union – having nuclear-power technology would deposit their natural uranium, enriched uranium and other nuclear materials with the IAEA, and the other countries would together think of ways to use these nuclear materials for peaceful purposes. This was followed by a big promotional pitch that successfully implanted in people's minds the dichotomy that "nuclear power and nuclear weapons are not the same thing".

Linked with this context were the efforts of Yasuhiro Nakasone and Matsutaro Shoriki, who in March 1954 helped pass a nuclear-power budget in Japan, and this was followed in April by the Science Council of Japan's proposal of three nuclear-power principles: autonomy, democracy, and openness. From that time on, the intent of the political, academic and economic circles in Washington and Tokyo was to create a "nuclear complex". The plan for the "peaceful use" of nuclear energy was in fact linked with the operation of a "nuclear umbrella" in conjunction with the military alliance.

Nuclear Power Accidents under the NPT System

The Nuclear Non-Proliferation Treaty (NPT) is part of the legal system to regulate arms. The true aim of this treaty, which was signed in New York in July 1968, was for the five nuclear powers to prohibit Germany, Japan and other countries from acquiring nuclear weapons. In legal terms, the nuclear powers alone would continue to monopolize nuclear weapons, while countries without nuclear weapons would be allowed to demand that nuclear disarmament be carried out, and given the right to develop research, production and use of nuclear energy for peaceful purposes. This right was even said to be "inalienable" owing to the perception that had been shaped by the end of the 1960s. Additionally, the Statute of the Vienna-based IAEA is actually a law assuring the peaceful use of nuclear energy, and until now that has been emphasized. Facilitating the peaceful use of nuclear energy is its true intent, and for that purpose it also attempts to carry out its role of guaranteeing that the nonproliferation system functions.

A number of nuclear power disasters befell the US and the Soviet Union nuclear superpowers, which had adopted this system. New questions were put to science and philosophy, and policies for nuclear safety and limitations to nuclear science and technology were exposed. First there was the US Three Mile Island accident in 1979. Even though an overwhelming number of researchers and engineers work in the US nuclear complex, no more nuclear power plants have been built since that time. In the following year, 1980, Sweden's Riksdag voted to close that country's nuclear-power plants. Then came the Chernobyl accident in 1986, followed five years later by the collapse of the Soviet empire. But because the radiation damage in the former Soviet republics of Belarus and Ukraine directly killed only 50 people, the IAEA grossly underestimated it. Nevertheless, European countries such as Germany and Belgium subsequently moved to discontinue nuclear power. Even France decided to close its fast breeder reactors. But Japan swam against the current. In Japan, Tokyo Electric's Fukushima I-1, which had been designed by the US company General Electric and in whose construction Toshiba and Hitachi were involved, started operating in March 1971. Further, in November 1987, the year after the Chernobyl accident, Japan and the US signed a new accord on nuclear power. Thus in terms of energy self-sufficiency, this arrangement put Japan under 4% in practical terms. This happened because Japan followed the US nuclear strategy and gave in to the temptation of money-first without thinking carefully. At the same time, Japan has now accumulated enough nuclear materials and technology to potentially enable it to quickly arm itself with nuclear weapons, to the extent that it is called a "quasi-nuclear power".

The Significance of Fukushima

First off, there was the mistake of taking no appropriate action within the first few hours after the first earthquake shock. After the earthquake on the afternoon of March 11, but before the tsunami came, operators shut down the emergency cooling-system in accordance with the manual, because core temperature and pressure had dropped. If the manual had not contained erroneous instructions and the cooling system had been operating, there should have been no hydrogen explosion. Also, belated venting, that led to the hydrogen explosion, was perhaps a greater instance of mismanagement in the initial response. Nine hours passed from the prime minister's order to vent until venting started.

The mythology of nuclear reactor safety, TEPCO's denial of the accident, and its culture of concealment led to these mistakes after the initial quake. On April 12, a month after the accident, Japan's Nuclear and Industrial Safety Agency (NISA) finally announced that the Fukushima accident was the same level 7 as the Chernobyl accident, as assessed using the International Nuclear and Radiological Event Scale (INES). Already by March 25 French and US experts had recommended that the accident be raised to level 6. The US Nuclear Regulatory Commission (NRC) and the IAEA had released their opinion made in the light of information obtained on and after March 18, and, faced with a strong pressure from the Obama administration, the Japanese government arrived at the assessment that the accident was actually level 7.

Conclusion

Lawyers against nuclear arms must take a new look at our starting point. This means that by redrawing a big picture of the nuclear age, we will overcome the dichotomy that "nuclear power plants and nuclear weapons are not the same thing", and help the nuclear victims, both "the atomic bombing hibakusha" and the "nuclear power-plants hibakusha". If the perspective is limited to a discussion on the legal aspects of Fukushima, it is as follows: Continuing nuclear power plant use and expanding it, even if we know its horrific consequences, violates all the principles of international law, environmental law, and international law pertaining to sustainable development. If government authorities do not act immediately to stop the construction of new nuclear power plants, they are committing crimes against future generations. What is more, it is a crime against humanity to allow currently-operating nuclear plants to continue operating. I suggest that present-day lawyers have the role and responsibility to academically and technologically elaborate on this legal consciousness and legal inquiry, and disseminate their results locally, regionally, and globally.

A Global Climate Community*

David GRACE

Professor John Pinder has proposed the creation of a Global Climate Community as a practical response to climate change and a step towards world federation[1]. There is now a branch of political science devoted to examining ideas of cosmopolitan democracy but I must begin with a warning to the academic. Some years ago at a Lothian Foundation Conference in Oxford a young Italian woman presented her doctoral thesis which sought to explain why Federal Union, which flourished and grew dramatically in Britain from 1938 to 1940, then became much less active and influential. Her analysis of the archives led her to the conclusion that Federal Union declined because of doctrinal differences between world federalists and European federalists. Unfortunately for her, at the conference was the author and journalist Richard Mayne who was active in Federal Union in 1940. He told her that the decline in activity was caused by a more immediate priority, the fear and threat of invasion. Our theories must not overlook the simplest of explanations.

The paradigm of actual existing global governance is the United Nations. I attended the UN Conference on Science and Technology for Development in Vienna in 1980, where I witnessed several models, formal and informal, of global dialogue but not much decision-making. First there were the plenary proceedings of the conference where national delegates made formal introductory statements and formal exits from the room when others of whom they disapproved made theirs in turn. We heard of but could not see the smaller gatherings of influential nations in smoke-filled rooms behind the scenes where the final *communiqué* was negotiated. There was also a very formal assembly of International NGOs following a set agenda established by a core of well-financed western organisations and chaired by an American called Harvey Wallbanger. If anything, this was less exciting than the plenary and certainly no place for new ideas or radical departures. Thirdly there was the alternative NGO forum in a less opulent venue and with more opportunity for spontaneity but none for decision. Finally there was the *öko-dorf* in the Prater, a temporary assortment of structures powered by wind, sun and methane

* Published in Issue 1/2011.

1 "Ventotene Papers", No. 5.

from recycled sewage. This enjoyed a self-consciously anti-authoritarian mode of governance, despite the earnest attempts of the Vienna City fire and health authorities to regulate it. Decisions, if any, were taken by a lunchtime meeting of whoever happened to be there at the time. Everyone sat upon the ground and when moved to contribute jumped up and spoke in whichever language they preferred. They spoke without reference to the previous speakers and were followed by others who spoke without reference to them. There was of course no chairman nor agenda nor interpretation. Thus at one UN conference you could find in miniature, indeed in caricature, all the existing systems of global governance. Federalists are often accused of utopian thinking, but is it not utopian to imagine that global problems can be solved by existing international mechanisms which are only copies of those mechanisms in formal dress.

We know that history is full of proposals to overcome the anarchy of the world and civilise the discourse of nations. In the seventeenth century William Penn suggested a European Diet. As a Quaker he included one of the kindest and oddest reasons, that princes might marry for love instead of as diplomatic gestures of interstate harmony. Immanuel Kant offered his project for perpetual peace. Having seen an inn named *Perpetual Peace* with a sign depicting a graveyard, he presented a project for the living. After the Napoleonic wars the great powers tried to keep peace through the Concert of Europe, a series of congresses, which crumbled in 1848. The next attempt, the League of Nations followed the vast slaughter of the First World War, which had also been known as the War to end all wars. The Second World War crowned the League's failure and from the ashes rose the United Nations. I do not denigrate much of the good work of UN agencies but let us examine how it has risen to the greatest global challenge other than peace itself – climate change.

What makes climate change such an intractable problem is its very scope. One may agree with Tony Blair – about this if nothing else – that the scope of the problem both in time and space escapes the capacity of national governments facing elections every few years. Our institutions do not measure up to the problem. Consider the time-lags in causing, understanding and responding to climate change. In 1820 Joseph Fourier recognised that the earth was 30 degrees hotter than it should be and hence something must be trapping the heat. In the 1850s John Tyndall identified carbon dioxide and water vapour as the gases responsible and in the 1890s Svante Arrhenius calculated the effects of a doubling of such gases. Since that time the concentration of greenhouse gases in the atmosphere has risen from 285ppm to 430ppm. According to Nicholas Stern[2] if we carry

2 Nicholas Stern, *A Blueprint for a Safer Planet: How to Manage Climate Change and Create a New Era of Progress and Prosperity* (London: Bodley Head, 2009).

on today with "business as usual" then by 2100 the figure will be 730ppm. There is now a 50% chance of the average temperature of the earth rising to 5 degrees above the temperature in 1850. Stern went on to calculate the cost for Britain of taking action to avoid this outcome: it would be 1% of Gross Domestic Product, whereas the cost of doing nothing would be 20%. Of course, action by the British government alone would solve nothing.

Here in front of us now is the global challenge. How has the world's existing global institution, the United Nations, responded? In 1979 the first ever World Climate Conference took place. Nine years later scientists formed the International Panel on Climate Change, which produced its first report two years later in 1990. The world considered the report two more years later at the Rio Earth Summit and after a further two years the United Nations Framework Convention on Climate Change (UNFCCC) came into effect. The main meeting of the Conference of the Parties (COP) to the convention takes place before Christmas every year. The first meeting in Berlin in 1995 proposed a menu of actions which member-states might like to consider – the Berlin Mandate, but it wasn't mandatory. The next year in Geneva the conference only noted but did not agree a declaration. Indeed it rejected ideas of harmonised policies on climate change. In 1997 came a breakthrough, the Kyoto protocol, which set targets for signatory states to reduce emissions between 2008 and 2012 to 5% below 1990 levels. The protocol could only come into force when a minimum of nations had signed it and this didn't happen until 2004 after some diplomatic reduction in the target required of Russia. The United States has still not ratified the protocol. As each year passed it became clear that developing countries in the South blamed the industrial countries of the North for the problem and would not take action which they thought could undermine their own development. Meanwhile the richer northern countries feared that any action imposing costs on their industries would damage their competitiveness. This mutual suspicion bedevilled all attempts at agreement. In 2007 in Bali the parties were able only to agree a timetable of preparation for Copenhagen two years later. Copenhagen was supposed to be the great occasion when all would be resolved and the countries of the world would finally face up to the magnitude of their common problem and unite in action from 2012 onward. Instead the outcome conformed to T.S. Elliot's poetic prediction, "This is the way the world ends, not with a bang but a whimper." 25 countries led by the USA and China ignored the patient work of the vast majority over the preceding two years, tore up the draft text and adopted instead a new accord, which contained no emissions targets and no binding commitments. The rest of the countries merely noted the accord.

Why after nearly twenty years did the UNFCCC fail to make progress? A worthwhile agreement would set out the size and distribution of cuts in emissions between countries and provide a method to scrutinise compliance. All these ingredients strike at national sovereignty and that is why the powerful nations who wrecked Copenhagen took action to avoid them. As one commentator wrote, "Why use the world's worst decision-making methods to take the most important decisions?". John Pinder draws the comparison between the establishment of the European Coal and Steel Community (ECSC) in the 1950s and a possible Global Climate Community (GCC) in the 21st century. Now as then the issue is security and the blockage is national sovereignty. The Schumann declaration called for pooling power on "a limited but decisive point". The ECSC involved a rule-based market mechanism administered by new institutions. Similarly the GCC would set up an emissions trading system agreed by a Council of Ministers and a parliamentary assembly. There would be an executive like the original High Executive and today's Commission to run the system, a task which the UNFCCC Secretariat is neither empowered nor equipped to handle. There would be a court to interpret and enforce the GCC's legislation. There might also be a central bank to facilitate emissions trading and a common market in low-carbon technology. Crucially the six countries which set up the ECSC did not wait for all nations to agree and, in particular, for one powerful nation – the United Kingdom. They began with a coalition of the willing and in time the community of six grew into the union of twenty-seven. Today the GCC must overcome the North-South divide and not wait for the USA or China. The key initial partners could be the European Union itself and India, joined by Brazil and African countries. For those not willing to join immediately there could even be external association agreements.

The challenge of global warming has been growing over a century. We cannot wait a century to solve it. The idea of a Global Climate Community was launched at an international conference at the British Foreign Office conference centre at Wiston House in 2004. A British civil servant commented on the proposal by saying that it was hard enough to negotiate international action. It would be almost impossible to seek further agreement on setting up new institutions. The federalist responds that with the existing institutions we have not and cannot reach agreement on action – "The definition of insanity is to keep repeating the same action over and over again expecting a different result". The UNFCCC has met every year for twenty years. Perhaps it is time to find another way.

From a League of Failing Nations to a Global Community for the Environment*

Joan Marc SIMON

Yet another Conference Of Parties (COP) finished in Durban in December 2011 with yet another decision to postpone action. Like in any European Council summit, after more than a fortnight of multilateral negotiations most national and regional delegations returned home and claimed victory in silence while, once again, the common interest was the main loser. A deafening silence that was reported as such by the national and international media who, after the failure of Copenhagen, have learnt to keep expectations low and dance along to the tune of the climate change requiem.

The expectations were so low that this time only 12 Heads of State assisted to the negotiations, not a single one from the G20, meaning that none of the leaders among the big polluters bothered to show up.

If we look at what was politically possible, the outcome of Durban can be qualified as acceptable; the process is alive and continues to move forward. Concretely, the COP17 succeeded to "agree to launch a process to develop a protocol, another legal instrument or a legal outcome under the Convention applicable to all Parties" (Art. 2) and it gave itself 4 years to do so "no later than 2015 […]", although a very late date to enter into force; "and for it to come into effect and be implemented from 2020" (Art. 4). It also managed to create a Green Climate Fund, with the World Bank as a trustee, which is supposed to receive $100bn a year but, with the exception of South Korea, Germany and Denmark, nobody has yet committed to chip money into it.

As a result, the Kyoto Protocol will expire, leaving it up to the countries to voluntarily reduce their emissions until 2020. The Kyoto protocol, with all its weaknesses of enforcement and limited scope, was the only legally binding treaty for its signatories. However, Canada for instance didn't hesitate to stab the dying protocol on the back with her withdrawal from the treaty right after Durban in order to avoid paying $14bn for having increased its emissions by one third – according to the protocol it should have reduced them by 6%. The move from Canada reminds us that no

* Published in Issue 1/2012.

matter how lengthy the negotiations, there is no guarantee that countries won't walk away from their commitments later down the line.

Indeed, even if Canada had opted for staying inside the Kyoto protocol and refused to pay the $14bn, there is little the feeble Compliance Committee could have done other than naming and shaming. After all, one may wonder whether is the end of the Kyoto protocol so sad when the case of Canada illustrates very well how, regardless of the commitments, it is up to the inner motivation of the parties to reduce emissions. The EU is a good example of how what matters when reducing emissions is the political will and not the protocol itself. It is an illusion to think that an international treaty can compel national decision makers to cut emissions faster than their domestic populations are willing to.

On the other hand, if we look at the results of Durban from the point of view of what was necessary to avoid catastrophe, the results are, once again, an unacceptable failure. While total emissions continue to grow, there are no short or mid-term legally binding measures to reduce or stabilize them.

If we take a step back to observe the evolution of the climate change negotiations, it is fair to claim that the weak link between the problem and the solution is the inadequate governance structure under which the negotiations take place. The current methodology consisting in identifying a common problem – excess of emissions – and trying to agree on national emission limits, the final enforcement of which, falling on the country itself, is just not working.

In fact, this methodology can be compared with the methodology that was used in Europe to manage a common problem – war – after World War I; the creation of an organization – the League of Nations – where countries would discuss matters and settle multilateral agreements the enforcement of which was inapplicable. In both cases, the methods have proven inadequate; the CO_2 emissions, far from stabilizing, have increased dramatically, same as the League of Nations couldn't settle the disagreements which led to World War II.

Same as in the post-WWI period, national governments lack the will to challenge entrenched constituencies to change their ways of life and their vision of the world. And even if one would dare to, this is a clear "prisoner's dilemma" case, in which in the short term there is an incentive to collaborate and it rather pays off to free-ride on the good behavior of others.

Another parallelism we can draw between the League of Nations and the UN Framework Convention on Climate Change (UNFCCC) is that in both cases the only reason for the parties to cooperate, to overcome the prisoner dilemma's syndrome, is that the cost of non-cooperation has revealed to be higher than the cost of cooperation. It took the Europeans two world wars to politically accept that the risks of integration were worth to be taken. However, so far the price of the cession of sovereignty to create a World Community for the Environment is considered to be higher than the costs of global warming. Considering the scientific evidence and the impressive costs associated to the effects of climate change (according to Lord Stern they amount to 5 to 20% of the world GDP), it is very telling that the national governments regard their sovereignty as something even more precious!

There is still one more thing about the European experience that can be extrapolated to the problem of global climate governance; that is the difficulty of providing common supranational goods without a supranational checks-and balances system – the judiciary and the legislative – and above all without a supranational government – the executive – and, as a consequence, a supranational budget. The current European economic crisis highlights how much the lack of a European government and of a European budget are responsible for inadequate action. The parallelism is valid for the UNFCCC negotiations; firstly, without a judiciary capable of penalizing the countries breaching the emission limits, there is no enforcement capacity. Secondly, without a body representing the citizens of the world – the Conference of Parties represents the governments of the world, and as such it can't represent the common will of the world peoples –, the global interest is not pursued. Reality illustrates very well how the sum of national interests is far from being the global interest, rather the opposite. Thirdly, without an empowered global executive, accountable to a global parliamentary assembly, taking the lead and showing the way towards de-carbonization of the world economy, it will be in the hands *of* the G20 – and in the end the G2, China and the US – to continue hijacking the fight against global warming. And finally, in the absence of the last three institutions, it will be very difficult to have a proper budget to invest in the transition to a new industrial model. So far, the absence of a global budget to fight climate change has meant that the financing has gone through bilateral deals in the Clean Development Mechanism and carbon markets, which have ended up increasing emissions and fueling speculation in these very lucrative markets.

The UNFCCC negotiations are providing acceptable deals as regards what is politically possible, but continue to fail to provide what is actually needed. Emissions continue to increase and speculation in carbon markets is more profitable than ever. Durban confirmed once again the frightening limitations of the UNFCCC model. In this sense, the precedent of the League of Nations can be a useful example to illustrate what could be the fate of the UNFCCC. The question that humankind faces once again is whether it will take a climate catastrophe of the scale of a world war to realize the real risk of non-integration, and to build the political momentum among the peoples of the world and its leaders necessary to create a World Community for the Environment.

Global Warming: with a View to the 2015 UN World Conference in Paris*

Roberto PALEA

A worrying record was set in 2013. According to the UN World Meteorological Organization, in 2013 the levels of greenhouse gases in the atmosphere reached a very high peak. These are only the latest data, which add to the critical scenario described by the IPCC (Intergovernmental Panel on Climate Change), the UN body on global warming consisting of approximately 2,000 scientists from 160 countries around the world[1].

In its increasingly alarmed periodic reports, the IPCC continues to warn us that global warming, resulting from mankind's higher and higher consumption of fossil fuels and increasing CO_2 and other greenhouse gas emissions into the atmosphere, is likely to exceed the "threshold of irreversibility" within ten year, (which is marked by the increase in global average temperature by 2°C this century) if strong and rapid action is not taken at the global level, and it will put on risk the very survival of the human species.

According to the most recent studies conducted by the IPCC, by 2050, global emissions in the atmosphere must be reduced by 40 to 70% compared to 2010. The results of this reduction have to be obtained in no more than 15 years, and be completed over the next 20 years[2]. Despite considerable but insufficient progress in reducing harmful emissions, China, the US and Europe account for over 55% of these emissions[3].

Therefore, a trend reversal in air pollution depends on these three economic zones, so that the situation does not go out of control. Through their essential cooperation, other polluting states (in particular Japan, India, Russia, Brazil, Indonesia, South Korea and South Africa) are also likely to be involved. This would allow a binding Agreement (or Convention) among the worst polluters on the planet on gradually

---

* Published in Issue 2/2015. This text is a memorandum prepared for the Holy See in view of the UN Climate Change World Conference held in Paris in December 2015.

1 Website: www.ipcc.ch.

2 IPCC – Fifth Assessment Report (AR5): Sectoral Reports.

3 IEA data – International Energy Agency (www.iea.org).

reducing CO_2 and other greenhouse gas emissions to be reached during the next international climate conference in Paris in 2015, as well as allow all the necessary measures to be taken to implement the commitments undertaken.

1. The New Energy Paradigm

The energy regime has indeed seriously affected the means of production and life style since the very beginning of human life on the Planet. More recently, since the mid-19th century, the Industrial Revolution has changed the world, as the solar energy stored over the centuries in coal, oil and natural gas has supplied "unlimited" cheap energy to steam and internal combustion engines. Since then, the pace, speed and flow of economic activities have increased. The boom of agricultural production, mass production of manufactured goods and the extensive use of natural resources of all kinds have led to an increase in the productivity of human activity and an unprecedented material well-being.

The above-mentioned energy regime (cheap fossil fuel consumption by machines) has contributed to the population growth and urbanisation, and, conversely, to the environmental degradation resulting from the unlimited consumption of natural resources, especially energy resources, and of their unrestrained depletion. Now, after more than a century, despite opposition and enforcement actions, including media actions, by fossil fuel-producing states and the large, powerful oil and car manufacturing lobbies, the technology of energy production from solar sources (to which wind source is also linked) has now been developed. Solar energy is an endless resource: in forty minutes, the sun radiates as much energy on earth as the whole of humanity consumes in a year[4]. It is not only abundant but completely free, and it spreads from North to South, albeit in varying degrees.

In general most of the "solar-rich" countries are less developed. Many of them are afflicted by the scourge of poverty, hunger and child mortality, while they benefit from solar radiation levels that are higher than those of other currently more economically developed areas, almost as a form of compensation. The solar energy (and wind energy, resulting from the different thermal fields produced by the sun) generated using different technologies (thermal storage, production through photovoltaic technology or concentrating solar technology) has now overcome the barriers of its cost-effectiveness, competitiveness, reliability and it still offers a very wide scope for further and rapid improvement.

---

4 John T. Houghton, *Global Warming* (Cambridge University Press, 1997).

According to the most recent studies:

- from 2007 to 2014, the production cost of photovoltaic solar panels has dropped from 3 euros per electric kW/h to 0.50 euros[5];
- the cost of lithium batteries for the storage of the electricity produced has plummeted from 1,100 euros per kW/h in 2010 to the current price of 350 euros, and is expected to reach less than 100 euros over the next 10 years;
- moreover, in the meantime, fuel cell technology for the storage of energy produced by solar/wind sources, which are intermittent, has become reliable, efficient and now economical in many cases. The fuel cells, through hydrogen production and its reuse in the same cells, allow excess energy to be stored if needed for times when the energy source is not available (night, winter, rain, weak or excessive wind).
- Companies producing fuel cells, including listed companies, now exist and thrive (Rolls Royce, Teledyne Inc., Hidrogenics etc.), although they are only focused on niche markets (e.g., backup of computer data);
- solar electricity distribution technology using the interactive power network (intergrid) has advanced and is now wide spread.
- high-end electric cars (hybrid and plug-in) are currently competitive, considering not only their initial purchase cost but also their longer life and lower operating costs (e.g., Tesla)[6]. Within a few years their competitiveness is also expected to extend to small and medium engine size cars which are already being produced and distributed on the market (e.g., Renault, Nissan, BMW, etc.).

The spread of solar (and wind) energy:

- will dramatically reduce carbon and other greenhouse gas emissions since the electricity produced and the use of electric motors do not release pollutant emissions;
- will powerfully free us from our dependence on fossil fuels, especially in "solar-rich" countries, which are currently suffering the consequences of underdevelopment (Africa and South East Asia), and have all suffered the negative effects of global warming (the drying up of watercourses, desertification, reduction in agricultural crops, typhoons, floods, hurricanes and other natural disasters due

---

5 European Photovoltaic Industry Association data, News 2014.

6 Tesla, Umicore, UBS "*Will Solar, Batteries and Electric Cars Re-Shape the Electricity System?*", Q series UBS, August 2014.

to an increase in extreme weather events linked to global warming) without reaping the benefits, all in favour of today's developed countries. They will be able to benefit from electricity production at almost no cost, thus triggering endogenous development processes in the sectors of traditional agriculture, handicraft, the on-site production and use of raw materials and the goods produced. One possible indirect effect, will be a reduction in migration flows and the population settlement in the countries of origin;

- will contribute to spreading not only wealth and reducing inequalities but also democracy, as all the people on earth will be able to produce the energy they need for themselves and their families almost for free, without having to depend on external producers to purchase fossil fuels.

This will provide all the evidence needed to prove what an inestimable gift the Sun is. This evokes and breathes life into the words of St. Francis of Assisi in his Canticle of the Creatures:

> "Be praised, my Lord, through all your creatures, especially through my lord Brother Sun, who brings the day; and you give light through him. And he is beautiful and radiant in all his splendour! Of you, Most High, he bears the likeness".

2. Make Binding Agreements Among Polluter States Possible

As aforementioned, in 2012, China, the United States and the European Union produced 55% of the total global CO_2 emissions in the atmosphere (34.5 billion tons, a 1.1% increase compared to the previous year). China is responsible for 29%, the US for 16% and the EU for 11% of the total emissions. Disaggregated data, country by country, show once again that *per capita* emissions in the US are more than double those of China and the EU, which are equal, however[7].

Consequently, developing countries cannot agree to the US proposals, clearly stated in the 2009 Copenhagen Conference and dictated by the US Congress (and so far maintained), to calculate the progressive reduction in CO_2 emissions in the atmosphere on the basis of the total emissions of each country (and not on the *per capita* emissions) because they are obviously contrary to the most elementary principles of fairness and justice. The longest-industrialised countries are, *inter alia*, the ones that have benefited most from the low-cost consumption of fossil fuels and are responsible for the majority of the CO_2 and other greenhouse

7 IEA data – International Energy Agency (www.iea.org).

gas accumulated in the atmosphere and should bear most of the costs of greening the economy.

However, the principle of cost-sharing on the basis of the total emissions would place the burden of higher costs on the developing countries that have most suffered the adverse effects of pollution, mainly caused by industrialised countries. Putting forward the US proposal again means making agreement impossible, despite the counterparties' willingness. Therefore, the United States needs to address negotiations with other states starting from a reduction in pollutant emissions on the basis of the *per capita* emissions of each country.

As with all international treaties, the loose Kyoto Protocol, which expires in 2020, lacks the necessary governance, sanction and coercion instruments. Therefore, it has been widely disregarded. When its targets were achieved in some countries, this was due to the country's ability and interest rather than to its willingness to observe the provisions of the international Treaty (which, however, was not ratified by many major polluting states). Therefore, it is necessary to go beyond the conclusion of a new international Treaty.

In Paris an Agreement must be reached that includes the establishment of a "World Environment Organization" under the auspices of the UN, at a higher level than polluting states and with the power of monitoring them. This Organization should be modelled on the European Coal and Steel Community (ECSC), which, after the war, European states entrusted with rationalising the energy resources of the time and regulating production and consumption in key areas for post-war reconstruction. The new Organization should be endowed with real powers and financial autonomy and be managed by an independent High Authority with the task of implementing a Global Plan to reduce CO_2 emissions in the atmosphere in a balanced manner – agreed upon under the above-mentioned binding Agreement – as well as of adapting the objectives to the evolving situation, implementing structured actions to combat global environmental emergencies, develop new technologies in the energy sector and transfer them to industrialising countries.

In the future, a global carbon tax should be introduced to discourage the use of fossil fuels, with different rates that vary according to the carbon content of each fuel. This tax would also provide the World Organization with the funds necessary to achieve the purpose for which it will be set up. It should operate under the democratic control of the UN General Assembly, and in the future of the UN Parliamentary Assembly (when it is established), in accordance with the principle of "no taxation without representation".

3. Conditions for feasibility

The aforementioned binding Agreement requires the total support of the European Union. However, considering its very advanced positions on CO_2 emissions reduction, it is being called upon to play a leading role in the green conversion of the world economy based on solar energy, which best suits its history, aspirations and interests. The introduction of a European carbon tax in Europe, at least in the Eurozone, aimed at financing a "Special European Fund for Growth and Employment", which should be achieved using the "enhanced cooperation" mechanism provided for in the Lisbon Treaty, falls within the objectives of providing the EU with the financial resources necessary to implement a "European Investment Plan", essential to promote sustainable development in the EU and reduce unemployment. Therefore, it is being advocated by the European Parliament and the Commission itself.

If it were approved in the EU, as hoped, also in the wake of the announcement-effect of its intent, this would provide a clear signal of its willingness and could act as an effective example, strongly encouraging other countries (primarily the United States and China) to emulate it. Therefore, a European carbon tax is of strategic importance to facilitate its extension to other industrialised countries. The European Union is the only economic area where the virtuous process of the green conversion of the world economy can be launched. This worldwide launch requires a starting point clearly identified in a major economic area. This is precisely the EU, which can trigger an emulation process that exceeds its own borders.

A European carbon tax should also play this important role. Its first target would be consumption, by imposing a European tax rate allocated to the above-mentioned "European Fund". At a later stage, this rate could be increased by an additional proportion used to finance the World Organization. Citizens would then realise that they are simultaneously citizens of their own country, the EU and the world. The new tax would be welcomed by European states and citizens, if the European investments needed to stimulate European economic recovery were financed at the European government level. National budgets would no longer bear the burden of these investments, and they could reduce the national tax burden with the new available resources for the corresponding amounts, especially on labour and corporate income, with additional benefits to boost demand and economic recovery.

4. Conclusion

An energy regime based on solar/wind energy, which does not release any harmful emissions into the atmosphere and on which the gradual mitigation of global warming depends because it reduces the number of the sources of the emissions, is within reach. Moreover, this regime will not be able to immediately replace the production systems in place in different countries and will require timescales for its introduction (consider, for example, the case of France where 80% of electricity production derives from nuclear power).

However, these timescales could be quickly reduced to the benefit of the environment, if the desired binding Agreement on CO_2 emissions reduction and the ensuing establishment of the above described new World Organization were reached at the Paris Climate Summit. The introduction of a global carbon tax would further accelerate progress towards the decarbonisation of the economy. However, this decision is linked to the EU's willingness to take the first step by internally introducing a carbon tax, which is necessary to finance investment in development and employment, aimed at stimulating economic recovery and halting the European Union's rapid decline.

The Foundation of a Cooperative Global Financial System*

A New Bretton Woods to Confront the Crisis of the International Role of the US Dollar

Alfonso Iozzo and Antonio Mosconi

The crisis of the international role of the US dollar is progressive and irreversible. In strictly financial terms it manifests itself in the unsustainable level of US foreign debt, heavier year after year because of the current account deficit, in turn growing and almost insensible to the devaluations of the dollar thus far decreed by the financial markets. In political terms, it manifests itself in the incapacity of the United States to supply those global public goods which constitute the counterpart of hegemony.

The globalisation of the world economy, made possible by scientific means of production and the end of the cold war, requires the provision on the same scale of the public goods (such as security, legality, equity and environmental sustainability) which can no longer be supplied by an hegemonic power and in whose absence the market is incapable of self-government. The United States, after the end of the cold war, attempted to ensure unilaterally the governance of the world economy, basing it on Wall Street and the Pentagon, thus forgetting the historical experience of the unsustainability of empires due to the growing costs of defence not justifying the advantages of dominion.

This attempt has failed. If it had succeeded the political superstructure corresponding to the era of the scientific means of production would have been the imperial. But this is not the case. On the contrary, throughout the world, the requirement for a multilateral, shared and democratic management of the globalised economy is being developed. A requirement which must be urgently satisfied if we want to arrest the forces of disruption which threaten to take history backwards: to protectionism, macro and micro nationalisms and war.

* Published in Issue 2/2006.

The crisis was written into the genetic code of the international monetary system created by the Bretton Woods Conference: with the dollar (that is, the currency of one of the participants in the game and not a neutral currency) at its centre, the system would have brought about situations of dollar shortage in the case of a positive US balance of payments, and dollar inflation in the opposite case, according to the famous "Triffin dilemma". In the early post-war years there was a shortage of dollars and subsequently inflation. The world became multipolar with the emergence of the economic power first of Europe and Japan, then the emerging countries, China today and soon India. The centrality of the dollar disappeared with the creation of the euro and the decoupling of the yuan and other currencies, such as the Argentinean peso, from the American currency. If we want to avoid a ruinous fall in the dollar and ensure exchange rate stability as a foundation for globalisation and development, it is necessary to start again from Bretton Woods, correct its defects, put a world basket at the centre of the system and entrust its management to truly multilateral institutions.

Bretton Woods

At the beginning of 1942, when the fortunes of war were already leaning towards the Allies, Keynes made a desperate attempt to salvage a role for the United Kingdom, alongside with the United States, in the structure of the postwar international monetary system. He thus proposed the construction of an international currency union based on a currency, the bancor, with a fixed, but not immutable, content in terms of gold and accepted by all the members for the payment of international debts, to stimulate the expansion of trade and world economic development. The proposal, which was intended to internationalise the creation of liquidity so as not to leave it completely in the hands of the United States, was made by the British government in 1943 and inspired the Bretton Woods Conference of 1944, in which however the plan designed by White, chief international economist at the US Treasury, prevailed. White's plan reflected the power relationships coming from the military and economic results of the war, imposing the recognition of the US as the new hegemonic power. The enormous British debt to the United States to support the war effort (*Lend Lease Act* of 1941) did not allow Keynes and his team to achieve anything but a saving of face. The Bretton Woods Agreements, ratified in Washington in 1945, impeded the internationalisation of the creation of liquidity. In substance, they identified the principal regulators of the new structure in fixed currency parities, modifiable only by common agreement in the face of fundamental disequilibria, and in multilateralisation of currency transfer. The freedom of individual States to sustain domestic demand through various instruments, such as the extension of the welfare state, was sheltered from the risk of "capital flight" through a complex and rigorous system of bureaucratic controls over "speculative" movements of capital (in practice all, except direct investments abroad). The creation of international liquidity was entrusted, in fact, to the United States, the only country to have substantial reserves of gold after the war, on the basis of a promise of convertibility of the dollar into gold at a fixed price of 35 dollars an ounce (gold exchange standard). Finally the International Monetary Fund and the International Bank for Reconstruction and Development (the World Bank) were established, but their functions did not reflect those proposed by Keynes: the UN Stabilization Fund and the Bank for Reconstruction and Development, notwithstanding the terminological maquillage used to hide the rejection of the British design. The system, moreover, included only convertible currencies, issued by a few advanced Western countries. It did not include the countries of the Soviet bloc, nor the rest of the world. It was, however, for the last time, an international monetary system based, at least formally, on an international conference, or on a multilateral basis, and ensured the successful phase of post-war reconstruction and development. The present system results, instead, from successive unilateral decisions.

The crisis of Bretton Woods

The Bretton Woods structure, having guaranteed the golden years of post-war prosperity, at least for the countries which participated, fell progressively into crisis in the 1960s, when the excessive creation of dollars, consequent also upon the financial needs of the Vietnam war, made the promise of convertibility of the dollar into gold incredible. In 1968, while Europe moved to a customs union and began the process of a common agricultural policy, the double gold market was established, i.e. the United States limited the convertibility of the dollar at 35 dollars an ounce only to central banks holding their official reserves in dollars. In the same year Triffin showed how a country cannot create international liquidity except by accumulating foreign debt to sustain a deficit in its own balance of payments, aimed at the acquisition of goods, services and foreign investments as well as military support of its possessions and the maintenance of influence/ complicity in the liberated/occupied countries. He denounced this system as the "international monetary scandal"[1]. In 1971 the United States declared the inconvertibility of the dollar, thus making official the move from gold exchange standard to dollar standard. Exchange rates were left to float according to free market forces, as envisaged by the monetarist school of Milton Friedman. The

[1] Robert Triffin, *Our International Monetary System: Yesterday, Today and Tomorrow,* (New York: Random House, 1968).

greatest economists, in fact largely American, abandoned the vulgate of fixed exchange rates for stability and development and began to preach that changes in exchange rates would impede the creation of important and persistent disequilibria in the balance of payments. The new world order would be ensured by the market's "invisible hand". Soon, however, it had to be admitted that the market was not so free as they pronounced and the phrase "dirty floating" arrived. The deficit in the US balance of payments was then determined by movements of capital, that is United States investments in the rest of the World. Only from 1982 did the US deficit change nature: the current account balance turned negative and the deficit was financed by attracting savings from the rest of the World not to be reinvested abroad but to finance domestic demand. For almost a quarter of a century this has been the structural situation of the United States, with the result of a frightening growth in its foreign debt.

European Economic and Monetary Union

The beginning of the extreme phase of dollarisation of the world economy and the launch of the first attempt, in Europe, to avoid a similar fate, occurred at the same time. In 1969, in The Hague, the summit of the heads of state and government of the EEC (European Economic Community) decided to launch a European economic and monetary union, which was to be fully realised, after a long and difficult journey, with the introduction into circulation of the euro, on 1 January 2002[2].

To support the argument put thus far, it is relevant to remember how the creation of the euro had been preceded by a phase of coupling together the European currencies to a basket made of the same currencies, whereas previously each currency was coupled to the dollar, with the result that the exchange rate volatility of the European currencies (crossrates) could be greater than the rates between them individually and the dollar. The Economic and Monetary Union, preceded and prepared by the European Monetary System, has preserved *l'acquis communautaire*, which would have been destroyed in a regime of currencies each freely fluctuating against the dollar; it has put next to the Parliament a second federal institution, the ECB (European Central Bank), in the concrete constitution of Europe; it has modified the expectations of many non-EMU countries, which already constitute a vast area of the euro, and of other countries which look at it with hope; it has allowed a programme of diversification of the official reserves and means of payment by countries such as Russia, China, the Arab oilproducing countries; it has given

2 For a history of the passage from the Werner Plan to the creation of the euro: Tommaso Padoa-Schioppa, *La lunga via per l'euro* (Bologna: Il Mulino, 2004); Matt Marshall, *The Bank* (London: Random House, 1999).

the example for other regional integrations. The value of the issues of international bonds denominated in euro has already surpassed that of bonds in dollars. On the other hand, consistently with the fact that the European Union has still not realized a common foreign and security policy, the determination of the external value of the euro has in fact been abandoned to the financial markets, even though the Treaty of Maastricht envisaged that exchange rate policy should lie with the economic and finance Ministers (Ecofin, therefore, and not the ECB). Since the degree of openness of exchanges in the euro zone[3] does not exceed 15% and this percentage is reduced in the larger area of the countries which accept the euro, also for payment of supplies of petroleum, gas and raw materials, the problem could seem of little relevance. A problem arises, instead, because the process of globalisation, so far ungoverned, has increased the volume of the international financial transactions to a point where they represent more than sixty times those of world exports and the exchange rates between currencies are determined by the expectations of financial markets rather than the fundamentals of the various economies. These expectations are distorted by the United States to allow them to finance the enormous deficit in the balance of payments from the savings formed in other countries.

The unpegging of the yuan from the dollar

The decision of the Chinese Authorities to unpeg the yuan from the dollar, to which it was linked at a fixed exchange rate, and to go instead for a basket of currencies, is not limited, as some reductive interpretations suggest, to allowing a modest revaluation of the yuan. On the announcement of this decision some American banks and some economists suggested that the weight of the dollar in the basket would have remained more than 50%. But the Chinese Authorities soon made known its composition (among the heavier currencies: dollar, euro, yen and Korean won; among the less important: sterling, Australian dollar, Canadian dollar, Singapore dollar, rouble, Malaysian ringgit and Thai baht). Although the weight of each currency in the basket has not been communicated, the governor of the People's Bank of China has explained that it depends on trading exchanges. JP Morgan analysts have drawn the conclusion that the weightings should be: 23% yen, 21% dollar, 15% euro, 8% won[4]; approximately a third divided among other currencies. This would have

[3] The degree of openness results from the ratio of the sum of import and exports of goods and services with external countries (in this case the 12 EMU countries) and their GDP.

[4] Riccardo Sorrentino, "Avanza la liberalizzazione dello yuan", in *Il Sole-24 Ore*, 11 Agosto 2005.

to be confirmed by a gradual reduction of the weight of the dollar in the composition of the Chinese currency reserves, by a revaluation of the yuan against the dollar and in future by yuan convertibility. The new exchange policy adopted by China, like the creation of the euro, reflects the crisis of the international role of the US dollar.

For a new Bretton Woods

The gradual acceptance of baskets, such as the ecu, the predecessor of the euro; the coupling to a basket of currencies fundamental for world stability, such as the yuan; the parallel failure of other attempts to couple only to a single currency of the hegemonic power; all these phenomena indicate the road already begun, that of multilateralisation, to bring the international monetary system up to date with an economy in course of globalisation, multipolar and interdependent.

The intellectual thread for a "new Bretton Woods" is something which unites the bancor of Keynes, the special drawing rights of Triffin/Ossola, the European monetary unification and the pressing criticism made by Stiglitz[5] of the catastrophes provoked by the rigid application of the *Washington Consensus* in situations such as those in South-East Asia, Russia, Argentina (where the dollarisation of the peso finished with a serious default of the country and damage to savers throughout the world). However, it is necessary also to take account of the fact that we face, in many ways, a new situation, both because of the extraordinary weight of the problems caused by the unilateral management of the global economy, and because of the complexity and linkage of the challenges for a peaceful and sustainable future. A "new Bretton Woods" ought thus to propose a solution together for the two orders of problem: 1) to consolidate/get over/use the immense foreign debt of the United States and of other debtor countries and introduce a discipline to impede the repetition of fundamental permanent and cumulative disequilibria, like that of the US current account deficit, financed with the savings of the rest of the world; 2) to guarantee the financing of the supply of the necessary public goods for the functioning of a globalised economy, to bring back under control the "World risk society"[6]. For that, in using the ideas, concepts, architectures and instruments in which the thread of Keynes-Triffin-Stiglitz is rich, and referring to the European experience from

---

5 Joseph E. Stiglitz, *Globalization and Its Discontents* (Torino: Einaudi, 2002).

6 Ulrich Beck, "The terrorist threat. World risk society revisited", in *Theory, Culture and Society*, XIX, 2002, no. 4, pp. 39-55. According to Beck we are entering a world of uncontrollable risk (a contradiction in terms), composed of uncertainties and unnatural dangers, created by man. The prospect we adopt discounts the possibility (the duty) of a control of global risks.

1969 to the creation of the euro and its stable and valuable functioning, we must have in mind a global vision, systemic and not only mechanical, ecological and not only economic, insurance and not only banking.

This time the problem cannot be resolved by passing the baton from one hegemonic power to another. We are talking about substituting an ordered system for a disordered order, a multilateral system (a system of systems) for a unilateral order, a cooperative system for a hegemonic order, a global system for a circumscribed order, and an equitable system for an unequal order.

A world monetary basket

It is now necessary to move to a world monetary standard: not a gold standard nor a gold-exchange standard, not a dollar standard and not even a euro standard, but simply a world standard. The objective is the creation of a world currency, but one can start with a unit of account based on a basket of currencies, a *world currency unit* (*wcu*)[7]. The weight of the various currencies in the basket would have to be set out in the agreements according to a valuation of each based on economic fundamentals which also include elements which are not today counted as economic, such as human development, ecological sustainability, the concentration/diffusion of assets and incomes, the demographic composition of the population and their tendencies. Since the measurement of these values is today still rough and can lead to discussions, a procedure would have to be designed to revise the agreement to modify the weights. In future, when reliable and shared measurements are available, the revisions could become automatic. The wcu has no need for coupling. It expresses a productive potential socially and ecologically compatible and a promise of payment in terms of goods and services which constitute world wealth redefined as above.

All currencies should have the possibility of joining the system. Among the participating currencies, some already represent regional monetary systems and also wider areas (dollar, euro, yen, yuan, rouble) others ought to be encouraged to form regional groups, within which to regulate the major part of their transactions and questions. In any case the value of every currency, whether as the expression of a system or a simple national currency, would be defined in terms of wcu in the initial agreements.

The markets would thus have at their disposal a powerful indicator to define the exchange rates among the different currencies, with the probable result of a substantial reduction in their volatility. Furthermore,

[7] One could think of *Sdrs* evolving into Wcu as happened with the *ecu*.

certain goods particularly important in the world market, such as for example the barrel of petroleum, could be quoted in wcu with a stabilising effect on prices, to represent the relationship between supply and demand without the effect of expectations in currency markets, a result which would not be obtained by substituting the quotation in dollars with any other currency. The move from quotation in wcu to payment in wcu could be swift since it would correspond, in the most effective and equitable manner, to the unsatisfied need for diversification in portfolios. Finally, the association of the unit of world measure of value with the value of non-renewable energy would provide a universal educational function.

The functioning of multilateral clearing, the concession of overdrafts to cover temporary disequilibria (excluding long-term support for poor countries and other projects, entrusted to the World Bank), the sterilisation of speculative attacks on a currency, ought to be governed by the agreements and use well tested instruments such as clearing unions, special drawing rights cooperation and monetary stabilization funds, adapted however to the new objectives of harmonic development and made consistent with the weights recognised in every economy/ system.

Consolidation of the US foreign debt and right of world seigniorage

Every central bank in the system, holding official reserves denominated in currencies issued by other central banks, would have to be able to ask for the conversion, total or partial, in wcu. At the moment of distribution of wcu, a premium ought to be levied according to a share fixed in the agreements and could be modified with their revision. It would be a real and proper right of world seigniorage, as transparent in drawdown as in the destination of funds: to give the UN its own resources, to finance the functioning of the system, to capitalize the related institutions, such as the World Bank, which could then access the market, within fixed leverage-ratios, to multiply the financial resources needed for its assigned aims. It may be observed that, differently from the Tobin Tax, this premium would be applied only to transactions between central banks, without "disturbing" the capital markets. It would in fact consist of an insurance premium, it would cost the world much less than the right of seigniorage which the United States today enjoys and would allow the financing of a system much more effective and efficient in supplying public goods and risk management at a global level.

The reform of the world economic institutions

We should have to configure a real and proper *World Monetary Systems' Organization* operating as a system of systems for the regional currencies and as a supplementary system for the currencies not yet participating in the regional systems.

The supervision of the new organization ought to be entrusted to the IMF, to be recognised as a real and proper Council of Economic Ministers of the UN (similar to Ecofin for the EU), as already proposed by Jacques Delors. The management of the new organization ought instead to be entrusted to the Bank for International Settlements (together with the collection of the conversion rate which the BIS will pass to the IMF for division among the final recipients).

Naturally, the IMF will have to be reformed to represent as democratically as possible the major regional monetary areas. It will have to be governed, cooperatively, by qualified majority voting based on the weight of the participants and present annual report to the UN General Assembly, in the context of a more general democratic strengthening of the UN itself[8].

The institutional architecture should be completed with the reform of another institution already in existence, the World Bank, and the creation of two new organisms: an Institute to manage risk and a Control Commission. The World Bank would be a specialised Agency of the IMF (and through it of the UN) for the financing of projects directed to promote security, human development and environmental and social sustainability of the globalised economy. The Bank would thus become the principal financial support for human development and could justify a change of name to Human Development Bank. The IMF ought also to institute a new agency (*World Risk Management Institute*) for the evaluation and management of global risks[9], such as economic, the financial crises and the physical and social global threats, which individual States uselessly attempt to confront with the logic of sovereignty. Finally, for the control of the markets and their controllers, a *World Financial Control Commission* should be established.

---

8 Among the many UN reform projects, we are referring to the federalist one proposed by Lucio Levi in *Crisi dello Stato e governo del mondo*, (Torino, Giappichelli Editore, 2005, Cap. 9 – "L'unificazione del mondo come progetto e come processo", pp. 295-335).

9 For the description of possible innovative approaches to the management of these risks, entrusted to the financial markets with the support of nation states, see Robert J. Shiller, *The New Financial Order*, (New Jersey, Princeton, 2003). The prospect we adopt is based instead on the conviction that an approach to global risks requires the establishment of an institution of corresponding level to direct the markets.

The World Supremacy of the Dollar at the Rendering (1917-2008)*

Antonio Mosconi

The "double entry" accounting system by Luca Pacioli[1], that of the "patrimonial system", (before the "revenue accounting system" began to give to the most talented accountants, to the most refined mathematicians and to the most clever financiers the possibility to let the destruction of assets pass for creation of profits), has finally rendered its arithmetic verdict on the end of the world supremacy of the dollar, which lasted for ninety years. Committed for trial for fraudulent bankruptcy. Waiting for the markets and the Courts to emit their respective judgements, it can be useful to go back over this currency in its two lives: currency of a creditor powerful country from the Twenties to the Sixties, currency of an "empire of debt"[2] from the Seventies up to now.

Three different Keynes allowed us to preview its evolution: the young officer of the English Treasury, who in 1919 resigned from the financial delegation at the peace table in protest against the reparations imposed on Germany[3]; the aged professor who, in 1936, introduced in the economic science expressions as animal spirits, state of expectations, liquidity traps and other strange things corresponding to observable real behaviours and able to give theoretical explanations to the experience of massive and long lasting unemployment[4]; finally, the plenipotentiary who at Bretton Woods in 1944, old and sick, was defeated, together with the British Empire, in his extreme attempt to avoid, with his *bancor*, the predominance of the dollar[5]. In the post-war period, the goal indicated by

* Published in Issue 1/2009.

1 Fra' Luca Pacioli (Borgo San Sepolcro 1445 – Rome 1517), pupil of Piero della Francesca, mathematician and Franciscan, is the inventor of the "double entry".

2 Bill Bonner and Addison Wiggin, *Empire of Debt. The rise of an Epic Financial Crisis* (Hoboken, 2006).

3 John Maynard Keynes, *The Economic Consequences of the Peace* (Cambridge, 1919).

4 J.M.K., *The General Theory of Employment, Interest and Money* (London, 1936).

5 Robert Skidelsky, John Maynard Keynes. Volume Three. *Fighting for Freedom 1937-1946* (New York, 2000).

Keynes, namely to create an international monetary base linked to a non-inflationary development of the world more than to the needs of a single powerful country, was pursued by Robert Triffin[6].

According to the masterly reconstruction made by Hudson[7], the dollar supremacy began in 1917, when the US Government financed the war efforts of Great Britain, France and Italy against the Central Empires, imposing the intergovernmental financing model instead of the private bank loans and of the friendly aids from allies, until then commonly used to tackle the financial needs of wars. The European States, to combat against each other, bought armaments from their ex-colony, got into debt with the American Government and were not even able to win the conflict by themselves. The final intervention of the US, when the European States were almost at the end of that horrible carnage, made it the real winner of the war.

The problem of the inter-alliance debt got intertwined with that of the German reparations. Germany, argued Keynes at Versailles, could not pay the reparations to Great Britain and to France without selling goods and services to the winners, who, nonetheless, did not mean to make room for that in their markets. At the same time, the "winning" European powers were not able to reimburse the debt contracted with the American Government without collecting the German reparations or getting the means needed through a commercial surplus. The reparations, in short, could and did eventually lead to a second world war. Ignored, Keynes resigned and wrote *The Economic Consequences of the Peace*. The prophecy was understood only when it came true, but at least it was useful for managing the second post-war period better than the first.

Roosevelt, just in office, was responsible for the failure of the 1933 London Conference, from which Great Britain and France expected, as the Hoover administration had let them hope, the remission of their debt or at least a moratorium, and therefore the possibility to come to a transaction with Germany. The formal explanation offered by the Roosevelt administration was that the US in 1917 was not yet an ally but only an "associate" in the war. The New Deal, which within the US was envisaging policies favourable to debtors, applied towards the European States a most rigorous creditor policy, together with protectionist measures. The debtor Countries, which wanted to honour their commitment towards

---

6 Triffin's works, from 1935 to 1988, were translated in Italian and collected in the volume "*Dollaro, euro e moneta mondiale*", with a preface by Alfonso Iozzo (Bologna, 1997). For this article, I make particular reference to: *Robert Triffin, Our International Monetary System: Yesterday, Today and Tomorrow* (New York, 1968).

7 Michael Hudson, *Super Imperialism. The Origin and Fundamentals of U.S. World Dominance* (London, 2003, second edition; first published in 1972).

the US, as the possibility of exports was excluded, asked more pressingly for the payment of the German reparations. This greatly favoured Hitler's campaign and pushed Europe towards its own destruction.

In 1936 Keynes published his *General Theory* and sided for the imitation of the New Deal by Great Britain. Undoubtedly, the New Deal, launched already some years before, put into place for the first time policies supporting the monetary demand and direct public interventions in the economy, that Keynes deemed essential to guarantee a stable level of income and an almost full employment in the capitalistic system characterized by complex financial institutions, whose instability was intrinsic in their investment-financing models[8]. However, the application of policies similar to those of the New Deal, therefore of a "beggar your neighbour" type, by the single national States could lead directly to war. This contradiction could be less visible to Roosevelt and Keynes, thanks to the size and richness of the internal market for the former and to the imperial space for the latter, but for the other European States its undervaluation was the most ruinous mistake of their economic nationalism. English federalists saw the contradiction, denounced it and supported a new international order, but the world had taken another path and Lionel Robbins himself, in the post-war period, regretted that he had opposed the "reflation" suggested by Keynes[9].

The financial tools with which the US Government supported the Allies before and during the Second World War (cash and carry and lend-lease) added a new and unsustainable weight to the previous debt, allowed the Americans to impose to Great Britain the renunciation to her imperial status, definitely strengthened the American position in the world and sanctioned the US succession to Great Britain as the hegemonic power. Therefore, the European national States' division handed the entire continent over to the US.

The agreement reached at Bretton Woods with the adoption of the White Plan (a gold exchange standard founded on the convertibility of the dollar

---

8 The introduction of financial instability is the most innovative aspect of the Keynesian economy. However, it is ignored by the neo-classical synthesis and it is seen as banal by the same neo-Keynesian models. A deeper examination of the Keynesian Theory, compared to the simplistic general opinion, was necessary only at the end of the golden years (1946-66) with the recurrence of longer and stronger financial crises. See the two main works by Minsky: Hyman P. Minsky, *John Maynard Keynes* (New York, 1975); *Stabilizing an Unstable Economy* (New York, 2008, first published in 1986).

9 Lionel Robbins, *Economic Planning and International Order,* 1937, London. On Robbins and Keynes, see Guido Montani, Introduction to the Italian edition of Robbins' works, *Il federalismo e l'ordine economico internazionale* (Bologna, 1985). On Robbins and the British federalists, see Lucio Levi, *Federalist Thinking,* chapter 6, *English Constitutional Federalism and the Crisis of the European System of States between the World Wars* (Lanham, 2008).

in gold at the price of 35 US$ per ounce) and the rejection of the proposal put forward by Keynes (an international currency denominated bancor), sealed the success of the American project of a unilateral dominance on the Western world. The success of the dollar as the international currency, the American power of veto at the International Monetary Fund, the use of the World Bank to support an international division of labour favourable to American exports, the double standard which became the GAAP rule in commercial matters, made up the bone structure of the economic system corresponding to the American hegemony.

The US obtained Europe's final renunciation to any colonial ambition during the Suez crisis (1956), when it asked the IMF to make its support to the pound conditional on the retreat of the Anglo-French troops from the Canal. The Americans, as illustrated by Hudson, were aiming at taking over the English Empire since the times of the first intergovernmental loan in 1917. The crisis of the pound in 1956 was caused mainly by the conversion of the sterling balances into dollars. They were Great Britain's debts vis-à-vis its Colonies for the supply of groceries to the US, the main British contribution to the war. At Bretton Woods, Keynes asked for a bilateral clearing regarding these "deposits" between Great Britain and its Colonies, in order to reimburse them gradually with the income coming from exports, but the US asked and obtained, together with the abandonment of the imperial status, the multilateralization of those British debts.

More than once (with regard to the 1917 loan, the London Conference and Bretton Woods) Hudson reflects on the reasons at the root of the British acquiescence to the American requests, and tries different answers. Firstly, that Great Britain was convinced of the need to keep the creditor policy strong, honouring the commitments even in a debtor position, because that policy, as well as private property, was a pillar of capitalism, and the British leading classes of the time, amongst which there were also supporters of fascism and nazism, feared communism more than anything else. Secondly, Hudson's hypothesis is that Great Britain resigned itself to pass the baton to the US, in order to realize through them the diffusion of the English language and culture (that is, their "race") worldwide. Each of these explanations includes relevant aspects, but one cannot forget that in reality Great Britain did not have other possibilities: the division of the national sovereign States and their wars delivered the entire Europe in the hands of the US.

The acceptance of the dollar as the international currency, when the US was in a leading position during the "golden years" between 1946 and 1965, can therefore be easily understood. The Bretton Woods monetary system had reorganized the "free world" around the dollar, as the British

Empire had been organized around the pound. The US represented more than half of the world's gross product, had almost the totality of the gold reserves and was the only one able to finance the reconstruction and the economic recovery in the post-war period. It did it in a masterly manner, for the clear correspondence between reconstruction and the American reason of State, for the improvement in the way economy was perceived (a quarter of a century had passed since the *Economic Consequences*), and finally, perhaps, for its idealism (at least in a minority always present in American history). The US was nevertheless able to prolong the international role of the dollar until today, forty years after the end of the gold convertibility (in 1968 it was limited to the Central Banks and in 1971 it was abolished by Nixon). The power exercised by the US as creditor is evident, but the one exercised as debtor needs some explanation. As guessed by Triffin, the adoption of the dollar as the international currency could end up in two opposite situations (the Triffin dilemma): a shortage of the international currency in the case of a surplus of the American balance of payments, and an excess of dollars in the opposite case. After the dollar-shortage of the Fifties, there came the dollar-inflation with the wars in Korea and above all in Vietnam. After the declaration of the end of the dollar convertibility in gold, the gold-exchange standard became, even formally, a dollar standard, which allowed the US to finance a series, until today almost uninterrupted, of export-balance deficits.

Until 1982, the deficits were caused by capital flows: the US bought, getting into debt, the companies of the rest of the world, 15 gained high profits and capital gains on its investments, and paid low interests on its Treasury Bills and on its Treasury Bonds. The balance of current payments did not present unbalances. Europe and Japan were in this phase the main investors in the US. However, from 1982, the deficit involved the current account balance of goods and services, and it worsened until it reached 5-7% of the GDP, not very affected by the changes in the dollar exchange rate (also because the dollar was devalued *vis-à-vis* the wrong currencies: too much versus the euro, too little versus the yuan). The military costs, continuously increasing, were financed with foreign debt without a corresponding increase in tax rates, which were on the contrary lowered for the upper classes. The Government therefore avoided to ask Congress, and the American people, to support the war costs. The "deficit without tears", opposed in vain by De Gaulle and Rueff, allowed to finance the cannons without renouncing to the butter.

Europe brought itself to safety with the creation of the euro, a process which lasted for thirty years. The main investors in the US were in this second phase the oil-exporting countries and the Asian countries, which were exporting industrial products (with extensive use of low-cost labour, without social dues, without environmental restrictions, with a strong State-control on the exchange rate). The export revenues of these countries, deposited in US banks and mainly reinvested in US Treasury bonds, made the US the largest world debtor. But the accumulation of the deficit made the debt unsustainable.

It would be really surprising if the American Government and the too many authorities in charge of controlling the US financial system, every day under pressure for the need to renew the old debts and to place new ones, were worried about exercising more stringent controls, about impeding the most dangerous financial experiments, about limiting the creation of financial institutions not subject to the Fed's rules, and about putting at last a limit to the leverage levels, tending to infinity. As illustrated by Minsky, in a capitalist system like ours (the true one, not that of the Chicago boys' books) instability is intrinsic, because the physiological financing phases (hedge financing) cause an increase in profits, and consequently an increase in the value of capital assets, which pushes towards a speculation on their prices through speculative financing tools, which can end up in the need to make new debts to just finance the interests alone on previous debts (the Ponzi financing). This is the path to bankruptcy. This is a different explanation from that given by Galbraith[10] or Shiller[11], of an irrational expectation of a continuous increase in the stock exchange, because Minsky underlined the endogenous character of instability: even if all the operators behave rationally, the sum of their rational behaviours is not sustainable by the economy as a whole.

The fundamental issue is therefore the international role played by a domestic currency: with the US Government busy with the placement of debts, and the controlling Authorities willing to take no notice, bankruptcy is not an enigma any more[12]. Market fundamentalism, deregulation, privatisation/expropriation of public properties and of natural monopolies, all the Chicago paraphernalia talked about by Reagan and his successors served only as a smokescreen to cover the US, while it was putting in place the most ruthless debtor policy, according to which debts are not to be paid.

This crisis is not like the others, but it is the last convulsion of the international role of the dollar. The world economic recovery cannot be pursued and the relapse into protectionism and war cannot be avoided without radical reforms[13]:

---

10 John Kenneth Galbraith, *The Great Crash* (Boston, 1961).

11 Robert J. Shiller, *Irrational Exuberance* (Princeton N.J., 2000).

12 A timeless reconstruction is given by Morris: Charles R. Morris, *The Trillion Dollar Meltdown: Easy Money, High Rollers, and the Great Credit Crash*, 2008, Public Affairs.

13 The suggested proposals can be found in the article by Alfonso Iozzo and Antonio Mosconi, "The Foundation of a Cooperative Global Financial System. A new Bretton

- the creation of a world currency unit, with functions similar to those of the European currency unit (ecu) in the phase preceding the creation of the euro;
- the entrusting of the world economic and financial supervision powers to the IMF, transformed into a true economic Council of Ministers of the UN (corresponding to the European Ecofin), as already suggested by Delors;
- the entrusting to the Bank of International Settlements of the functions of Central Bank of the world system (or of the system of monetary systems);
- the entrusting to the European Central Bank of banking and financial supervision functions in the Eurozone, and to the BIS of the corresponding functions at the world level;
- the institution of independent authorities, in Europe and worldwide, with the functions today entrusted, with a conflict of interests, to the rating agencies;
- the institution of a public insurance company at world level for the coverage of global risks, or, at least, of an authority for the independent evaluation of risks, to be a reference for the insurance market;
- the commitment to a common struggle against illegal financial flows, disguised and secret, which make drugs, international crime and terrorism possible and profitable, to be pursued even in their off-shore havens;
- the use of the World Bank to pursue goals of human development and for the battle against poverty.

Woods to confront the crisis of the international role of the US dollar", in *The Federalist Debate*, 2/2006. See above pp. 403-411.

Adding the RMB into the SDR Basket: an Evaluation*

Yide QIAO and Jiafei GE

The Special Drawing Rights (SDR) is an international reserve asset, created by the IMF in 1969 to supplement member countries' official reserves. Its value is based on a basket, which currently consists of four key international currencies, the USD, the EUR, the GBP and the JPY. The IMF reviews the currency composition of the SDR basket every five years guided by several long-standing principles aiming at enhancing the attractiveness of the SDR as a reserve asset. IMF's criteria for the SDR basket currencies are: 1) the "major trading country" criterion, specifically the currency is to be issued by IMF members (or by monetary unions that include IMF members), whose exports of goods and services during the five-year period ending 12 months before the effective date of the revision had the largest value[1]; and 2) the "free usable" criterion (FU), namely the currency is to be widely used to make payments for international transactions and to be widely traded in the principal exchange markets[2]. In the 2010 review of the SDR basket, the RMB was deemed to be a currency meeting the "major trading country" criterion. But there were some shortages in the RMB in terms of the FU criterion. In the almost five years after last review, the RMB has made a phenomenal growth in international use and trade. So what are the prospects for the RMB in the review in 2015?

* Published in Issue 1/2015.

1 It refers to the five years before the inclusion into SDR basket. I.e. if 2010 is the evaluation year for SDR currency basket, the ranking in goods and service exporting volume for previous five years from 2005 to 2009 issuing country of the currency (or currency union) will be examined.

2 See the Articles XXX(f) of Articles of agreement of International monetary fund, "A freely usable currency means a member's currency that the Fund determines (i) is, in fact, widely used to make payments for international transactions, and (ii) is widely traded in the principal exchange markets", p. 61.

Discussions and studies on the criteria for the SDR basket currencies

There were some misunderstandings over the criteria for the SDR basket currencies in these years. For example, the United States Former Treasury Secretary Timothy Geithner once expressed his view that convertibility is a precondition for a currency to be added into the SDR basket. This is wrong. There are only two criteria for the SDR basket currencies according to the IMF. Convertibility is not a criterion or a prerequisite although it is important for any currency being a reserve one. To clarify the criteria for the SDR basket currencies, the IMF staff made a study in September 2011: it reconfirmed the FU "widely used" and "widely traded" criteria and proposed a revision of the indicators of the FU according to the improvement of data availability and the development of financial markets. At the same time, it proposed an alternative to the FU, which is the "reserve asset criterion" (RAC).

The revised indicators of the FU are:1) the currency composition of reserves (possible supplementary indicator: number of countries holding a currency in their reserves), 2) the currency denomination of international banking liabilities and 3) the currency denomination of international debt securities, for assessing the "widely used" criterion, and 4) the volume of transactions in foreign exchange spot markets (possible supplementary indicator: the bid-offer spreads) for assessing the "widely traded" criterion. The indicators of the RAC are similar for indicator 1), the same for indicator 4), while for indicators 2) and 3) it selects the volume of transactions in foreign exchange derivatives markets and over the counter derivatives trade, and the appropriate market based interest rate instrument to replace respectively the currency denomination of international banking liabilities and international debt securities in the FU[3]. Executive Directors of the IMF broadly concurred that the revised indicators should be important factors in the assessment of the FU and some of them were open to exploring alternatives to the FU, such as the RAC[4]. The 2015 review of the SDR basket may not adopt the RAC because it might need an eighty-five percent majority of the total voting power according to our understanding of Section 2 Articles XV of IMF's

---

3 See "Criteria for Broadening the SDR Currency Basket [R]", International Monetary Fund, September 23, 2011a.

4 See Articles of Agreement of International Monetary Fund, "The method of valuation of the special drawing right shall be determined by the Fund by a seventy percent majority of the total voting power, provided, however, that an eighty-five percent majority of the total voting power shall be required for a change in the principle of valuation or a fundamental change in the application of the principle in effect", p. 40.

articles of agreement[5]. So we will assess whether the RMB meets IMF's criteria in terms of the revised FU indicators.

Does the RMB meet the FU?

In terms of official reserves, more and more countries (or regions) are considering making or already have made the RMB one of their reserve assets denomination currencies. Such as the UK, Nigeria, Belarus, Malaysia, Australia, South Korea, Chile and so on[6]. Although there is no RMB statistics in the IMF COFER (Currency Composition of Official Exchange Reserves), the RMB is already the 7th largest reserve currency according to the People's Bank of China[7]. Since the 6th and the 7th largest currencies, AUD and CHF, accounted for 1.90% and 0.27% in allocated reserves in the IMF COFER in the 2nd quarter of 2014 respectively, the RMB might account for 0.27% to 1.90% in reserves. Considering the 47.39% of unallocated reserves in IMF COFER, there might be missing value bias. Besides, according to the *Balance of Payments and International Investment Position Manual*, "Deposits (in foreign exchange) acquired by the central bank initiating the arrangement are treated as reserve assets because the exchange provides the central bank with assets that can be used to meet the economy's balance of payments financing needs and other related purposes". As a result, central bank swap arrangements can be regarded as supplements for reserve assets although the amount of it can't be equivalent to that of reserves. In the recent three years, RMB swap arrangements have seen a significant accumulation. The People's Bank of China maintains currency swap arrangements with 28 countries or regions, reaching a total amount of 3.1 trillion Yuan.

In terms of international debt securities, the amount outstanding in the RMB is 110 billion dollars in the 2nd quarter of 2014, ranking 9th of the world. While the amounts in the basket currencies, the EUR, the USD, the GPB and the JPY, are 10,108 billion dollars, 8,525 billion dollars, 2,309 billion dollars and 512 billion dollars. The amount in the JPY, the 4th currency in international debt securities, is 4.7 times of that denominated in RMB. Although the use of the RMB is still less than

5 See Articles of Agreement of International Monetary Fund, "The method of valuation of the special drawing right shall be determined by the Fund by a seventy percent majority of the total voting power, provided, however, that an eighty-five percent majority of the total voting power shall be required for a change in the principle of valuation or a fundamental change in the application of the principle in effect", p. 40.

6 See "*Why the reserve role of RMB is inevitable?*" China Economic Net, Oct. 14th, 2014 http://finance.ce.cn/rolling/201410/14/t20141014_3692859.shtml.

7 See "The Vice President of Central Bank of China released that the RMB has become the seventh largest reserve currency", *China's Economy*, 21st Oct. 2014, http://finance.ce.cn/rolling/201410/21/t20141021_3742517.shtml.

that of basket currencies in terms of amounts outstanding, its growth is phenomenal. From the first time of a non-zero value, 0.26 billion dollars in the BIS statistics in the 4th quarter of 2005, to 110.2 billion dollars in the 2nd quarter of 2014, there was a growth of 423.8 times and a quarterly rate of 19.5%. According to the quarterly rate of the last 4 years[8], 16.1%, the amount outstanding of international debt securities denominated in the RMB will reach the level of that in the JPY by the end of 2016.

In view of the net issuing of international debt securities, according to the statistics of the BIS, the average quarterly amount denominated in the RMB is 5.99 billion dollars from the 3rd quarter of 2010 to the 2nd quarter of 2014, exceeding that in EUR, in GBP and in JPY in the same period, which are 2.42 billion dollars, 2.24 billion dollars and -6.80 billion dollars respectively. Besides, RMB-denominated money market instruments increased from 0.9 million dollars, the first non-zero data in the BIS statistics recorded in the 3rd quarter of 2010, to 29.56 billion dollars in the 2nd quarter of 2014. It expanded 33,018 times in 4 years with a yearly rate of about 13.5 times. The RMB has been the 4th largest denomination currency in international money market instruments, exceeding the JPY from the 2nd quarter of 2013. In terms of foreign exchange spot markets, the turnover of the RMB has had a rapid growth in recent years. The average daily exchange volume was 33.95 billion dollars, ranking 11th in the world, in April 2013, while the turnover of the USD, the EUR, the JPY and the GBP was 1,691.24 billion dollars, 754.28 billion dollars, 612.34 billion dollars and 226.74 billion dollars respectively in the same period. Besides, nearly 90% of the RMB transactions were traded against the USD, reaching 30.49 billion dollars. The international trade of the RMB is expected to increase with the start of direct transactions between the RMB and other currencies.

Although there is a discrepancy between the RMB and the SDR basket currencies in international foreign exchange spot transactions from the perspective of absolute value, the share of the RMB is increasing quickly. It grew by 11 times from 0.07% of total in 2004 to 0.83% in 2013 and nearly 3 times from 2010 to 2013. According to this rate, the RMB may account for 7.47% of international foreign exchange spot transactions in the 2019 survey of foreign exchange by the BIS. In general, 1) although there is no RMB statistics in the IMF's COFER, RMB is already the 7th largest reserve currency according to the People's Bank of China. 2) The RMB ranks 9th in the amount outstanding of international debt securities, and the amount denominated in the RMB will nearly reach the level of that in JPY at the end of 2016, based on current growth. It ranks 4th in the amount outstanding of international money market instruments just

---

[8] From the 3rd quarter of 2010 to the 2nd quarter of 2014.

following close behind the USD, the EUR and the GBP. 3) The daily turnover of the RMB ranks 11th in foreign exchange spot markets and will exceed the current level of the GBP in the 2019 survey of exchange markets by the BIS in light of the increase rate at which the share of the RMB grew from 2010 to 2013. Therefore, the RMB basically meets the FU for the SDR basket currencies according to the available data.

The significance of including the RMB into the SDR basket

Besides the wider and wider international use and trade of the RMB which was illustrated above to support the point of adding RMB into the SDR basket, the inclusion of the RMB will improve the representativeness and stability of the SDR. Considering that the RMB is not fully floating, there are some arguments that the inclusion of the RMB into the SDR basket is pointless and it may ultimately reinforce the role of the USD in the SDR basket and have no help for enhancing the representativeness of the SDR. These concerns are reasonable to some extent and it would be much more helpful for the representativeness of the SDR if the RMB were fully floating. But the RMB is not anchored to the USD or the SDR now. 1) China is implementing a managed floating exchange rate system based on supply and demand in the market and with reference to a basket of currencies. This basket includes 20 currencies with about half of them issued by developed countries and another half or so issued by emerging countries. They are not the same to the currencies included in the SDR basket. 2) The correlation between the RMB and the USD has decreased sharply since the inception of review of exchange rate formation mechanism in 2005. The correlation between the RMB and the USD, and between the RMB and the EUR is -0.138 and 0.028, respectively, which is lower than those between the GBP and the USD, and between the GBP and the EUR, which were 0.196 and 0.118, respectively. As a result, the inclusion of the RMB into the SDR basket will contribute to improve representativeness and stability of the SDR under current conditions. Firstly, the introduction of RMB will improve the representativeness of the SDR in terms of GDP. In 1980, the GDP of the SDR currencies issuers accounted for more than 60% of the global GDP. Currently, the currencies in the SDR basket are the USD, the EUR, the GBP and the JPY. The proportion of these countries in respect of GDP keeps falling, reaching a new low of 40% in 2012. If the RMB would be added into the SDR basket, the GDP representativeness of the SDR currency countries would have been enhanced to about 55%, and the descending trend would have been largely relieved. Secondly, the introduction of the RMB will strengthen the stability of the SDR in terms of exchange rate. With the falling representativeness of the SDR and the taking-off of emerging economies since 1981, the stability of the SDR fell. The average variances of the GBP, the EUR, the

USD, the JPY, the RUB and the INR in the period from November 2008 to September 2014 were 2.7 times, 2.2 times, 1.4 times, 1.2 times, 11.8 times and 3.0 times comparing the data in the period from June 2003 to September 2008, respectively. The inclusion of the RMB into the SDR basket can strengthen the stability of it. Had the RMB been added in 2010, based on relevant calculation of the IMF, the proportion of RMB in the SDR basket would have reached 12%, exceeding that of the JPY and the GBP, while the proportion of the USD, the EUR, the GBP and the JPY would have been 37%, 33%, 10%, and 8% respectively. From January 1, 2011 to September 30, 2014, if the value of the SDR had been calculated with the above proportion structure, despite certain concession in the stability of the SDR to the EUR and the JPY, the fluctuation[9] between the SDR and the RMB, the USD and the GBP would have seen a decrease of 13%, 21% and 7% respectively.

Conclusion

Ultimately, we concluded that the RMB basically meets the FU for SDR basket currencies and the inclusion of it will improve the representativeness and stability of the SDR. So, the introduction of RMB is in accordance with IMF's long-standing principle in reviews of the SDR basket of enhancing the attractiveness of the SDR as a reserve asset. Besides, the introduction of the RMB into the SDR basket will be beneficial to the progress of the RMB internationalization and contribute to reforming the international monetary system towards a stable direction by reinforcing the role of SDR in it. Thus, we suggest that the RMB should be added into the SDR basket in 2015.

9 The fluctuation here refers to the time-series standard deviation of relevant currencies in regarding the SDR as the base currency.

A Constitution for the Internet*

Stefano RODOTÀ

Is the Internet in need of a Constitution? The question is topical after the news of censoring initiatives by the Chinese government, leading to the arrest of a dissident there, and even of the cooperation offered by an American portal, Yahoo!. The question cannot be dodged by arguing that any attempt to impose rules on the Web is impossible or unnecessary. The Internet is the widest public space mankind has ever known, where every day millions of people exchange messages, produce and acquire knowledge, build up political and social participation, play, buy and exchange goods and services. Can all this be left to the bullying of authoritarian regimes or to the conveniences of the market?

Some months ago Microsoft already started agreeing to warn its Chinese customers not to use words like liberty, democracy, participation in their electronic messages. More seriously, Yahoo! provided the information necessary to trace back an e-mail that a journalist, Shi Tao, had sent to the United States, reporting on a warning issued by the government to journalists over the risks of the presence of dissidents at the Tienanmen Square's anniversary. Shi Tao was later sentenced to ten years in prison for spreading allegedly secret news. Finally, a law was passed that subjects messages over the Internet to strict control, authorizing only the "good" ones, in order to avoid a democratic contagion spreading via the Web that might foster the influence of voluntary organizations, make mobilization possible among the more than one hundred million Chinese web-surfers, and thus bring about not only dissent, but also rebellion. Do we have to draw the conclusion that the Internet is by its very nature democratic, and incompatible with authoritarian regimes?

All these facts show very clearly that Internet problems cannot be analyzed from the viewpoint of the traditional libertarian idea that considers the Web to be an intrinsically anarchical space capable of autonomously redressing a violated liberty and which cannot bear any regulation. But to justify the information against the journalist, one of the founders of Yahoo! stated that his company abides by the laws of the country in which it operates. Rules, therefore, exist, and they are severe,

* Published in Issue 1/2006.

and are reinforced by disquieting alliances between States and enterprises, becoming instruments that do limit liberty.

Thinking of legal rules to counter that possibility becomes a necessity, and almost a democratic duty. But one is immediately faced with concrete obstacles, raised in every sector against any attempt to devise legal guarantees adequate to meet the realities of a globalized world and of the new "spaces without borders" like the Internet: namely the sovereignty of national states, and the deep-rooted habit among trans-national companies of claiming to be themselves the issuers of the rules affecting them.

Have we no choice but to give up, or should we simply trust in the virtues of the Internet? Looking around, one can spot other possibilities. A fine analyst, Franco Carlini, is proposing a social reaction: let us immediately exploit the opportunities offered by the Web itself, the sensitiveness of the surfers and the possibility of immediate mobilization, replying in this way to any message coming from a Yahoo! mailbox: "Your message is refused, but we will be pleased to read it if it comes from any mail service other than Yahoo! and is respectful of human rights". In Italy, the members of *Magistratura Democratica* (Democratic Magistracy) are already doing that, and the Peacelink association offers a mailbox to those who quit Yahoo!. Lacking guarantee rules, citizens all over the world are trying to give shape to a kind of counter-power.

Initiatives of this nature, that take advantage of every means the Internet can give, have been defined as "poacher's strategies", and in other situations have produced significant results, as in the case of the boycott of transnational companies exploiting juvenile labour. At present, Reporters sans Frontières provides instructions about how to spread information over the Internet without being detected. This is more difficult because of the presence of a national state determined to maintain a hard line, and Yahoo!'s interest in conquering China's enormous market. However, should the type of reaction illustrated above succeed in getting a sufficient critical mass, it would surely have more than symbolic importance. That is why the thesis of those arguing that it is better to accept what Yahoo! is doing rather than leave Chinese customers to a much more oppressive national monopoly is not convincing. The very fact that the problem has been raised highlights the concrete risk of a "market censorship". This is a matter on which I have long ago tried to focus people's attention, and it cannot be dodged, considering that the Web's commercial uses have surpassed the non-commercial, thus opening up the prospect of deep changes in the nature of the Internet itself.

The chances of success for strategies from below increase if they are also backed by institutional strategies. When I speak of a Constitution for the Internet, I am not thinking, of course, of a document similar to national Constitutions, but of the necessity to define the principles on which to base rights relevant to the situations in which those using the Internet find themselves. As a constituent assembly to promulgate those rights is unthinkable, it is necessary to follow different paths, seizing all the opportunities in any part of the world as they arise.

A good starting point could be the European Union's Charter of Fundamental Rights, in which the right to protection of personal data is actually recognized as an autonomous fundamental right. This means going beyond the traditional notion of privacy, and considering the strong protection of personal information as an inalienable aspect of the liberty of a person. It is important to keep this in mind, because the European Union constitutes at present the region in the world with the highest level of protection of personal data, and this fact is influencing decisions in many other countries.

At the World Conference on Privacy, held in Venice in September 2000, the Chief of the Italian Authority launched the project of an international Conference on this topic. This proposal was upheld by the World Conference recently held in Montreux. As past experience shows, reaching agreement will require lengthy negotiations between governments. In the meantime, all the bodies involved in managing the Internet – whether states, citizens, providers, producers, enterprises, or other authorities – are required to start strengthening and enforcing the rules already written down in several documents, experimenting the "new-generation" codes of self-discipline – that is, those which are not the product of sectorial interests only, but are the result of a joint discussion with public bodies – while ascertaining which problems can be solved through better design and usage of existing technologies, thus helping to establish what a new Convention should include in practice.

Along this road, the opportunity offered by the World Summit on the Information Society, to be held in November in Tunis on the initiative of the United Nations, should not be missed. In fact, there is a proposal that at that meeting a Charter of Rights for the Web be approved, which starts from the recognition that the Internet is bringing about a new, great redistribution of power. Lest censorship-oriented attitudes prevail, it is high time to demand some "constitutional" principles as part of a new planetary citizenship: freedom of access, freedom of usage, the right to knowledge, respect for privacy, recognition of new public goods. In Tunis there will be an opportunity to decide whether technical management of the Internet should pass from the United States to the United Nations.

Meanwhile the European Union, which could act as the motor for this process and has taken a courageous stance on the issue of Internet's management, is going through a period that risks being dominated solely by security concerns. The Italian journalist Federico Rampini writes that "the authorities in Shanghai have installed cameras in Internet Cafés and check the documents of people entering them". That happens in Europe too, while the Commission in Brussels, mainly under pressure from Great Britain, is proposing to redraft in a restrictive sense the legal framework concerning phone communications, electronic mail and the Internet, beginning with how long the data concerning them should be kept. Reacting to this development, the European Parliament and the Warrant Authorities point out that we are dealing here with fundamental rights which cannot be restrained without upsetting the democratic character of our societies.

This confrontation highlights the constitutional dimension of the Internet. It is all the more necessary that the legitimate call for a widespread protest against Yahoo! should apply equally to those European rules that go well beyond the requirements of security protection.

A People's Assembly for the UN*

Jo Leinen

The UN is in urgent need of reform to meet the challenges of the 21st century. The global governance system in the UN must be made more efficient and more democratic. Decisions on the global level influence the daily lives of people everywhere, whether it concerns the economy, the environment, security issues or health policy. The current UN system is basically the structure of the founding year 1945. The world has changed dramatically in the last 60 years. It is unacceptable that the allied powers of the Second World War and China can still veto every decision. It is also unacceptable that only governments and executive bodies have full representation at the UN level.

The UN needs the participation of civil society and the representation of the member states' parliaments. The democratic deficit in the UN must be overcome. Governments are not necessarily representing the people of their country. They do not represent the opposition and other forces of society. They must be democratically accompanied and controlled by a citizens' chamber in the UN. The voice of the citizens is not only an additional voice on the international scene. The voice of the citizens is a qualitatively different power. Governments very often embody the competition between states and act according to the *raison d'état*. A people's assembly would act more directly towards people's interests and human development.

One important element of any UN reform must therefore be the establishment of a parliamentary assembly in the UN system. This world parliament could be constituted, according to art. 22 of the UN Charter, by a simple majority of the general assembly. The parliamentary assembly could start as a consultative body with a delegation from each national parliament. The parliament assembly would deal with all topics discussed in the general assembly. It would organise itself as a plenary, in committees and political groups.

The European Parliament could be a good example how this process can start off and how it might continue. The early Coal and Steel Community of 1951 between six European states (Germany, France, Italy, Belgium, Netherlands, Luxemburg) and the European Community of 1957 started

* Published in Issue 3/2004.

with a parliamentary assembly which had a purely consultative status. The national parliaments sent their delegations to this European assembly. Already in the sixties, however, a broad public debate began, calling for legislative power for the parliamentary assembly and for direct elections of its members. The Union of European Federalists (UEF) has been in the forefront of a broad coalition of forces promoting the transformation of the parliamentary assembly into a real European Parliament and the direct election of the European parliamentarians. This campaign is a success story which continues until the present day. In June 1979 the first direct elections to the European Parliament were organised.

On June 13th, 2004, the Europeans elected the 6th European Parliament. 450 million people from 25 member states could vote for 736 deputies in this European people's assembly. The European Parliament has step by step acquired more powers. The first European Constitution, signed on June 18th, 2004 by the heads of state and government of the 25 member states, will give the EP nearly the full range of powers of an elected parliament. The Constitution states the rule that European laws will be made by a two-chamber system: the citizens, represented by the European Parliament, and the states, represented in the Council of Ministers. The European Parliament will get full control over the EU budget and is entitled to elect the president of the European Commission which is the government of the European Union. After the federal parliament of India, the European Parliament represents the second largest democracy in the world. It is the first supranational parliament on this globe.

The story of the European Parliament could be a basis for similar developments in other continents as well as on the UN level. It is interesting to see that the newly created African Union (AU) will set up its own parliamentary assembly very soon. Similarly the Latin American association of Mercosur is debating a parliamentary assembly. The time has therefore come to push for a parliamentary body also in the UN system.

For the democratic development of global governance, it would be best to have one single parliamentary assembly and not one for every UN organization (WTO, World Bank, *etc.*) as it is debated here and there. The resources of parliamentarians are not as big as to make such a disaggregation feasible. A single people's assembly could also ensure the coherence of policies and decisions within the UN. The number of parliamentarians in the people's assembly should be below 1000 in order to facilitate debates and efficient decision-making. Every country should have a minimum of two parliamentarians and be represented according to its population by up to 18 MPs for the largest countries.

For a start, an amount of 100 to 120 million Dollars would be enough to provide for plenary sessions, committee meetings and a general secretariat. Compared with the 1.000 billion dollars spent on weapons every year, the necessary financial resources to achieve global democracy should not be an argument against the world parliament. Of course there are undemocratic countries in this world and there are doubts regarding the character of their parliamentary envoys. Yet, Freedom House have calculated that among the 192 member states of the UN there are 117 democracies, a clear majority. There is the hope that parliamentary debates in the new assembly would be a political and educational help for undemocratic countries to develop democratic cultures of their own. In my opinion it is necessary to start with parliamentarians from all UN-members to preserve the equality of the states and their population in this world.

A world parliament is an instrument for a world citizenship. The representation of the citizens in this assembly would increase the identity with global problems. The opening phrase of the UN-Charta "We the people" could finally fulfil its true meaning. The parliamentary assembly would also be an invaluable push for the development of a global civil society. NGOs are very important but by definition they do not have the same democratic legitimacy as parliamentarians emerging from direct and general elections. With the world parliament, NGOs and civil society would have a clear focus and a strong partner in the UN.

How is it possible to realize a parliamentary assembly in the UN? A worldwide campaign of citizens, organisations, parliamentarians and governments will be necessary to achieve this goal. Civil society has a special role to promote this idea because those who have the power are reluctant to change and do not want to share power. We therefore cannot wait for governments and national parliaments to start this process. There is of course a famous success story in recent years for a global coalition to promote UN-institutions. The World Federalist Movement (WFM) coordinated about 4.000 NGOs in favour of the International Criminal Court (ICC). I would like to see WFM or another coalition to unite world citizens for a world parliament.

The San Francisco People's Assembly 2004 was a starting point for such a global campaign. Let's get going to have first results next year, when the world community will be meeting for the 60th anniversary of UN. I will do my utmost so that the newly elected European Parliament will be a strong partner for this important idea and this innovative project. We are living in one world. The citizens of this globe need direct representation: a world parliament is a necessity for the 21st century.

Problems of Democratization*

George MODELSKI

Democratization is one of the central phenomena of our times. Let us bring together, with the help of an attractive image, some basic facts about it, viewing it as the process whereby democratic practices have been spreading world-wide for a considerable time now. We set out to accomplish this task with the help of the image displayed on page 438 that succinctly summarizes the information about the condition and the progress of democratization at various points in time in the past century and a half.

By condition we mean to indicate the relative importance of democracies in the world picture. With progress we intend to show this to be a dynamic picture that opens out a window to the future. The image "World Democratization" is simple but it displays this crucial information in two ways. First, it shows seventeen discrete data points that depict, at ten year intervals, the proportion of the world's peoples that at that point in time lived in democracies. The first of these data points refers to 1840, and indicates that in that year some 3.9 per cent of the world population lived in democratic countries, and more specifically, in the United States, and the United Kingdom, the only two that could thus be described. By the year 2000, the last of the data points, following the collapse of the Soviet bloc, that figure had risen to 57.1 per cent, and the number of democracies to 87.

The second feature of our table is more analytical, and traces the best part of an S-shaped curve that not only fits our 'hard' data quite accurately but also extends well into the future, to the 22nd century. We might call this the learning curve of world democratization.

Here we have two sets of basic information; so what to make of it? Let us highlight four of its features: democratization is a powerful process; it is world-wide, it has a long reach in time, and it might be seen as a learning experience. We then ask: what are the implications of these arguments?

---

* Published in Issue 1/2008.

A powerful trend

A glance at the seventeen actual data points confirms, first of all, that these are not scattered or random bits of information but rather a series or sequence pointing to the existence of a trend, and not just any trend but one that is persistent and powerful. Viewed over a time span of 160 years, the trend shows both ups and downs, and registers some setbacks (including a notable one centered on the 1930s, and World War II), but overall it moves clearly, and strongly, upward. In absolute numbers, the expansive force of democracy is simply staggering, from some 40-plus million people in mid-19th century, to close to 3.5 billion at the turn to the 21st. A trend of such power is not easily reversed, or aborted.

A world-wide trend

In our chart, democracy takes off as a transatlantic project, and for a long while, appears, in the main, as a 'Western' phenomenon. But over time, and since the mid-20th century, its spread has been to most parts of the world, and (as shown) it now engages more than half of the world's population. It has diffused via a demonstration effect because, by and large, democracies work better, know better how to cooperate, win wars but do not engage in mass killings, fight hunger more effectively, and, on the whole, are more productive and more prosperous. That makes democratization a likely universal process spreading by imitation.

A long-term trend

Our poster 'World Democratization' covers more than two centuries, making it plain that while undoubtedly powerful, this is a process whose progress is measured, deliberate, even slow, and not really to be hurried. It took over a century for democracy to move from a 'market share' of under ten per cent, to a majority position (in which India plays a large role) a few years ago. We suppose that for the bulk of the world system to be 'saturated' with democratic practices it will take many decades, and the path taken by China will be a key factor.

A learning process

Roughly connecting the dots in our chart is a line in the generic form of a learning curve. That curve marks not just the path of world-wide democracy over the past century and a half but also projects that path forward one century into the future, on the assumption that what we are observing is a learning process: humans settling into a cooperative mode; humans learning to live with each other. That strongly suggests that the trend we have charted is not just a summary of events past but a process of some regularity that (jointly with others) is likely evolutionary.

Democracy has for some time been a subject of contention between foreign policy Idealists and Realists. Idealists, advocating the spreading of democracy, speak sometimes in grandiose terms of principle, even morality, point to the record of successful societies and claim to represent the wave of the future. Realists warily eye the problems of the day, discount the future and counsel prudence. Our presentation suggests that both sides score in that argument and that both are in effect right.

Implications

What are the implications, for the next decade or two, of these basic facts about democratization? First, if democratization is indeed such a powerful process then it might be expected to proceed, we might say, under its own steam or, as it might be put more technically, as a form of self-organization. That is, in the ordinary course of world events, humankind seems on track, gradually, albeit slowly, to build a growing domain of democracy, and that is why what is called for, above all else, is patience.

There is no "duty to export democracy" nor is there any requirement for extraordinary measures such as costly military interventions, or risky preventive wars, to foster it. Arguably, such measures are likely to prove counter-productive rather than facilitative. Indeed, as we look at the chart once again, we see that the point reached in the year 2000, a high point of the entire story, and following the spectacular expansion of democracy at the end of the Cold War, is well above the trend line (or the learning curve). That suggests that we may be 'ahead of schedule', and that a slowdown of the process could well lie ahead. And that suggests caution. Second, if in fact we are at present 'ahead of the curve', then the other watchword must be consolidation. The greater urgency lies with safeguarding and solidifying the gains of the recent past, and building up the links among existing democracies.

That might take two forms: protecting the elements of the emerging global democratic community, and continuing to strengthen the institutions that have proved their value and effectiveness. The elements of an emerging global democratic community are now in place. They include North America, the European Union, India, Japan-Korea, and Australia-New Zealand: components of what might be called an 'oceanic' grouping whose linkages are not due primarily to geographical propinquity but rather to participating in long standing networks of social, maritime and air connections.

This is a prosperous and active ensemble now accounting for the majority of the world's population, but its cohesion is not to be taken for granted and must be assiduously maintained in the face of rising pressure on at least two fronts: the demographic and the Islamist. Population might soon start declining both in Europe, and in Japan, reducing their weight in the democratic world. Democracy, moreover, is under challenge from the Islamists and the Jihadists, notably so in the Middle East, but also in Europe and Central Asia. In more narrowly political contexts, the way to consolidate the gains of the past is to cultivate and to strengthen the institutions that have proved their worth in the past century. One example is NATO, that since its inception in 1949 has been animated by strong transatlantic relationships; the organization has expanded its membership and could of course broaden its functions. Then there are the Bretton Woods institutions, and indeed the entire United Nations system that has a strong potential for democratic development. In all of this, of course, the role and policies of the United States remain of key significance.

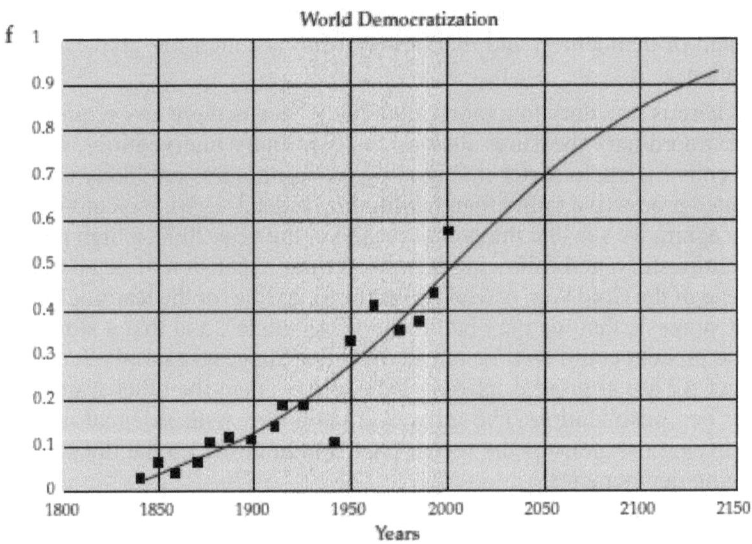

The figure shows, at ten-year intervals, the proportion of the world population living in democracies (left scale). Fitting the data is a classic learning curve. Graph by T. Devezas, based on data in: "Democratization in long perspective' revisited", by G. Modelski and G. Perry III, in *Technological Forecasting and Social Change*, 69 (2002), 359-376

Opinion on World Government in the USA*

Joseph Baratta

> "Notwithstanding this prospect of a very full and respectable meeting [the Philadelphia Convention of 1787], no very sanguine expectations can be well indulged. The probable diversity of opinions and prejudices, and of supposed or real interests among the States, renders the issue totally uncertain. The existing embarrassments and mortal diseases of the Confederation form the only ground of hope that a spirit of concession on all sides may be produced by the general chaos [...]"
>
> James Madison[1]

Anyone who seeks principled guidance for establishing a republic of the world, and hence the beginnings of a world governed by universal law, would do well to study the records of the American constitutional convention at Philadelphia and *The Federalist Papers*, which justified it. The diversity of people brought into the American Union was certainly not so great as in Europe, and far less than in the whole world, but the courage with which the Founding Fathers faced the necessity of a government will continue to inspire humanity in search of peace. "If we are in earnest about giving the Union energy and duration", wrote Hamilton, "we must abandon the vain project of legislating upon the States in their collective capacities; we must extend the laws of the federal government to the individual citizens of America"[2].

Thomas G. Weiss has written another challenging book on the United Nations, starting from the perspective of global governance, but what is unusual about this one is that he concludes with some regret that the idea of world government seems to have dropped out of contemporary thinking about international relations. Governance lacks, he admits, "prescriptive power in pointing to where we should be headed". Their assumptive framework (world government is unattainable) reduces

* Published in Issue 3/2010. Review of Thomas G. Weiss, *What's Wrong with the United Nations, and How to Fix It.* Foreword by Sir Brian Urquhart. (Polity Press, 2008).

1 *Letters and Other Writings of James Madison*, Vol. I, 1769-1793 (New York, 1884), pp. 286-87.

2 *The Federalist*, No. 23. Other numbers relevant to UN reform include 9, 10, 15, 16, 17, 21, 39, 46, 51.

governance scholars to observers at most of creative initiatives mostly within the UN Secretariat (what Weiss calls the "Second UN") to solving global problems, while those efforts mostly fail in the face of state ("First UN") resistance. "We have strayed too far", he writes, "from the kind of paradigmatic rethinking of human relations that is absolutely critical if we are to solve the more intractable problems faced by the United Nations".

What is also surprising, Sir Brian Urquhart in his preface praises Weiss for going further from the present stage of thought on "international governance" toward "world government". "Weiss suggests", writes Urquhart, "that world government is the necessary conceptual basis for adequate future management of the major problems of our planet". Since Urquhart refused to write a preface for my book, *The Politics of World Federation*, we wonder what has changed his mind? In the last chapter of *What's Wrong with the United Nations*, Weiss does not fail to appeal to the prejudices of fellow scholars in the mainstream with remarks about "rabid world federalists" and "idealism beyond the pale", "naive and demented". But later he actually makes quite an argument, as he did in his 2009 International Studies Association presidential address[3], for restoring the idea of world government to the spectrum of thinking about international relations. His last line is, "[…] how soon will we revert to an old-fashioned concept, world government?". His next book is said to be, *The UN and Global Governance: An Unfinished Journey*.

The very term, "world government", in the hands of most mainstream scholars in the United States, is pejorative, since they imagine it means a unitary world state built on the destruction of the national states. Hence, we prefer the term, "world federal government", since no historic proposal since first use of atomic bombs in war was unitary and all aimed to preserve the states: Robert M. Hutchins, G.A. Borgese, and the University of Chicago's *Preliminary Draft of a World Constitution* (1948), Grenville Clark and Louis B. Sohn's *World Peace through World Law* (1958), and Philip Isley's *Constitution for the Federation of Earth* (1977). The whole point of these proposals was to preserve the United States, like other states, in a world grown too interdependent for isolationism, another name for absolute sovereignty.

Weiss at least uses "world government" fairly as the fundamental alternative to an organization of sovereign states (a "confederation") like the United Nations. The idea of world federal government has historically functioned as the extreme of the spectrum of thinking about international organization. UN introductory documents take care to define the UN as "not a world government". Until recently, it was possible for such a

3 Thomas G. Weiss, "What Happened to the Idea of World Government?", *International Studies Quarterly*, (2009) 53, 253–271.

person as Gillian Sorenson, advisor to the UN Foundation, to deflect "UN bashing" by the Heritage Foundation with bashing "world government" – at least until she was challenged in Cambridge by someone who knew *The Federalist*, Nos. 23 and 51! What is significant about Weiss and Campbell Craig, as reviewed here in *The Federalist Debate*, Year XXIII, Number 2, July 2010, is that they are not ridiculing the idea any more but taking it seriously. Even Paul Kennedy, in *The Parliament of Man*, cites my book in his first note. He treats world federalism as beyond the pale, but at least he does not ignore it[4]. Joshua Goldstein and Jon Pevehouse, in their standard text, *International Relations*, used in many courses including my own, repeatedly discuss world government as the theoretical alternative to anarchy, especially in the field of positive peace[5]. World federal government may be difficult to establish, but it is adequate to the problem of the anarchy of states.

The philosopher Arthur Schopenhauer wrote: "Truth passes through three stages: first it is ridiculed, then it is violently opposed, and finally it is accepted as self-evident"[6]. World federalism is currently in the first stage, yet, since the end of the Cold War, it is slipping into the more serious category. Weiss's book exhibits the strain. The whole book goes by without a mention of the rule of law until p. 218, when "laws" are mentioned as elements in the notion of global governance. Does he mean domestic or international law? A little later in a context closer to world federalism (described there as "rabid"), there is a second mention of "law". The good man cannot even imagine that what is seriously proposed is the rule of world law, enacted by a world legislature, enforced by a world executive, with the assistance of a world judiciary, exactly as in any of the 30 historic national federations. Weiss makes no mention of a Second Chamber of the UN General Assembly, as proposed by Andrew Strauss and Richard Falk[7], which is exactly the kind of current, shrewd proposals to move the world toward the inauguration of the rule of world law. The idea is building a constituency in the Campaign for the Establishment of a United Nations Parliamentary Assembly, which as of 2009 has been supported by 731 members of national parliaments from 96 countries[8].

---

4 Paul Kennedy, *The Parliament of Man: The Past, Present, and Future of the United Nations* (New York: Random House, 2006), 3, 295.

5 Joshua S. Goldstein and Jon C. Pevehouse, *International Relations* (Longman Pearson, 9th ed., 2009), 134.

6 Arthur Schopenhauer, *The World as Will and Idea*, Foreword to the First Edition (1818), p. xv.

7 Andrew Strauss and Richard A. Falk, "*Toward Global Parliament*", Foreign Affairs, 80 (2001): 212-20; Strauss, "Envisioning a More Democratic Global System", *Widener Law Review*, 13, 2 (2007).

8 http://www.unpacampaign.org/.

What is needed to break the current impasse at the UN – however naïve and unrealistic it may seem – is to find ways to enlist the people in the work of the United Nations. In Weiss's book, there is virtually nothing on the people, prospective world citizens, representative government (even like that of the EU), and law enacted with the consent of the governed. As long as global governance scholars cannot bring the people into their thinking, they will be unable to take the step toward world federal government. For what world federalists demand is to abandon the distinction between "domestic" and "international" affairs, just as is happening now with the weakening of the Charter's Article 2(7), the shift in peacekeeping to peace enforcement, repeated humanitarian intervention to protect human rights, and the emerging norm of the responsibility to protect (R2P). After 2007, in the fifth edition of his mainstream text, *The United Nations and Changing World Politics*, Weiss introduced a term for the people's role in the work of the UN (the "Third UN", mostly NGOs, Multinational Corporations, and the occasional individual), but it needs to be greatly developed and encouraged.

The notion of world politics, we submit, has to change if we are to move to world federal government. Weiss seems to think, with Goldstein and most mainstream international relations scholars, that world politics means the relations between states and occasional non-state actors. But that includes war and all the violence that goes under the head of the threat and use of force, despite the Charter's effort to forbid it in Article 2(4). To call such things politics, seems to me like calling rape, love. It is not politics as the completion of ethics (Aristotle), nor the process by which a free people choose their governors and enact the laws (American usage). If the US invasion of Iraq, without UN Security Council mandate, and then the killing of at least 100,000 people and the making of 2,000,000 refugees is politics, then it must be extremely primitive politics, suitable for Men emerging from the Stone Age.

One difficulty in going still further toward world federal government is that federalist plans like the Chicago Committee's or Clark and Sohn's have run against the conventional wisdom of the inadvisability of Charter amendment. Yet the Charter has been amended (1965, 1973), so it is not impossible, and the old plans deal with conditions not very different from those today. Even my history of the federalist movement, read with a little imagination, recounts events rather like those today. Probably the last significant proposal for the practical federation of modern states was Altiero Spinelli's *Draft Treaty Establishing the European Union* (1984), which was enacted by the European Parliament after it was made directly elected by the people. It passed by a vote of 237 to 31, with 43 abstentions. Although rejected by the Council of Ministers, it led to the Maastricht Treaty and the European Union we have today since Lisbon. At the world level, a similar proposal based on democratic legitimacy could lead to similar achievements.

Weiss's book will be useful for both global governance theorists and scholars inclined toward world federal government. His views draw attention to the post-Cold War developments (like the decline of sovereignty and the growth of new partnerships) that point toward greater centralization in international organization. He informs the public about the great continuing difficulties (like the North–South imbalance) that cannot be wished away by projects to increase popular representation in the General Assembly or strengthen the rudimentary international court system (ICC). He draws his guidance, if not from the world federalist literature, then from such Second UN critical works as Robert Jackson's *Capacity Study* (1969); the International Commission on Intervention and State Sovereignty's report (2001), which gave us R2P; the High-Level Panel on Threats, Challenges, and Change's report (2004), which outlined Security Council reform for the ill-fated 2005 summit on UN reform; and especially the High-Level Panel on Coherence's report, *Delivering as One* (2006), which Weiss cites revealingly for his critique of development. Any scholar or aspiring world citizen would do well to consult these works for current information on the difficulties before any form of international organization.

We conclude with some world federalist comments on the UN's delivery of international peace and security. It is time to admit that most of Chapter VII is misconceived; it amounts to international war on the pattern of World War II, starting with aerial bombing (Art. 45). There is a reason why collective security has worked only twice (1950, 1990), if threatened perhaps eleven times, as Daniel Ellsberg once pointed out: Such "action" is so indiscriminate that national states will not agree to its use, except in the now exceptional case of cross-border aggression. Meanwhile, the threat of UN force corrupts the whole development of peaceful settlement (Chapter VI) and of proper institutions of world law, including treaties to protect and promote human rights, state reporting systems, and slow progress toward courts like the European Court. Madison, faced with the problem of enforcement by the federal government, once argued that "the use of force against a State would look more like a declaration of war, than an infliction of punishment, and would probably be considered by the party attacked as a dissolution of all previous compacts by which it might be bound"[9]. There is a need for a military power at the world level, true, but it cannot be the usual meaning of "enforcement".

9 Max Farrand, ed., *Records of the Federal Convention of 1787* (New Haven: Yale University Press, 1911, 1966), I: 54.

Experience shows that cooperation among sovereigns is almost worthless in building lasting peace. Jean Monnet understood this when turning to the European Community, looking forward to its outcome in a federal union[10]. In a European context, to suppose that voluntary cooperation is enough to undo a history of war and hatred would be to suppose that the Council of Europe could succeed better than the still emerging European Union, which already, even if not yet a strict federation, has abolished war among its 27 members.

Almost certainly, for a change from cooperation to binding law, a crisis will be necessary, as Mark Malloch Brown fears. Jean Monnet did, too, saying, for the hard work of uniting sovereignties, people will act only when faced by a crisis[11]. Thomas Jefferson said much the same when he wrote, "All experience hath shown that mankind are more disposed to suffer, while evils are sufferable, than they are to right themselves by changing the forms to which they are accustomed"[12]. Judging by current trends, this crisis will come when America falls, as did Britain, from the rank of world hegemon. Then we will need world federal government. Scholars should prepare for such a day.

Let me conclude by pointing out that there exists a vast, unworked literature on world federation and general international relations scholarship that looks in that direction. In *The United Nations System: Meeting the World Constitutional Crisis* (1995), we surveyed the most progressive literature since the end of the Cold War[13]. The book is an annotated bibliography, organized from most to least consensus on effective international organization from the Universal Postal Union to the UN Environment Program. In *The Politics of World Federation* (2004), we included another annotated bibliography on world federal government, pro and con[14].

[10] Jean Monnet, *Memoirs,* trans. Richard Mayne, intro. George Ball (Garden City, NY: Doubleday, 1978), 17-20, 87, 271, 295, 316, motto.

[11] *Ibid.*, 13, 421.

[12] Declaration of Independence, 1776.

[13] Joseph Preston Baratta, *The United Nations System: Meeting the World Constitutional Crisis*. (Oxford: ABC-Clio; New Brunswick, NJ: Transaction Press, 1995).

[14] Baratta, *The Politics of World Federation*. Vol. 1: *United Nations, UN Reform, Atomic Control*. Vol. 2: *From World Federalism to Global Governance*. (Westport, CT: Praeger Press, 2004).

The Security Council Reform*

Lucio LEVI

Punctually, like the comet of Halley, the problem of the Security Council reform has appeared again on the horizon. And yet it continues to be formulated in a way that does not fit the most recent tendencies of international politics.

The current structure of the Security Council was devised in an age of domination and inequality. At a distance of 60 years from the creation of the UN, the substance of the decision-making power in the UN is still concentrated in the hands of only five states out of 191. That structure has become wholly inadequate to present needs of the world and inconsistent with the goals of equality and justice in international politics. Hence the need to enlarge and transform it from the five big powers' directory into a more representative body.

The traditional way to address this problem is to open the Security Council doors to the strongest states that have risen to prominent positions in the world power hierarchy and to entrust them the representation of the smaller states belonging to the same region. The decline in US international influence, as shown by the failure of the strategy of preventive war, suggests to entrust regional gendarmes (such as Germany, Japan, India, Brazil and a still-unidentified African country) with the responsibility of sharing the burden of maintaining the world order.

This solution arouses the hostility of the states left out, particularly of those most qualified to a seat in that assembly. For instance, Pakistan is not willing to accept the candidacy of India, Argentina that of Brazil, Italy that of Germany and so forth. The bestowal of two new seats on the North and three on the South would indeed strengthen the representation of the South in the Security Council, but would also confirm the supremacy of the North and especially of Europe, which would get three seats, an entirely disproportionate weight, if we consider that the EU population amounts to 455 million inhabitants. In conclusion, this proposal reflects the principles of domination and inequality that have shaped the present Security Council structure, but are by now inadequate to meet the present needs of the world and incompatible with the objectives of equality and justice that are becoming paramount in international relations.

---

* Published in Issue 3/2004.

The best way to achieve an equitable reform of the Security Council is that involving the formation of regional groupings of states. The reorganization of the world order on the basis of groupings of states represents not only an alternative to the power hierarchies determined by the difference between states of varying sizes, but also to the world fragmentation into a cloud of small states and statelets, contrasted with very large states.

In fact, the huge disparity in size and power of member states represents the most serious shortcoming of the current structure of the UN. The constant increase in the number of member states (today they are approximately four times as many as in 1945) shows an alarming trend toward fragmentation and anarchy. It is necessary to let regional groupings form within the General Assembly, and increase their cohesion, so that they can later express themselves in the Security Council.

The growing cohesion of the EU as a player in the UN is closely correlated to the degree of advancement in the unification process. It is not to be forgotten that, in spite of the dramatic split of the EU brought about by the US attack on Iraq, member states' decisions in the sphere of external relations show a high rate of convergence. This is true particularly in the field of economic, monetary and environmental policies, where Europe can speak with one single voice. In the WTO and the FAO the European Commission represents member states. But within the UN, the EU already acts in the great majority of cases as one single actor. For instance, in 1999 it took a common position in almost 95% of the General Assembly votes. Moreover, the forthcoming European Constitution, recognizing the international legal personality of the EU, creating the European Foreign Minister and promoting a single security and defense system through the "structured co-operations", is destined to strengthen the international role of Europe. The weakness of Europe lies in the fact that its political decisions on foreign and security policy are to be made unanimously. This is the vacuum that has to be filled to make possible the entrance of the EU into the Security Council.

EU membership in the Council would also be an alternative to the hegemony of the three most powerful countries in the EU and to Germany's demand for representation. It must be considered that the admission of Germany to the Security Council would encourage, in that country, the development of a foreign policy independent of that of the EU and thus provide a stimulus for the revival of German nationalism. If Germany's reasons are recognized, how to ignore those of Italy, Spain, Poland and so on? If the Europeans decide to return to giving priority to national interests, the whole design of the European unity will be irretrievably damaged. Paradoxically this occurs when the ratification of the European Constitution is on the agenda.

A strong independent EU represents the first pillar of a renewed UN building based on regional groupings of states. The principal teaching that can be deduced from the history of international law and international organizations is that a well-functioning system of rules depends on a balance of power between the members of the states system. If one state is preponderant, it may afford to disregard the rights of other states. This means that the overcoming of the asymmetry that, due to the American hegemony, currently characterizes international relations, is the necessary step forward which can pave the way to the UN reform.

The integration processes under way in Africa, the Arab World, Southern Asia, South-East Asia and Latin America appear to be creating the conditions to attain the economic size required for the development of modern production techniques and to acquire the political weight needed to obtain a real independence from the great powers. If the European Union (which, having nurtured a process of economic integration, is now moving towards political union) can be seen as a pilot project, it is foreseeable that the other great regions which are taking shape in other parts of the world may, in the future, become the protagonists of the new multipolar world order.

The extraordinary novelty of the regional representation in the Security Council lies in the recognition of the rights of all the states of the EU to be represented in the Security Council, with no distinction made between permanent and non-permanent members. The achievement of this principle in Europe will open the way to its extension to the other great regions of the world.

The transformation of the Security Council into the Council of the great regions of the world will allow all the states to be represented in this body through their respective regional organization. This is the way to overcome the unjust discrimination between permanent and non-permanent member states. This is the way leading to the replacement of the right of veto with the majority vote.

The ICC is a Reality International Law Applied over Individuals*

William R. PACE

On April 11, 2002 ten nations simultaneously deposited their instruments of ratification to the Rome Statute of the International Criminal Court (RS) taking the number of nations ratifying the ICC treaty from 56 to 66 and triggering the entry into force of the new system of international criminal justice on July 1, 2002. In the address to the special ratification plenary at the UN, the World Federalist Movement, speaking on behalf of the NGO Coalition for the ICC, recalled our statement in Rome in 1998, that world history has almost always been the story of wars won and peace lost, but that the RS represented a historic achievement by the international community in which peace has won and war lost.

The World Federalist Movement (WFM) was founded to promote the vision of a world in which the global rule of law would replace the rule of violence, brute power and anarchy. The WFM worldwide peace movement was essentially alone in the 1945-52 period in recognizing that the great institutions established at the end of WWII were fundamentally flawed and democratically deficient.

The rush by most WWII victors to reoccupy their empires, the victors control in UN Charter, the victors justice of the Nuremberg and Tokyo tribunals, and the victors one-dollar-one-vote control of the Bretton Woods institutions all foreclosed the possibility of the UN being able to achieve its most fundamental purpose, "to save succeeding generations from the scourge of war."

The fear of the world plunging into world war III wherein the use of atomic weapons would incinerate most of human life and civilization motivated the world federalists, like Emery Reves, Einstein, and Russell to call for world government and world peace through world law. International treaties and step by step disarmament efforts were proclaimed illusory because, they argued, the step by step forces that lead to war always proceed faster. They did not like it but they reluctantly argued that if it required an autocratic world government imposed by the USA and Russia, perhaps with the UK and France, to "outlaw" war then

* Published in Issue 2/2002.

this was far preferable to the "better dead than Red" political-military mindset of the USA. They argued that it was better to establish world government and then fight to make it democratic, if that was necessary to avoid certain nuclear war. They had been through two terrible "world wars" in less than 30 years.

The Cold War descended upon the world, the disastrous efforts of WWII victors to reoccupy their empires turned into 45 years of wars of independence and decolonization, and the world federalists were almost marginalized out of existence by the Realpolitik of "mutual assured destruction." The dangerousness, recklessness and insanity of world politics in the Cold War may never be properly recorded.

It is wonderfully ironic that after 40 years wandering in the wilderness the first really focused and successful global project of the World Federalist Movement was to help organize and lead the effort to create a permanent International Criminal Court. It is a treaty, but it is a treaty establishing international law not only between nation states, but international law over individuals. States and UN officials are describing the ICC as the greatest advance in international law since the founding of the UN. The USA claims the Rome Statute is "supranational" and threatens to undermine both national sovereignty and the exclusive powers given to the UN Security Council in the Charter. It will be decades before we know the fate of the ICC, and years before historians will explain why this extraordinary effort succeeded, and why it proceeded so quickly, achieving 60 ratifications five to twenty-five years faster than almost all experts predicted in 1998. I believe historians will recognize that in addition to the much-heralded economic globalization sweeping the planet in the late 20th century, the globalization of democracy, justice and the rule of law was also extending throughout the world. Emery Reves made a powerful case in 1945 that unless the collision between industrialization and nationalism was vanquished by law there was no hope for the survival of civilization. Since WWII, the victimization of civilians in war has, incredibly, increased three-fold! The ICC represents not only a major step forward in the development of international democracy, it represents a major step forward in the goal to rid the world of the scourge of war.

Reforming the United Nations by the Convention Method

Learning from the EU[*]

Antonio PAPISCA

In one way the difficult transition towards a new, more humane and sustainable world order resembles the problem of constructing a mosaic. It cannot be done without tesserae which someone must arrange for the mosaic to be completed.

With this metaphor my intention is to emphasise that the tesserae for our mosaic – that is, key elements of a sustainable world order – already exist in the internationally recognised moral and juridical paradigm of human rights, international law rooted in the United Nations Charter, multilateral institutions, actions, and precedents. But no coherent outcome has yet appeared because the political bodies which have the capacity to arrange the tesserae have so far lacked the courage to face up to that task: that is, they must make the blueprint for world order visible and ensure that people become aware that we are not groping in the dark and that it is possible to resist the ideology of *Realpolitk* determinism.

The second half of the 20th century saw some positive achievements (epiphanies of global good governance) which it is unreasonable to abandon: especially the UN Charter, the Universal Declaration of Human Rights, the United Nations Organisation, the UN system of Specialised Agencies, and regional integration processes such as, primarily, the European Union. Thus the planet has become like a house filled with a lot of useful appliances that are not properly exploited.

The "DNA" of a more humane world order

In the mid-20th century a human-centric revolution already changed the DNA of the world system. Today, people would no longer maintain as a matter of principle that respect for human dignity should be subordinated to state sovereignty. Apartheid and colonialism are now taboo. Security and development are increasingly seen as essential to the human condition.

---

* Published in Issue 1/2006.

Unilateralism, although emphasised by the superpower leadership, is now considered unnatural and costly in both moral and economic terms.

The European system and processes as a fertile lesson for the world

With the European Union presenting a mixed picture of conflict and confusion, though also offering a wealth of opportunities, we may wonder whether it is truly capable of collecting and arranging the tesserae of the mosaic portraying our emerging world order. Its biggest task is to develop and improve our common heritage of universal values into a coherent strategy for building world peace.

That requires moral consistency, general appeal, the ability to govern and lead by example. Can the European Union live up to these standards? Empirical evidence says yes, provided we assume it is also capable of doing so within its own system. My arguments are as follows.

The European integration process has been a model of how it is possible to construct lasting peace between states, peoples and religious entities which for many centuries were fighting each other.

The European system is a living laboratory of mutual learning between differing political systems and cultures. It is a real yardstick of intercultural dialogue in a very complex historical context.

The European system is also a laboratory of multi- and supra-national governance based on the principle of subsidiarity, both territorial and functional. We can actually say that the system is proving to be successful in carrying out the twofold task of 'agenda development' and 'institution building', in order to suitably meet the governance needs stemming from the structural crisis of traditional statehood, namely the crisis in both state 'capacities' and state 'form', and of the democratic practice. The European Union is the trans-national system in which new and more sophisticated forms of governance – better, of statehood – are actually pursued.

The European system is pioneering international democracy – that is, genuine transnational democracy with supranational political institutions legitimatised through the direct election of a parliamentary body and the participation of civil society organisations and groups in the decision-making process at the supranational level.

The European Union is metabolising the pattern of internationally recognised human rights both in its own practices and externally. Its Charter of Fundamental Rights, proclaimed in Nice in December 2000 and now included in the draft Treaty establishing a Constitution for Europe, advocates the full "constitutionalisation" of the EU system. In treaties with third countries the EU is developing the practice of including a "human rights clause" and by means of speeches and financial largesse it has also campaigned for the establishment of a functioning International Criminal Court.

Furthermore, the European Union is gradually extending both the concept and the practice of citizenship. While the Maastricht Treaty established EU citizenship as a basket of additional rights available only to member states' citizens – *ad alios excludendos* –, the EU Charter of Fundamental Rights covers all human beings, thus in effect extending citizenship *ad includendum*: a universal and plural citizenship. This challenges the discriminatory approach of the original Maastricht provisions. In this respect the EU is acting as a laboratory for structural change in line with universal ethics and therefore offers an example for the entire world.

The "convention method" used in the ongoing European institution-building process of the EU's comprehensive democratisation. So far two European Conventions have been held, the first on human rights and the second dealing with EU's future structure and resulting in the draft Constitutional Treaty. The rationale behind this innovative practice is that, in accordance with subsidiarity, the traditional Summit Conferences need to be complemented by a more extensive and diversified input when deciding on major statutory revisions. The intrinsic value of the convention method lies in the plurality and diversity of its membership. This allows for a more representative participation, thereby drawing on a wider range of ideas and experience, and increasing legitimacy.

Strengthening & democratising the United Nations as a EU priority

Everything mentioned above should be sufficient to make the European integration process an impressive example for all, and the European Union a credible actor in world politics. But being "an example" is a boomerang for the EU. Globally it is expected to act in accordance with the magnitude of its achievements, and that it has a moral duty to act as a power characterised by successful human rights mainstreaming, peace-building and democratisation. Yet, though it has a single domestic currency, the absence of a EU "single voice" in world politics means that it still lacks the capacity to use those successes as a power resource.

In playing a major role, the EU should give priority to the arrangement of the "world order" mosaic's tesserae, bearing in mind (a) that behind economic deregulation lies a strategy of institutional deregulation, undermining systems of organised multilateralism, supranational criminal justice, collective security, and non-profit transnationalism; and (b) that the destiny of (new) International Law based on human rights is inevitably linked with the future of the United Nations, of multilateral cooperation, and of the entire network of international organisations. If we abandon these we shall be left without the mechanisms necessary to implement human rights, pursue collective security and human development goals, even that to extend democracy.

The EU task regarding the United Nations

The United Nations Organisation has had its failures and its successes. Nevertheless it contributes to a positive future for the world. To quote but a few of its achievements, it has helped create respect for an international law of human rights, with its complementary philosophy of concern for human security and human development, the enhanced culture and practice of multilateral cooperation, the ongoing pressure to improve the status of women and their role in the world's political agenda, collaboration with NGOs and civil society movements, the development of international criminal law and the establishment of a supranational criminal justice machinery, etc.

As a matter of priority, in its foreign and security policy the European Union should therefore make what I would call a "preferential choice" in favour of strengthening and democratising the United Nations in accordance with Article I-3 (The Union's objectives) of the draft EU Constitution: "In its relations with the wider world, the Union shall uphold and promote its values and interests. It shall contribute to peace, security, the sustainable development of the Earth, solidarity and mutual respect among peoples, free and fair trade, eradication of poverty and protection of human rights, and in particular the rights of the child, as well as to strict observance and development of international law, including respect for the principles of the United Nations Charter".

Seen from this perspective, the question of the UN reform cannot be regarded as simply one aspect of a wider agenda of world order issues. It is in fact central to this agenda.

Over the past four decades innumerable working groups, panels, *comités de sages*, eminent personalities both within and outside the UN itself have produced a plethora of largely empty reports and dossiers on the UN reform. They lie scattered across the landscape like tombstones in a mediaeval graveyard. And yet the need for reform remains urgent, for there is no reasonable alternative to an effective United Nations Organisation.

Needed: a "Universal Convention" to strengthen & democratise the UN!

Reform of the UN should be undertaken in accordance with the principles enshrined in the UN Charter and other human-centric legal instruments, including the Universal Declaration of Human Rights whose Preamble contains the key message, namely: "the recognition of the inherent dignity and of the equal and inalienable rights of all members of the human family is the foundation of freedom, justice and peace in the world".

The reform strategy should pursue two main objectives: democratisation of UN organs and their decision-making processes; and balancing the two thematic elements in the Charter represented institutionally by the Security Council and the present Economic and Social Council. New headings for these two thematic elements could be, respectively, human security and human development.

Democratisation of the UN is an absolute priority. Without it, no further changes, developments or improvements are possible. But it must be emphasized that international democracy means genuine democracy: not simply "one state, one vote", but more direct legitimacy of the international organs, involving increased popular participation in the way decisions are taken, with autonomous civil society initiatives at the world political level.

- making the Security Council more representative, preferably by reorganising or complementing its membership on regional basis,
- establishing a UN Parliamentary Assembly and a permanent Global Civil Society Forum,
- enhancing the role both of non-governmental organisations and local government institutions,
- reinforcing the ECOSOC functions in pursuing social justice goals, including the empowerment of the UN human rights machinery,
- establishing a permanent UN police force (both civil and military),
- enlarging the mandate of the International Criminal Court and strengthening its structure,
- endowing the International Court of Justice with the right to assess the legitimacy of the Security Council acts.

The practice of representative and participatory democracy in the UN would almost certainly have a huge impact among its member states, for international democracy would then be seen as the independent variable of internal democracy. Through dialogue, peaceful exchange, and cooperation, it would have an increasingly positive influence.

Balancing the two main thematic elements of the Charter also means that the Economic and Social Council should be endowed with the powers needed to orient the world economy and world affairs towards social and economic justice. As we know, the area at present covered by ECOSOC is both extensive and relevant. It includes economic and social affairs as well as the human rights mechanisms and rather loose advisory functions of coordination vis-à-vis the Bretton Woods institutions. Yet, notwithstanding the crucial relevance of these policy areas, its powers are not in any way comparable with those of the Security Council.

Within and around the UN system we speak of human security and human development as two sides of the same coin, both being multi-dimensional and affecting the same subjects, namely individuals, groups and peoples. Why then, in comparison with the Security Council, is ECOSOC so feeble and endowed with so few powers?

To make ECOSOC genuinely a Council for economic, social and environmental security, its functions and powers should be increased to the level of the present Security Council. Such a package, which would be fully consistent with the principles of interdependence and the indivisibility of all human rights, would enormously strengthen the entire UN system.

The practice of democracy within the UN should start already during the preparatory phase of drafting a comprehensive document on its reform: that is, a framework document having both moral and political authority. It is needless to emphasise the delicacy of this phase and the influence it will have on the subsequent formal decision-taking process.

Drafting should take place in a plural and participatory context, by which I mean that the reform document should be prepared by an ad hoc body whose membership should be broader and more diversified than in strictly intergovernmental bodies, as the General Assembly or the Security Council. Its composition must break away from the usual stagnant, inconclusive self-referentialism of the debate at the United Nations headquarters, and also from the hidden agendas of powerful governmental lobbies.

My proposal is that by means of a resolution endorsed by the General Assembly – where veto power does not exist – a "Global Convention for strengthening and democratising the United Nations" should be established, whose composition would ideally be comprised of the following representative segments:

- UN member states, by regional groupings
- relevant institutions of the UN system
- regional organisations

- national parliaments and the parliamentary assemblies of regional bodies
- local government authorities (through a newly established NGO of "United Cities and Local Governments")
- NGOs having consultative status at the UN and in global civil society networks
- Women's global movement
- Permanent Observers to the UN.

In practice, this Global Convention for UN Reform would bring reality to the UN Charter's introductory words: "We, the Peoples of the United Nations". Their anticipatory message of a truly trans-national democracy would find an echo in the minds of millions active members of global civil society organisations and movements. A special website would ensure the widest possible access to the Convention's proceedings, and its final conclusions would then be submitted to the General Assembly as the mandatory institution of this ad hoc body.

As we have seen, the European Union has twice used the convention method with positive results. Its experience entitles it to take the initiative and propose that the question of UN reform should be addressed by the same pluralistic method, duly adapted, of course, to the world context.

The UN Convention would be more than a mere 'working group'. It would be a constituent entity with a mandate to draft a coherent set of formal proposals. In this way it should be possible to finally overcome the sterile inter-governmental approach, which until now has proved to be the real obstacle to the UN reform.

Editors

Giampiero Bordino

Author of historical essays and manuals, in particular about contemporary history. President of the Einstein Centre for International Studies (CESI) in Torino, Italy. Member of the editorial staff of and contributor to the review *The Federalist Debate*

Lucio Levi

Former Professor of Political Science and Comparative Politics at the University of Torino, Italy. President of the European Federalist Movement from 2009 to 2015. Editor of the review *The Federalist Debate*. Scientific Director of the International Democracy Watch. Editor with Giovanni Finizio and Nicola Vallinoto of the First International Democracy Report published as *The Democratization of International Institutions*, London-New York, Routledge, 2013

Antonio Mosconi

He has been Controller of Fiat Group and Managing Director of Teksid, Fiatimpresit, Toro Assicurazioni and Utet. Former President of the Einstein Centre for International Studies (CESI), in Torino. He is a member of the editorial staff and contributor to the review *The Federalist Debate*. He has published several essays on the automotive sector and the international monetary system

Authors

Yossi Amitay

Lecturer on Middle East Studies at Ben Gurion University, Beer Sheva, Israel. Former Director of the Israeli Academic Center in Cairo

James Arputharaj

Member of WFM Executive Committee, and President of South Asian Federalists, currently working in Afghanistan as Chief of Party for a USAID Project

Joseph Preston Baratta

Professor of World History and International Relations at the Worcester State College, USA

Seyla Benhabib

Eugene Meyer Professor of Political Science and Philosophy at Yale University and Director of its Program in Ethics, Politics and Economics. President of the Eastern Division of the American Philosophical Association in 2006-07

Carsten Berg

Vice-Chairman of Democracy International. Founder of the Initiative & Referendum Institute Europe

Jean-Francis Billion

Vice President UEF France. Member of UEF Federal Committee and the WMF Council

Giampiero Bordino

(See *Editors* above)

Josep Borrell

Former President of the European Parliament and former President of the European University Institute

Pier Virgilio Dastoli

President of the Italian Council of the European Movement (CIME)

Garry Davis

World Coordinator -World Government of World Citizens

Ludo Dierickx

Former member of Belgian Senate and former President of B-Plus

Andrew Duff

Visiting Fellow at the European Policy Centre. He was a British Liberal MEP 1999-2014, and President of the Union of European Federalists 2008-13

Daniel J. Elazar

He was the Director of the Center for the Study of Federalism in Philadelphia and of the Jerusalem Center for Public Affairs, as well as Professor at the Bar Ilan University in Jerusalem. He was also the founder and editor of *Publius, The Journal of Federalism* since 1970

Ken Endo

Professor of International Politics, Hokkaido University, Japan and Fernand Braudel Senior Fellow, European University Institute, Italy

Jiafei Ge

Researcher for the Shanghai Development and Research Foundation

Jean-Pierre Gouzy

Honorary President of the Association of European Journalists/French Section, Journalist and Historian of European unification

David Grace

Secretary at James Madison Trust

Pietro Greco

Scientific journalist and writer. Director of the Study Centre of "Città della Scienza", Napoli

Daniel Gros

Director of the Centre for European Policy Studies (CEPS), Brussels

Hazem Hanafi

Researcher of the Arab Foundation for Federal Studies, MA in Comparative Federalism, University of Kent

Fernand Herman

Former President of UEF Belgium and member of the UEF Executive Bureau, former MEP and former Minister of the Belgian Government

Fernando A. Iglesias

WMF Council Chair. Director of the Campaign for the Latin-American Criminal Court. Holder of the Spinelli Chair in Buenos Aires (CUIA)

Alfonso Iozzo

Former Managing Director of Sanpaolo IMI, President of Cassa Depositi e Prestiti S.p.A. in Rome and Prometeia S.p.A. in Bologna. Honorary Member of the Executive Bureau of the UEF. Vice-President of Robert Triffin International. President of the Centre for Studies on Federalism

Raymond M. Jung d'Arsac

Rapporteur at the Hertenstein Conference (1946)

Sylvia-Yvonne Kaufmann

Former Vice-President of the European Parliament, member of the Presidium of the UEF Federal Committee

Sir Charles Kimber

One of the original founders of the Federal Union

Robert Lafont

Former Professor at Paul Valéry University of Montpellier. Social linguist and writer

Jo Leinen

MEP, member of the Constitutional Affairs Committee (AFCO) and Co-Rapporteur for the reform of the European Electoral Law. President of the European Movement International (EMI)

Lucio Levi

(See *Editors* above)

Alberto Majocchi

Professor of Public Finance at the University of Pavia. Vice President of the Centre for Studies on Federalism

George Modelski

Former Professor of Political Science at the University of Washington, author and editor of a number of important books, including *Long Cycles of World Politics*

Antonio Mosconi

(See *Editors* above)

Paul Oriol

Member of the Editorial board of the journal *Lettre de la Citoyenneté*. Organizer of the Campaign "One Million Signatures for European Citizenship to Residents"

William R. Pace

Executive Director, World Federalist Movement-Institute for Global Policy (WFM-IGP). Convenor, Coalition for the International Criminal Court (CICC). Steering Committee member, International Coalition for the Responsibility to Protect (ICRtoP)

Tommaso Padoa-Schioppa

Italy's Minister of Economy and Finances from 2006 to 2008. Member of the Executive Board of the European Central Bank from 1997 to 2006.

Roberto Palea

Board member and former President of the Centre for Studies on Federalism

Giannis F. Papageorgiou

Assistant Professor of European Politics and of Comparative Politics at the School of Political Science of the Aristotle University of Thessaloniki, Greece. Former President of JEF

Antonio Papisca

Professor Emeritus of International Relations and UNESCO Chair Human Rights, Democracy and Peace at the University of Padova

John Parry

Honorary member of the UEF Bureau

John Pinder

Former Chairman of the Federal Trust, President of UEF from 1984 to 1990, former Professor at the College of Europe in Bruges, Belgium. Director of Political and Economic Planning from 1964 to 1985

Romano Prodi

President of the European Commission from 1999 to 2004. Prime Minister of the Italian Government from 1996 to 1998 and from 2006 to 2008

Yide Qiao

Deputy Chairman and General Secretary of the Shanghai Development and Research Foundation (SDRF)

Stefano Rodotà

Professor Emeritus of Civil Law at the University "La Sapienza" of Rome. Former member of the Convention which drafted the Charter of Fundamental Rights of the EU

Francesco Rossolillo

President of the Union for European Federalists from 1991 to 1997. Editor of the review *The Federalist* from 1997 to 2004

Amartya Sen

Lamont University Professor Emeritus at Harvard University. He was awarded the Nobel Prize in Economics in 1998

Dusan Sidjanski

Professor Emeritus at the University of Geneva. Honorary Chairman of the Centre Européen de la Culture and Special Advisor to the President of the European Commission

Joan Marc Simon

Board member of the WFM-IGP, Federal Committee member of the European Federalists and Coordinator of the UNPA Campaign in Spain

Barbara Spinelli

Vice-President of the Committee on Constitutional Affairs of the European Parliament

Ira Straus

US Coordinator, Committee on Eastern Europe and Russia in NATO. Fulbright Professor of International Relations, MGU and MGIMO.

Former Executive Director of Federal Union and the Association to Unite the Democracies. Lecturer in Euro-Atlantic Integration Studies at the Moscow State Institute of International Relations

Peter Sutherland

President of The Federal Trust, Former EU Commissioner and DG of WTO

Heinz Timmermann

Associate Researcher at the Stiftung Wissenschaft und Politik, Berlin, Germany

Tzvetan Todorov

Franco Bulgarian historian and essayist

Robert Toulemon

Honorary Director at the European Commission, author of *Aimer l'Europe*, Paris

Kenji Urata

Vice President, International Association of Lawyers Against Nuclear Arms and Professor Emeritus, Waseda University, Tokio

Nadia Urbinati

Kyriakos Tsakopoulos Professor of Political Theory, Department of Political Science, Columbia University, New York

Sir Brian Urquhart

Former Undersecretary-General of the United Nations, he organized the first peace-keeping force under UN mandate (in Egypt after the Suez crisis)

Peter Ustinov

Actor, writer and dramatist. He served as a Goodwill Ambassador for UNICEF and President of the World Federalist Movement from 1991 to 2004

Guy Verhofstadt

President of the Liberals and Democrats group in the European Parliament and former Prime Minister of Belgium from 1999 to 2008

Fergus Watt

Executive Director, WFM-Canada

Ernest Wistrich

Director of the Campaign “Britain in Europe” and of the European Movement UK from 1969 to 1986

Federalism

The book series Federalism, run by the Centro Studi sul Federalismo/ Centre for Studies on Federalism (CSF) aims to disseminate knowledge in the field of studies on federalism, as well as to feed the academic and public debate and support the activity of decision-makers, confronted with demands for autonomy by local governments, along with forms of regional and world integration needed to govern global processes.

The book series is divided into two sub-series: Studies and Classics. The former contains the research outcome and the proceedings of conferences and seminars promoted by the Centre, while the latter consists in reprints of the federalist classic works and English translations of Italian federalists' works.

The CSF is a think tank that carries out activities of interdisciplinary research, documentation, information regarding domestic and supra-national federalism, developments in the area of regional and continental integration – first and foremost the European Union – and problems related to the world order and the process of democratisation of the international system. The CSF has been founded under the auspices of the Compagnia di San Paolo and the Universities of Turin, Pavia and Milan.

***Series Editor**: Umberto Morelli, University of Turin*

Centro Studi sul Federalismo
via Real Collegio, 30
10024 Moncalieri (To) – Italy
Tel. + 39 011.6705024
Fax + 39 011.6705081
E-mail: info@csfederalismo.it
Website: www.csfederalismo.it

Series titles

No. 1 – Giovanni Finizio and Ernesto Gallo (eds.), *Democracy at the United Nations. UN Reform in the Age of Globalisation*, 2012.

No. 2 – Roberto Castaldi (ed.), *Immanuel Kant and Alexander Hamilton, the Founders of Federalism. A Political Theory for Our Time*, 2013.

No. 3 – Claudio Giulio Anta (ed.), *Lord Lothian: The Paths of Federalism. Writings and Speeches*, 2014.

No. 4 – Filippo Maria Giordano and Stefano dell'Acqua (eds.), *„Die Welt war meine Gemeinde". Willem A. Visser 't Hoof – A Theologian for Europe between Ecumenism and Federalism*, 2014.

No. 5 – Giampiero Bordino (ed.), *A New Right for Democracy and Development in Europe*, 2015.

No. 6 – Filippo Maria Giordano, *"United through Diversity". An Insight into Federalism and Ecumenism within Italian Protestantism*, 2016.

www.peterlang.com